COLLAPSE

Civilization on the Brink

By
Chaitanya Davé

PublishAmerica
Baltimore

PublishAmerica has allowed this work to remain exactly as the author intended, verbatim, without editorial input.

Hardcover 978-1-4512-9769-0
Softcover 978-1-4489-4456-9
PUBLISHED BY PUBLISHAMERICA, LLLP
www.publishamerica.com
Baltimore

Printed in the United States of America

Also by Chaitanya Davé

CRIMES AGAINST HUMANITY:
A Shocking History of U.S. Crimes since 1776

To my wife who gave me a life of love
To my sons who have made our lives so wonderful and worth living
and
To my parents who gave us such a joyful childhood and taught us
about how to live life with
pride, honor, and dignity, and to love nature and to treat it with the
utmost respect.

PREFACE

As both a chemical engineer heading a metal-finishing-product manufacturing company, and the founder of the non-profit rural development organization *Pragati,* I have been involved with the environment for the last 35 years. Working in these capacities has made me acutely aware of the environmental problems we face. However, upon reading Jared Diamond's *Collapse: How Societies Choose to Fail or Succeed,* and Joseph Tainter's The *Collapse of Complex Societies,* my eyes were truly opened. I began wondering if such a collapse as what beset the Easter Islanders, the Anasazi, or the Mayas could happen to our current civilization; the similarities were frightening. Studying the subject of global warming extensively, I realized that such a reality is not only plausible but approaching certainty because this civilization, like other collapsed ones of the past, is not sustainable and has devastated both the global environment and the planetary ecosystem.

These facts inspired me to write this book and to inform the public that on humanity's current course a worldwide total ecosystem breakdown is nigh—If not in our own lifetime than in our children's or in their children's—with the result being planetary collapse. The Earth can only take so much abuse. What is at stake is the very survival of our current civilization. Rather than offer false hopes, I have tried to be realistic about the fate of present human society globally; a fate that is not very optimistic as so many diverse, selfish, myopic, and rather foolish forces are at work within and between nations that an equitable, just, and efficiently workable agreement might elude us before it is too late.

Fortunately, many books have emerged in recent years by activists and experts on climate change and related subjects. In addition, many articles by several progressive magazines, newspapers, and sometimes the mass media have covered this subject often. This has indeed created more awareness among the populace of a hand-full of countries, though by and large the masses of people around the world are yet unaware of the extent the threat of global warming poses to our civilization. Indeed a very small percentage of people, besides climate scientists, experts, and activists realize that current civilization is on the brink of an anthropogenic cataclysmic disaster, that there is a limited window of opportunity…just a few years to do something drastic to avert this catastrophe, and that if we fail to act now, we will cross the brink from which there is no return. We will all sink together.

In this book, I have tried to cover all the facets of global warming and the other challenges we face, and have attempted to give the reader the unadulterated facts.

Rancho Palos Verdes, California

April 21, 2010

ACKNOWLEDGEMENT

I would like to thank my family: my wife Amita, and my sons Maurya and Aditya for their help in the shaping of this book. Their moral support and patience were very inspirational for me to undertake and finish this project. Maurya's ideas and suggestions and Aditya's editing and structuring of this book were of vital importance.

Table of Contents

INTRODUCTION

10,000 years ago, what a beautiful place was this Earth? Vast forests covering most of our planet: tropical, subtropical, lush-green, and rainforests harboring great varieties of plants and trees and with a wide variety of animals roaming freely. Big animals, small ones, insects, butterflies, birds...all lived in harmony with each other and thrived. The rivers and lakes were filled with clean water that was in abundance. The oceans were pure, teeming with diverse sea creatures making it their home. The air was brisk and life-giving. Even people lived with respect for and in harmony with nature.

Humans then were a hunting-gathering species eking out their subsistence from plants, herbs, and animals. But they eventually discovered how to cultivate plants for food. That was the dawn of the agricultural revolution. This had two crucial ramifications: ecological and political. Ecologically, the invention of agriculture kicked off an invasive assault on natural systems. Today's large-scale commercial agriculture is rooted all the way back to then. Politically, the availability of sufficient food enabled societies to form tribes, villages, and kingdoms with chiefs, and then kings. Political control, repression, and subjugation with the formation of nation-states followed.

The industrial revolution that followed in the mid-18th century in England intensified the human assault on ecosystems everywhere.

Unleashing the concentrated energy of coal, oil, and natural gas to run a machine-based world gave us unparalleled material comfort. But within two centuries, this industrial revolution fortified with capitalism has gobbled up the resources of the planet, polluted the global environment beyond belief, and destroyed the ecosystems of the Earth. It has polluted the planet's rivers, oceans, and lakes. Corporate greed, over consumption in the developed world, and poverty-driven burgeoning population growth in the developing world has devastated our forests. Also, the dominance and exploitation of weaker nations by the few strong ones in the last 500 years has created in the world today an inequity that is shameful at best. According to U.N. reports, more than a billion people don't have enough food to eat or clean water to drink. There is no question that humanity is in trouble, deep trouble. We are on the verge of the worst man-made disaster our world has ever faced: global warming and a heated planet. The 'March of Folly' that began in England in the early eighteenth century has over-consumed the Earth's resources, exhausting our very basis of life.

According to UN-Habitat, more than a billion people live in slums and that number is expected to double by 2030. The world in 2030 will be unimaginable when the convergent impacts of climate change, peak oil, rising oceans, peak water, and an additional 1.5 billion people on our planet will begin to throttle growth and destroy what remains of the planet's ecosystems. Our pristine world that we have inhabited for the last 10,000 years has ended, even if no newspaper in America or Europe has published its obituary.

It seems we in the 'modern' world suffer from delusion. We are being duped by the mass-media all over into believing that some high-advanced-technology fixes will enable our troubled world to overcome the massive problems confronting humanity. The mass-media owned and run by corporate interests is committed to maintaining this delusional state and the status quo. But the real solutions, if even they exist, will come through a significant paradigm shift in how we humans live and how quickly we are able to down-scale the level at which we live in developed world. I used the word 'if' because there certainly is no guarantee that there are solutions. History and nature do not owe us a chance to remedy our mistakes just because we want it.

I have tried to be as truthful and frank as possible to impart the dire situation that we humans find ourselves in. I, for one, do not believe in painting a rosy scenario if it is not true. The purpose of this book is not to mislead you into believing that all will be fine and technology will take care of the problem. The purpose is to make people aware of just the kind of catastrophe facing humanity, what our options are, and what are the probabilities of success.

There is no question that humanity has already overshot the Earth's long-term carrying capacity for the human race. Industrial civilization has so vastly overused and squandered the Earth's resources that some form of societal collapse is now inevitable. The word '*Collapse*' in this book is reverently echoed from Joseph Tainter's and Jared Diamond's books which I found to be extremely interesting and reveling.

This collapse will not be sudden, but gradual. The first two centuries of the industrial revolution will go down in history as an unbridled growth period. However, the period from 2000 onwards, for a century or two, will be a period of collapse—a drastic downsizing of human society. We are already in the first phase of this collapse evidenced by the breaking down of ecosystems around the planet, decline in per capita global grain production, depletion of energy resources, cascading extinction of species, highly polluted environments, melting glaciers, increasing world-wide water scarcities, and higher frequencies of storms and floods. Humanity can either control itself population-wise and consumption-wise or nature will inevitably do it for us.

The book is divided into four parts:

Part-I- Ancient Civilizations describes how ancient societies just a few hundred years ago flourished. Yet unbeknownst to them, they over-consumed their natural resources, devastated their environment and their societies succumbed to tragic drought-ridden demise.

This first section will reveal the connection between these ancient societies and our current industrial civilization: how both have flourished, how they shockingly similar, and—if we do not take drastic steps to change our life-styles now—how we could meet the same fate as the Anasazi, the Easter Islanders, and others.

Part-II- Industrial Nations and their Impact on Earth covers the ecological impact of major industrial nations on planet Earth—how they have polluted the environment and how humanity finds itself in such dire situation.

Part-III- Early Symptoms of Peril concerns the early symptoms of the catastrophe developing on the horizon.

Part-IV- The Sustainable Ways describes how, as individuals, we can help save the environment by making some changes in our lives. It also describes what various nations are doing on the course towards sustainability. Finally, a chapter is included that points out a few societies which are unique, sustainable, and likely to survive a forthcoming collapse.

Chapter-14- Is Collapse Really Imminent? is the last and perhaps the most important chapter of the book. This chapter poses the key questions: Will world leaders be able to steer their countries' economies towards renewable energies in time and will people be able to reduce their consumption levels to a sustainable way of life? If this does not happen in time, the chapter describes a grim scenario of massive collapse where millions will perish and chaos will reign supreme.

This is a defining moment in the entire history of humanity. The very survival of the human race and the other beautiful creatures of the planet depend on what the major powers decide to do or not do now. There are few choices left for humanity. The developed nations who are largely responsible for creating this problem have a huge debt to pay to the rest of the world. Unless they come up with reasonable sum of money and free transfer of technology to help other nations cope with and change to renewable sources of energy, business as usual will certainly invite catastrophe of epic proportions. Unless major nations of the world unite, forego their own selfish interests, and act in a responsible manner to switch their economies to sustainable sources of energy and ways of life, unless people of the developed nations in particular but also of developing nations voluntarily reduce their consumption levels, and unless the human population of the planet stabilizes and reduces gradually, our planet is doomed. This book makes this clear in no uncertain way.

SECTION I
ANCIENT CIVILIZATIONS

CHAPTER 1
THE MAYAS, ANASAZI, MESA VERDE, NORSE & OTHERS

Forests to precede civilizations, deserts to follow.
—Francois René Chateaubriand (ca. 1840)

THE ANASAZI, MESA VERDE, MIMBRES, AND HOHOKAM

These forgotten ancient societies lived less than 600 miles from Los Angeles, California in the state of New Mexico—the American Southwest. The Anasazi lived in today's Chaco National Historical Park, and the Mesa Verde at the Mesa Verde National Park lying in the southwest United States, on New Mexico Highway 57 and near U.S. Highway 666 respectively. The populations of these ancient societies numbered in the thousands—small when compared to the Mesoamerican Mayas, which were in the millions. A series of ancient southwestern cultures flourished, reached their peaks, and then collapsed at different times. The Mimbres collapsed around A.D. 1130; Chaco Canyon, North Black Mesa and the Virgin Anasazi in the middle or late 12th century; Mesa Verde and Kayenta Anasazi around A.D. 1300; Mogollon around 1400, and possibly around the late 15th century for the Hohokam. The Anasazi did not completely vanish as a people; rather, their descendants have been incorporated within other southwestern Native American societies living today such as Hopi and Zuni pueblos.

The first humans to reach the Americas, living as primitive hunter-gatherers, arrived in the American Southwest by 11,000 B.C., perhaps even earlier. This was part of the colonization of the new world by an Asian people, ancestors of modern Native Americans. Because of the scarcity of domesticable wild plants and native species, agriculture did not develop indigenously in the American Southwest. It arrived from Mexico instead where corn, beans, squash and several other crops were domesticated. Corn arrived by 2000 B.C., squash by 800 B.C., beans a little later and cotton by A.D. 400. Turkeys were domesticated either arriving from Mexico or vice versa. These people adopted agriculture as part of their hunter-gatherer life-style. By A.D. 1, they were already living in villages, depending on agriculture with ditch irrigation. As years went by, more food was produced, their populations exploded, and spread around the surrounding areas and thrived.[1]

What happened to these thriving societies who flourished for so long and suddenly disappeared one by one from A.D. 1130 to the late 15th century? What triggered their collapse?

The Anasazi were the largest and most spectacular of the southwestern societies. This Chaco Anasazi society flourished from about A.D. 600 for more than five centuries until it disappeared between 1150 A.D. and 1200 A.D.. It was a geographically widespread, well organized, and a regionally integrated society. They built the largest structures in North America. Yet today, we are astonished to see the barren treeless landscape of Chaco Canyon consisting of deep-cut arroyos and sparse vegetation of only salt-tolerant bushes because the canyon is now completely uninhibited. Why would anyone build an advanced city in this wasteland and having done all that work, abandon it?

When Native American peoples first moved into the Chaco Canyon area, they lived in underground pit houses like other Native Americans in the southwest. Around A.D. 700, the Chaco Anasazi independently invented the stone construction techniques, ultimately learning to adapt rubble cores with veneers of cut stone facing. In the beginning those structures were only one story high. But by A.D. 920, they were two stories, becoming the largest Chacoan site of Pueblo Bonito. Then it rose to five or six stories, with the largest houses having 600 rooms, over the next two centuries. Its roof supports were logs up to 16 feet long and weighing as much as 700 pounds.

Why was it at Chaco Canyon that construction techniques and political and societal organization reached its highest point? The environmental advantages of Chaco Canyon were the most likely reason. Initially, the environment must have been quite favorable: an oasis. The rain runoff from side channels was caught by the narrow canyon and the large upland area resulted in high ground water levels allowing farming regardless of local rainfall. Also, the soil was being renewed from the runoff, increasing its fertility. For such a dry habitat, the large habitable area, and everything within 50 miles of it, could support large populations. The Chaco region offered a diverse variety of wild plants and animal species. The relative low elevation provided a long growing season for the crops. In the beginning, nearby juniper and pinyon woodlands supplied the construction logs and firewood. The Anasazi diet depended heavily on growing corn, squash, and beans. Early archaeological levels also indicate consumption of wild plants such as pinyon nuts with 75% protein, and hunting of deer.[2]

But the Southwest was environmentally fragile. With the passage of time, the Anasazi were confronted with two major problems: water management and deforestation. Initially, rain runoff over the flat canyon bottom would have been like a broad sheet, permitting floodplain agriculture watered by runoff and by a high alluvial ground water table. When the Anasazi started diverting water into channels for irrigation, the fast water-flow and the clearing of vegetation for agriculture, combining with natural processes, started cutting deep canyons around A.D. 900. The water levels in the canyons were below field levels, hence the irrigation agriculture and agriculture based on groundwater became impossible. The Anasazi dealt with this problem by building dams inside side-canyons above the elevation of the main canyon to store rainwater. They also laid out field canyons so that rainwater would irrigate as well. Additionally, they stored rainwater coming down over the cliffs rimming the canyon's north wall between each pair of side-canyon and they built rock dams across the main canyon.[3]

The second major problem was deforestation in the Chaco Canyon. It was deforested quite fast taking only a few centuries, like Easter Island, because its climate was dry and the rate of tree regrowth on the logged land was too slow to keep up with the rate of logging. The pinyon nuts as a local food supply vanished due to the loss of woodland, forcing Chaco residents to look for different timber sources for their construction needs as shown by a complete disappearance of pinyon beams from Chaco architecture. Chacoans now had to go far into forests of fir trees, ponderosa pine, and spruce which grew in mountains up to 50 miles away and at several thousand feet higher elevation. Even without any draft animals, about 200,000 logs weighing 700 pounds each were dragged down the mountains over this distance to Chaco Canyon by human muscle power only.[4]

The Chaco Canyon was now like a black hole into which everything was imported but nothing went out. Lots of items came in: tens of thousands of big trees for construction, pottery (most of late-period pottery in Chaco Canyon was imported probably because local firing wood supplies were exhausted precluding firing pots within the canyon itself), quality stones for making tools, turquoise for making ornaments, and from other parts of New Mexico: Macaws, copper bells, and shell jewelry from Hohokam and from Mexico: luxury goods. As evidenced by a recent study tracing the origins of corncobs excavated from Pueblo Bonito, even food had to be imported. It turns out that already in the 9th century, corn was being brought in from the Chuska Mountains 50 miles to the west while corncobs from the last years of Pueblo Bonito came from San Juan River system 60 miles to the north in the 12th century.

Doesn't this remind one of America on a massive scale in the 21ˢᵗ century as almost everything is imported from other countries?

Despite the two environmental problems that reduced crop production and eliminated timber supply within the canyon, the population of Chacoans here continued to increase at A.D. 1029. Many archaeologists surmise the Chaco Anasazi population at its peak to be much higher than 5000. Now the Chaco society had turned into a mini empire: a well fed elite living in luxury with an underfed poor peasantry doing the labor and growing the food. Chacoans started living in a complex, interdependent society with outlying settlements of peasantry supporting the center where the elite lived in luxury—somewhat similar to today's modern cities.

Tree ring tests show that the final blow to Chacoans came in the form of a drought around A.D. 1130. Previously, there had been similar droughts around A.D. 1040 and 1090. The difference this time, however, was that Chaco Canyon held many more people, was more dependent on outlying settlements, and had no unoccupied land left. The ground water level went down below the level where it could be tapped by plant roots that could support agriculture; the drought also made rainfall supported dryland agriculture and irrigation agriculture impossible. A drought that lasted longer than three years would have been fatal because even the modern Puebloans can not store corn longer than two to three years after which it is too rotten or infested to consume. Outlying settlements that had formerly supplied the Chaco political and religious centers with food lost faith in the priests whose prayers for rain were unanswered and they now refused to make food deliveries.[5]

Once the food scarcity set in, strife within the society began. The last identified construction of Pueblo Bonito, dating from the decade after A.D. 1110, was of a wall that enclosed the south side of the plaza. This was formerly open to the outside. This shows strife. People were now visiting Pueblo Bonito not just to attend the ceremonies or to receive orders but also to create trouble. The last wooden beam at Pueblo Bonito and at the nearby Great House of Chetro Ketl was cut in A.D. 1117, and the last beam in Chaco Canyon in A.D. 1170.

Other Anasazi sites show more evidence of unrest, including the presence of cannibalism such as at the Kayenta Anasazi settlements at the top of steep cliffs which were far from fields and water. At these southwestern settlements which outlasted Chaco and survived until A.D. 1250, warfare was intense as evident by the presence of defensive walls, moats, and towers and a clustering of small hamlets into larger hilltop fortresses. Also found is evidence of deliberately burned villages containing unburied bodies, skulls with cut marks caused by scalping, and skeletons with arrowheads within the body cavity. The strongest evidence comes from an Anasazi site at which a house and its contents had been smashed. The scattered bones of seven persons were left inside the house suggesting their death occurred during a war raid as they were not properly buried. Just as bones of animals had been cracked, some of these peoples' bones had been cracked to extract the bone marrow. Consistent with human flesh having been cooked in the pots, the broken pots themselves from that Anasazi site contained residues of human muscle protein myoglobin on the pots' interiors. The most convincing evidence of cannibalism at the site is that of dried human feces, found in the house's hearth—still well preserved after nearly a thousand years in that dry climate— which was determined to contain human muscle proteins, which is absent from normal human feces, even from feces of people injured and with bleeding intestines. Hence it is quite probable that whoever attacked that house, killed its inhabitants, cracked open their bones, boiled their flesh in pots, scattered the bones, and relieved themselves by depositing feces in that hearth that actually contained the flesh of their victims.[6]

An explosion of population growth and deepening environmental problems resulted in civil unrest and warfare for the Anasazi and a once complex society rapidly disintegrated to the point of people actually consuming each other.

Some time between A.D. 1150 and 1200, the inhabitants of the Chaco Canyons finally abandoned their home. The canyon remained largely empty until Navajo sheepherders, some 600 years later, reoccupied it. The Navajo found these great ruins. Not knowing who had built them, they referred to these vanished inhabitants as "the Anasazi", or "the Ancient Ones". What really happened to the thousands of the inhabitants of Chaco Canyon? By analogy with historically witnessed abandonment of other pueblos during a drought in the 1670s, most of them likely starved to death, some people killed each other, and the survivors fled to other settled areas in the southwest. It seems the evacuation was planned because most rooms at Anasazi sites are devoid of pottery and other useful items that people would be expected to take with them in a planned evacuation except for the presence of pottery in the above mentioned sites whose unlucky occupants were killed and eaten. The other settlements where these evacuees fled to include Zuni pueblos where rooms built in Chaco Canyon style houses containing Chaco style pottery have been found at dates corresponding to the time of Chaco's abandonment.

The aforementioned Kayenta Anasazi, living not far from Chaco Canyon in Long House Valley in northeastern Arizona, although surviving longer than those in Chaco, also completely abandoned their valley at around A.D. 1300. Numbering around a thousand people from A.D. 800 to A.D. 1350, these Anasazi succumbed to greatly reduced corn harvests resulting from reduced rainfall and drought, largely due to greatly reduced soil fertility and deforestation that had taken place all over the area, reducing the supply of timber for construction and firewood for living.[7]

The inhabitants of other nearby areas known as the Mesa Verdeans, Mimbres, Hohokam, Mogollon, and others also underwent reorganizations, collapses, or abandonments at various times within the period from A.D. 1100 to 1500. Though different factors influenced collapses at different areas, all of them lived in fragile and difficult environments. They all found clever solutions in the 'short run' but were not able to cope up with problems in the 'long run'. Their societies all finally yielded to a combination of long lasting droughts, environmental degradation, soil erosion, and reduction in water supply or water table levels.

My family and I visited the cliff dwellings of Arizona and Mesa Verde of Colorado in 1998. It was amazing to see the cliff dwellings of Arizona built on the side of a mountain cliff at such a high elevation. Though they would have been safe from predators at such heights, living on the cliff, they must have been very cold in the harsh winter, being not far from Flagstaff, Arizona. We also found the site of Mesa Verde remarkable. The dwellings are extensive and well built on the side of a mountain. They had various rooms, back rooms against the rocks, which would be cool in summer while the front areas and little front yards were open, getting sunshine and keeping the women warm while they did their daily household chores including making pottery and baskets.

Amazingly, the Anasazi and others survived for 600 years or more (the United States is not yet 250). At their peak, none of them would have realized how quickly their economy and their world would collapse. Yet when it did, it happened very fast. The Chaco society collapsed after its peak in the decade A.D. 1110-1120, and to the Chacoans of that decade, how implausible might that have seemed!

Perhaps, we modern humans of this industrialized world should not be so sure that our world would remain the same forever foolishly thinking that we would be enjoying the same or better amenities for ever. It would not be too surprising if our own world might change drastically in not too distant a future. The change may be slow but the world is surely changing around us whether we like it or not. Change is the law of nature.

THE MAYA CIVILIZATION

Some of you might have visited the ruins of the ancient Maya civilization that flourished over a thousand years ago in Mexico's Yucatan Peninsula and in surrounding parts of Central America. A visitor there finds many ruins with their gigantic pyramids, temples, and monuments still surrounded by jungle, far from present human settlements. Yet, these were the sites of the most advanced Native American civilization of the New World, long before the arrival of the Spaniards.

Many Maya cities remained deserted and hidden by the growth of jungles, totally unknown to the outside world. In 1839, a wealthy American lawyer named John Stephen along with an English draftsman Frederick Catherwood, having heard the rumors about the ruins in the jungle, set out to search for them. They explored 44 sites and various cities. Looking at the extraordinary quality of structures and art, they realized that these were not the work of 'savages', but rather that of a highly advanced civilization that had vanished. Stunned by these sites, Stephen wrote:

> The city was desolate. No remnants of the ruins hangs round the ruins, with tradition handed down from father to son and from generation to generation. It lay before us like a shattered bark in the midst of the ocean, her mast gone, her name effaced, her crew perished, and none to tell whence she came, to whom she belonged, how long on her journey, or what caused her destruction...Architecture, sculpture, and painting, all the arts which embellish life, had flourished in this overgrown forest; orators, warriors, and statesmen, beauty, ambition, and glory had lived and passed away, and none knew such things had been, or could tell of their past existence...Here were the remains of a cultivated, polished, and peculiar people, who had passed through all the stages incident to the rise and fall of nations; reached their golden age and perished...We went up to their desolate temples and fallen altars; and wherever we moved we saw the evidence of their taste, their skill in arts...We called back into life the strange people who gazed in sadness from the wall; pictured them, in fanciful costumes and adorned with plumes of feather, ascending the terraces of the palace and steps leading to the temples...In the romance of the world history nothing ever impressed me more forcibly than the spectacle of

this once great and lovely city, overturned, desolate, and lost…overgrown with trees for miles around, and without even a name to distinguish it.[8]

The Maya society consisted of small kingdoms, politically divided and perpetually at war with each other, and never became unified into large empires like the Aztec Empire of the valley of Mexico or the Inca Empire of the Andes. Maya armies and bureaucracies were small, unable to undertake lengthy campaigns over long distances. Most of these Maya kingdoms had populations of 25,000 to 50,000 people, none over half a million; all living within a radius of two or three days' walk from the king's palace. It was possible to see the tops of the temples of the nearest Maya kingdom from the top of the temple of one Maya kingdom. These Maya cities remained small, and the royalty didn't manage food storage or trade.

The Maya region is part of the larger Native American cultural region known as Mesoamerica. It extended approximately from Central Mexico to Guatemala, Honduras, and Belize. It was, along with the Andes of South America, one of the two new world centers of innovation before the arrival of the Europeans.

Within the Maya region, villages and pottery appeared around or after 1000 B.C., major buildings around 500 B.C. and writing around 400 B.C. All preserved ancient Maya writing, a total of about 15,000 inscriptions, is on stone and pottery. It relates only with the kings, nobles, and their conquests. No mention of commoners is found. The Maya were still using bark paper coated with plaster to write books, of which only four survived; the rest were burned by the Spanish bishop Landa. The four that survived are treatises on astronomy and the calendar.

The classical period of Maya civilization begins around A.D. 250 when the kings and dynasties appeared. The Maya kings had their own name glyphs and palaces; many nobles also had their own inscriptions and palaces in the kingdom. In Maya society the king was also the highest priest, responsible for attending to astronomical and calendrical rituals, thereby to bring rain and prosperity which the king claimed to possess the supernatural powers to deliver due to his special relationship with the Gods. That is why the peasants supported the luxurious life style of the kings and their courts, feeding them corn and venison, and building their palaces. Implicit in this were their promises to the peasants of good rain and plentiful harvests. As it finally occurred, the kings were in trouble when the long drought came and they could no longer keep their promises [9]

From A.D. 250, the Maya population started expanding exponentially, as did the largest buildings and monuments. The population and construction reached its peak in the 8th century. The largest monuments were erected towards the end of that classic period. Then, throughout the 9th century, both construction and population began declining, until the last known date of any monument constructed which fell on the year A.D. 909. That final decline in Maya population, its architecture, and the Long Count calendar constitutes what is known as the Classic Maya Collapse.[10]

One of these kingdoms was Copan, which was situated in southwestern Honduras. We find densely built ruins here. The population in Copan Valley steeply grew to about 27,000 people around A.D. 750-900. Construction of royal monuments glorifying kings was massive between A.D. 650 and 750. After A.D. 700, nobles other than kings also got into the practice of building huge palaces for themselves. Around A.D. 800, there were about twenty such palaces. One of those palaces had 50 buildings with room for about 250 people. These palaces, though spectacular, amounted to an increasingly tremendous burden on the peasants. The last date on an incomplete altar likely bearing a king's name is of A.D. 822.

So, why did such a thriving society collapse? Around A.D. 650, people had begun cutting down the forest on the hill top and had started living there. Huge number of trees was being cut down to clear the sites; the cut trees were being used for construction and fuel. The deforestation must have caused a man made drought in the valley bottom because forests play a major role in water recycling so that massive deforestation tends to lower rainfall. Hundreds of skeletons recovered from Copan archaeological sites show that the health of Copan's inhabitants deteriorated from A.D. 650 to 850, both amongst the elites as well as among the commoners.

The drought that continued produced less and less food, more and more people must have started depending on the fertile valley at the bottom of the hills for their food. Fighting amongst the farmers for the best land must have ensued—just as it happened in modern Rwanda. People must have been extremely angry at the king for his failure to provide the rains and prosperity. That explains why the last we hear from any Copan king is in A.D. 822. As per evidence, the royal palace was burned around A.D. 850. Some nobles continued their luxurious life style after the king's fall, until around A.D. 975. Copan's total population declined more gradually than its king or nobles. The population estimate around A.D. 950 was still 15,000, a 54% decline from its peak of 27,000. That population still continued to dwindle until there was no one left in the Copan Valley by around A.D. 1250.[11]

Similarly, there were other collapses at other sites at different times. A smaller collapse occurred earlier around A.D. 150 when north of Copan, El Mirador in Guatemala, and other Maya cities collapsed. El Mirador, a huge site in the middle of Maya region, was settled around 200 B.C. It boasted one of the largest Maya pyramids ever. It was abandoned around A.D. 150, long before the rise of Copan. A society living at Tikal, a site south of El Mirador in Guatemala seems to have collapsed between the late 6th and early 7th century. Some societies, however, survived the classic collapse or even increased after it. Chichen Itza of Mexico fell around A.D. 1250 and Mayapan collapsed around 1450. In 1995, this author, with family, saw the ruins of Chichen Itza including its massive pyramid which I climbed (reluctantly as it was quite steep). But it was indeed awe inspiring. Chichen Itza, located in northern peninsula, grew after A.D. 850. It was the main northern center around A.D. 1000, only to be totally destroyed around 1250 in a civil war. In Belize, there had arisen a society which built one of the largest pyramids. Once again, during our December 2004 visit of Panama, we also visited parts of Belize. In Belize, we stopped at this pyramid site. The pyramid was very high, solidly built and huge in size. Though it was very steep, my friend and myself climbed the pyramid all the way to its summit. The last part close to top had no fence or steps. I dared and climbed that also and stood on the top of the pyramid. All around, I could see nothing but forest. It reminded me of how advanced these ancient people must have been to build such a massive structure.

Cities in the Maya region rose and fell at different times. So what caused this Maya civilization of millions of people to collapse at seemingly arbitrary times? There were several reasons that contributed towards their decline and disappearance. Two major ones were warfare and drought. For a long time, archaeologists believed that the Mayas were peaceful and gentle people. But from evidence, we now know that Maya warfare was chronic, intense, and not solvable because limitations on food resources and transportation made it impossible for any Maya king to unite the whole region in an empire, in the way that Aztecs of Central Mexico and Incas of the Andes did. Archaeological records indicate that towards the time of the Classic Collapse, wars became more frequent and intense. Maya kings fought to take one another captive. The captives were tortured and killed. Maya warfare was violent and costly; wars between different kingdoms, cities within a kingdom revolting against the capitol to secede, and frequent violent attempts by would be kings to usurp power, resulted often in civil wars. All this took its heavy toll on the limited resources of the kingdoms.

Another important cause of Maya Collapses was the phenomenon of repeated droughts. Climatologists and paleoecologists, based on the studies of radiocarbon-dated layers from lake sediment cores, conclude that from about 5500 B.C. until 500 B.C., the Maya area was relatively wet. The following period—just before the rise of pre-Classic Maya civilization—from 475 to 250 B.C., was dry. The pre-Classic rise must have been facilitated by the return of wetter conditions after 250 B.C., but then a drought from A.D. 125 until A.D. 250 was connected with the pre-Classic collapse at El Mirador and other sites nearby. Then, wetter conditions returned causing Classic Maya cities to spring up, temporarily interrupting their rise further by a drought around A.D. 600 which caused a decline at Tikal and other cities nearby. Finally, around A.D. 760, a worst drought in the last 7000 years began, peaking around the year A.D. 800, and is conspicuously associated with the Classic Collapse.[12]

Analyzing frequency of droughts in Maya area, it is obvious that they recur at the intervals of approximately 208 years. These drought cycles may be as a result of small variations in the sun's radiation, likely made more severe in the Yucatan (drier in the north, wetter in the south) shifting southwards. This effect might be true in other areas of the world. As a matter of fact, some other prehistoric collapses far from the Maya area appear to coincide with peaks of those drought cycles. According to Professor Jared Diamond, the collapse of world's first empire, the Akkadin Empire of Mesopotamia around 2170 B.C., the collapse of the Moche IV civilization in the Peruvian coast around A.D. 600, and the collapse of Tiwanaku civilization in the Andes around A.D. 1100 are some examples of other collapses due to the same reasons. The Mayas were not able to store corn, their staple food, longer than 12 months due to increased humidity in the area. So any drought lasting longer than one year would have been devastating.

Southern lowlands were the areas most affected by the Classic Collapse for two reasons. It was the region with the densest population and it may have had the most serious water problems because it was situated too high above the water table for water to be obtained from cenotes or wells when rains failed. In the course of the Classic Collapse, the southern lowlands lost 99% of their population. For example, in Guatemala around Central Petén, at the peak of the Classic Maya period, the population was estimated at between 3000,000 to 14,000,000, and perhaps as many as 24,000,000 people. But at the time of Spanish arrival, there were only 30,000 people there. In 1524 and 1525, when Cortez and his Spanish army passed through Central Petén, they nearly starved because they came across so few villages from which to acquire corn. Cortez passed just within a few miles of the ruins of the great Classic cities of Tikal and Palenque, but he heard or saw no signs of them because they were covered by forest and almost no one was living in their vicinity.[13]

Once again, how did such a huge population of people disappear? Some of that Maya population decline surely involved people starving to death or dying due to thirst, or killing each other over struggles for dwindling resources. The other aspect of decrease may reflect a slower birth rate or higher child mortality rate over the course of many decades. Thus, it is likely that depopulation consisted of both, higher death rate and lower birth rate. But this was all because of underlying deforestation, persistent droughts resulting in lower agricultural production and scarcity of water, and constant warfare. One wonders why the kings and nobles failed to recognize and solve these seemingly obvious problems threatening their society. Unfortunately, more of their attention was focused on their short-term concerns of enriching themselves, erecting monuments wasting vast resources, conducting wars, competing with each other and extracting enough food from poor farmers to support these activities. The Maya kings, like most short-sighted leaders throughout history, did not heed long-term problems as they perceived them.

NORSE PEOPLE OF GREENLAND

This is another grim story of the collapse of a society of Norse people who had settled in Greenland, survived for some 450 years and ultimately met the same fate as the Anasazi and the Mayas. The Norse were Vikings who had come from Scandinavia, especially Norway, and had occupied Greenland around A.D. 980. Actually, around A.D. 980, a hot blooded, violent man named Eric the Red was charged with murder and was forced to leave for Iceland. There too, he ended up killing more people, and was subsequently exiled from Iceland as well. In the end, he set sail with 25 ships and came to Greenland's south coast. Finding good pastureland inside deep fjords, he named this island Greenland. Many more would arrive from Norway and Iceland and the colony eventually grew into 5000 or more people. Unfortunately for the Norse, Greenland's climate fluctuated periodically: from cold to bitter cold.

The climate in Greenland had warmed up after the last ice age some14,000 years ago. The first settlement there occurred around 2500 B.C. by Paleo-Eskimo cultures. Later they declined or disappeared around 1500 B.C. and again they returned, declined and then completely abandoned southern Greenland some time before the arrival of the Norse around A.D. 980. Initially, the Norse didn't encounter the natives there though they did come across ruins left by these people. The warmer climate though allowed the Inuit people again to enter northwestern Greenland from Canada around A.D. 1200 which would bear big consequences for the Norse people.

From the ice core analysis, we learn that the climate in Greenland was mild around A.D. 800 to 1300, similar to Greenland's weather today or even slightly warmer. These mild centuries are called the Medieval Warm Period. Regarding Greenland's average climate over the last 14,000 years, the Norse had arrived in Greenland during a period good for growing hay and pasturing animals. But around A.D. 1300, the climate in the North Atlantic began to get colder, ushering in a cold period called the Little Ice Age that lasted into the 1800's. This Ice Age was in full swing by 1420 and the increased summer drift ice between Norway, Greenland, and Iceland ended shipping relations between the Greenland Norse and the outside world. While this cold weather was bad news for the Norse, it was tolerable or even beneficial for the Inuit, who could also hunt the ringed seals while the Norse depended on growing hay.[14]

So why did the Norse people survive for 450 years and then died off in Greenland? The onset of the Little Ice Age was a major factor behind the collapse of the Norse, though other factors indeed also played major parts. Additionally, they inadvertently damaged their environment on which their survival depended by destroying the natural vegetation by cutting down the trees, stripping turf, overgrazing, and causing soil erosion. As soon as they arrived, they started cutting down the woodlands to clear land for pasture. The remaining trees were cut down for lumber and firewood. Livestock grazing and trampling prevented trees from regenerating, especially in winter, when the plants were most vulnerable. While the Inuit learned to burn blubber for heating and lighting their dwellings, the Norse kept burning willow and alder wood in their houses, accelerating the deforestation. Another major demand for firewood was in manufacturing dairy. The vessels which stored milk and milk products—a major protein source in the Norse diet—needed to be washed with boiled water frequently, twice a day for the milk buckets. All this required wood burning and contributed to deforestation. Hence, their impact on natural vegetation left them short of lumber, and fuel. Their impact on soil and turf left them short of useful land. They, by cutting and burning the cover of trees and shrubs, contributed heavily to soil erosion. With the trees and shrubs gone, the sheep and goats began to graze down the grass, which could regenerate only slowly in Greenland's cold weather. Once this grass cover was broken and the soil was exposed, it was carried away by strong winds and the pounding by heavy rains. Top soil was removed and washed miles from the entire valley. Where the sand was exposed, it was picked up by the winds and dumped downwind. Lake cores and soil profiles attest to the development of serious soil erosion in Greenland after the arrival of the Norse.[15]

The Inuit people, unlike the Norse, had a major advantage. They had inherited thousands of years of cultural developments by Arctic people learning to master Arctic conditions. Unlike the Norse, who used wood and timber for heating, building or illuminating their houses, the Inuit built igloos for winter housing out of snow, and they burned whale and seal blubber both for fuel and for lighting lamps. Instead of wood, they used stretched seal skins over frameworks to build kayaks and boats big enough to take out in unprotected waters for hunting whales.

The Norse and the Inuit had shared the same island for several centuries. They did have face to face contact at some times. As a matter of fact, when they met for the first time, the Norse killed some of the Inuit and their relations from the beginning were tarnished. Unfortunately for the Norse, failure to trade with or learn from the Inuit, particularly of their hunting techniques, turned out to be a major setback because the Inuit were very skilled hunters. The Inuit had more sophisticated techniques to hunt the Walruses and the seals with their light skin boats and hunting methods. The Inuit exhibited amazing speed and maneuverability with their kayaks when hunting in the waters. When the Norse were chronically at risk of exhausting their stored winter food supply and on the verge of starving, they could have traded with the Inuit for ringed seals to eat. Ringed seals were Greenland's most abundant seal species available during winter. These seals were successfully hunted by the Inuit but not by the Norse, at a time which was crucial to acquire food. Though Inuit arrived later than the Norse to Greenland, their hunting methods were far superior while the Norse depended more on storing hay, raising cattle, sheep and goats, getting milk, cheese etc. from these animals and slaughtering these animals for food in winter when necessary.[16]

Greenland's natural resources were only marginally sufficient to support a European pastoral society of viable size. The hay production in Greenland fluctuated significantly from year to year depending on the severity of winter and moisture. Hence, in poor years, the society's survival was threatened due to the depletion of the resources.

Thus, five factors were responsible for the ultimate demise of the Norse in the Greenland: Climate change, Norse adversely affecting their environment (including deforestation, overgrazing, soil erosion etc.), decline in friendly contacts and trade with Norway, increasing hostility between them and the Inuit, and a conservative non-adaptive outlook on their ways of life. Severe cold weather lowered hay production inducing the starvation of the cattle first. Ice sheet clogged the sea lanes between Norway and Greenland, thus ending the vital contacts between the two, depriving the Norse the Iron, some timber, and their identity. The demand in Europe for Greenland's principal export, Walrus ivory, declined when the crusades enabled Christian Europe's access again to

Asia's and East Africa's Elephant ivory whose deliveries had been cut off by the Arab conquest of Mediterranean shores. By the 1400s, carving was out of fashion whether with Walrus or with Elephant ivory. A combination of these factors undermined Norway's resources and motivation for sending ships to Greenland. Finally, the arrival of the Inuit and Norse's inability to establish cordial relations with them and to learn from their superior hunting techniques brought an end to Norse settlements in Greenland. These five factors impacted the Norse gradually over a long period of time and by the 15th century the Norse settlements had vanished.[17]

Perhaps, future generations will wonder at our current industrial nations who keep using fossil fuels which are leading us on a self destructive path of environmental degradation and climate change despite the over abundance of other clean sources of energy such as sun and wind. They might look at us with the same incredulity as we look at the Norse today and their inability to change leading to their inability to survive.

CHAPTER 2
THE EASTER ISLANDERS

Civilizations die from suicide, not by murder
—Arnold Toynbee

The story of Easter Island is both tragic and mysterious. Easter Island, located in the South Pacific, is the most remote habitable piece of land in the world—the nearest place is the coast of Chile, 2,300 miles to the east. To its west, some 1,300 miles away, are Polynesia's Pitcairn Islands. By jet, Easter Island is a five hour flight from Chile, over endless Pacific Ocean stretching hundreds of miles from one horizon to the other with nothing else below. It is advisable to reach the island before nightfall as, if pilots miss this little spec of land, they may not have enough fuel to make the 2,500 mile return trip to Chile.

Easter Island's mysteries were first unearthed by the Dutch explorer Jacob Roggeveen, who spotted the island on Easter Day, April 5, 1722—a namesake which remains to this day. It took Roggeveen, sailing in three large European ships, 17 days crossing the Pacific without sighting any land, leading to his wonder at how these Polynesians who greeted him upon landing at the coast of Easter Island could reach such a remote place. Upon arriving, he and subsequent visitors were surprised to learn that the islanders had but small and leaky canoes as their watercrafts. They were hardly 10 feet long and capable of carrying one or two persons. They wondered, how could a band of such primitive colonists with their crops, drinking water, and some chickens survive such a long journey of two and a half weeks in such rackety watercrafts?[1]

When Roggeveen and his crew started exploring the island, they were awe struck to see hundreds of gigantic stone statues scattered throughout the island. These statues were erected on stone platforms and were on average 30 feet tall and weighed about 10 tons. One was as high as 32 feet, weighing some 75 tons. The statues were of a human torso with a head and a head-cover, all carved from solid stone. Yet, among these monoliths, what Roggeveen saw was a wasteland with not a single tree or brush over ten feet high.[2] Like other Polynesian paradises, what had happened to all the trees that must have stood there in abundance, he wondered. How could the people at this island have transported these giant statues and erected them on these platforms, some up to 30 feet high, without any ropes or timber? Roggeveen would have puzzled further if he knew that these islanders had no draft animals, no wheels, and no source of power except their own muscles. To add to the mystery, these statues were still standing in 1770, but by 1864 all of them were tossed down by the islanders themselves. Why did they carve them in the first place and why did they stop?[3]

Easter Island is a triangular island which entirely consists of three volcanoes that emerged from the sea in close proximity to each other but at varying times in the last million to several million years. These volcanoes have been dormant for the island's history of human settlement. Between 600,000 and 3000,000 years ago, the oldest volcano Poike erupted and formed the southeast corner of the island while the subsequent eruption of Rano Kau formed the southwest corner. The eruption of the youngest volcano Terravaka, situated to the triangle's northern corner, some 200,000 years ago released lavas that covered 95% of the island's surface.

According to archaeologists, at least 30,000 years before the arrival and during the early years of Polynesian settlement, Easter Island was anything but a wasteland. Instead, it was a subtropical forest of trees and woody brushes that towered over a ground of shrubs, ferns, grasses, and herbs. In this forest grew rope-yielding hauhau trees, tree daisies, and toromiro trees that furnish dense, mesquite-like firewood. The most common tree on the island was a species of palm, now absent, that was closely related to the still-surviving Chilean wine palm, which grows up to 80 or 90 feet tall and 6 to 7 feet in diameter. The tall, strong and un-branched trunks of these palms would have been most suitable for constructing large canoes as well as for transporting and erecting the giant statues. They may also have been a valued source of food as its Chilean varieties yield edible nuts as well as sap from which Chileans make syrup, sugar, honey, and wine.[4]

By Polynesian standards, Easter Island's area of 66 square miles and its elevation of 1,670 feet are both modest. The island's topography is mostly gentle with none of the deep valleys you come across in the Hawaiian Islands. The subtropical location gives it a mild climate while its soil is fertile due to its recent volcanic origin. While the subtropical climate is warm by the standards of European and North American winters, it is cool by the standards of most of Polynesia. Unlike other Polynesian Islands, Easter does not lie close to the equator. Hence, some tropical crops such as coconuts that grow in abundance elsewhere grow poorly in Easter. The surrounding ocean is too cold for coral reefs that could rise to the surface creating an abundance of fish and shellfish. Easter Island is generally deficient in fish and coral-fish, with only 127 species compared with more than a thousand species in Fiji. Easter is also a windy place, likely posing problems to the early farmers. All these factors offered fewer food resources to the Easter Islanders than to most of the Pacific Islanders.

Additional problems are associated with its geography and its rainfall. It receives on average 50 inches per year—low by Polynesian standards. In addition to this limited rainfall, its volcanic surface is very porous so what little rain falls percolates quickly through the surface—limiting its fresh water supplies. It has just one intermittent stream on Mt. Teravaka's slope, which is often dry at times. Still, the islanders managed to collect sufficient water for drinking, cooking, and growing crops, though perhaps through considerable effort.

In prehistoric times, Polynesian expansion was the most dramatic over-water exploration in human history. The spread of ancient humans from the Asian mainland through Indonesia's islands to Australia and New Guinea had advanced no farther into the Pacific than the Solomon Islands east of New Guinea. Around this time, a seafaring and farming people who produced ceramics known as Lapita-style pottery, originating from Bismarck Archipelago northeast of New Guinea, sailed nearly a thousand miles across open ocean east of the Solomons to reach Fiji, Samoa, and Tonga. They became the ancestors of the Polynesians. Though these Polynesians lacked the knowledge of compasses, writing or metal tools, they were masters of navigational arts and sailing with canoe technology. By around 1200 A.D., the Polynesians had reached every habitable piece of land in the vast triangle of ocean from Hawaii to New Zealand to Easter Island. It is now clear that both the discoveries and settlements of these islands were meticulously planned rather than being accidental. Contrary to what one would expect, much of Polynesia was settled in a west-to-east direction, opposite to the prevailing winds and currents. Transfers of many species of crops and livestock, from bananas to taro and from dogs to pigs and chickens, proves beyond doubt that these settlements were by well-prepared colonists carrying products of their homelands essential for survival in their new colonies.

The first expansion wave of the Lapita-potters ancestral to the Polynesians, spread eastwards across the Pacific only as far as Fiji, Samoa, and Tonga which lie only about a few days' sail from each other. A much larger gap of water separates these West Polynesian islands from the East Polynesian islands: the Societies, Cooks, Australs, Marquesas, Tuamotus, Hawaii, New Zealand, Pitcairn Group, and Easter. Following a long time interval of some 1,500 years, that gap was breached. Sometime around A.D. 600-800, the East Polynesian islands Cooks, Societies, and Marquesas were colonized. Finally, they became the sources of colonists for the remaining islands. Across the huge water gap of 2,000 miles, with New Zealand's occupation around A.D. 1200, the settlement of the Pacific islands was finally complete. By what route, the farthest island in the east, was Easter itself occupied? Though Marquesas supported a large population, and they were the source for Hawaii's settlement, the wind and current conditions would rule it out as the source for Easter Island's inhabitants. The most likely 'jumping-off' points for the Easter's colonization have been Pitcairn, Henderson, and Mangareva as they are located about halfway between Marquesas and Easter. Archaeological evidence also points towards these sources for Easter's occupation. A reconstructed Polynesian canoe *Hokule'a* succeeded in 1999 in reaching Easter Island from Mangareva after a voyage of 17 days, further supporting this theory.[5]

The Easter Islanders have a tradition that the leader of the expedition to settle their island was a chief known as Hotu Matu'a (the great parent)—who sailed in one or two large canoes with his wife, six sons, and extended family. The populations of many other Polynesian islands kept in contact with each other through inter-island two way travels after their initial discovery and settlements. But Easter Island lacked dogs, pigs, and certain Polynesian crops that one would have expected to find. If they did not survive the journey with the Hotu Matu'a, or after his party came in, then perhaps other subsequent voyagers from other islands would have brought these basic animals with them. Additionally the discovery of tools made of stone with a chemical composition typical for one specific island turning up in another island unquestionably prove that there existed inter-island trade between Pitcairn, Mangareva, Marquesas, Henderson, and Societies. Yet, no stone of Easter Island origin has been found on any other island or vice versa. Thus, it is quite likely that Easter Islanders were totally isolated at the end of their world, with no contact with other islanders or the outside world for the thousand years from Hotu Matu'a's arrival to Roggeveen's or later.

Though other islands were settled around A.D. 600-800, the most reliable radiocarbon dates for early occupation of Easter Island are of

A.D. 900. This is based on paleontological evidence, obtained on wood charcoal and on bones of porpoises eaten by islanders, from the oldest archaeological layers offering evidence of human presence at Easter's Anakena beach. Anakena, being the best canoe landing beach on the island, would have been the obvious site where the first settlers would have based themselves. But the canoes to hunt the porpoises soon became unavailable. So the current estimate of Easter's occupation is somewhat before A.D. 900.[6]

At its peak, how many people inhabited Easter Island? The best estimates put the number of people inhabiting the island is anywhere between 15,000 and 30,000. Both archeological surveys and oral traditions indicate that Easter's land surface was divided into about a dozen territories like a pizza pie—each part belonging to one clan or lineage group. Each started from the sea coast and extended inland to form a territory with its own chief, platform, and statues. The different clans competed peacefully in the building of platforms and statues. Yet this competition would eventually result in ferocious fighting. These competing clan territories were integrated religiously, and to some degree politically and economically under the leadership of one supreme chief. Easter's pie did not consist of identical slices. Different territories were endowed with different resources. Some contained quarries of the best stone for carving statues; other contained the red stone for carving the crown of the statues. Still others consisted of the fine grained volcanic stones for making tools, and some contained the best land for agriculture, water streams, and the best beaches.[7]

The archaeological evidence of cooperation between the different clans of various territories is that the stone statues and their red crowns from quarries of the Tongariki and Hanga Poukura clans were transported to the platforms of all 11 or 12 territories distributed all over the island. The roads to transport the statues and their crowns out of those quarries had to traverse many territories and the clan whose statues were transported needed permission to pass through the territories of the other clan chiefs. All localized foods, fish etc. had to be distributed all over the island making it an integrated island unlike Marquesas or others.

The most mysterious things on the Easter Island are its statues (moai) and the platforms (ahu) on which they stood. About 300 ahu have been found. Many were small and had no moai on them but at least 113 did have moai. Twenty five of them were quite large and elaborate. Every one of the dozen of the island's territories had from one to five of those large ahu. Most of the statue bearing ahus are scattered around the coast oriented so that ahu and its statues faced the interior over the clan's territory. The statues do not look towards the sea.

The ahu is a platform, rectangular in shape and made not of stone but of rubble fill kept in place by four stone retaining walls of gray basalt. Some of these walls such as those of Ahu Vinapu have beautifully fitted stones reminiscent of Inca architecture. The ahu are about 13 feet high and many have side wings up to 500 feet wide. So an ahu's total weight could have been from about 300 tons for a small one to more than 9000 tons for Ahu Tongariki. Unimaginable efforts must have been undertaken in building these ahus and their moais. The front walls of the ahus slope down to a rectangular plaza, 160 feet on each side, while the back side (sea side) retaining walls are vertical. In the back of an ahu are the crematorias which contain the remains of thousands of bodies. Unlike other Polynesian islands, the Easter Islanders cremated their dead. The ahus were originally colorful, white, yellow and red. The facing slabs were encrusted with white coral. The freshly cut moai were yellow and its crown and horizontal band of stone coursing on the walls in front of some ahu were red.

The moai represented high-ranking ancestors of which 887 were carved. Nearly half of them still remain in the Rano Raraku quarry. Most of the rest were transported out of the quarry and were erected on ahu, between 1 and 15 per ahu. One statue, a shorter but bulkier version, on ahu tongariki, weighs about 87 tons. Rano Raraku quarry contains bigger unfinished statues, with one 70 feet long and weighing about 270 tons.[8]

Looking at their sheer size one would wonder how such mammoth statues could have been carved, transported, and erected on platforms by humans! The task almost seems impossible to accomplish. The Swiss author Erich Von Deniken even claimed in his book *Chariots of the Gods* that these statues were carved and erected by extra terrestrials who visited Earth thousands of years ago. Actually, these statues have many precedents in Polynesia, especially in East Polynesia. Stone platforms used as shrines and often supporting temples are widespread; three were present in Pitcairn Island from which the settlers of Easter might have come. The Marquesas, Pitcairn, and Australs had large statues carved of red scoria, similar to the material used for some Easter's statues. Another type of stone called 'tuff' was also used in the Marquesas; Mangareva and Tonga also had other stone structures. Similar wooden statues also exist in Tahiti and elsewhere. Thus Easter Island architecture was likely a part of existing Polynesian tradition.

From the radiocarbon dating of the coral eyes of the statues and other indirect methods, it is clear that the ahu building period was between A.D. 1000 and 1600. Most statues were carved from volcanic tuff from the Rano Raraku region, as it was infinitely superior for carving. As time passed, these statues became larger, more stylized, rectangular, and nearly mass-produced, though each one was different.

The increase in size of the statues suggests that competition existed between rival chiefs to outdo one another. Many statues had a head crown called Pukao, a cylinder carved from red scoria, weighing up to 12 tons, mounted as a separate piece to rest on top of the moai's flat head. How could these ancient people mount a 12 ton crown on the head of a 32 feet statue? The answer is that they were both erected together. Once the statues were erected, eyes of white coral with a pupil of red scoria were inserted in the eyes' socket. These eyes were few and guarded by the priests who inserted them only at the time of certain ceremonies. Once inserted, the eyes create a penetrating and blinding gaze, awesome to look at.[9]

How did they transport such massive statues as far as 9 miles from the quarries to various platforms around the coast without any wheels or equipments and, once there, how did they raise them on the platforms? The transport roads are still visible. Well, many other people have accomplished such feats in the past such as at the pyramids of Egypt, Stonehenge in Britain, the Mayan pyramids in Latin America and the Aztec Teotihuacan. The Hawaiians have moved some of their biggest canoes, weighing more than an average size Easter Island moai, over canoe ladders miles away. The canoes were made after felling huge trees and after hollowing them out. So the method is quite plausible.

The statues were slided on so-called canoe wooden ladders made from the giant trees. Experts surmise that the Easter people modified these wooden ladders that were widespread on many islands. The ladders consisted of a pair of parallel wooden rails joined by fixed wooden cross bars. According to modern archeologists, the statues must have first been mounted on a wooden sled, then attached by ropes (likely made from hauhau trees) to the sled and hauled over the ladder. It was found that 50 to 70 people, working five hours a day, could drag the sled five yards at each pull. Thus, they could transport an average size statue nine miles in a week! The key was that all these people must synchronize their pulling effort similar to canoe peddlers synchronizing their paddling strokes. So a team of 500 adults could have transported even a bigger statue like Paro. This could have been within the manpower capabilities of an Easter Island clan which consisted of one to two thousand people.

As per how the statues were erected on the platforms, the remaining islanders now have told the investigators how their ancestors did this. They even erected a statue for them to prove their point. Subsequent experiments by others have now confirmed how these giant statues were erected on the platforms which were as much as 13 feet high. The islanders first built a gently sloping ramp of stones from the plaza up to the top of the front of the platform. Then they pulled the stone statue with its base end towards up the ramp. After the base reached the platform, they levered the statue's head an inch or two upwards with logs, slipping stones under the head to support it in its new position. Thus they continued to lever up the head and thus tilted the statue all the way towards vertical. The Pukao was probably erected at the same time as the statue itself, both being mounted together in the same frame that supported them. The long ramp of stones left must have been dismantled and reused to create the lateral wings of ahus.[10]

Anywhere between 20 to 25 carvers had to be fed for a month by the chief who was commissioning the statue. They also must have been paid in food for their families. For transporting these giant statues some nine miles away, a crew of 50 to 500 strong workers and a similar erecting crew had to be fed while doing this hard physical job. This would have required much more food than usual as well. There must have been feasting and celebrating within the whole clan owning the ahu and for the clans across whose territory the statue was transported. Much more food had to be consumed for transportation of huge stones for the construction of the ahus which outweighed the statues by twenty times. Archaeologists and others have concluded that given the number and size of ahus and moais, the work of constructing them added at least 25% to the food requirements of Easter's population over the 300 peak years of construction.

* * *

As a result of extensive research by archaeologist Dave Steadman who analyzed middens at Anakena Beach (the likely site of first human landing and settlement), it was concluded that Easter was formerly home to six native land birds including heron, two parrots, a barn owl, and two chicken-like rails. More impressive was it being the nesting place for 25 species of seabirds, making it perhaps the richest breeding site in all of Polynesia, perhaps the whole Pacific. Albatross, boobies, petrels, prions, shearwaters, storm-petrels, frigate birds, fulmars, terns and tropicbirds...all were attracted to Easter's remote location and complete lack of any predators. This made it an ideal haven as a breeding site—until the humans arrived.[11]

These Anakena excavations tell us much about the diet and the life-style of Easter's first human settlers. From bone studies, one third belonged to the largest animal available to them, the Common Dolphins, a porpoise which weighed up to 165 pounds. This is amazing as elsewhere in Polynesia, Dolphins accounted for not even 1% of the bones in the middens. These porpoises could not have been hunted by line-fishing or spear-fishing from shore as they live out in the sea. Instead, they must have been harpooned far offshore, in the seaworthy canoes that were built from the tall trees that grew there when the settlers arrived. About 23% of the bones in the middens are fish bones while elsewhere in Polynesia they were the main foods accounting for 90% of their diet. This was because Easter had a rugged coastline and steep drop-offs of the ocean bottom, so there were few places to catch fish by net or by handline in shallow water. The Easter Islander diet was low in mollusks and sea urchins for the same reasons. The abundance of sea birds and the land birds compensated for this. Bird stew seasoned with meat from the large number of rats which must have reached Easter as stowaways in the canoes of the first Polynesian colonists was common. Only at Easter archaeological sites in Polynesia, rat's bones outnumber fish bones.[12]

Birds, fish, porpoises, and rats were not the only meat sources available to Easter's first settlers. Seals, turtles, and large lizards were other sources to feed on. All these delicacies were cooked over firewood that came from Easter Island's subsequently vanishing forests.

Trees were being burned for firewood. They were also being burned to cremate bodies. The presence of remains of thousands of bodies and huge amount of human bone ash implies massive fuel consumption needed for the cremation. Most of Easter's land area except at high elevations was being used to grow crops, so trees were cleared for gardens. From the abundance of bones of open-ocean porpoises and tuna found in early middens, one can infer that big trees were being felled to make seaworthy canoes. Trees supplied timber and ropes for transporting and erecting statues and for a host of other purposes. The rats introduced accidentally as stowaways used palm trees and other trees as a nut source:

every Easter palm nut recovered shows tooth marks from rats gnawing on it; thus making them unable to germinate; this will be a disastrous consequence for the islanders.

So what happened to this whole society of 20,000 to 30,000 people who inhabited this Polynesian paradise with a forest of huge palm trees, other trees, and large numbers of land and sea birds breeding there? Deforestation started after the Polynesians' arrival by A.D. 900, and must have been over by 1722 when Roggeveen arrived and saw no trees taller than 10 feet. Most radiocarbon dates on the palm nuts are before 1500, indicating that the palm became rare or extinct thereafter. The Poike Peninsula which is Easter's most infertile region was deforested first and the palms there disappeared around 1400. Radiocarbon dated charcoal samples from ovens and garbage pits show wood charcoal being replaced by herb and grass fuels after 1640, even at the houses of the upper class who might have access to the last precious trees after none were available for the peasants. Pollen cores show the disappearance of palm, toromiro, tree daisy, shrub pollen, with grass and herbs replacing them between 900 and 1300. These and other test results suggest that soon after the human arrival, deforestation began, reached its peak around 1400, and was virtually complete by locally varying dates between the early 1400s and the 1600s.[13]

Easter Island is one of the most extreme cases of forest destruction in the world. The whole forest was gone and most of its tree species became extinct over a period of several hundred years. The ultimate consequences for islanders were losses of raw materials, wild caught foods, massive soil erosion, and decreased crop yields.

Raw materials including everything made from native plants and birds, timber, ropes, bark to make bark clothes, and feathers etc. were lost or became less available with the passage of time. Construction, transport, and erection of statues came to an end with the lack of large timber and ropes. When, in 1838, a French ship anchored at Easter Island, five of Easter's two-man canoes came out to trade with him. The captain of the

French ship reported that all the natives excitedly repeated the word 'miru' often and became very impatient when the ship crew didn't understand. 'Miru' is the name of the timber used by the Polynesians to make their canoes. This was what they wanted most. Easter's highest mountain is 'Teravaka', means 'place to get canoes'. Its slopes were used for timber before they were stripped of their trees for plantations. They are still littered with scrapers, knives, stone drills, chisels and other tools for woodworking and canoe building from that period. Easter has winter nights of wind, driving rain, and cold temperature of 50°F. A lack of large timber meant they didn't have wood for fuel any more. Hence, after 1650, Easter's inhabitants were reduced to burning grasses, herbs, sugarcane scraps, and other crop waste for fuel. Fierce competition must have arisen for the remaining woody shrubs among people trying to collect wood for houses, thatching, implements, and bark cloth. Even cremation practices had to be abandoned due to lack of wood. Instead, the Islanders turned to mummification and bone burials.

Most wild food sources were gone. Without sea worthy canoes, the islanders could not catch porpoises—their principal meat during the first centuries of inhabitance. Their bones as well as those of tuna and pelagic fish bones virtually disappeared from middens by 1500. Only whatever fish they could catch from shallow waters from the shore remained part of their diet. The land birds disappeared completely and sea birds were reduced by one third, and confined their breeding on a few offshore islets. Apple nuts, palm nuts, and all other wild fruits dropped out from their diet. Only one wild food source remained available unchanged. That was rats.

Deforestation led locally to soil erosion by rain and wind and the clearance of palms led to massive erosion causing reduced crop yields from nutrient leaching and desiccation. Farmers could not even find any more wild plants, fruits, leaves or twigs that they were using for compost.

According to Jared Diamond, these were the immediate consequences of deforestation and other human impacts on environments. The further consequences were starvation, a population crash and a descent into cannibalism. Surviving islanders' accounts of starvation is confirmed by the proliferation of little statues called moai kavakava. They depict a starving people with hollow cheeks and protruding ribs. No wonder, in 1776, Captain Cook described the islanders as "small, lean, timid, and miserable." From the peak values around 1400-1600 to the 1700s, the number of house sites in the coastal lowlands where almost everyone lived, declined by 70%. This suggested a corresponding decline in population numbers. Now, as wild sources of meat became scarce, the Easter Islanders turned to the unused largest source of meat available to them: humans, whose bones became more common not only in burials but also (cracked to extract marrow) in late Easter Island garbage heaps.

Easter's chiefs and priests had formerly justified their higher status by claiming their relationship to Gods and so by promising to deliver prosperity through bountiful harvests. This belief was enhanced by undertaking monumental construction of statues to impress the masses, and made possible by surplus food. But as their promises turned hollow, their power was overthrown around 1680 by military leaders called matatoa, and Easter's former integrated society collapsed in an epidemic of civil war. Now the commoners built their homes in the coastal zones which were previously reserved for the houses of the elite and many started living in caves for safety. The caves were enlarged by excavation and their entrances were partly sealed to create narrow tunnels for easier defense. Food-remains, woodworking implements, bone sewing needles etc. found in these caves clearly show that these caves were being used as permanent residences rather than temporary shelters.[14]

In the twilight of Easter's Polynesian society, not only did the political ideology fail, but with the end of the chief's power, religion was also discarded. According to oral traditions, the last ahu and moai were erected around 1620 and Paro (the tallest statue) was among the last. The upland plantations which fed the statue workers were progressively abandoned between 1600 and 1680. The progressive increase in the size of the statues may reflect not only the chiefs trying to outdo each other, but they were urgent appeals, necessitated by the environmental crises, to their ancestors. At the time of the military coup around 1680, the rival clans instead of building larger statues, started throwing down each other's statues by toppling a statue forwards onto a slab placed so that upon falling, the statue would break. Thus it is evident that after Easter's society reached its peak population, monument construction, and the environmental impact, its collapse swiftly followed.

Captain Cook, upon visiting the island in 1774, has commented on some statues being thrown down as well as some standing. The last European visitors in 1838 have mentioned fewer statues still standing. None had been reported still standing in 1868. Traditions relate that Paro was the last statue to be toppled and broken. When investigators Jo Anne Van Tilburg, Claudio Cristino, Barry Rolett, Sonia Haoa and University of California professor Jared Diamond visited the island a few years ago, they saw ahu after ahu turned into a rubble pile with broken statues reflecting the great tragedy that had occurred on this island. The islanders whose forefathers had undertaken enormous efforts carving, transporting, and erecting these giant statues on huge ahus, themselves destroyed their ancestors' monumental achievement with utter rage and hopelessness.

Survivors after 1680 adapted as best as they could, both in their religion and in their subsistence. Both, cannibalism, and chicken houses (for raising chicken) underwent explosive growth after 1650. Those who survived carried on with their lives the best they could. In 1888, Chilean government annexed Easter Island but it was not until 1966 that the islanders became Chilean citizens. Today, the islanders are undergoing a resurgence of cultural pride. The economy is being stimulated by visitors arriving via several plane flights a week from Santiago and Tahiti.

The parallels between the Easter Island and our current industrial world are chilling. Just as Easter's dozen clans, today, due to globalization and international trade, all countries affect one another. Just as the Easter Islanders had nowhere to go when environmental disaster finally struck, we humans have nowhere to go if and when Earth's polluted environment along with global warming makes it uninhabitable for all living species, including us.[15]

MANGAREVA, PITCAIRN, AND HENDERSON ISLANDS

These islands are the sole habitable islands in Southeast Polynesia. These three islands—just like Easter Island—were settled by Polynesians. Unfortunately, they too met the same fate as their brothers in Easter.

Mangareva, Pitcairn, and Henderson were settled sometime around A.D. 800 as part of the eastward Polynesian expansion. The western most of these three, Mangareva, lies about a thousand miles from the previously settled parts of Polynesia, namely the Marquesas to the northeast and Societies to the west. Marquesas and Societies were occupied 2000 years after west Polynesia's settlement. Yet, they were occupied long before these three. Thus, these three were quite isolated and were likely occupied via Marquesas or Societies during the same colonizing expeditions that settled even more remote Hawaiian Islands and Easter. This finally completed the outgrowth of Polynesia. Of these three islands, Mangareva was the most abundantly endowed with natural resources vital for human settlement, making it suitable for a larger population.

Mangareva, Pitcairn, and Henderson continued their inter-island trade for several centuries. Mangareva was rich, but whatever it lacked, it obtained it from Pitcairn and Henderson while these two received much more materials from Mangareva and soon became heavily dependent on Mangareva for their survival. Being very fertile and possessing a multitude of raw materials such as big forests, good agriculture, water etc., Mangareva's population multiplied beyond its carrying capacity for human survival. The trade within these three islands continued from about A.D. 1000 to 1450 but stopped by A.D. 1500. At Henderson, canoes were no longer arriving from Mangareva or Pitcairn. Henderson's few dozen people were now trapped in a most remote island with little means to survive. In all three islands, massive deforestation had taken place. Disastrous environmental damages on Mangareva and Pitcairn forced them to stop their trade with Henderson or with each other.

Mangareva's forests were cut down beyond replenishment. The top soil had eroded—carried away by rain from the hillside that had been deforested to plant crops—reducing the agricultural food supply. Trees large enough to build canoes were gone and fish yields were consequently devastated. When the Europeans arrived at Mangareva in 1797, the islanders had no canoes, only rafts.

With too many people fighting for a limited supply of food, Mangarevans slid into the familiar nightmare of civil war and starvation. The islanders turned to cannibalism, not only by eating the dead but also by digging up dead corpses. For the precious remaining available cultivable land, intense fighting erupted. Chiefs were overthrown by warriors and disorder was abundant. Among the chaos, trade voyages with other islanders—i.e. leaving one's house and land unattended—was unthinkable. Mangareva was the hub of this trade which was vital for the survival of Pitcairn and Henderson. Hence, environmental damage led to social and political turmoil. It also led to the loss of timber for canoes, ending southeast Polynesia's inter-island trade. For the inhabitants of Henderson and Pitcairn, the loss of trade was tantamount to cutting off of their umbilical cord. The results were catastrophic. Eventually, no one was left alive on these islands.

The environmental damage caused by the people of these islands was so severe that it endangered their very survival. Pitcairn and Henderson were also so dependent on trade with Mangareva, and with each other, that they collapsed when this trade could not be carried on. With its decline and inability to support its neighbors, Mangareva was on the way to ultimate doom but it also carried with it the demise of the inhabitants of Pitcairn and Henderson.[16]

SECTION II
INDUSTRIALIAL NATIONS AND THEIR
IMPACT ON EARTH

CHAPTER 3
AMERICA & ITS EARTHLY FOOTPRINTS

Anyone who believes that exponential growth can go on forever in a finite world is either a madman or an economist.
—Kenneth Boulding (ca. 1980)

For 200 years we've been conquering nature. Now we're beating it to death.
—Tom McMillan, quoted in Francesca Lyman, The Greenhouse Trap, 1990

We shall continue to have worsening ecologic crisis until we reject the Christian axiom that nature has no reason for existence save to serve man.
—Lynn White, Jr., "The Historical Roots of Our Ecological Crisis," 1967

The United States constitutes 5 percent of the world's population but consumes roughly 25 percent of its resources. If just 15 percent more of the world's population reaches America's level of consumption, then 100 percent of the Earth's resources would be consumed by 20 percent of the people of the planet. The remaining 80 percent would have to die. So far, few if any of these people have volunteered.[1] Few Americans realize that America is an empire with 761 military bases in more than 180 countries of the world. America is the largest gobbler of oil in the world with a daily consumption of 20.8 million barrels. Naturally, with that colossal appetite, America is one of the biggest emitters of greenhouse gases. One quarter of the world's greenhouse gases are emitted by the United States. So, the United States has the distinction of being one of the biggest polluters in the world. In America today, for every four citizens, there are three cars, the highest per capita car usage anywhere. Being an economic giant, America is the biggest producer of chemicals, pharmaceutical drugs, airplanes, home appliances, houses, construction materials, hardware, metals etc.—you name it. With bigger armaments expenditures than the rest of the world combined, totaling $650 billion, America is also the biggest arms producer in the world. Fighter planes, aircrafts, tanks, guns, bombs, ammunitions, naval ships, aircraft carriers, rockets, missiles, nuclear weapons, submarines...the list goes on and on. All this manufacturing does not come easy. It bears a heavy price in terms of capitol, materials, and pollutants. With the manufacture of all this vast variety of items, America generates the highest pollutants in waters, atmosphere, and soil. China is steadily taking over the United States in some of these areas now. But China is a recent entrant as a great polluter. America has been at it since World War II.

OIL & THE AUTOMOBILE INDUSTRY

Since early twentieth century, automobiles have dominated the American psyche more than any other industry. Around a hundred years ago, the first car was made and Americans fell in love with it. Soon after, the car manufacturing industry spawned. First came the Ford Motor Company, then General Motors and others followed. These companies started rolling out cars after cars, each model getting better and more attractive, year after year. This was happening in America while the world was still dependent on bicycles, horse-driven carts, and for longer distance, coal-powered trains. While more and more people in America started owning cars, only the super rich in other countries, except perhaps in parts of Western Europe, could afford them.

With the advent of cars, America was transformed from a rural horse-driven, train riding old fashioned nation, into the first 'modern' nation dominated by mega-cities and its suburbs joined by an extensive network of highway systems extending thousands of miles all across the nation. Shopping centers, gas stations, accessory industries to the automobile industry, repair shops, all sprang up over several decades. By now—with the exception of parts of Western Europe —while the rest of the world was walking or bicycling to work, cars in America were no longer a luxury but a necessity.

Today, there are more than 240 million cars and trucks in America; more vehicles than licensed drivers. Some 35% of Americans have three or more cars.[2]

Anybody who has visited the United States back in 50s or 60s could not help but be fascinated by its car culture. One could go across the country comfortably by car enjoying the beautiful countryside from the east coast to the west or from north to south. When I came to America in 1966, I traveled from New York to Las Cruces, New Mexico by luxurious bus. During the Christmas vacation, my brother, a fellow student, and I went to New York from Las Cruces driving all the way through. It was indeed fascinating to see the beautiful country during the first trip (by bus) in September. The second trip to New York during December by car offered a completely different picture. We came across miles upon miles of countryside that was blanketed with snow as if we were passing through a wonderland.

No doubt, cars gives one the freedom to go anywhere in America. The whole country is geared towards and around cars. Today, three out of four Americans own a car. An average American family owns more than one car: two, three or four. In addition to the cars, there are millions of trucks on our highways. Oil provides 96% of the fuel for our transportation. The United States is the world's largest oil consumer, consuming nearly a quarter of the world's oil. We use more than 24 % of the world's total supply, followed by China at 9%; Japan at 6%; and Russia, Germany, and

India at just around 3% each. An average American consumes approximately 2.8 gallons per day. In Japan, that number is 1.8 gallons; in Germany, 1.4 gallons; and in China, 0.2 gallons. The United States is to oil consumption what Saudi Arabia is to oil production—the largest by far.

U.S. oil imports have grown from 34% in 1973 to more than 60% today. Europe buys 17% of its oil from the Persian Gulf while Japan imports 78%. Forty-four percent of America's energy-related carbon dioxide emissions come from oil—more than from coal or natural gas. Approximately, 16 million new cars and trucks are sold every year. The average car in the United States emits more than 1.5 tons of carbon into the atmosphere every year. In the United States as well as in the world, total emissions are climbing sharply.

Our transportation sector alone consumes roughly 69% of our oil. We in the United States use about 20.8 million barrels of oil per day. Of these, more than 9 million barrels per day are used for gasoline alone. Diesel trucks, buses, and trains consume more than 3 million barrels per day. Airplanes consume about 1.7 million barrels per day. A smaller amount is consumed for home heating, in industrial boilers, and as a chemical feedstock. Average Americans drive more than 12,000 miles per year. With close to 240 million vehicles on the roads, that means we Americans drive 3 trillion miles every year. Unfortunately, with an increasingly mobile society, vehicle miles traveled in the United States is constantly increasing.

As the figures on page 63 show, there are basically two energy markets in this country. For the first market of transportation, oil is overwhelmingly dominant. The second market of electricity generation, oil is a minor factor. Half of our electricity is derived from coal; 19% comes from natural gas; nuclear power generates another 19%; 9% comes from renewable sources such as sun, wind and hydro; and a mere 3% is derived from oil.

Fuel Sources – U.S. vehicles

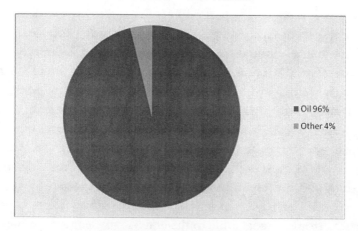

Fuel Sources – U.S. Electricity

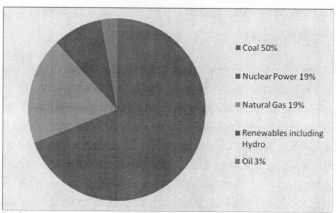

Source: David Sandalow, Freedom from Oil, pp. 14-19

Thus, oil provides more than 96% of the fuel for America's transportation sector but less than 3% of electricity of the country. Oil is responsible for 44% of America's energy-related carbon dioxide emissions—more than from coal or natural gas. It is obvious why the United States is the biggest polluter in the world as per transportation sector. [3]

COAL AND ELECTRICITY

America is quite rich in coal. The United States possesses the world's largest deposits of coal. After China, it is the largest producer of coal. It was more than a hundred years ago on the shores of lower East River in New York City that Thomas Edison opened the Pearl Street Station, the first centralized Coal-fired power plant in the country. More than a century later, more than half of our electricity comes from coal-fired power plants. In 2006, a record 1.161 billion tons of coal was mined, most of which went straight to electricity production. Unfortunately, coal being one of the most polluting sources of energy available, it jeopardizes our health and our environment. The pollution created by generating electricity from coal does not start or stop at the power plants. It stretches all the way from the coal mine to the end use of electricity in our homes and businesses. Mining and burning coal scars our lungs, tears up the land, pollutes water, devastates (particularly poor) communities, and worsens global warming.

Coal was formed from dead plants that had been heated and compressed beneath the surface of the Earth for millions of years. The main ingredient of coal is carbon. It also contains sulfur, mercury, and other elements in trace amounts. More than 27% of world's coal deposits are in the United States. Coal is found in 70 countries and mined in 50 of them worldwide. In the U.S., the coal producing areas are the Appalachian and rocky mountain states, as well as in the deep South and Midwest. It is cheap to make electricity from coal. It costs half or a quarter to produce a kilowatt-hour of electricity from a coal-fired plant than it does from a natural gas plant. Coal is also a little cheaper than wind and much cheaper than solar energy.

Coal mining is a major source of water pollution too as acid mine drainage that occurs when abandoned mines fill with water that mixes with heavy metals and then leaks into groundwater and streams. Coal preparation called "washing" also causes water pollution as water and chemicals are used to separate impurities from mined coal. Every year, up to 90 million gallons of coal preparation slurry is produced in the U.S., most of which are stored in huge waste pits known as impoundments. Impoundments can leak into local water supplies and can even burst suddenly, sending millions of gallons of wastes flowing as mudflows and destroying property and lives.[5]

One of the most severe blows to the environment is imparted in the United States by coal mining from the mountain tops in Appalachia, Virginia and other regions. It involves blasting off mountain tops to reach the coal bearing seams where the coal is mined. The huge pile of debris that is produced as a result is thrown in the surrounding areas burying water streams and acres of forests in the surrounding areas, devastating the environment in the whole region. This practice started in 1970 and since then, an estimated 1.5 million acres of hardwood forest have been lost, over 470 mountain tops have been blasted, and 1,200 miles of Appalachian streams have been buried.[6]

Coal-fired power plants are one of the biggest sources of air pollution in the U.S. Its consequences are shocking, especially with regards to particle pollution or soot, one of the deadliest types of air pollution in America. Soot can trigger heart attacks, strokes, and it can cause asthma or irregular heartbeat that can lead to premature death. Many studies have shown that communities of color are disproportionately exposed to harmful air pollution from coal-fired power plants as these plants are often located near these communities. Besides major sources of soot pollution, these power plants are the greatest contributors to smog in the nation. Smog also harms plants and trees.

The Antelope Valley Coal-Fired Power Plant in North Dakota uses 14,000 gallons of water every second. It generates 900 megawatts of electricity, lighting 360,000 homes. But to provide that, it mines, crushes and burns 16,000 tons of coal every day. Imagine the carbon emissions by this plant! There are many more in the United States and around the world.[7]

Burning coal also releases carbon dioxide (CO2) pollution, the primary culprit in global warming. Coal-fired power plants generate about half of America's electricity, and count for almost 40 percent of its carbon dioxide pollution from all sources including transportation. [8]. Actually, coal-fired power plants possess the highest output rate of carbon dioxide per unit of electricity among all fossil fuels.[9]

Burning coal for electricity also generates various types of liquid and solid wastes known collectively as "coal combustion wastes". Taken together, the amount of coal combustion waste in the United States is simply staggering: more than 120 million solid tons. This waste alone can fill a million railcars every year, or a 9,600 mile long train.[10] Even after it is stored, this combustion waste can leak out and pollute the surrounding environment and ground water. Containing poisonous elements like mercury, lead, and arsenic in toxic amount, coal combustion wastes and their pollution are known to cause illness in plants and animals. In humans, where the greatest exposure risk is from contaminated ground water and drinking water, the toxins have been linked to increased cancer, respiratory illness, organ disease, neurological damage, and developmental problems. In one study by EPA, it was estimated that more than 21 million people, including six million children, live within five miles of a coal-fired power plant, a dangerous situation considering that most coal combustion wastes are stored onsite.[11] As if to testify to the fears of this polluting coal combustion waste's danger to the communities, on December 22, 2008, an earthen dike collapsed at the Tennessee Valley Authority's (TVA's) Kingston coal-fired power plant, spilling coal ash across as much as 400 acres. The ash, from decades of coal burning, had been stored in a sludge pond. The spill extended into a waterway, blocked a road, and destroyed few homes, according to TVA.

The environmental group's tests on this TVA accident took place on December 27; it showed higher levels of pollutants of mercury, arsenic and lead than reported by the TVA and the EPA. For example, arsenic levels from Kingston power plant canal tested close to 300 times the allowable limits in drinking water. A sample taken two miles downstream, revealed arsenic at about 30 times the limit.[12]

Thus, the biggest hurdle in using coal is its pollution. Many experts believe that coal seems cheaper because the producers are able to pass on the environmental and social costs of production on the society as a whole. Mining coal devastates natural landscapes and pollutes waterways and the environment. Burning of coal releases mercury, sulfur dioxide, and other pollutants into the atmosphere. Hence, coal—despite technological advances—remains the biggest polluter of the environment in the United States. It is also the leading cause of global warming. Upon burning, the carbon in the coal bonds with the oxygen in the atmosphere forming carbon dioxide, the leading heat-trapping gas.

The following table shows that China and the United States are the biggest producers of coal:

WORLD COAL PRODUCTION

World Coal Production

Top Ten Hard Coal Producers (2008e)

PR China	2761Mt	Indonesia	246Mt
USA	1007Mt	South Africa	236Mt
India	490Mt	Kazakhstan	104Mt
Australia	325Mt	Poland	84Mt
Russia	247Mt	Colombia	79Mt

Global Hard Coal Consumption

	1990	2007	2008e
World	3461Mt	5415Mt	5814Mt

Source: World Coal Institute

United States has the biggest reserves, followed by Russia, China, India, and Australia.

There are still an estimated 909 billion tonnes of proven coal reserves worldwide, enough to last at least 155 years, according to experts as reported by The Independent/UK, June 24, 2007.

CUMULATIVE CO2 EMISSIONS

Greenhouse gases remain in the atmosphere and contribute to global warming long after they are emitted (in most cases, for a century or more), so cumulative emissions are an important measure of a country's contribution to climate change. From 1850 to 2000, the United States and the European Union were responsible for about 60% of energy-related CO_2 emissions, while China contributed 7% and India 2%.

THE PENTAGON

The nation's biggest polluter is the Pentagon. Every year, the U.S. Department of Defense produces more than 750,000 tons of hazardous waste—more than the combined total of top three chemical companies. For the past five decades, by the combined efforts of the federal government, the chemical industry and defense contractors, public health protections against perchlorate—a component of rocket fuel that affects children's growth and mental progress by disrupting the function of the thyroid gland which regulates brain development—have been blocked. All across the country, perchlorate has been leaking from hundreds of defense plants and military installations. According to EPA, perchlorate is present in drinking and groundwater supplies in 35 states. Studies by Center for Disease Control and other independent groups have shown that our food supplies, cow's milk and human breast milk, all contain perchlorate. Thus, every American carries some level of perchlorate in his body. In the Colorado River which provides water to 20 million Americans, perchlorate levels are high.

Cumulative CO$_2$ Emissions* (1850-2000)

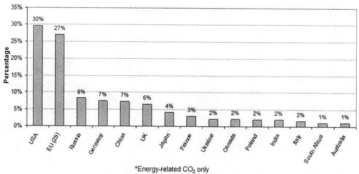

*Energy-related CO$_2$ only

Source: Climate Analysis Indicators Tool (CAIT) version 5.0. (Washington, DC: World Resources Institute, 2008).

Source: PEW CENTER: Global Climate Change. http://www.pewclimate.org/facts-and-figures/international/cumulative

Federal Energy Subsidies in 2006 ($74 billion total—excludes military spending)

Federal Energy Subsidies in 2006
($74 billion total – excludes military spending)

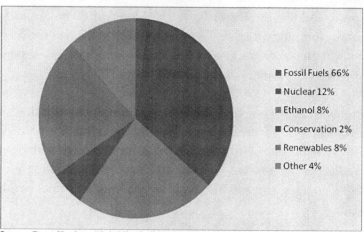

- Fossil Fuels 66%
- Nuclear 12%
- Ethanol 8%
- Conservation 2%
- Renewables 8%
- Other 4%

Source: Doug Koplow, "Subsidies in the US Energy Sector: Magnitude, Causes, and Options for Reform", exhibit 2, p.4, www.earthtrack.net

Due to the presence of a large number of military operations and defense contractors in the region, the chemical is most prevalent in the southwest and California.

In 2001, as per an EPA estimate, the total liability for the cleanup of toxic military sites would have exceeded $350 billion, five times the Superfund Act liability of private industries. Due to federal government's complacency, perchlorate levels run rampant in our water supplies. No wonder, some call Pentagon the nation's "premier environmental villain".

> "If they can spend $1 million on cruise missile, it seems ridiculous they won't spend $200,000 to see if our food is contaminated with rocket fuel", complains Renee Sharp, a scientist with Environmental Working Group.[13]

These military sites which possess more than 50 million acres, are among the most insidious and dangerous legacies left by the Pentagon. They are strewn with fuel dumps, buried hazardous waste, unexploded munitions, and toxic bomb fragments, open pits filled with debris, burned piles, and yes, rocket fuels. A 1998 internal memo from EPA warned of the looming problem: "As measured by acres, and probably as measured by number of sites, ranges and buried munitions, they represent the largest cleanup program in the United States." [14]

When the site is too polluted, the Pentagon simply closes it down and turns it over to another federal agency. The Pentagon has thus transferred more than 16 million acres over the last three decades often with none or little remediation. So now we find city and state parks, wildlife refuges, landfills, golf courses, airports and shopping malls upon former bombing areas.

Near every military training ground, streams, soil and ground water are contaminated. Heavy metals and other pollutants such as unexploded weapons saturate many sites today. The unexploded weapons include rockets, hand grenades, guided missiles, mortars, projectiles, rifle grenades and bombs according to the Government Accountability Office's list.

It seems our government has colluded with the Pentagon, defense contractors ,and perchlorate manufacturers to down play the deadly effects of all these pollutants on the American public.[15]

THE CHEMICAL INDUSTRY

Rachel Carson's prophetic words reverberate in our minds even after more than 45 years after her explosive book, *The Silent Spring* was published in 1962, warning us of the dangers of pesticides that were being used widely in America and around the world. She warned:

The chemicals to which life is asked to make its adjustment are no longer merely the calcium and silica and copper and all the rest of the minerals washed out of the rocks and carried in rivers to the sea; they are the synthetic creations of man's inventive mind, brewed in his laboratories, and having no counterparts in nature.

Carson (1962a, 24) warned further:

For the first time in the history of the world, every human being is now subjected to contact with dangerous chemicals, from the moment of conception until death. In the less than two decades of their rise, the synthetic pesticides have been so thoroughly distributed throughout the animate and inanimate world that they occur virtually everywhere.

Rachel Carson, with her daringly reveling book, exposed for the first time the danger of pesticides such as DDT and others. She herself succumbed to breast cancer after her book was published.

Annual global production of pesticides has increased twenty-seven fold since 1945, from 0.1 million tons to 2.7 million tons. The pesticide formulations that are marketed today are more potent: current pesticide formulas are ten to a hundred times as toxic as they were in 1975. Today, about 11,000 organocarbons are in production. The most common plastic is polyvinyl chloride (PVC). Global production of PVC rose more than 70 percent, from 12.8 million tons to 22 million tons, between 1988 and 1996.[16]

Every single day, 42 billion pounds of chemicals are either produced or imported in the United States; about 140 pounds for every American. An average person in the United States has 700 different chemicals in his body, a shocking fact indeed! Many people in the United States drink coffee from either metallic cups or drink water from polycarbonate plastic bottles or drink beverages or eat food from cans or containers that are lined with or coated with bisphenol-A, a chemical commonly used for lining these containers. Bisphenol-A is a harmful chemical suspected of increasing the chances of breast cancer or polycystic ovary syndrome in women, a leading cause of infertility; and men to have increased odds of prostate cancer and reduced sperm counts. A U.S. Center for Disease Control study has detected bisphenol-A in 93 percent of all Americans.[17]

One wonders whether advancement in many fields including chemical technology has really been good or rather disastrous for the human race just as the development of nuclear bombs or creation of biological weapons and poisons. Since the early twentieth century, humans have learned to synthesize chemicals which have been terribly harmful to all living creatures, including us humans. Beginning at that time, thousands of synthetic chemicals have been and are being discharged into the environment with little thought given to their effect on the biological landscape. These were some of the most potent toxins ever developed. For example, a single drop of Dioxin, if dispersed among 1,200 people, could kill all of them.[18]

Countless chemicals many of which turned out to be highly harmful to the humans and the living creatures were developed and released in the environment by the United States and European countries in the twentieth century. Chlorinated hydrocarbons, DDT, synthetic organochlorines such as Dioxins, polyvinyl chlorides (PVCs), polychlorinated biphenyls (PCBs), and a host of Persistent Organic Pollutants (POPs) were developed and marketed by the chemical industries of the United States and also those of Europe. They were marketed as pesticides (DDT), herbicides, defoliants (Dioxins) and others which were widely used by the people in America and Europe, polluting the environment such as water, soil and air. They were also marketed in other developing countries of South and Southeast Asia, Latin America and others.

At least, 11,000 organochlorines are manufactured commercially today. Many thousands more are created as by-products during the manufacture, use and disposal of these 11,000. Only a few of them are tested for carcinogenicity and other effects. Fewer still have been tested for their abilities to disrupt the human endocrine system, alter the sexual, immunological, and neurological development of pre and postnatal periods, or for any of a long list of equally subtle but potentially devastating effects. Today, it takes more than five years and hundreds of thousands of dollars to gather basic data on one single chemical.

Commercial organochlorines have become pervasive in our daily lives. They are found in soaps, shampoos, cosmetics, deodorants, toothpastes, and mouth rinses; also in lubricants and refrigerants. Many of today's children's toys such as the 'Barbie Doll' are made up of flexible PVCs.[19]

A report by the Pesticide Network North America and Commonwealth documents widespread contamination of U.S. food with many POPs which had been banned in the United States for many years. The report says that an average American may encounter as many as seventy exposures a day to POPs, most of them in food. The report titled, 'Nowhere to Hide: Persistent Toxic Chemicals in the U.S. Food Supply,' analyses chemical residue data collected by the Food and Drug

Administration (FDA) and finds POPs present in all our food groups, from baked goods and meats to fresh fruits and vegetables.

Virtually all of our food products are contaminated with POPs. That includes fruits, vegetables, baked foods, poultry and dairy products. It is not unusual to find three to seven POPs in our daily diets. A typical holiday menu of 11 food items can give 38 'hits' of exposes to POPs, where a 'hit' is one persistent toxic chemical on one food item. The top ten contaminated food items are: butter, cantaloupe, cucumbers (pickles), meatloaf, peanuts, popcorn, radishes, spinach, summer squash, and winter squash.[20]

A Greenpeace report published in March 2000 warned that much of the world's food is contaminated with POPs. The report, 'Recipe for Disaster', reviewed existing data on worldwide food and revealed that some foodstuffs, especially meat, fish, and dairy products contain levels of POPs that exceed internationally agreed-upon limits.[21]

Today, commercially manufactured organochlorines and those created unintentionally can be found in soils, air, lakes, ocean sediments and animals including humans, in most regions of the earth. If you visit villages in the remote Arctic West Greenland, people there have higher concentrations of PCBs than anywhere in the world. They are at the top of a food chain composed mainly of PCB-laced polar bears and other large animals found there.

Persistent Organic Pollutants (POPs), of which PCBs are but one, are insoluble in water. But they dissolve easily in fats and oils. Because of their resistance to biodegrade and their affinity for fat, POPs accumulate in the body of living organisms and become more concentrated as they move from one creature to another onward and upward in the food chain. This way, extremely small levels of these contaminants in water or soil can magnify into major hazards to predators who feed at the top of the food web such as polar bears, dolphins, herring gulls, and human beings. Thus, these chemicals bioaccumulate (intensify in potency) along the food chain, often to thousands of times their original toxicity, posing special perils to animals and humans who consume the meat of these animals and fish. Their toxicity is acute especially in the Polar Regions, where currents in the atmosphere and the oceans cause organochlorines to accumulate.

New chemicals, as many as 1000 are invented and introduced everyday in the United States. According to National Institute of Safety and Health, there are 100,000 substances officially listed as toxic and/or hazardous, and one third of the 700,000 different chemicals in current use have never been tested for their effects on human health.[22]

Certain types of cancer rates have risen markedly in the country. According to Phil Landrigan, a pediatrician and chairman of preventive medicine at Mount Sinai School of Medicine, since 1972, the date at which national records began in the U.S., the rate of brain cancer incidence has accelerated 41 percent among children.[23] Robert Napier commented as follows in London's Guardian:

Currently one person in three will get cancer and this figure will rise. The idea that cancer is due to poor lifestyle, bad genes, or viruses is being increasingly discredited. The massive increase in cancer in industrialized nations is partially due to the increase of 100,000 synthetic chemicals into the environment, their concentration in the food chain, and their bioaccumulation in humans. Each of us carries 300 to 500 man-made chemicals in our body.[24]

Millions of tons of wastes are generated in the United States (to the environment) every year, out of which some 60 million tons are classified as hazardous which means it increases the risk of serious or even fatal illness to the populace. After World War II, a totally new industry created an entirely new class of toxic wastes: Uranium mining and the radioactive waste generated by the nuclear industry.[25] It is also reported that more than a billion pounds of pesticides are released in the environment— mostly into soil—in the United States, mainly from its huge agricultural industry, and from other pesticide using sectors.

In the U.S., polluters dump about 240 million pounds of toxins—rocket fuels, pesticides and pharmaceuticals—into our waterways each year. [26] Louisiana and Texas emit more neurological and developmental toxins to air and water than any other state. Ohio, Illinois, Georgia, Tennessee, Virginia, Michigan, Pennsylvania and Florida are other major emitters.[27] Roughly 12 million U.S. children under eighteen years of age (one out of every six) now suffer developmental, learning, or behavioral disabilities, including mental retardation, birth defects, autism, and attention-deficit hyperactivity disorder.[28]

As mentioned above, there are many incidents of toxic waste accidents in the United States such as the Love Canal, Cancer Alley, Exxon Valdez oil spill, and within New York's Hudson River.

In 1983, two hundred miles of the Hudson River were declared a Superfund hazardous- waste site. For thirty years, General Electric was dumping PCBs in the Hudson River. The company had discharged PCBs into the Hudson from its manufacturing plants in Fort Edward and Hudson Falls between 1947 and 1977. Two GE capacitor plants, located between Albany and Fort Edward, dumped more than 1.3 million pounds of PCBs into the Hudson River before PCBs were outlawed in 1977. But the damage was done. In August 2001, the EPA ordered GE to pay $480 million to dredge the toxic chemicals, mainly PCBs off the floor of the upper Hudson River. GE has spent millions of dollars on lobbying and advertizing, in a failed attempt to persuade state and federal officials that this is unnecessary and environmentally risky. But the EPA has stuck to its guns. Now, G.E. has begun dredging for PCBs in the river. The contaminated sediment will be transported by train to hazardous waste site at Andrews, Texas, near the U.S.-Mexico border. The Sierra Club has opposed the plan, saying, "All they are doing is moving hazardous waste from one location to another, leaving it for future generation to solve the problem." GE is paying for the project but is still challenging the legality of Superfund law.[31]

Besides chemical pollution of our water, high quantities of pesticides, antibiotics, and hormones are also present in our food, water, soil, and air. Arsenic and lead concentrations above the health based limits established by the U.S. EPA are found in more than 12,000 wells that supply water to 100 million Americans. Since 1867 arsenic, and since 1890 lead-arsenic, has been used on crops in the U.S...Even today, arsenic is widely used in the U.S. on turf crops, soy, cotton, and corn as an herbicide or defoliant.

Nearly 30 million Americans are drinking water contaminated with atrazine, simazine, telone II, 2,4-D, or 2,4,5-T. All these chemicals are related to DDT and were first sold in the 1940s after being developed during World War II. Registrations of simazine and 2,4,5-T have been cancelled by the EPA, yet millions of Americans drink water contaminated with these deadly toxins. These chemicals are known to cause birth defects and cancers in laboratory animals. Their use is the farm industry continues to damage bird populations.[32]

A December 2009 story in the New York Times reported that more than 20 percent of the nation's water treatment systems have violated key provisions of the Safe Drinking Act over the last five years. Since 2004, water provided to more than 49 million people contained illegal concentrations of chemicals like arsenic or radioactive substances like uranium, as well as bacteria often found in sewage.

Factory farmers still continue to use enormous quantities of highly toxic poisons. In 2006, four out of the six most used farm pesticides were among the most dangerous chemicals around. Farmers in the United States applied more than 35.7 million pounds of four pesticides: Metam sodium, methyl bromide, telone II, and Chloropicrin. Metam sodium, the third most used California pesticide, is the close relative of the chemical gas that escaped in Bhopal, India in 1984 and killed 30,000 people while injuring 200,000. As much as 14.8 million pounds were used in California in 2006. Metam sodium is a biocide, causes multiple birth defects, injures farm workers, and is highly toxic to wild birds and fish.

In 2006, California farmers used 7 million pounds of methyl bromide, the fourth most used farm pesticide in the state. It is also a notorious destroyer of the ozone in the atmosphere. Methyl bromide additionally causes cardiac arrest, birth defects, nervous system damage, and is responsible for many thousands of deaths since 1936. The biggest sufferers are the poor Mexican farm workers working on California farms for a pittance, while their bodies are contaminated with this pesticide leading to early deaths.

The sixth most widely used chemical in California was Chloropicrin, another deadly biocide. This chemical is same as tear gas. Using in conjunction with methyl bromide, it greatly enhances the fumigation toxicity of both the poisons. It causes severe respiratory damage, birth defects, and is highly toxic to fish. California farmers used 6.9 million pounds of this biocide in 2006.

The extent to which California farmers use these deadly pesticides is evidenced by the fact that California strawberry growers used 184 different pesticides in 2004. On average, they applied more than 335 pounds of pesticides per acre. Metam sodium, methyl bromide, chloropicrin, and telone II accounted for 74% (or 248 pounds) of the pesticides used on each acre of strawberries. These four of the most toxic chemicals in the world, accounted for almost three quarters of all pesticides used.[33]

U.S. WARS

The United States has been involved in many armed conflicts, especially after World War II. These wars—in Korea, Vietnam, Cambodia, and Laos, Kosovo, two Iraq wars and the current Afghanistan war—have left their indelible mark on the planet's environment. Millions of gallons of Agent Orange were sprayed in Vietnam, Cambodia, and Laos destroying vast areas of vegetation, contaminating huge areas of jungle, and sickening millions of people in these countries with devastating birth defects. In Iraq, huge quantities of depleted uranium were used, contaminating the air and soil of Iraq and surrounding countries. This has increased significantly the rate of cancer and other diseases among the Iraqis. The Gulf War in Iraq was an environmental disaster as millions of tons of CO2 were emitted during conflict by the bombing of refineries, oil storage tanks, burning oil wells, and the incessant bombing and burning of infrastructure. War is clearly not only a crime against people, but also against nature itself.

THE NUCLEAR INDUSTRY

This industry, after the Second World War has become a menacing polluter of the environment in the United States. At the peak of the cold war, around 1965-68, the United States possessed tens of thousands of nuclear bombs; Russia perhaps a few thousand less. The cold war itself was the height of folly.

To make these weapons, United States needed tons of nuclear material. That came from mining uranium ore. Uranium mining companies in Arizona and New Mexico sent many innocent Navajos into the mines to mine radioactive uranium with no protective gear, as if it was coal or iron. The miners, during their lunch breaks, washed their food down with radioactive water that flowed through the mines. Lacking toilet paper, the miners often cleaned themselves with wads of radioactive yellowcake. Thirty years later, a large number of these miners died of lung cancer, in the area where the disease was practically unknown.[34] A similar fate of early death awaited many other Americans who—unaware of the danger—worked in other uranium mines around the country.

Atomic bombs gave the United States its 'superpower' status. But at what cost to the ordinary American workers who died by the thousands contracting cancer working in the uranium mines and atomic weapons manufacturing industry in the 1940s, 50s and 60s? A similar fate was realized by the unfortunate Russian miners or to a lesser degree by the British and French workers. Safely disposing of radioactive nuclear waste generated by the nuclear-weapons manufacturing and the nuclear power industries is a major problem for all nuclear powers.

During the years following World War II, this new industry created a new generation of industrial waste, the best known components of which are uranium and plutonium. But there are other transuranic elements that are created by nuclear reactions. All these substances pose a grave danger to humans through their radioactivity. Even in minute doses, they can damage or destroy human tissues and organs.

Nuclear waste cannot simply be dumped. It must be stored in a safe place while they degrade: a process that can take hundreds of thousands of years. No nuclear power has yet found a safe way of disposing this deadly waste. America possesses millions of tons of this waste lying all over the country at nuclear plants. It is struggling to find a way to safely store this waste. The base of Yucca Mountain in Nevada is being hotly considered now. But it is fraught with many problems including leakage in case of earthquakes.

THE HI-TECH INDUSTRY

The computer related hi-tech industry is another big polluter. Close to 300 million Americans own over two billion high-tech electronics items: computers, televisions, cell phones, printers, fax machines, microwaves, personal data devices and entertainment systems…just to list a few. Americans own over 200 million computers, over 200 million televisions and more than 150 million cell phones. In America today, 130,000 computers are thrown away every day while 100 million cell-phones are discarded every year. As some five to seven million tons of all these items become obsolete every year, high-tech electronics are now the fastest growing part of the municipal waste dump, both in America as well as in Europe. Europe creates some six million tons of solid waste each year. The volume of this e-waste as it is known today is growing three times faster than the rest of the European Union's municipal solid waste combined. Similarly, e-waste is accumulating rapidly in other high tech countries such as China, India, and Taiwan. The United Nations Environment Program estimates that some 20 to 50 million tons of e-waste is generated worldwide each year. This is the price for technology the world is paying now.[35]

Large amount of chemicals are used to treat or clean computer components as well. Computers also use several metals such as lead, cadmium, copper etc., all of which pollute the environment. Electronics are a particularly complex kind of trash. They contain a virtual alphabet soup of various plastics, among them polyvinyl chloride (PVC), polystyrene, and acrylonitrile butadiene styrene (ABS). A typical desktop computer uses about fourteen pounds of plastics, most of which are never recycled. PVC which is used in wire insulation and in other electronics parts pose a particular hazard as when burned it produces dioxins and furans, both persistent organic pollutants (POPs). The Hi-tech industry also uses antimony, beryllium, barium, zinc, chromium, silver, nickel and chlorinated and phosphorous based compounds as well as polychlorinated biphenyls (PCBs), nonylphenols, and phthalates. These are some of the other hazardous and toxic substances used in hi-tech electronics. A report by the EPA in 2001 estimated that discarded electronics account for almost 70 percent of the heavy metals and 40 percent of the lead now found in U.S. landfills.

The semiconductor industry also uses a variety of solvents in its manufacture—Ammonia, trichloroethylene (a carcinogen), methanol, and glycol ethers—all of them adversely affect human health and the environment. They end up in local rivers, streams, and aquifers, often in big volume. Semiconductor production commonly uses volatile organic solvents and other hazardous solvents such as methylene chloride, Freon, and other perfluorocarbons that pollute the air as well as adversely affect the health of those who work with them.[36]

PLASTICS

Consider the plastics manufacturing industry in the United States. Plastics are made from oil. Today, wide ranges of plastics are produced: soft, hard, transparent, semi-soft, semi-hard...you name it. They are used in thousands of applications. As a matter of fact, it is inconceivable to see our lives without these all pervasive plastics. From medical devices, computers, electronics, televisions, cars, buses, shoes, aircrafts, ships, trains, to home furnishings and omnipresent plastic bags...the list is limitless. This means, billions of tons of plastics waste is generated each year in the United States. The same is true with other countries too. Most of it finds its way to the dump site. This plastic is non-biodegradable. That means it will be there forever. No rain, sunlight or any weather condition affects them significantly. When McDonald's, the fast food chain restaurant, used to supply its hamburgers in styrofoam containers, it was said that these styrofoam containers will outlast the pyramids. McDonald's changed the containers to paper to avoid the bad publicity. But the fact remains that these plastics will stay in our soil forever polluting our environment. One of the worst such plastic polluters are the all pervasive plastic bags that are used all over the world. They find their way into the ocean along with other plastics where harm wildlife and form a part of continent size floating ocean garbage pile in the Pacific Ocean near Hawaii.

CONSTRUCTION INDUSTRY

Construction is another great polluter damaging the world's environment. Much of the deforestation worldwide can be attributed to the unquenchable American appetite for wood used in its construction industry. All over the U.S., millions of homes are constantly being built using artificial materials, plastics, wood and concrete. Of course people do need homes to live. But while the world lives in 500 square feet homes or less, the average American home is 2 to 4 times bigger, consuming far more wood and other materials.

THE AIRCRAFT INDUSTRY

This is yet another industry that heavily pollutes the environment. Each aircraft that the Boeing Company produces contains thousands of parts. They are made up of steel, stainless steel, aluminum, titanium, copper, plastics, rubber, and much more. They are treated with chemicals, some are anodized, chem.-filmed, painted, or treated with acids; thus they go through a wide variety of chemical treatments. When these huge planes are made, their lifetime could range from 25 to 30 years. During that life span, they emit millions of tons of carbon in the air from burning huge amount of gasoline while flying.

THE ARMAMENTS INDUSTRY

America is the world's biggest arms producer and exporter. The U.S. defense budget is bigger than that of next ten highest countries combined. Its arms sales are by far larger than any other country of the world. The U.S. arms industry or 'Defense Contractors' constantly come up with and manufacture newer and newer weapons of war: faster supersonic fighter planes, longer distance radar evading bombers, more sophisticated helicopters, and faster and more agile tanks, more precise missiles, bigger, more destructive bombs, better and faster ships, destroyers, aircraft carriers, and anti-aircraft guns or cruise missiles. The United States, one can say, is obsessed with weapons of war. The United States today generates only 20 percent of the world's GDP, yet it accounts for 43 percent of the world's arms expenditure.[37]

The United States defense budgets itself is enormous, colossal and wasteful. For 2008 and 2009, it was $667 billion each. For 2010, it is $693 billion. In the first week of February, 2010, U.S. Defense Secretary Robert Gates set out a defense budget proposal of whopping a $708 billion for 2011.[38]

U.S. global arms sales in 2008 skyrocketed to $32 billion—triple the already excessive $12 billion in 2005—and 45% higher than in 2007.[39] Pollution created in terms of emitted carbon in the manufacture and ultimate use of this enormous amount of arms is colossal. Assuming that the fiscal year 2009 war costs are $170 billion, an estimate provided by Secretary of Defense Robert Gates, the United States is likely to spend

$711 billion on national defense in the fiscal year that began on October 1, 2008.[40]

It is obvious to any knowledgeable person that the world cannot afford such a wasteful American lifestyle. We Americans must reduce our consumption level and change our lifestyles to sustainable level.

CHAPTER 4
CHINA AND PLANET EARTH

If Chinese lived like Americans—and that is what they are aspiring and trying for—we will need 6 planet earths.
—'Crude Impact' Documentary.

In the broadest ecological context, economic development is the development of more intensive ways of exploiting the natural environment.
—Richard Wilkinson

In August of 2001, my family and I toured China for 16 days. We traveled from Beijing to Chunking, boarded a cruise on the Yangtze River, and then traveled to Shanghai. We found it a fascinating country. We saw its people: smart, hardworking, and friendly. We got a glimpse of its ancient customs, culture, and some of its vast countryside. We were indeed captivated with this country, its people, and its culture. Everywhere we went, we saw the ongoing construction, particularly in preparation for the Olympics: the country was definitely on the move.

China is the world's most populous country with some 1.3 billion people. One in five persons in the world is Chinese. Area wise, it is the third largest country, and in plant species diversity, the third richest. China's economic miracle is unparalleled in history. Its economy, already huge, is growing at the fastest rate of any major country, at between 10 to 11 percent a year. This is four times the growth rate of most "first-world" economies. Today, it produces and consumes the highest quantities of steel, cement, television sets, coal, fertilizers, tobacco, and aquaculture food; it is close to the top in production of electricity and (soon) motor vehicles, and in consumption of timber; it has already built the world's largest water-diversion dam, the Three Gorges Dam and is planning another major water-diversion project joining the Yangtze river to the Yellow river.

Its economic miracle has come at a price though; a heavy price. Barring these spectacular achievements, China is today the world's biggest polluter and the most polluted country. According to the Netherland Environmental Agency's late 2007 report, China has surpassed the United States as the world's biggest emitter of the carbon dioxide, a greenhouse gas.

Its environmental problems are monumental, and are getting worse. The list is long, ranging from severe air pollution, cropland losses, disappearing wetlands, biodiversity losses, desertification, grassland degradation, and intensifying human-induced natural disasters, to overgrazing, invasive species, soil erosion, river flow cessation, salinization, trash accumulation, and water pollution and shortages. The result is enormous economic losses, social conflicts and upheaval, and major health problems including increasing rates of cancers and diseases among its vast population.

China's massive environmental problems and the impact on its people are enough as a subject of major concern. But its huge economy, massive population and vast area qualifies it not as just a domestic problem but one that spills over to rest of the world. China's environmental problems impact us, as we all share the same planet, the same oceans, and the same atmosphere while the world affects China through globalization.

And the problems are escalating. Its economy is now increasingly being hampered by water pollution and water scarcity. Rising levels of air pollution are endangering the health and well-being of millions of Chinese, and much of its land is rapidly turning into desert. China has become a world leader in water and air pollution, and land degradation. It is now the top contributor to many of the world's vexing environmental problems, such as the climate change, marine pollution, and illegal trade in timber. As China's pollution woes mount, so do the risks to its economy, public health, social stability, and international standing. In 2005, Pan Yue, a vice minister of China's State Environmental Protection Administration (SEPA) warned, "The (economic) miracle will end soon because the environment can no longer keep pace."[1]

The coal that has powered China's economic growth is unfortunately also choking its people. Seventy percent of China's energy needs are provided by coal: it consumed some 2.4 billion tons in 2006—more than the United States, Japan, and the United Kingdom combined. In 2000, China expected to double its coal consumption by 2020; it did that by 2007. Inefficiency is partly to blame for the huge consumption; as one Chinese official has reportedly lamented in 2006, "To produce goods worth $10,000, we need seven times the resources used by Japan, almost six times the resources used by the U.S. and—a particular source of embarrassment—almost three times the resources used by India."

Meanwhile, reliance on coal is devastating China's environment. China is home to 16 of the world's 20 most polluted cities. Four of the worst-off among them are in the coal-rich province of Shanxi, in northeastern China. Coal usage is responsible for 90 percent of its sulfur dioxide emissions and 50 percent of its particulate emissions. Particulates are responsible for widespread respiratory problems among its population, and acid rain—which is caused by the sulfur dioxide emissions—falls on one-quarter of China's territory and on one-third of its agricultural land, diminishing its agricultural output and eroding its buildings.

Yet, massive use of coal may be the least of China's air-quality problems. It is the transportation boom that poses a major threat to its air-quality. While Chinese builders are laying more than 52,700 miles of new highways throughout the country, some 14,000 new cars hit its roads every day. By 2020, China is expected to have 130 million cars, and by 2050—or maybe even by earlier—it is expected to have more cars than the United States, a dangerous situation air-quality-wise. Beijing is already paying a price for this boom. Due largely to increased congestion and pollution, in a 2006 survey, Chinese respondents rated Beijing the 15th most livable city in China, down from the 4th place in 2005. Air-born particulates are now six times higher in Beijing than in New York City.[2]

With its colossal use of coal to produce badly needed electricity—China builds one coal-fired power plant every week—China is today the world's largest producer of global warming accelerating CO2 emissions. It is also the largest contributor of Chlorofluorocarbons, sulfur dioxides, and many other ozone-depleting gases to the atmosphere. Aerial pollutants and dust particles emanating from China travel eastwards in the atmosphere to neighboring countries and even to North America; it is also one of the two leading importers of tropical rainforest timber, thus making it a driving force behind tropical deforestation in other countries.

China is the world's largest producer and consumer of fertilizer, accounting for more than 20% of world use and more than 90% of global increase in fertilizer use since 1981, thanks to the quintupling of its own fertilizer consumption, now three times the world average per acre. It is the second largest producer and consumer of pesticides, accounting for 14% or more of the world total and is now a net exporter. Above all this, it is the largest producer of steel, the biggest user of agricultural films for mulching, the second largest producer of electricity and textiles, and one of the top three and fastest growing oil consumers.

The primary meat consumed in China for decades was pork. But now, the demand for beef, lamb, and chicken products has increased rapidly, so the per-capita egg consumption now equals that of the first world. Per capita consumption of meat, eggs, and milk increased four times between 1978 and 2001. As it takes 10 to 20 pounds of plants to produce one pound of meat, this corresponds to much more agricultural waste. The annual output of animal droppings on land already exceeds by three times the output of industrial wastes. To this is added an increase in fish droppings, fish food, and fertilizer for aquaculture, thus increasing aquatic pollution in addition to terrestrial.[3]

Climate Action Network-Europe issued a report in 2006, ranking China fifty-fourth out of fifty-six countries for its climate change response, just behind (not surprisingly) the United States and ahead only of Malaysia and Saudi Arabia. Because of its heavy reliance on coal to fuel its economy, its emissions of greenhouse gas carbon dioxide have tripled over the past thirty years and are now higher than those of the United States.

Unfortunately, China's development strategy suggests that there will be little change in the foreseeable future. With plans on the books to urbanize half of its population by 2020, energy consumption will soar. City-dwellers consume 250 percent more power than their rural counterparts. China's newly found love affair with the private car now rivals that of the United States. Asian Development Bank's conservative estimate predicts that the number of cars in China could increase by fifteen times the present levels over the next thirty years, more than tripling its CO2 emissions.[4]

These grand-scale urbanization plans will aggravate matters. China plans to relocate more than 400 million people—i.e. more than the entire population of the United States—to newly developed urban centers between 2000 and 2030. In doing this, they will erect half of all the buildings expected to be constructed in the *entire world* during that period. This is indeed troubling as the Chinese buildings are highly energy inefficient—as a matter of fact, they are two and half times less so than those in Germany. Additionally, newly urbanized Chinese, who use televisions, refrigerators, and air conditioners, consume almost three and half times more energy than their rural counterparts. Though China is the world's largest producer of compact fluorescent lights, solar cells, and energy-efficient windows, these items are mainly for export, going to Germany, Spain, and other countries. Unless these energy-saving goods stay at home, the building boom will result in skyrocketing energy consumption and pollution.

China's land has also suffered from environmental neglect and unfettered development. Much of China's north and northwest has been left degraded from centuries of deforestation, along with overgrazing of grasslands, and over cultivation of cropland. Additionally, over the past half century, forests and farmlands have had to make way for sprawling cities and industrial zones. The result is diminished crop yields, a loss of biodiversity, and local climatic change. The Gobi Desert, which now engulfs much of western and northern China, is spreading by about 1,900 square miles annually. According to some reports, one quarter of the entire country is now desert despite Beijing's aggressive reforestation efforts. As per China's State Forestry Administration estimates, desertification has hurt some 400 million Chinese, converting tens of millions of them into environmental refugees, in search of new jobs and homes. Meanwhile, most of China's arable soil is contaminated, raising concerns about food security. Today, as much as ten percent of China's farmland is believed to be polluted, and each year, some 12 million tons of grain are contaminated with heavy metals absorbed from the soil.[5]

China's cropland has been reduced by the aforementioned problems such as soil erosion, fertility losses, salinization, and desertification; to this add urbanization and land appropriation for mining, forestry, and aquaculture and we see its cropland significantly decline. This is posing a big problem for its food security because while its cropland is declining, its population and per-capita food consumption is increasing, and its cultivable land potentially is limited. Its cropland per person is only one hectare today, barely half of the world average and almost as low as northwest Rwanda. Additionally, as China recycles very little trash, large quantities of domestic and industrial trash are simply dumped into open fields, taking over or damaging the cropland and polluting soil. Today, trash surrounds more than two third of China's cities. Its composition has dramatically changed from vegetable leftovers, dust and coal residues to plastics, metals, glass and wrapping paper.

China's deforestation is massive. It is one of the world's most forest-poor countries; with only 0.3 acres of forest per-capita compared to a world average of 1.6 acres and with forests covering only 16% of its land area compared to 74% of Japan's. Due to governmental efforts, the single-tree plantation areas have increased, but the natural forests especially the old-growth forests have been shrinking. This deforestation is a major contributor to China's soil erosion and floods. The great floods of 1996 caused $25 billion in damages, and even bigger floods of 1998 affected 240 million people (one fifth of its population at the time), shocking its government into action. It banned any further logging of natural forests. With climate change, deforestation likely has contributed to China's frequency of droughts, which now affect 30% of its cropland every year.

Besides deforestation, the two most serious forms of habitat destruction in China are destruction and degradation of grasslands and wetlands. China is second only to Australia in the extent of its natural grasslands that cover 40% of its area, mainly in the drier north. But, due to its huge population, this amounts to only half of the per-capita grassland of the world average. Its grasslands are so damaged by overgrazing, climate change, and mining and other types of developments that 90% of its grasslands are now degraded. Since the 1950s, the grass production per hectare has decreased by about 40%, and weeds and poisonous grass species have spread at the expense of high-quality grass species. This degradation of grasslands has major implications besides its usefulness to China's grassland food production as these grasslands of the Tibetan Plateau—the world's largest high-altitude plateau—are the headwaters for major rivers of India, Pakistan, Bangladesh, Vietnam, Laos, Cambodia and Thailand as well as for China. As an example, grassland degradation has increased the frequency and severity of floods on China's Yellow and Yangtze rivers and has also increased the frequency and severity of dust storms in eastern China. Hence the effects in these other countries will be similar as a result.[6]

If China's development strategy continues as planned, its increase in greenhouse gas emissions will likely exceed that of all industrialized nations combined over the next twenty-five years. This will surpass by five times the reduction in such emissions that the Kyoto Protocol has sought; a nightmarish and dangerous outlook.[7]

Recently, extensive algal blooms have developed in Qingdao caused, in large part, by massive misuses of fertilizer. As the world's largest fertilizer user, China consumes more than 50 million tons annually. Too often, untrained peasants apply far too much fertilizer to their meager plots in the false hope of boosting yields. This has resulted in excess fertilizer runoff flooding into rivers and streams.

Algal blooms now continually plague China's third largest lake, Lake Tai. Famous for its classic beauty, the lake is more than simply a tourist attraction. It also provides water for 30 million Chinese. It will cost China US$ 14 billion to clean up this lake. Panic buying of bottled water during Lake Tai's repeated algal blooms have driven the price of bottled water as high as $1.50 per liter.

Unfortunately, China's algal blooms are hardly restricted to its rivers and lakes. Its coastal waters are also suffering major growth epidemics of "red tides"—a version of eutrophication. The problem is particularly acute in the shallow waters of the Bohai and Yellow seas off northern China where Qingdao is located and where there is minimal tidal exchange.

While China has experienced a 40-fold increase in the incidence of red tides in just the past few years, these red tides are destroying fish stocks and devastating marine life for both China and its neighbors. The broader picture emerging from these small stories is that this big country is choking to death on a wide variety of pollutants.[8]

We may select three factors giving us an indication of health consequences of all this pollution. The average level of lead in the blood of Chinese city-dwellers are nearly double the levels considered in the world to be dangerously high and so puts at risk the mental development of its children. Air pollution in China is responsible for more than 300,000 deaths per year, and $54 billion in health costs. Deaths due to smoking are more than 730,000 per year and are rising because China is the world's biggest consumer and producer of tobacco and is home to the maximum number of smokers. More than 320 millions of these smokers—one quarter of the world total—smoke an average of 1,800 cigarettes per year per person.[9]

WATER PROBLEMS

Access to clean water is a problem in China today. Although China possesses the fourth-largest freshwater resources in the world (after Brazil, Russia and Canada), a situation has developed due to overuse, skyrocketing demand, inefficiencies, pollution and unequal distribution, where two-thirds of China's approximately 660 cities have less water than they need and 110 of them suffer serious shortages. According to the leading Chinese water expert Ma Jun, several cities near Beijing and Tianjin, in the northeastern part of the country, could run out of water in five to seven years.

Besides growing demand, enormous waste is a major problem. Sixty-six percent of the water is claimed by the agricultural sector, mostly for irrigation. But it manages to waste half of that. In the same way, Chinese industries too are highly inefficient. They usually use 10-20 percent more water than do their counterparts. Urban China loses 20 percent of its water through leaky pipes. As urbanization and a rise in income takes place, the Chinese, like the Americans and the Europeans, will become even larger consumers of water. They now take lengthy showers, use washing machines and dishwashers, and buy second homes with lawns that need to be watered. China's cities saw water consumption jump 6.6 percent during 2004-5. Due to a plundering of its ground water reserves, massive underground tunnels are created and as a result; its cities are sinking. Shanghai and Tianjin have sunk more than six feet during the past fifteen years.

Today, fully 70 percent of China's seven major rivers are heavily polluted, 80 percent of its rivers fall short to meet standards of fishing, while in rural areas, liver and stomach cancers related to water pollution are among the leading causes of death. 21 cities along the Yellow River are characterized by the highest measurable levels of pollution.

Its ground water that provides 70 percent of the country's total drinking water is threatened from a variety of sources: hazardous waste sites, polluted ground surface water, pesticides and fertilizers. The government-run Xinhua News Agency reports that 90 percent of Chinese cities' aquifers are polluted. More than 75 percent of the river water flowing through China's urban areas is deemed unsuitable for drinking or fishing. The Chinese government deems about 30 percent of the river water throughout the country to be unfit for use in agriculture or industry. As a result, almost 700 million people drink water contaminated with animal and human waste. The World Bank has found that the failure to provide fully two-thirds of the rural population with piped water is a leading cause of death among children under the age five and is responsible for about 11 percent of the cases of gastrointestinal cancer in the country.[10]

China is one of the world's most severely damaged countries by soil erosion. It now affects more than 19% of its land area resulting in soil loss at 5 billion tons annually. Erosion is especially devastating around Loess Plateau—the central stretch of the Yellow River where about 70% of the plateau has eroded—and increasingly on the Yangtze River, where the sediments discharge from erosion exceeds the combined discharges of the Amazon and Nile, the two longest rivers in the world. The sediment, by filling up China's rivers—as well as its lakes and reservoirs—has shortened its navigable river channels by 50% and thus has restricted the size of ships that can traverse them. The soil quality, its fertility, and soil quantity have declined, partly due to long term fertilizer use and pesticide-related significant declines in soil renewing earthworms, thereby causing a 50% decrease in the area of cropland considered high quality. Salinization has affected more than 9% of China's lands, mainly because of poor design and mismanagement of irrigation systems in dry areas. (This is one problem that the government programs have made good progress in combating and reversing).[11]

DAMAGE TO OTHER COUNTRIES

China's environmental problems are already affecting the world. Japan and Korea have long suffered from acid rains produced by the sulfur dioxide emitted by China's vast number of coal-fired power plants and from the eastbound dust storms that sweep across the Gobi Desert in the spring dumping toxic yellow dust on their land. Even this dust, sulfur, soot, and trace metals travel across the Pacific from China to the United States and are being tracked by researchers there. The Environmental Protection Agency in the U.S. estimates that at least one percent of the particulates in the atmosphere in Los Angeles have originated in China. Rising levels of mercury deposits on U.S. soil are traced by the scientists to the coal-fired power plants and cement factories of China. Mercury is a poisonous metal that when ingested in sufficient quantities, causes birth defects and developmental problems. Of the world's mercury emissions, 25-40 percent originates in China.

It is indeed amazing how much effect China exerts on the world. What it dumps in its waters is also polluting the rest of the world. The World Wildlife Fund reports that China is now the largest polluter of the Pacific Ocean. "Almost no river that flows into the Bo Hai (a sea along China's north coast) is clean," says Liu Quangfeng, an adviser to the National People's Congress. Today, China releases about 2.8 billion tons of contaminated water into the Bo Hai annually. The heavy metal content in the mud at its bottom is now 2,000 times as high as China's own safety standards. Over the past 15 years, the prawn catch has dropped 90 percent. Almost 8.3 billion tons of untreated sewage was discharged in China's industrialized southeastern provinces of Guangdong and Fujian in 2006, 60 percent more than in 2001. More than 80 percent of East China Sea, one of the world's biggest fisheries, is now rated unsuitable for fishing, 53 percent higher from 2000.[12]

Faith Birol, the chief economist of the International Energy Agency warned that unless China rethinks its use of various sources of energy and adopts cutting-edge environmentally friendly technologies, it will emit twice as much carbon dioxide as all the countries of the Organization for Economic Cooperation and Development combined; an ominous possibility for our planet.

China's economic partners in the developing world carry additional environmental burdens from China's economic activities. To fuel China's continued economic growth, its multinationals that are exploiting natural resources in Southeast Asia, Africa and Latin America, are devastating habitats of these regions in the process. Since 1998, when devastating floods led Beijing to crack down on domestic logging, China's appetite for timber has exploded. Between 1993 and 2005, China's timber imports more than tripled. The World Wildlife Fund reports that China's demand for timber, paper, and pulp will likely increase by 33 percent between 2005 and 2010.

Thus, China has become a huge exporter of deforestation, devastating the forests of several other countries. It ranks third in the world in timber consumption and is closing in to be second soon as wood provides 40% of the nation's rural energy in the form of firewood, and furnishes almost all the raw materials for the pulp and paper industry. It also supplies panels and lumber for the construction industry which is the fastest growing in the world. There has developed a growing gap between its own supply and its increasing demand for wood products. This is especially so since its own ban on domestic logging after 1998 floods.

Hence China's wood imports have increased more than six fold since the ban. China now stands only second to Japan—which it is rapidly overtaking—as an importer of tropical lumber from countries on all three continents that span the tropics, especially from Malaysia, Papua New Guinea, and Brazil to Gabon. It also imports from the temperate zone countries such as Russia, the U.S., Germany, Australia and New Zealand. With its entry in the WTO, these imports are increasing rapidly as tariffs on wood products are being reduced. So, like Japan, China will be conserving its own forests but exporting deforestation to other countries, several of which—Australia, Papua New Guinea and Malaysia—have already reached or are on the way to catastrophic deforestation.

Illegal logging is especially damaging to the environment as it often cuts rare old-growth forests, endangers biodiversity, and disregards sustainable forestry practices. China unfortunately is already the biggest importer of illegally logged timber in the world. For example, the government of Cambodia in 2006, ignoring its own laws, granted China's Wuzhishan LS Group a 99-year concession that was 20 times as large as the size permitted by Cambodian law. Local Cambodians had to repeatedly protest at the company's practices of spraying large quantities of herbicides. The Chinese companies, according to the international NGO Global Witness, have destroyed huge parts of the forests along the Chinese-Myanmar border and are now moving deeper into Myanmar's forests in search of timber. In most cases, illicit logging activity takes place with the active connivance of corrupt local officials. Central government officials in Myanmar and Indonesia, the countries where China's loggers are active, have protested such arrangements to Beijing, but to no avail. The local populations in the developing world are seriously concerned for their environment at these activities along with those of Chinese mining and energy companies.[13]

The social unrest over this environmental disaster is rising in China today. In the spring of 2006, China's top environmental official, Zhou Shengxian warned that there were 51,000 pollution related protests in 2005. This amounts to 1,000 protests each week. Citizens complain regarding the environment in letters to local officials and complaints on official hotlines are increasing at the rate of 30 percent a year; in 2007, they topped 450,000. Few of them are resolved satisfactorily. So people are increasingly taking to the streets. Most demonstrations are relatively small and peaceful. But when they fail, the protesters sometimes resort to violence. In the spring of 2005, despite petitioning local, provincial, and central government failed to redress their complaints for their failed crops and poisoned air, some 30,000-40,000 villagers from Zhejiang Province stormed 13 chemical plants, broke windows and overturned buses, attacked government officials, and torched police cars. The government sent in 10,000 men from the People's Armed Police in response.

The leaders of China know and understand this. They are very concerned about their mounting environmental woes. These environmental problems stem as much from its corrupt and undemocratic political system as from Beijing's continued focus on economic growth.

China's leaders have shown the capacity and wisdom of taking bold decisions in the past. Deng Xiaoping and his supporters launched a series of drastic reforms despite stiff political resistance and set the country on the path to its current economic miracle. [14]

Whatever they may do, at present it is apparent that China's economic miracle has also become their environmental disaster. It seems nothing comes without a price.

CHAPTER 5
THE OTHER NATIONS

For the first time in the history of the world, every human being is now subjected to contact with dangerous chemicals, from the moment of conception until death.
—Rachel Carson, Silent Spring, 1962

Besides America and China, the world's biggest greenhouse gases contributors today, other industrial nations— the European Union, Russia, Canada, India, Brazil and Indonesia—are leaving their own carbon emission footprints on the planet Earth. The developed nations of Europe and Russia have already indeed left behind heavy footprints on the global environment. These developed nations have all built their economies at a huge cost to the environment and exacerbated global warming.

The European Union nations and Russia have their own industries— nuclear, chemical, defense, car manufacturing, aircraft manufacturing, plastics or electronics—similar to the United States' but on a smaller scale, with the exception of the former Soviet Union. But together, their collective carbon emissions and pollution of the environment is enormous.

GLOBAL ARMS TRADE

The world spent 1.3 trillion dollars from 2007-8 on their militaries. Countries enmeshed in conflicts are often flooded with weapons—which many of them can ill-afford—and are then turned against helpless civilian populations. In all wars, it is the civilians who pay the highest price, often with their very lives.

Many, however, wisely talk about disarmament. The U.N. Peacekeeping Force's former commander in the Democratic Republic of Congo, General Patrick Cammaert, saw firsthand the futility of disarmament without controlling the supply of arms at the same time. "You had the feeling," he said last year, "that you were mopping up the floor when the tap was open. One moment you disarm a group, and then a week later the same group has fresh arms and ammunition." [1] A new report by Oxfam International reveals how irresponsible arms trade undermines many developing countries' chances of achieving their developmental objectives. Either this trade is draining these governments' resources or fuelling armed conflict, most often both. According to Transparency International—the leading global organization monitoring corruption—the international arms trade is also one of the most corrupt businesses in the world. Nothing good comes out of it.

"What is clear is that if you want to achieve the developmental goals, with poverty reduction, improved healthcare, and education, you need to control arms transfers," opined Katherine Nightingale, author of the Oxfam Report.[2]

According to U.N. statistics, at least, 22 of the 34 countries least likely to reach the U.N.'s Millennium Developmental Goals are in the midst of, or emerging from conflict. According to Oxfam Report, between 1990 and 2005, 23 African nations together lost an estimated 284 billion dollars as a result of armed conflicts, fueled by transfers of arms and ammunition; some 95 percent of it came from outside Africa.[3] In other words, arms suppliers, by supplying their deadly weapons, kept the poor people of

Africa in perpetual poverty because this vast some of money could have been used instead to uplift the desperately poor millions of this unfortunate continent.

The number one arms exporter in the world is the United States. Russia, Britain, China and others are other major exporters though smaller in comparison to the United States. The global arms industry does hundreds of billions of dollars' worth of business worldwide annually. This industry is crucial to every major economy and is served, either with overt collusion or discreet silence, by the governments and the mass media. It is interesting to note that the top five countries profiting from arms trade are the five permanent members of the United Nations Security Council: the United States, the U.K., France, Russia and China. Aren't these five countries supposed to make sure that peace is maintained around the world? Yet, they are the ones who by selling their deadly cargo to various countries promote wars and conflicts around the globe! Hypocrisy at its maximum!

The arms manufacturing industries in all these exporting countries utilize huge quantities of oil, gas, coal, and water in the manufacturing process. The manufactures of these arms—using vast amount of diverse materials such as steel, rubber, plastics, other metals such as aluminum, zinc, lead, depleted uranium, and high-tech electronics etc.—gobbles up huge quantities of fuel (oil, gas, coal) as well as significant quantities of chemicals and water. Together, these leave significant carbon footprints on the planet and with no constructive purpose. Can today's world, on the brink of a global warming catastrophe afford such foolish trade? A few companies in few countries gather their wealth while millions of poor around the world suffer—along with mother earth—due to their greed and avarice.

CANADA AND THE ARCTIC

There are roughly 140,000 Inuit people living in the arctic, spanning around the North Pole from Nunavut (meaning "our home" in Inuktitut language) to Alaska and Russia. There is also an Inuit community living in the northern Quebec province of Canada. Nunavut itself, a territory four times the size of France, has a population of around 27,000; 85 percent of whom are Inuit. To a tourist uninterested in environmental toxicity, the Inuit Arctic homeland may seem as pristine as ever during its long snow-swept winters. Many Inuit today even guide dogsleds onto the pack ice surrounding their Arctic-island homelands to hunt seals and polar bears. Such a scene looks pristine until you realize that the polar bears' and seals' body fats are laced with dioxins and PCBs.

The native people of the Canadian Arctic are pay heavily the price of modern industry. These native people whose diets consist largely of sea animals—whales, fish, polar bears and seals—have been consuming concentrated toxic chemicals. Inuit mothers' breast milk has been found to contain abnormally high levels of dioxins and other industrial chemicals. The persistent organic pollutants (POPs) such as DDT, PCBs and dioxins are multiplying up the food chain of the Inuit as air and water currents take with them the effluvia of southern industry into the Polar Regions. Geographically, the Arctic is in the worst situation for toxic pollution, as a ring of industry in North America, Russia, and Europe pour their pollutants northward.

Global warming is accelerating in the Arctic much faster than anywhere else on the Earth. Some Inuit villages are even being washed into the sea or slowly swallowed by melting permafrost as and the sea-ice that is shrinking imperils the survival of species on which they depend. Accelerating Ozone depletion over the Arctic is threatening both the Inuit and the endemic animals with cancer from strong ultraviolet radiation.

Not long ago, it was disclosed by Canada that, in its Alberta province, a day's drive from Glacier National Park, enormous deposits of 'tar sands' has been discovered. The material is a mud-like thick mixture of sand and clay surrounded by a dense hydrocarbon called bitumen. To extract this resource from the ground, gigantic shovels and bulldozers are required.

Then steam is used to separate the bitumen from clay and sand; or steam is pumped underground to 'cook' the bitumen for two weeks. Finally, it is pumped out of the ground. Canada, in 2003, for the first time, decided to report its bitumen as economically recordable "proven reserves" of petroleum. With a simple stroke of the pen, Canada increased its oil reserves 3,600% to 180 billion barrels. This qualified Canada as the possessor of world's second largest oil reserves—after Saudi Arabia, which boasts 256 billion barrels. The tar sands now provide a third of that country's oil output. These tar sands now could theoretically quench enormous U.S. thirst for oil for years to come. Many companies, Canadian, American and even Chinese have moved in to exploit this resource. But there is one major problem: its extraction cost is enormous—both in terms of financial expense and energy consumed. Environmentally, it is disastrous. Canada's current output is about one million barrels per day, amounting to one twentieth of total U.S. daily demand.

So, what is involved to keep up this rate of production? Every day, huge trucks as big as small apartment buildings—more than 50 feet high and 30 feet wide—motorized shovels and other heavy equipment remove in three or four scoops more than 400 tons of rock and mud from fields in northern Alberta—enough to fill Yankee Stadium every 48 hours—so as to expose the underlying tar sands; tons of these sands are then mined and hauled away to processing plants; the trucks at times go up to forty-five miles per hour, burning fifty gallons per hour of gas. There, the natural gas and gasoline-like substance, naphtha are used to separate and process the bitumen. Basically, the oil is dispersed in millions of tons of sand. Principally, there are two ways of extracting the oil from this resource: by either mining it with gigantic shovels and bulldozers, then using steam to separate bitumen from sand and clay, or by cooking the bitumen by pumping steam underground over a period of two weeks and then pumping the liquefied bitumen out of the ground. Oil production from these tar sands is poised to triple from one million barrels a day in 2007 to 3.4 million barrels a day in 2017, according to documents obtained by *The Toronto Star*.[4] Though this huge resource of oil in Canada may be enough to supply bitumen to a thirsty U.S. market for decades to come, a single barrel of synthetic crude gobbles up from 500 to 700 cubic feet of natural gas. The alternate method of cooking bitumen requires twice as much natural gas. Both processes require immense water supplies. Thus, producing oil from these tar sands is highly carbon-intensive. According to reports, "Currently, two tons of sands must be mined to yield one barrel of oil."[5]

Tar sands oil production generates several times more greenhouse gases than conventional oil. Its production destroys fresh drinking water, pollutes air, and razes some of the world's last remaining endangered forests.

Europe

Europe is not immune from these chemical poisons. How an accident can imperil the food web of an entire nation was revealed in 1999, when animal feed became contaminated with PCB-laced oils in Belgium. As a result, chickens were contaminated at up to 5,000 times safety levels. Some were used for breeding chicks, contaminating the egg supply.

Belgium quarantined a thousand poultry and pig farms in the summer of 1999, after contamination tests revealed PCBs, revealing the presence of dioxins in the animal feed. Dioxin was introduced into the Belgian food supply through contaminated fat used in animal feeds supplied to Belgian, Dutch, and French farms. Hens, pigs and cattle also consumed the contaminated feed.

Many parts of Europe have been contaminated with these poisonous chemicals. For example, the manufacture of vinyl chloride monomer has caused extensive dioxin contamination of Rotterdam harbor in Netherlands. Greenpeace analyzed sediments from Porto Marghera in Venice and it showed dioxin contamination of the lagoon by the Enichem plant, where vinyl chloride monomer is manufactured. At the wastewater treatment plant at Wilhelmshaven, Germany, the Environmental

Ministry of Lower Saxony found extremely high levels of dioxins. Dioxins were also found in the dump where these sludges were disposed.[6]

There are more incidents of accidents where civilians were endangered. An explosion took place on July 10, 1976 at a trichlorophenol manufacturing plant in the northern Italian town of Seveso, pumping clouds of dioxins in the air as a reaction went out of control. The plume of smoke consisted of pure dioxin. Four days later, the flowers and other plants in Seveso began to die. Birds, fish and other animals too began to die in large numbers. Hundreds of ailing people started overcrowding the town's hospitals. Their dioxin dusted homes became inhospitable. Many pregnant women were faced with the dilemma, whether to have deformed children or to abort against the wishes of the Catholic Church. This 1976 dioxin release near Seveso turned out to be the highest level of dioxin ever recorded in humans. As a result, first studies confirmed that elevated levels of dioxin remained in the people even after twenty years. Also the study confirmed that women retained higher dioxin levels than men, thus harming unborn children.[7]

INDIA AND SOUTH ASIA

God forbid that India should ever take to industrialism after the manner of the west…keeping the world in chains. If (our nation) took to similar economic exploitation, it would strip the world bare like locusts.
—Mahatma Gandhi

India has close to 18% of the world's population and just 2.4% of the world's total area. With more than 1.1 billion people, likely to grow into 1.26 billion by 2016 and posed to surpass China in the year 2050, the population has increased its pressure on Earth's natural resources. Air and water pollution, water shortages, soil exhaustion, deforestation, and erosion afflict many areas of the country.[8]

The country's economy may be growing second fastest in the world, but pollution in India is quickly spiraling out of control and rivers are dying by the dozen. Three billion liters of waste are pumped into Delhi's Yamuna River alone each day.

"The river is dead, it just has not been cremated," says Sunita Narain, director of the New Delhi-based Centre for Science and Environment— one of India's top environmental watchdog groups.

The problem is not limited to Delhi's Yamuna River. Ganges, Brahmaputra, and a host of other rivers face utter pollution in their flowing waters. Fully 80% of urban waste in India ends up in the country's rivers. Unchecked urban growth across the country with little government oversight means the problem is getting worse by the day. A growing number of bodies of water in India are highly polluted and unfit for human consumption, and the Ganges, holy to 82% of India's Hindu majority, has become highly polluted.[9]

Air pollution is also rapidly worsening. Indications are that soot and smog from India and China may even be changing weather patterns in North America. But closer to home, the effects are clear: As brown clouds block out more and more sunlight, the rice crop yields are falling. The brilliant white of Taj Mahal is turning sickly yellow. The country is getting less and less sunlight. It is getting about 5% less sunlight than it did 20 years ago according to a study by Padma Kumari and colleagues at the Indian Institute of Tropical Meteorology in Pune. "Solar Dimming," as this phenomenon is known, is happening in India because of a cloud of tiny air-born particles released by the nation's industries hovers above the subcontinent, blocking the sunlight.

Dr. Shreekant Gupta, a professor at the Delhi School of Economics specializing in the environment says factoring in the cost of environmental damage in India would shave off 4% off the country's GDP. Lost productivity from disease and death are the primary culprits.

Much of the river pollution in India emanates from untreated sewage. Samples taken from Ganges River near Varanasi show high levels of fecal coliforms, dangerous bacteria that comes from untreated sewage, were some 3000% higher than what is considered to be safe for bathing.[10]

One of the primary causes of environmental degradation in a country could be attributed to rapid population growth, which adversely affects the environment and natural resources. India fits this scenario perfectly. Population growth and economic development are heavily contributing to serious environmental problems there. This includes heavy pressure on land, land degradation, deforestation, habitat destruction, and loss of biodiversity. Better economic conditions have led to higher consumption resulting in rising demand for energy. The end result is air pollution, global warming, climate change, water pollution, and water scarcity.

India is home to many environmental issues that include various natural hazards, cyclones, flooding and droughts, increasing population, higher individual consumption, industrialization, infrastructural develop-ment, poor agricultural practices, and resource misdistribution. An estimated 60% of cultivable land suffers from soil erosion, water logging, and salinity. It is also estimated that between 4.7 and 12 billion tons of topsoil are lost every year from soil erosion. Between 1947 and 2002, average annual per capita water availability declined by almost 70% to 1,822 cubic meters, and the states of Punjab, Haryana, and Uttar Pradesh saw overexploitation of ground water.

Today, forest area covers 18.34% of India's geographic area (637,000 km²). The forest cover is declining because of harvesting for fuel wood and agricultural land expansion. These trends along with increasing industrial and transport vehicle exhaust, have led to increases in atmospheric temperature, shifting rain patterns, and declining intervals of drought recurrence in many regions.[11]

It is estimated by the Indian Agricultural Research Institute of Parvati that a 3°C rise in temperature will result in a 15% to 20% loss in yearly wheat yields, a dangerous possibility. Civil conflicts involving natural resources—most notably forests and arable lands—have taken place in eastern and northeastern states.[12]

From a total of 3,119 towns and cities, only 209 have partial treatment facilities, and just 8 have full water treatment facilities (WHO 1992). 114 cities dump untreated sewage directly into the Ganges River while further downstream people use the untreated water for bathing, washing, and drinking.[13] The same is true for many rivers in India. Whenever there is intense population pressure, as in many developing countries around the world, this situation is familiar.

Major Indian cities suffer from air pollution coming from countless vehicles in its roads and many industries. Vehicles raise road dust into the air contributing further to pollution. Thus, one of the biggest problems of pollution stems from the transport system. Indian diesel engines have 200 times the amount of sulphur of European engines. Hundreds of thousands of them are burning away diesel emitting sulphur and CO2 continuously. Big cities have huge concentrations of these vehicles continuously transporting goods.

The government of India has noticed this huge source of pollution affecting peoples' health and is slowly taking measures. In New Delhi, all buses were forced to convert from diesel to compressed gas (CPG). Electric rickshaws in Delhi are being designed and will be subsidized by the government. Today, New Delhi has one of the most modern railway transport systems.

The wonderful Taj Mahal was also being damaged by countless industrial factories scattered around. After the court ruling, all these polluting factories and transport surrounding this beautiful monument have now been banned by the government.

One of India's biggest industrial group, Tata Motors, has come up with the cheapest car in the world, the aptly named Nano (small), priced at mere $2,500. Imagine when hundreds of thousands of Indian middle class start buying them—they will be available in near future—and driving them around in already overcrowded Indian cities! Perhaps, Tatas will be better off selling them exclusively in foreign markets only. What

India needs are not cheap cars running on gasoline but cheap cars and bicycles running on electricity with zero emissions as well as mass transit systems or fast trains covering various locations in each major city.

Air pollution in big cities is rising so high that it is now 2.3 times higher than the amount recommended by the World Health Organization and land pollution in India is due to vast amount of pesticides and fertilizers used on the farms.

Since independence in 1947, human encroachments have deforested Indian forests and threatened its wildlife. In response, the government of India has wisely substantially expanded the system of national parks and protected areas first established in 1935. Also, in 1972, the Indian government enacted the Wildlife Protection Act and Project Tiger to safeguard crucial habitats; federal protections were promulgated in the 1980s. India now has over 500 wildlife sanctuaries, and hosts 14 biosphere reserves, four of which are part of the World Network of Biosphere Reserves. There are now 25 wetlands registered under the Ramsar Convention.

DDT, aldrin, chlordane, dieldrin and heptachlor: these life threatening poisons are banned or severely restricted in most countries. But, according to an investigative report released by Greenpeace, these poisons continue to be manufactured, stored, used, and traded freely in South Asia.[14] According to Nityanand Jayaraman, a Greenpeace campaigner, "Asia faces a frightening scenario of historic, current and potential poisoning by the most dangerous variety of persistent poisons. This situation is a result of existing stockpiles of obsolete pesticides, the continuing production of organochlorines and other chemical pesticides and unmitigated expansion of dirty chlorine-based industries in the region."[15]

I remember, as a child some fifty years ago, when we were growing up in the city of Bhavnagar, Gujarat—located in northwest India, population at the time, 150,000—remember once or twice a year, our city municipality men used to come with a barrel and hand sprayer. They would spray DDT in our houses, bathrooms, and some other areas of the house or outside in the yards where there would be mosquitoes. Right after they left, we would use the toilets and bathrooms smelling the pesticide and breathing it in. My wife who is from Pune, Maharashtra— in Midwest India— experienced the same fumes of DDT sprayed by the municipality in her house some 40-45 years back. The story was the same all over India.

Fortunately, India has many NGOs (Non-Governmental Organizations) who look after the health of the people and carry out campaigns of protest whenever they find any substance harmful to the masses. Greenpeace International, fortunately, is also very active in India. For example, in 2002, Indian environmentalists carried out a campaign for banning endosulfan, a pesticide that was outlawed in many parts of the world but was still being used in India. The pesticide was being sprayed on Kerala's cashew crops. Higher prevalence of learning disabilities, low I.Q., and scholastic backwardness was found as a result amongst the children in the region. Additionally, congenital and reproductive abnormalities were also found amongst people in the region. The workers in the cashew plantations suffered from neurological problems such as trembling hands.[16]

The famous leak at a Union Carbide Chemical Company in Bhopal in 1986 is a grim reminder of what happens when something goes wrong in our 'advanced society'. Over 20,000 people lost their lives. Naiveté on the part of the Indian government was evidenced there when they allowed such a dangerous chemical manufacturing plant in the midst of a highly populated city. A plant manufacturing poisonous pesticide would never have been allowed in the midst of a populated area in the U.S., to which Union Carbide belonged. Also, Union Carbide officials' negligence was the main reason that such a catastrophe happened in the first place.[17]

One of the worst polluting industries in India is ship-breaking at Alang, a coastal village some 40 kilometers from my hometown

Bhavnagar, Gujarat, India. When I visited it several years ago, I saw a busy coastline: a ship anchored and hundreds of workers working in hazardous conditions, cutting and welding metals, and busy with other harmful activities. Thousands of workers work there in unhealthy conditions dismantling ships from world over. The workers there are exposed daily to hazardous compounds such as PCBs, tributyltin (TBT), and asbestos. Worker mortality has been estimated at one death per day: either the slow death resulting from exposure to a cocktail of deadly chemicals or due to common explosions caused by the torching of residual fuels from unclean vessels. Continual oil spillage there has contaminated the whole coastline. A similar ship-breaking industry is active in Bangladesh, where the worker conditions are even worse.[18]

"Our rivers, lakes, and groundwaters are irreversibly poisoned because of the government's inability to control and monitor the rapacious chemical industry that continues to release deadly chemical wastes and effluents into our water, air and land. Entire eco-systems and species dependent on them are under threat. So much so that traces of these toxic chemicals have shown up in breast milk and human blood too," complained Vinuta Gopal, Toxics Campaigner, Greenpeace-India. She said further, "Greenpeace, independent scientists and civil society groups have presented enough instances of toxic chemical pollution and its impacts on human health and our environment. Bahut Ho Gaya (it is too much), we now want action!" But fast action is hard to come by.

There are many other examples of pollution. The Kodaikanal community is impacted by the mercury poisoning of their pristine hill forests, a sensitive water-shed area, polluted because of the malpractices at Hindustan Lever's thermometer factory. In the same way, the community of Eloor, living by the Periyar River in God's own country (Kerala), has suffered due to the environmental havoc caused by the unregulated industries of the Eloor Industrial Estate. Other examples include the people of Patancheru, where the lakes have borne the brunt of chemical poisoning from the Medak Industrial Estate and the fishing communities of Orissa, who are literally sandwiched between hell and high water, trapped between Oswal Chemicals and poisoned sea-inlets. These are just a few of many examples of polluted waters, air, or soil by the industries and the Indian government's total inaction to remedy the situation.

The Supreme Court of India has repeatedly ordered closure of the factories across the country for violation of pollution laws, but unfortunately, nothing has changed.[19]

The Indian Automobile Association rate India as the second fastest growing market, some 14% growth rate for cars. In addition, Tata Motors forthcoming Nano means a huge number of middleclass Indians would be able to afford cars. This will lead to an indelible surge in fuel consumption and CO_2 emissions in the next few years. According to Greenpeace, legislation for progressive mandatory fuel efficiency is a critical step necessary to tackle the fuel crisis and pollution problem the country faces with a booming car population. India already imports 78% of its crude oil needs. This will rise to 94% by 2030 as estimated by the International Energy Agency. While Indian consumers are familiar with noxious fumes, and the pollution that vehicular emissions cause, they are not aware that vehicles emit CO_2, a major greenhouse gas, the biggest contributor in fact to global warming. India needs to require car manufacturers to have mandatory "CO_2 emissions-rate labeling" on all new cars to enable consumers to make sensible decisions before buying a car. The government also needs mandate CO_2 emissions standards for the auto industry which will require car manufacturers to progressively reduce CO_2 emissions from new cars to achieve a fleet efficiency of 80gm CO_2/km by 2020. India won't be the first country to require these standards; it will simply be following the global trend. Vehicular fuel efficiency and CO_2 emissions regulation is in practice in various countries including the EU, China, Japan, Taiwan and South Korea.[20]

Although India currently lags behind China in its overall consumption of coal, it is nonetheless on track to becoming a major CO_2 contributor over the next decade and is already the fifth-largest emitter of greenhouse gases globally.

INDONESIA

A country of thousands of islands, Indonesia is rich in minerals, timber, palm oil, rubber, coal and other resources. It is home to a wide range of animal and plant species. Its islands of Borneo and Bali possess a dense tropical forest home to countless number of animal, bird and plant species, some of which cannot be find anywhere else.

Unfortunately, Indonesia also exhibits massive environmental degradation with huge pollution problems, deforestation, soil erosion, monumental land degradation due to extensive mining, illegal tree cutting, and forest clearing. The island of Borneo is divided between Indonesia, Malaysia, and Brunei, with the major part controlled by Indonesia, a smaller north-western portion under Malaysia and about one percent under Brunei in the north. Ruled for thirty two years by the dictator Suharto who treated Indonesian forests and many other resources as his personal family wealth, Indonesia suffers from rampant corruption even today, a decade or more after Suharto was forced to leave due to massive protests by students.

In the past 20 years, single-crop plantations of oil palm have spread across Borneo to meet the world demand for versatile and vastly profitable oil derived from its fruit. Since 1991, palm oil plantations have spread into forests and peat lands on the Sumatra and Borneo islands, making Indonesia the world's third-highest emitter of greenhouse gases. Increasingly, palm oil plantations are taking over the habitat of a number of animal species including the famous Orangutans and Clouded Leopards. Currently, there are 40,000 wild orangutans in Borneo but the United Nations estimates there could be fewer than 1,000 by 2023. The Centre for Orangutan Protection warns orangutans living outside Central Kalimantan's conservation areas could be wiped out within three years.

Of approximately 20,000 individuals in Central Kalimantan province, close to 3,000 die every year, it says.[21]

Palm oil is used for cooking and a seemingly endless number of products such as cosmetics, soaps, desserts, and today as a biofuel. Indonesia (19.7 million metric tons in 2008) and Malaysia (17.4 million metric tons in 2008) supply 86% of the world's demand as growing conditions are perfect for this newly found green gold. While environmentalists are spreading the news about palm oil's contribution to global warming, some calling for palm oil products' boycott, Indonesia has become the world's largest producer with 15 million acres under cultivation, a number that may double by 2020. As if palm oil is not enough, Borneo possesses another resource that is both economic blessing and environmental disaster. Some 300 million years ago, extensive plant material grew on what is now Borneo. It now lies underground, transformed into coal. Surface mines for gold and coal, spread across southern and eastern Borneo like pockmarks, are replacing forests and polluting rivers with waste. Sadly, nearly a third of the rainforest that stood on Borneo in 1985 has disappeared by 2005.

Under today's looming threat of global warming, Borneo has gained the world's attention for yet another reason: A specialized ecosystem known as peat swamp forest covers about 11 percent of the island. Here, trees grow on highly organic soil, built by centuries of accumulation of water-logged plant material. Sometimes, as deep as 60 feet, peat soil is a massive store of the world's carbon. Tropical peat, stripped of its trees and drained, decays and releases its carbon into the atmosphere. When it dries, it becomes very susceptible to intentional or accidental burning. Massive fires set deliberately every year to clear forested land for new palm oil plantations—exacerbated by frequent droughts—have burned uncontrollably filling Borneo's skies with smoke, closing some airports and making millions of people suffer from respiratory problems as far away as mainland Asia. The carbon released by these fires, decaying peat soil, and rampant deforestation has placed Indonesia third among nations as a source of greenhouse gases, just behind highly industrialized China and the United States.

It is the extreme poverty of most Indonesians who inhabit three quarters of the island that influences conservation in Borneo. Any strategy that environmentalists may pursue to save its forests and biodiversity in the future must include ways for these inhabitants to improve their lives.[22]

BRAZIL

Brazil, whose Amazon forests are the lungs of this Earth, is deforesting this invaluable forest at an alarming rate. Brazil's forests are being cut down by powerful corporations for timber as well as for agriculture plantations, including corn plantations, as corn supplies a major proportion—more than 50 percent—of transportation energy requirements in the form of ethanol biofuel. Two countries, Brazil and Indonesia, account for more than half the deforestation in the world. The Democratic Republic of Congo is also high on the list but it is a failing state, so forest management is difficult to pursue.

EXPORT OF TOXIC WASTES

It is saddening that many countries export their industrial, electronics or nuclear waste to other poorer countries of Africa, China, India, Pakistan, Bangladesh and Nepal.

Canada is an exception. It is a rich country. Yet, it has been accepting shipments of PCB contaminated waste from America's foreign bases that the U.S. government itself will not accept. Greenpeace International released a U.S. Defense Department document prepared for the U.S. Congress during March 1999 that refers to "current shipments of foreign-manufactured waste to Canada". More than 200 truckloads of U.S. toxic waste undergoing treatment in Alberta became a target of controversy...[23]

Tanzania has become home to huge stockpiles of agricultural pesticides and veterinary drugs, including DDT which pose significant threat to its environment and its people's health. Some stocks are older than thirty years and are stored with no or few safety precautions. The stocks of toxic chemicals are growing in Tanzania because there is no environmentally safe way to dispose them off. According to environmentalists, Tanzania has more than 500 tons of agricultural compounds dumped or stored at more than a hundred sites. Most of this waste was imported in Tanzania more than a decade ago as 'donations' by Japan, China, Italy, the United States and other wealthier countries seeking to dispose off toxic chemicals that are now illegal and unusable at home.[24]

Exports of 'Gift Waste' are growing worldwide. The United Nations' Food and Agriculture Organization (FAO), in early May 2001, said that more than 500,000 tons of banned or expired pesticides are seriously threatening the environment and health of millions of people worldwide in developing countries. According to the FAO news release, in Asia, the quantities of obsolete pesticides are estimated at over 200,000 tons, in Africa and the Near East at over 100,000 tons, and in Eastern Europe and the former Soviet Union at more than 200,000 tons.[25] These pesticides can leak into the ground, contaminating the water and the soil. Leaking pesticides can poison a very large area, making it unfit for crop production according to the FAO 2001 press release. [26]

Export of e-waste has also become big business with the advent of computer technology. According to a Greenpeace investigation, significant quantities of electronic waste are being exported to China, India, Nigeria, Ghana and others. Containers filled with old and often broken computers, monitors, TVs—famous brands including Philips, Microsoft, Nokia, Canon, Dell, Sony and Siemens—arrive in Ghana from Germany, the U.S., Korea, Switzerland, and the Netherlands under dubious label of "second hand goods". Export of e-waste from Europe is banned but exporting of old electronics for 're-use' allows unscrupulous traders to profit from dumping old electronics in Ghana.

Most of the contents of the containers end up in Ghana's scrap yards to be crushed and burned by unprotected workers.

In these scrap yards, the unprotected workers, many of them children, dismantle TVs and computers with little more than stones in search of metals that can be sold. The remaining plastic, cables and casing are either burnt or simply dumped, creating pollution. Some of the electronics contain toxic metals including lead in high quantities. Chemicals such as phthalates, some of which are known to interfere with sexual reproduction, are found in many items. Some even were found to contain high level of dioxins, known to promote cancer. According to Greenpeace's Dr. Kevin Bridgen from their science unit, who visited the scrap yards in China, India, and Ghana, "Many of the chemicals released are highly toxic, some may affect children's developing reproductive systems, while others can affect brain development and the nervous system. In Ghana, China, and India, workers, many of them children, may be exposed to these hazardous chemicals."[27]

As mentioned above, China, besides others, is a big receiver of electronic waste and garbage from around the world. Some first world countries get rid of their mountains of garbage by paying China to accept this stuff. This garbage includes toxic chemicals and discarded electronics such as old computers, TVs, cell-phones, monitors, keyboards etc. China's expanding manufacturing industries accept this garbage/scrap as it serves as a source of cheap raw materials. The quantity of this garbage increased from one million tons to 11 million tons from 1990 to 1997. The first world garbage shipped to China via Hong Kong increased from 2.3 million tons to over 3 million tons annually from 1998 to 2002.

When this garbage arrives in China, at certain locations it is dismantled by the poor Chinese, who contaminate their bodies with toxic chemicals working in very unhygienic conditions. It is thus that the first world transfers its pollution to China, endangering the lives of many Chinese workers.[28]

NUCLEAR ACCIDENTS

Ever since nuclear power has been discovered and nuclear power plants have been built, several nuclear accidents have occurred worldwide, clearly proving the fact that nuclear energy is not safe. It is not safe to operate the nuclear power plants, and there is no safe way yet found to dispose off the nuclear waste generated.

Nuclear accidents such as Chernobyl and Three Mile Island are famous. The Chernobyl disaster occurred at a powerful nuclear reactor in the Chernobyl Nuclear Power Plant in the Soviet Union. It was the worst nuclear power plant disaster ever. Huge amounts of radioactivity were released into the environment following a massive explosion that destroyed the reactor.

The radioactive plume drifted over extensive areas of the Soviet Union, Eastern Europe, Western Europe, northern Europe, and eastern North America. Wide areas of Ukraine, Belarus, and Russia were terribly contaminated, resulting in the evacuation and resettlement of more than 336,000 people. About 60% of the radioactive fallout fell on Belarus, according to official post-Soviet data.[29] For years now, these three countries are burdened with continuing decontamination and healthcare costs of the Chernobyl disaster.

According to Soviet estimates, between 300,000 to 600,000 people were involved in the cleanup of the 30 km. evacuation zone around the reactor, but many of them entered the zone two years after the disaster.[30] Estimates of nuclear "liquidators"—workers brought into the area for disaster management and recovery job—vary. For example, the World Health Organization puts the figure at around 800,000; in the first year after the disaster, the number of cleanup workers was estimated to be 211,000. These workers received a heavy dose (165 millisieverts) of radiation; many of them would succumb to this radiation in the years to come. The plume of the deadly radioactive debris has been said to be equal to the contamination of 400 Hiroshima bombs.

Plant and animal health were adversely affected by the disaster. A large swath of pine forest killed by acute radiation was named the Red Forest. The dead pines were bulldozed and buried. Livestock were removed during the human evacuations.[31] Elsewhere in Europe, radiation levels were examined in various food stocks. In both, Sweden and Finland, fish in deep freshwater lakes were banned for resale and land owners were advised not to consume certain types.

The number of people whose lives were affected by the disaster is enormous. Some reports indicate that over 300,000 people were resettled because of the disaster; millions, however, lived and continue to live in the contaminated area. Greenpeace suggested that there will be 270,000 cases of cancer attributable to Chernobyl fallout, and that 93,000 of these will probably be fatal. Further they add in their report that in Belarus, Ukraine, and Russia alone, the accident could have resulted in an estimated 200,000 additional deaths in the period between 1990 and 2004.[32]

The total cost of the disaster is estimated at $200 billion USD, taking inflation into account: the costliest disaster in the modern history.[33]

* * *

In 1960, I had occasion to make a trip by car (to) a place near Chelyabinsk in the Southern Urals (from northeast of), the city of Sverdlovsk in the Northern Urals. We began our trip shortly after midnight and reached the main highway leading from Sverdlovsk to the south at approximately 5 a.m. when it was clear enough to see the surrounding area.

About 100 kilometers from Sverdlovsk, a road sign warned drivers not to stop for next 30 kilometers and to drive through at maximum speed.

On both sides of the road as far as one can see the land was "dead": no villages, no towns, only chimneys of destroyed houses, no cultivated fields or pastures, no herds, no people...nothing.

The whole country around Sverdlovsk was exceedingly "hot". An enormous area, some hundreds of square kilometers, had been laid waste, rendered useless and unproductive for a very long time, tens or perhaps hundreds of years.

I was later told that this was the site of famous "Kyshtim Catastrophe" in which many hundreds of people had been killed or disabled.

I cannot say with certainty whether the accident was caused by buried nuclear waste, as Zhores Medvedev wrote in the New Scientist and *The Jerusalem Post* or by the explosion of a plutonium producing plant, as intelligence sources (quoted by A.P) and the Times have said. However, all people with whom I spoke—scientists as well as laymen—had no doubt that blame lay with Soviet officialdom that were negligent and careless in storing the nuclear wastes.

Thus wrote Professor L. Tumerman of the Weismann Institute of Science, Rehoboth, to *The Jerusalem Post* in Israel. Dr. Zhore A. Medvedev, a Soviet biochemist first broke the story in an article in the *New Scientist* about the nuclear explosion. The story about the nuclear accident was also reported in the *New York Times, Denver Post,* and *Los Angeles Times* on November 8, 10 and 11, 1976 respectively.

Late in 1957 or in early 1958, a huge explosion occurred in the disposal section of the Soviet atomic weapons industry located in the southern Urals where atomic wastes had been stored for more than ten years. The consequences were devastating. The main radioactive contamination covered between 800 and 1200 square miles, an area the size of Rhode Island. Several people died. Many were injured. Whole villages had to be evacuated and bulldozed. The remaining plant and animal life received such a massive dose of radiation that its effects will last for a century or more.[34]

There are other nuclear accidents which are unknown to the general public. Citing the July, 2007 accident in Japan where fire and leakage from the Kashiwazaki-Kariwa Nuclear Power Plant, Greenpeace's Climate and Energy Expert, Srinivas Krishnaswamy warned, "The leakage from the nuclear power plant in Japan is a grim reminder of how natural disasters and terrorist attacks pose a big challenge to nuclear power stations and can lead to very serious accidents, the impacts of which would be felt not just locally." He added, "The Japanese and Global nuclear industry has been marred by a series of accidents and cover-ups." A similar incident occurred at the German nuclear power plant Krummel in June the same year. It was first claimed that the fire had no impact on the safety of the reactor. In reality, the fire caused the reactor to malfunction and according to German nuclear regulators, directly threatened its safety.

POLLUTING MULTINATIONALS

Multinationals, in their greed for profit, are some of the biggest polluters around the globe. Take for example Nigeria. It is the most populous country of Africa, and is endowed with substantial natural resources. Yet, it is one of the poorest countries of the world. As is the case with many oil rich developing countries, oil reserves have proved a mixed blessing for this country. Since 1974, oil exports are the main source of revenue for the country. Today, oil sales account for more than 40% of gross domestic product (GDP), 80 % of government's budgetary revenue, and more than 95% of its exports.

The Niger Delta of Nigeria is home to substantial oil deposits. Several multinational oil companies, mainly from the U.S. such as Shell, Mobil, and Chevron, but also those from other countries such as Italy's Agip and France's Elf Aquitaine are there. All these oil companies operate there on the basis of joint venture with the government. While pumping gasoline, these companies are devastating the Niger Delta environment with no regard to the wellbeing of the citizens to whom this oil belongs. While these companies are making windfall profits, the poor Nigerians are as deprived as ever. The oil exploration is having a severe impact on the local environment, and on agricultural and fish production throughout the Niger Delta region. Many communities complain that they rarely receive sufficient compensation for the land taken by the oil companies, or rendered unusable by oil spills, acid rains, and other forms of pollution. Protests by the people have met with often violent reprisals by the government militias with the complicity of the oil companies as these government police and security forces are bribed by them.

A big polluter here is constantly burning gas flares. Natural gas is a by-product of oil industry operations. Most of them burn 24 hours a day and some have been burning for 40 years! Communities living near these flares are deprived of even the comfort of night's natural darkness. Natural gas does not have to be flared off, and in many countries there is little flaring. The gas can be reinjected in the subsoil and can be stored as a source of energy for the locals. But these companies opt for flaring because, even by paying minimal fines per barrel of gas burned—that they have to pay to the government—it is by far much cheaper than the alternatives.

Thus these communities are losing a valuable resource and have to live in the polluted environment due to flaring. Though full assessment is not done, the impact of gas flares on the local ecology and climate, as well as the health of people and property is evident. The extremely high levels of carbon dioxide and methane gases that are released into the atmosphere also impact the environment beyond the immediate areas. The flares are so hot, that one cannot go near them. A constant roar accompanies the thick column of smoke emanating from these flares, fouling the air. Hundreds of meters away, a noxious odor emanates from these flares.

Besides depriving the communities of drinkable rainwater and stunting the crop growth, acid rain is also affecting people's homes due to this flaring. In the Iko, Eket and Etagberi regions, people used zinc roofs as they lasted 7-10 years and were good replacements to labor-intensive thatched roofs. But with the acid rain, they are destroyed within 1 or 2 years. So many of the home owners now have resorted to asbestos roofing which, though more resistant to acid rain, are more expensive and hazardous to their health.

Besides grave problems with gas flares, on-site oil leaks and ruptured pipelines have become a serious problem here. Some of these decrepit pipelines are more than 40 years old. They criss-cross villages and land; some of them are above ground. These pipes are rusted and obviously need repair.

On average, each month, three major oil spills are recorded here. Shell recorded 35 incidents of oil spills in its operations in the first quarter of 1997 alone. It was reported in June 1998 that a leak near the Otuegwe community that had been going on for months had spilled over 800,000 barrels of crude from a 16-inch buried pipeline owned by Shell. The Otuegwe community was seriously affected by the resulting ecological devastation. Villagers in many areas complain that when pipelines corrode and leak, oil workers will inspect but not repair the leak. Instead, according to the villagers, the oil companies often claimed sabotage. Under Nigerian law, companies are not obligated to clean up or compensate for the effects of spills caused by sabotage.

Activists from 'Essential Action and Global Exchange' had visited the Niger Delta between September 8 to18, 1999. Most of what they found is mentioned above. They found that oil companies are illegally acquiring the land belonging to the people of Niger Delta. By their spills, large swaths of land are being destroyed along with its flora and fauna. The Niger Delta is the third largest mangrove forest in the world and the largest in Africa. Mangrove forests are essential for the locals for sustaining their lives as they provide soil stability, medicines, wood for fuel, shelter, healthy fisheries, tannins and dyes, and critical wildlife habitats. But these oil spills are contaminating, degrading and destroying these mangrove forests. Endangered species—delta elephants, the river hippopotamus, the white-crested monkeys and crocodiles—are increasingly endangered by the oil exploitation and devastation caused by the spills.

Though Nigeria is world's 13th largest oil producer, it was until a few years ago chronically short of fuel, having to import it from other oil-producing nations. The government of Nigeria is a 55-60% shareholder in oil operations and earns billions in royalties each year; the local infrastructure at the source of these billions is in shambles according to the activists who visited the Niger Delta. According to them, food shortages abound, malnutrition is common among children, power blackouts occur regularly and roads are in terrible condition.

Everywhere the above activists visited, they witnessed the destruction of the local environment, and oppression of communities affected by what they called an 'outlaw oil industry'. Millions of Niger Delta residents barely survive under the sober shadow of this industry's wealth. The tragedy is real where so much oil is being extracted from the same lands where abject poverty has become institutionalized. Billions of dollars in profits have been earned each year over the last 40 years. Meanwhile, the very life blood of the region and its people is being drained by high unemployment, failing crops, poisoned waters, declining wild fisheries, dying forests and vanishing wildlife. Indeed, this is a tragedy that still continues to this day.[35]

The situation is no different in Congo. According to the Congolese government reports, 80% of the Congolese people live on mere 30 cents or less a day while billions of dollars go out through the back door into the pockets of the mining companies many of which are American and Canadian.[36]

This is just one example of polluting multinationals. There are many around the globe such as in Ecuador, Bolivia, Myanmar and others.

SECTION III
EARLY SYMPTOMS OF PERIL

CHAPTER 6
CURRENT CIVILIZATION IN TROUBLE

The earth we abuse and the living things we kill will, in the end, take their revenge; for in exploiting
their presence we are diminishing our future.
—Marya Mannes, More in Anger, 1958

The industrial civilization of ours that began in eighteenth century in England and spread around the world is now, without a doubt in peril. We see the ominous signs everywhere. The Earth's temperature is warming. The climate is changing. Six of the last ten years have been the warmest in history. From Antarctica to the Arctic, from the Himalayas to the Pyrenees, from the Andes to the Alps and from Hindukush to the Pamir, the glaciers which abode there for thousands of years are melting at an alarming rate. Our environment is polluted terribly. The oceans of the world, from the Pacific to the Atlantic, from the Indian Ocean to the Gulf of Mexico, are also heavily polluted. There are plastics and other garbage islands many miles long freely floating in our oceans. From the Ganges to Brahmaputra, from Yangtze to the Yellow river, the world's rivers, once the cradles of rising civilizations, are contaminated with toxic waste. Our planet's forests which once covered most of the Earth are dangerously depleting in front of our eyes. Animal and plant species are dying, going extinct day by day, year after year. Our grand children may not see the lions or Rhinos in Africa, Tigers in India or Orangutans in Borneo,

Indonesia. The world's top soils, the pivotal necessity of planet's food supply and human survival is being eroded at a dangerous rate, threatening the very survival of humans. The climate is warming, the rainfall pattern is shifting, the ocean waters are rising and the tropical storms' frequency and intensity is increasing menacingly.

RISING TEMPERATURES & SWELLING OCEANS

Our current civilization has evolved during a period that was remarkably stable for the last several thousand years. But that stability is now ending. Now, we are entering a period of global warming, thanks especially to the industrial revolution and the civilization that followed. It is beyond doubt according to all scientific data that it is we humans who have triggered this global warming catastrophe. Besides the scientific data, we ourselves are seeing and experiencing the effects of climate change. All around the planet, mountain glaciers are melting. Rivers of the mighty Himalaya that feed millions of people of China, India and Tibet by irrigating their rice and wheat fields are fast drying up.[1]

The ice sheets of Antarctica and Greenland are melting at an alarming rate. The resultant trillions of gallons of water being added to the seas could raise the sea level by as much as 12 meters (39 feet). As a result, many of the world's coastal cities will be under water in the not too distant future. As many as over 600 million coastal inhabitants will be forced to abandon their homes and become eco-refugees.[2] The frequency of heat waves has increased. The year 2003 experienced record high temperatures and drought. The 2003 heat wave, unheard of in Europe before, took a heavy human toll there. This searing heat wave that broke all the records across Europe claimed more than 52,000 lives in nine countries. Italy alone lost 18,000 people while France lost 14, 800.[3]

Meteorologists point out that the 23 warmest years on record have all come since 1980; and since record keeping began in 1880, the seven warmest years have been experienced in the last nine. Four of these years—2002, 2003, 2005 and 2006—were years in which major food producing regions saw their crops wither due to these record temperatures.

Since the beginning of the industrial revolution, the quantity of carbon dioxide (CO2) in the atmosphere has risen significantly. It has grown from 227 parts per million (ppm) to 384 ppm in 2007. The annual rise in atmospheric CO2 levels is one of the planet's most predictable environmental trends resulting from the annual discharge into the atmosphere of 7.5 billion tons of carbon from burned fossil fuels and 1.5 billion tons of carbon coming from deforestation. Largely resulting from increased emissions from burning fossil fuels, the current annual increase is nearly four times what it was in the 1950s. The temperature of the planet goes up as more and more as CO2 accumulates in the atmosphere.[4]

Looking at these increases, the projections that Earth's average temperature will increase by 1.1 to 6.4 degrees Celsius (2.0 to 11.5 degrees Fahrenheit) during this century seem all too likely. These are the latest projections from United Nations' Intergovernmental Panel on Climate Change (IPCC), the body of 2,500 scientists from around the world that in 2007 released a consensus report affirming humanity's role in climate change.[5]

The IPCC's projected rise in temperature is the global average. But in real terms, the rise will be very uneven. It will be much greater over land than over oceans, in the high northern latitudes than over the equator, and in the continental interiors than in the coastal areas.[6]

A recent new study, released in September 2009 says the global warming is increasing at a higher rate than previously thought. The study by the United Nation's Environmental Program reports that the planet's temperature will rise by 6.30 °F by the end of this century even if the most ambitious of the proposals to combat climate change are enacted. The temperature rise is two times higher than what scientists have previously identified as a maximum the humans can afford to avert the climate disaster.

Higher temperatures reduce crop yields, increase the area affected by drought, and melt the snow and ice of glaciers in the mountains that feed the Earth's rivers, cause more destructive storms and increase the frequency of more destructive storms and wildfires.

MELTING GLACIERS

Mountain Glaciers are giant natural reservoirs of water feeding the major rivers of the world that irrigate millions of acres of fertile lands which feed hundreds of millions of people around the world. Unfortunately, the burning of fossil fuels by us humans has triggered global warming that is melting these glaciers at an alarming rate. These glaciers accumulate more snow in the winter and melt at a normal rate in the summer. So the rivers that these glaciers feed keep flowing throughout the year. But even one degree rise in temperature in the mountains can significantly reduce the snowfall there and boost rainfall instead. This then increases the flooding during the rainy season and reduces the snowmelt that flows into the rivers. Besides, glaciers that feed the rivers during the dry season are also melting. Some have already disappeared completely. At no place is the melting of glaciers of more concern than in Asia. There as many as 1.3 billion people depend on their water supply on rivers and their tributaries originating in the Himalayas and the nearby Tibet-Qinghai Plateau.[7]

The Gangotri Glacier of India which supplies 70 percent of water to the Ganges is not only melting but is doing it at a disturbing rate. If this continues, Gangotri's life expectancy will be measured in decades. That means Ganges will become a seasonal river, flowing only during the monsoons. This will be a life threatening catastrophe for some 407 million Indians and Bangladeshis who inhabit the Ganges and Brahmaputra basin.[8]

All the great rivers of Asia—the Ganges, the Indus, and the Brahmaputra in India, Pakistan and Bangladesh; the Yangtze and the Yellow Rivers in China; and the Mekong and Salween Rivers in Southeast

Asia—are sustained by giant glaciers stretching across the towering Tibetan-Qinghai plateau.

"With climate change, all these rivers will have greatly reduced flows," warns Carter Brandon, director of the World Bank's China Environment Program in Beijing. "There will also be much more seasonal variation—when flow is more dependent on rainfall, as opposed to the steady inflow of snowmelt from glaciers."[9]

The glacier system delivers water to more than 300 million people in China—and one billion across south Asia. Unfortunately, the region is among the world's most rapidly warming. Average temperature on the "rooftop of the world" has climbed 2 °F in last two decades.

Chinese scientists expect the total area of the glaciers to halve every 10 years. They predict that by 2100, the glaciers may have largely vanished.[10]

For China, which is even more dependent on river water for irrigation than India, the situation is even more threatening. According to Chinese government data, the glaciers on the Tibet-Qinghai Plateau that feed both the Yangtze and Yellow Rivers are melting at 7 percent per year. The Yellow River Basin—home to some 107 million Chinese—could experience a large dry-season flow reduction. The larger Yangtze River is also threatened by the disappearance of the glacier. Some 369 million Chinese living in its basin depend heavily on rice fields irrigated with its water.[11]

A leading Chinese glaciologist named Yao Tandong predicts that two thirds of China's glaciers could be gone by year 2060. "The full-scale glacier shrinkage in the plateau region," Yao warns, "will eventually lead to an ecological catastrophe."[12]

There are other Asian rivers originating in the Himalayas. They include the Indus, in whose basin 178 million people live in India and Pakistan;

Brahmaputra which flows through Bangladesh; and the Mekong, which supplies waters to Cambodia, Laos, Thailand and Vietnam.[13]

For decades, scientists have been warning that glaciers not only in Asia, but also in Africa, and Latin America—particularly Peru—are melting. In 2007 the United Nations' Intergovernmental Panel on Climate Change (IPCC) issued a report concluding that due to rising global temperatures, Latin America's glaciers could melt away within 15 years. Glaciers have been disappearing throughout Bolivia, Colombia, Ecuador, and Peru, but the impact is felt hardest in Peru, which is home to 70 percent of the world's tropical glaciers.[14]

The French government's Research Director for the Institute of Research and Development, Bernard Francou believes that within the next 15 years, 80 percent of South American glaciers will disappear. For countries like Peru, Ecuador and Bolivia, which depend on waters from glaciers for irrigation and household use, the consequences could be dire.[15]

Peru stretches some 1,600 kilometers along the vast mountain range of the Andes. My family, some friends, and I visited this beautiful country and Ecuador in 2004. Both these countries, especially Peru have a large population of indigenous people. These countries and their people are beautiful and innocent. But a catastrophe awaits these friendly peoples, a catastrophe not of their making. Already, 22 percent of Peru's glacial endowment, which feed many Peruvian rivers that provide water to the cities in the semi-arid coastal regions, have disappeared. Lonnie Thompson warns that the Quelccaya Glacier in southern Peru, which was retreating by 6 meters per year in the 1960s, is now retreating by 60 meters annually.[16]

Most of Peru's farmers irrigate their wheat and potato farms with river water from these disappearing glaciers. These farmers are completely dependent on irrigation water during the dry season. The shrinking glaciers for Peru's 28 million people means a shrinking food supply.[17]

The three rivers high in the Andes which are fed partly by glacial melt, supply most of the water for the 7 million people of the city of Lima. The river flows are above normal while the glaciers are melting, but once they disappear, the river flows will sharply decline, creating severe water crises for the residents of Lima.[18] Peruvians are not alone in their predicament. According to the World Bank report, 82% of the glaciers are lost in the Bolivian Andes as well. This means a significant shrinking in water supply for the Bolivians too. The report predicts complete disappearance of these vast ice fields in the next 20 years, a catastrophe that these people have nothing to do with in its creation.[19]

Africa is yet another continent threatened. In 1999, my family and I were amazed looking at majestic, partially snow capped Kilimanjaro Mountain from a distance in Tanzania. We were traveling enjoying Serengeti forest in Tanzania and other areas in Kenya. It is sad to know now that Kilimanjaro may soon be snow and ice-free for the first time in thousands of years. A study done by Ohio State University glaciologist Lonnie Thompson shows that Africa's tallest mountain, Kilimanjaro lost 33 percent of its ice field between 1989 and 2000. Thompson projects that by 2015, its snow-cap could entirely disappear.

While traveling in Kenya in 1999, we stayed at Mount Kenya Lodge, a beautiful place nestled in the mountain at several thousand feet elevation with lush green surroundings. Little did we realize then that Mount Kenya has lost 7 of its 18 glaciers. The local rivers which are being fed by these glaciers are becoming seasonal rivers. This is creating conflict among the 2 million people who depend on them for their water supplies during the dry season.[20]

As one can see from above, in many agricultural regions, the leading source of irrigation and drinking water are glaciers and masses of ice. In the southwestern United States, the Colorado River—the region's main source of irrigation water—derives its water from the snowfields of the Rockies. California, where I live, is not only heavily dependent on the Colorado River, but relies primarily on the snowmelt from the Sierra

Nevada in the eastern part of the state. The Sierra Nevada and the coastal range provides irrigation water to California's Central Valley, a major source of America's fruits and vegetables.[21]

An analysis of the effects of rising temperatures on three river systems in the western United States—Colorado, Sacramento and Columbia Rivers—shows that the winter snow pack in the mountains feeding them will be dramatically reduced and that winter rainfall and flooding will increase.[22]

The global climate models with the status quo energy policy predict that by mid-century, there will be 70 percent reduction in the amount of snow pack for the western United States. A detailed study of the Yakima River Valley—a vast fruit-growing region in Washington State—carried out by the U.S. Department of Energy's Pacific Northwest National Laboratory shows progressively heavier harvest losses as the snow pack shrinks, reducing irrigation water flows.[23]

Meanwhile, in Europe, the Pyrenees Mountains have lost almost 90% of their glacier ice over the past century, according to the scientists who warn that global warming means they will disappear totally within a few years.

While glaciers covered 3,300 hectares of land on the mountain range that divides Spain and France, at the turn of the century, only 390 hectares remain, according to Spain's environment ministry.[24]

Among the first to disappear from the continent over the coming decades are the most southerly glaciers in Europe which are losing the battle against warming. Their loss will have a severe impact on summer water supplies in the foothills and southern plains south of the Pyrenees. "This century could experience (perhaps within a few decades) the total, or almost total, disappearance of the last reserves of ice in the Spanish Pyrenees and, as a result, a major change in the current nature of upper reaches of the mountains," the author of the report on Spain's glaciers said.[25] Scientists have ruled out the idea that progressive deterioration of glaciers around the planet is part of normal, long-term fluctuations in their size. Europe's glaciers are thought to have lost a quarter of their mass in the last 8 years.

Prof. Wilfried Haeberli, director of the World Climate Monitoring Service has warned that glaciers under threat in Spain feed rivers such as Ga"ego, the Cinca, and the Garona which water the foothills and plains of the south Pyrenees. "During the dry season, especially in Spain, they are nourished by glacier and snow melt," said Prof. Haeberli. He said that smaller glaciers, such as those in Spain and some in tropical countries such as Colombia and Kenya, would soon disappear as the planet warms. Even the Alps are likely to lose up to 75% of their glacial area by the mid-century.[26]

The World Glacier Monitoring Service last year reported that glaciers around the planet were melting at a rate unseen for 5,000 years. "It has become obvious that the ongoing trend of worldwide and fast glacier shrinkage...is of a non-cyclic nature," the service's report for the decade up to 2005 warned. The rate of melting, when compared to the previous decade, more than doubled over that period.

Changes were "without precedent in history" and would produce "dramatic scenarios", including the complete loss of glaciers in some mountain systems, according to the report.[27]

Looking at Central Asia, the snowmelt from Hindu Kush, Tien Shan, and Pamir mountain ranges is the major source of water for irrigation on which the countries of Uzbekistan, Tajikistan, Kyrgyzstan, Kazakhstan and Afghanistan are heavily dependent; similarly, the snowmelt of the 5,700-meter-high Alborz Mountains between Tehran and the Caspian Sea provide most of the water to Iran.[28]

We take for granted the snow and ice masses in the world's major mountains because they have been there for millions of years before humans. But that is all changing now. Unless we change our ways drastically and stop burning fossil fuels and deforesting forests, these vast reservoirs of water in the mountains will be gone forever bringing unimaginable catastrophe to hundreds of millions of people who depend on them.

MELTING ICE AND RISING OCEANS

The new projections by IPCC, the body that compiles findings of international scientists, of ocean levels rising by a 4.6 foot, or 55-inches, is higher than 23-inch estimate of 2007 and are direr than previously thought. In their 2007 calculations, the panel didn't include melt from the Greenland and Antarctic ice sheets, which have accelerated in the past decade. The scientists have now begun to forecast even higher ocean-level rises.[29]

Another report sketches much higher sea levels. With ice melting in the mountains, the river flows are affected and the sea levels will start rising. According to this report, when one takes into account the huge ice sheets of Greenland and Antarctica, their melting could raise the sea levels by as much as 7 meters (23 feet). On the other hand, if the West Antarctic Ice Sheet melts, the sea level could rise further 5 meters (16 feet). But even partial melting of these ice sheets could dramatically raise ocean levels. Scientists have noted that the IPCC projections of the sea level rise of 18 to 59 centimeters during this century are already obsolete and 2 meters rises during this time are quite possible.[30]

A 2005 study, *Impacts of a Warming Arctic,* has come to a conclusion that the Arctic is warming at double the speed as rest of the planet. The study conducted by the Arctic Climate Impact Assessment (ACIA) team, a group of 300 international scientists, has found that the temperatures, in the regions surrounding the Arctic, including western Canada, Alaska and eastern Russia, have risen by 3-4 °C (4-7 °F) over the last half century. The Chair of ACIA, Robert Corell warns that this region "is experiencing some of the most rapid and severe climate change on Earth."[31]

The ACIA report tells that the retreat of the sea ice has devastating consequences for polar bears whose very survival is now at stake. A subsequent report mentions that polar bears, in their struggle to just survive, are resorting to cannibalism. Also, ice-dwelling seals—the basic food source of the Inuit—are threatened.

There is new evidence since this 2005 report that the problem could be worse than previously thought. A team of scientists from the National Snow and Ice Data Center has compiled data on Arctic Ocean ice melting in the summer from 1953 to 2006. They have concluded that ice is melting much faster than previous models had predicted. As per their findings, from 1979 to 2006, the summer sea ice shrinkage accelerated to 9.1 percent a decade. In 2007, the Arctic sea ice shrank about 20 percent below the previous record set in 2005.

All this means the sea could be ice-free long before 2050, the earliest date projected by the IPCC in its 2007 report. Julienne Stroeve, an Arctic scientist, has noted that the shrinking Arctic sea ice may have reached "a tipping point that could trigger a cascade of climate change reaching into Earth's temperate regions."[32]

Senior NASA scientists reported that even the winter ice cover in the Arctic Ocean shrank by 6 percent in 2005 and 2006. This new development along with the news that the sea ice cover is now thinning, is a clear evidence of ice not recovering after its melt season. That means summer ice in the Arctic Ocean could disappear much sooner than previously thought possible.[33]

A researcher named Walt Meier at the U.S. National Snow and Ice Data Center, who tracks the changes in Arctic sea ice, views the winter shrinkage with great concern. He thinks there is all likelihood that the Arctic tipping point has been reached. "People have tried to think of ways we could get back to where we were. We keep going further and further in the hole, and it's getting harder and harder to get out of it" he laments.

Some scientists are now convinced that the Arctic Ocean could be ice-free in the summer as early as 2030.[34]

Expert after expert is warning us of ice covers melting in the Polar Regions at an alarming rate and the resultant impending catastrophe the world faces.

"The Arctic is warming so quickly that the region's sea ice cover in summer could vanish as early as 2013, decades earlier than some had predicted," a leading polar expert said on March 5, 2009. Warwick Vincent, director of the Center for Northern Studies at Laval University in Quebec, said recent data on the ice cover "appear to be tracking the most pessimistic of the models, which call for an ice free summer in 2013." He told Reuters that the year "2013 is starting to look as though it is a lot more reasonable as a prediction. But each year we've been wrong—each year we're finding that it's a little bit faster than expected."[35]

Vincent's scientific team has spent the last 10 summers on Ward Hunt Island, a remote spot some 2,500 miles northwest of Ottawa. He told Reuters last September that it was clear some of the damage would be permanent and that the warming in the Arctic was a sign of what the rest of the world could expect. "Some of this is unstoppable. We're in a train of events at the moment where there are changes taking place that we are unable to reverse, the loss of these ice shelves, for example," he said.[36]

Some scientists now think that "positive feedback loops" may be starting to kick in. One is in the Arctic, the albedo effect. When the incoming sun light strikes the ice in the Arctic Ocean, about 70 percent is reflected back in the space. Only around 30 percent is absorbed as heat. But as the Arctic ice melts, the incoming sunlight strikes the dark waters there and only 6 percent is reflected back into space and 94 percent is converted into heat. This accounts for accelerating shrinkage of the Arctic sea ice and increasing temperatures in the region that directly affects the Greenland ice sheet.[37]

The sea level will not be affected if all the ice in the Arctic Ocean melts because the ice is already in the ocean. But as more of the incoming sunlight is absorbed there as heat, the arctic region will get much warmer. But as Greenland lies within the Arctic Circle, this is much cause of worry. As the Arctic region heats up, Greenland's ice sheet—up to 1.6 kilometers (1 mile) thick in some places, starts to melt.[38]

The second positive feedback mechanism is also connected to melting. As surface ice begins to melt, some water filters down through cracks in the glacier, lubricating the surface between the rock and the glacier above it. This accelerates the glacial flow and the calving of icebergs into the surrounding ocean. The warm water that flows through the glacier also takes with it the surface heat deep inside the ice sheet much faster than it would otherwise penetrate by conduction.[39]

Looking at the other end of the Earth, a 2-kilometer-thick Antarctic ice sheet covers a continent twice the size of Australia. It contains 70 percent of world's fresh water. This ice sheet has also begun to melt. Ice shelves that extend from the continent into the surrounding oceans are also now breaking up at an alarming rate.[40]

What would melting of the world's largest ice sheets and a 10-meter rise in sea level mean? This scenario is analyzed by The International Institute for Environment and Development (IIED). The IIED study first points out that 634 million people inhabit the coasts at or below 10 meters of sea level, in what they term Low Elevation Coastal Zone. This huge group of people consists of one eighth of world's urban population.[41]

China is one of the most threatened countries with 144 million potential climate refugees. Next are India and Bangladesh with 63 and 62 million respectively. Vietnam has 43 million vulnerable people while Indonesia has 42 million. The top 10 includes Japan with 30 million, Egypt with 26 million, and the United States with 23 million. [42]

Scientists, gathered at the International Climate Change Conference in March, 2009 at Copenhagen have warned that rising sea levels triggered by global warming pose a far greater danger to the planet than previously thought. Now, a major risk exists that many coastal areas around the world will be inundated by the end of the century because Antarctic and Greenland ice sheets are melting faster than previously believed. According to them, low-lying areas including Florida, Bangladesh, the Maldives and the Netherlands face catastrophic flooding. In Britain, large areas of the Norfolk Broads and Thames estuary are likely to disappear by 2100.[43]

Dr. Jason Lowe of the Hadley Centre, the UK's foremost climate change research centre warns, "It is still not clear exactly how much the sea will rise by the end of this century, but it is certain that rises will continue for hundreds of years beyond that—even if we do manage to stabilize carbon dioxide emissions and halt the rise in atmospheric temperature. The sea will continue to heat up and expand. In addition, the Greenland ice sheets will continue to melt." [44]

This later effect could be especially destructive. Scientists have calculated that if emissions of carbon dioxide and other greenhouse gases eventually produce a global temperature increase of around 4°C, there is a risk that Greenland's ice covering could completely melt. This could take from several hundred years or even a couple thousand. The end result is beyond doubt however. It would add around seven meters to the global sea levels, devastating many regions of the planet.

Such a scenario is distant but real, scientists warn. However, they argue, at present the most important issue is that of short-term sea-level rises of around one meter by 2100. When that occurs, Maldives will be submerged, so would the islands like the Sunder bans in the Bay of Bengal, and Kiribati and Tuvalu in the Pacific. The U.S.—which has roughly 12,400 miles of coastline and more than 19,900 square miles of coastal wetlands—would need around $156 billion to protect these areas. Cities such as London would need massive investments to create defenses against the rising waters, while other cities such as Alexandria in Egypt would simply be inundated.

However, there's more. The rising water will also contaminate both surface and underground fresh water supplies, worsening the world's existing fresh-water shortage. Underground water sources in China, Thailand, Vietnam and Israel are already experiencing salt-water contamination.

The farmlands in coastal areas around the planet will be wiped out, triggering massive displacements of men, women and children, seeking housing, jobs, and sustenance. It is now estimated that a one-meter rise in sea-level could flood 17% of Bangladesh, one of the world's poorest countries. Its rice-farming land will be reduced by 50%, leaving tens of millions or more without homes. Rising sea levels will not be the only problem. Adding to this mayhem, much stronger storms worldwide will afflict coastal areas.[45]

Millions of these climate refugees would be forced to move to higher grounds when sea inundates their homes and dwellings. Others, with extreme overcrowding in their own countries, could seek refuge into the neighboring countries. Bangladesh's 62 millions would be forced to join in with the horribly overcrowded 97 million living in the interior higher grounds or many would try to sneak into India which itself is overwhelmed: there supposedly exists today some 25 million illegal economic Bangladeshi refugees.[46]

Not only would the world's largest cities such as London, Kolkata, Shanghai, and New York be partly or entirely inundated, but in addition, vast areas of world's productive farmland would be gone. Part of Asia's food supply will be lost as its rice-growing river deltas and floodplains would be covered with salt water. This loss of farmland in addition to the loss of rivers as Himalayan glaciers disappear would be devastating to Asia.[47]

This massive uprooting of millions of people could destabilize several countries and their governments as violent social upheaval could ensue. Resource wars between countries and peoples could be the outcome.

The new forecast, announced at an international meeting of climate scientists in Copenhagen, is based on more research since the IPCC's fourth assessment report. At this meeting held in Copenhagen in March of 2009, the scientists have said that due to a much higher sea level rise than previously thought, island states and populous delta areas in Bangladesh, Myanmar, South East Asia and Africa would be most at risk from sea level rise.

Rob Baily, Climate Change Policy Advisor for Oxfam International (UK), said: "These startling new predictions on sea level rise spell disaster for millions of the world's poorest people...Rich countries who created the climate change crisis, must cut their emissions from 1990 levels by at least 40 percent by 2020 and provide the $50 billion that is the minimum needed each year to help the world's poorest people adapt to the unavoidable impacts of climate change."[48]

DEPLETING FORESTS

The Earth's forested area was estimated at 5 billion hectares at the beginning of the twentieth century. It has shrunk to just under 4 billion hectares since then. The remaining forests are evenly divided between tropical and subtropical forests in developing and temperate/boreal forests in industrial countries.[49]

The developing world has lost some 13 million hectares of forest a year since 1990. This loss of about 3 percent a decade equals an area the size of Greece. The industrial countries meanwhile are gaining an estimated 5.6 million hectares of forestland each year, mainly because of abandoned cropland turning into forests on their own and from the spread of commercial forestry plantations. Hence, the world incurs a net forest loss of more than 7 million hectares a year.[50]

Pressures on forests continue to mount worldwide, especially in developing countries.

We humans are constantly using more firewood and an increasing quantity of paper and lumber. Of the 3.5 billion cubic meters of wood harvested worldwide in 2005, over half of it was used for fuel. Fuel wood accounts for nearly three fourth of the total in developing countries.[51]

The Indian subcontinent and the Sahelian zone of Africa top the list of regions where deforestation to supply fuel wood is most extensive. When urban firewood demand surpasses the sustainable yield of nearby forests, the woods slowly disappear from the city in an ever larger radius, a phenomenon clearly discernible from satellite photographs taken over time. As the size of the radius enlarges, the cost of transporting the firewood increases, resulting in the development of a charcoal—a more concentrated form of energy—industry. Thus, large Sahelian towns are surrounded by a sterile moonscape. In Dakar and Khartoum, one has to go 500 kilometers or more to get the charcoal, sometimes into neighboring countries.[52]

Logging companies take a heavy toll on world's forests. Usually, logging is carried out by foreign corporations interested in maximizing their profits rather than managing a sustainable forest in perpetuity. So once a country's forests are gone, they move on to another country leaving behind a devastated forest or its remnants. The Philippines and Nigeria have lost their once thriving forests supplying the tropical hardwood for export and both are now net importers of forest products.[53]

Perhaps the most devastating effect on the world's remaining natural forests in this new century is the explosive growth of wood products made by China, now supplying the world with furniture, other building materials, flooring, particle boards, and a vast array of other products made from wood. To quench its appetite for logs, China has gone wildly into logging outside its borders, often illegally, to cut the forests of Myanmar, Indonesia, Papua New Guinea and Siberia. At present, the aggressive Chinese firms have entered the Amazon and the Congo Basin.[54]

In an interesting article in April 2007 by reporters Peter Goodman and Peter Finn in *Washington Post*, they report in details how the Chinese entered across the border into Myanmar to get the remaining natural teak wood. Two agents connected to Burmese borderlands were bribed by the Chinese, handing them rice stack stuffed with $8,000 worth of Chinese currency. The agents used this money to bribe everyone standing between the teak and China…Then came the Chinese loggers using Chinese built roads…[55]

According to *Forest Trends*, a nongovernmental organization made up of industry and conservation groups, the natural forests in Indonesia and Myanmar will disappear in a decade or so at the current rate of logging. Papua New Guinea's forests will last for 16 years and vast Russian Far East's forests may not last longer than 20 years.[56]

As reported in the earlier chapter, rising demands for palm oil have led to alarming deforestation in the tropical island of Borneo, Indonesia. The palm plantations were expanded at the annual rate of 8 percent in the Malaysian Borneo (Sarawak and Sabah) between 1998 and 2003, clearing the beautiful tropical forests. The rate is higher at 11 percent in Kalimantan, the Indonesian part of Borneo. Malaysia is the biggest exporter of timber in the world; its timber coming from the forests of Sarawak in Borneo. It is a $2 billion industry and the rain forest in Sarawak has virtually disappeared with less than 20% standing today. Unfortunately, now palm oil is used as a biofuel; this will increase its demand even higher, threatening the remaining tropical forests of Borneo.[57]

It had previously been thought that it would be safe for the trees and other vegetation, and the vast number of animals living among them in the Amazonian rainforest if temperatures rose no more than 2 °C. But researchers have now found that up to 40 percent of the rainforest will be lost if such temperature rises are restricted to 2 °C, which most climatologists regard as the least that can be expected by 2050. Researchers have found that even such an increase will destroy large tracts of land, but the die-back is a slow process and will take up to a century to realize its full effect.

Dr. Chris Jones, of the Met Office Hadley Center in Exeter, told a conference in Copenhagen recently that the time delay had masked the full impact of the temperatures. A team of researchers led by him calculated that 20 to 40 percent of the forest will be killed off by 2050 under a 2 °C rise.

Dr. Vicky Pope, the head of the climate change advice at the Met Office Hadley Center, warned that the findings showed the threat to the forest is much higher than expected. "Impacts could be much worse than previously thought," she said in Copenhagen as scientists met there to discuss the latest research into climate change and its effects. "Even if temperature rises are limited to 2 °C above pre-industrial levels, as much as 20 to 40 percent of the Amazonian rainforest could be lost if this temperature is sustained for 100 years or more."[58]

According to these researchers, a 3 °C rise is likely to result in 75 percent of the forest disappearing while a 4 °C rise, regarded as the most likely increase this century unless greenhouse gas emissions are slashed significantly, will kill off 85 percent of the forest. All these scenarios are gloomy and catastrophic.

Other research unveiled at the conference showed that it is quite likely that even though greenhouse gas emissions are reduced, temperatures may not start falling for at least 100 years or more.

Professor Peter Cox, of the University of Exeter, said of the finding that at least a fifth of the Amazonian forest is almost certainly doomed: "Ecologically it could be a catastrophe and it would be taking a huge chance with our own climate. The tropics are drivers of the world's weather systems and killing the Amazon is likely to change them forever. We don't know exactly what would happen but we could expect more extreme weather. Destroying the Amazon would also turn what is a significant carbon sink into a significant source. It would amplify global warming significantly. Just as an example, at the moment deforestation adds about a fifth of the world's carbon to the atmosphere."[59] All this does not bode well for the Amazon which is the lungs of this planet. It is shocking to know that deforestation in the tropics destroys an area the size of Greece every year—that amounts to more than 25 million acres.[60]

The Brazilian Amazon suffers devastating losses from clearing land for farming and ranching, usually done by burning; similar losses are the fate of the Borneo and Congo Basin. After losing 93 percent of its Atlantic rainforest, Brazil is now on the path to total destruction of the Amazon rainforest. Anyone who has traveled to the Brazilian Amazon has to be amazed at the sheer beauty and the vastness of the Amazonian rainforest, its animal inhabitants, its birds and the indigenous peoples. Until 1970, this huge forest, roughly the size of Europe, was mostly intact. Since then, close to 20 percent has been destroyed.[61]

The world's forests maintain ecological systems that are essential for life. According to the Met Office Hadley Centre, (2008), "The Amazon rainforest contains about one tenth of the total carbon stored in land ecosystems and recycles a large fraction of the rainfall that falls upon it. So any major change to its vegetation brought about by events like deforestation or drought, has an impact on the global climate system."

On the Amazon's good health depends the cultural survival of many forest dwelling peoples and communities. They also play a critical role in the preservation of biodiversity—over half of the world's land-based plant and animal species are found in forests. The Amazon is estimated to store 80-120 billion tons of carbon. If destroyed, some fifty times the yearly green house gas emissions of the USA could be emitted.

Brazil is the world's fourth largest producer of green house gas emissions, predominately from the clearance and burning of the Amazon rainforest. Globally, tropical rainforest destruction is responsible for around 20% of global green house gas emissions.

Imagine one hectare of Brazilian rainforest being lost every 18 seconds! Well, that is the recent reality in Brazil; its rainforest is rapidly succumbing to cattle ranching. The Brazilian Amazon has the greatest annual average deforestation by area of anywhere in the world.[62]

In the Brazilian Amazon, the world's most important forest carbon store, the cattle sector is the main driver of deforestation. According to the Brazilian government: "Cattle are responsible for about 80% of all deforestation" in the Amazon region and 14% of the entire world's annual deforestation. It is the world's biggest driver of deforestation, responsible for more forest loss than the total deforestation in any country outside of Brazil except Indonesia.

The world's largest commercial cattle herd is in Brazil and it is the world's biggest beef exporter. Additionally, according to the Brazilian government, its share of global trade in beef products is going to double by 2018 as this sector has seen rapid export-oriented growth over the last decade.[63]

Cattle Ranchers are the biggest culprits. Successive reports by The World Bank, the Brazilian government and research institutes, and analyses by Greenpeace repeatedly conclude that cattle ranching occupies about 80% of all deforested land in the Amazon region. Lack of governance gives the largest economic incentive for the expansion of Brazil's cattle sector there. Contributing factors include corruption, disorganization, limited capacity and lack of coordination between different government departments. Land grabbing in the Amazon is rampant. The land titles there are in disarray, with the legal status of roughly half of the area uncertain.

Analysis by Greenpeace of 2006-2007 satellite data and forest clearance permits reveals that more than 90% of current Amazon deforestation is illegal. Brazil presents itself as a world leader on action to cut deforestation. "Brazil does not wish to shy away from its responsibilities," said President Lula in 2007 as reported by *Guardian*, June 1, 2007. The Brazilian government, at the 2008 international climate summit at Poznan, announced its National Climate Change Plan that included a pledge to pursue 72% cuts in the rate of deforestation by 2018. These cuts which it claims are designed to prevent the emissions of 4.8 Gt. of CO2 are to be achieved mainly by tackling illegal deforestation. Yet, the Brazilian government is a funder and shareholder in the major players in the Amazonian cattle sector. It is bankrolling the expansion of the cattle sector there in order to dominate the global market in agricultural commodities, including beef. Brazil is offering a credit worth $41 billion to farmers to boost agricultural and livestock production.[64]

The world's multinationals from Brazil, China, USA, Italy and UK are major consumers of the products from the Brazilian rainforests. They play a significant part in driving the Brazilian deforestation as these companies get their supply of beef, wood products, and leather from the Brazilian rainforests.[65] The minimum these multinationals can do is to stop trading with companies that are implicated in forest destruction. Corporate greed and profit over people and over the Earth's resources at enormous costs to the environment is the mantra that reigns supreme in our current industrialized world. The Earth cannot and will not take it anymore.

The Amazon forest is being devastated in other surrounding countries too such as Bolivia and Ecuador. Ecuador's 100,000 square kilometers of the world's richest rainforest sits atop 4.4 billion proven barrels of oil, the 26th largest reserve in the world. Since 1960s, international oil companies have taken oil from Ecuador's eastern province, known as the *Oriente*, and much of it goes to the United States, leaving behind vast environmental and public health disasters while the people of Ecuador suffer from extreme poverty. During our visit to Ecuador, the Galapagos Islands, and

Peru in 2004, we saw and met some people of these countries. They are poor but very friendly and trusting, many being indigenous dressed in their beautiful traditional dresses. We saw that the U. S. dominance is so strong there that even Ecuador's currency is in U.S. dollars. Despite Ecuador's vast natural resources, 70 percent of Ecuadorians live below the poverty line.

The impoverished Ecuadorian government, in debt and dependent on petro-dollars for revenues, has put some 80 percent of its oil-flush lands up for grabs according to Amazon Watch, a California-based watchdog group. Most of the time, the corrupt Ecuadorian military or government officials are bribed, highly one-sided contracts are signed and more than 16 international oil companies loot Ecuador's mineral and oil resources leaving the Amazon and its other lands deforested and devastated while oil and mining companies fill their coffers with millions of dollars. According to Bolivar Beltran, an Ecuadorian congressional aide and activist, highly unfair contracts are signed between American, Italian, or Chinese oil companies and the government of Ecuador, transferring subsoil rights for oil and minerals of vast tracts of lands to these multinational companies. Ecuador's military protects these international predators for small sums of money, medicine or food and in exchange these companies loot Ecuador's oil, and mineral resources, devastating their Amazon rainforests.[66]

Haiti, a country of 9.6 million people, was once a beautiful tropical paradise largely covered with forests. But growing demand for firewood and land clearing for farming have devastated the whole country, left barren with scarcely 4 percent of its land now sustaining its forest. It is a clear case of a scenario being repeated like the one in Easter Island several centuries ago. First the forest goes, and then goes the soil.[67]

Thus, Haiti is a country which has destroyed its forests and is now caught in an ecological disaster from which it will be difficult to come out. An estimated 2 % of its trees are remaining as trees have long been burned to make charcoal. Tons and tons of its top soil is now being washed away into the ocean. Haiti's coral reef and marine life, once beautiful are now devastated. Its fish and sea-creatures are so contaminated with toxins that anyone who eats them could get sick. It has become a failed state, and is sustained by international economic assistance and food aid.[68]

Another island country, Madagascar, biologically rich with rainforest, with a population of 18 million people and possessing unique species of wild life, is going the same way as Haiti.

There, trees are being cut unsustainably either to produce charcoal or to clear land for farming, destroying Madagascar's unique tropical rainforest cover. As per environmentalists, Madagascar could soon become an island of scrub growth and sand.[69]

A similar situation is proceeding rapidly in the East African country of Malawi where 14 million people live. There, deforestation and land clearing are proceeding at a rapid pace with mounting use of firewood and speedy clearance of large tracts of virgin forests. Its forest cover has shrunk by close to 25 percent since the early 1970s, a loss of up to 1 million hectares. Malawi is sliding fast into the same grim fate as Haiti, with constant logging of trees for charcoal production and for curing tobacco.[70]

Fortunately, today, more and more countries are realizing the risks inherent in deforestation. Countries which have now enforced total or partial ban on logging in primary forests are China, Vietnam, Thailand, the Philippines, Sri Lanka and New Zealand. Unfortunately, sometimes the countries shift their logging into other countries or import huge quantities of wood from abroad, exporting the deforestation to other countries. Japan was very smart. During the times of Shogun Emperors, they realized that Japan was rapidly being deforested as wood was a major source of house-construction there. So since that period, the Shogun Emperors put total ban on logging in Japan. Today, as a result, Japan is 75 percent forested.

SOIL EROSION

It has taken millions of years or more to form the top soil, about six inches deep, that is the foundation of civilization. Civilization could not exist without this soil which is the very basis of all the food that living beings eat to survive. Accumulated over the eons, it has provided the medium over which the plants and crops grow. In return, the plants protect the soil from erosion. Unfortunately and dangerously, we humans are disrupting this vital relationship.

New soil formation has continued over long geological stretches of time. But sometime in the midst of the last century, soil erosion has begun to exceed soil formation over large areas of the Earth. Now, land's inherent productivity is reducing as about a third of all cropland is losing topsoil faster than new soil formation. In other words, the very foundation of current civilization is being threatened.[71]

The familiar pattern of deforestation, overgrazing, and agricultural expansion onto marginal land, followed by withdrawal as soil begins to disappear...is related to accelerating soil erosion around the globe. It can be seen in the dust bowls that form as vegetation is destroyed and wind erosion soars out of control. Most prominent among these were the dust bowls in America's Great Plains during the 1930s, the dust bowls in the Soviet Virgin Lands in the 1960s, the large one that is being formed currently in northwest China, and the one that is shaping up in the Sahelian region of Africa.[72]

Many nations saw population growth of the twentieth century extend agriculture into highly vulnerable regions. During the late nineteenth or early twentieth centuries, overplowing of the U.S. Great Plains resulted in the 1930s Dust Bowl, coinciding with the Great Depression. This tragic period in American history forced hundreds of thousands of farm families to leave the Great Plains. Many of them migrated to California in search of a new life.

Some 30 years later, history repeated itself in the Soviet Union. The Soviets, under The Virgin Lands Project between 1954 and 1960 undertook plowing an area of grassland for wheat that was larger than the wheatland of Canada and Australia combined. Initially, the Soviet grain production went up impressively. But the success turned into a disaster as soon a dust bowl developed there.[73]

At the center of this project was Kazakhstan which saw its grainland area peak at just over 25 million hectares around 1980. But since then it has shrunk to 15 million hectares today. On the rest of the land, the average wheat yield is hardly 1 ton per hectare, a far cry from close to 7 tons per hectare that French farmers achieve in France, Western Europe's leading wheat producer.[74]

The same fate has befallen Mongolia, where over the last 20 years, half of the wheatland has been abandoned and wheat yields have declined by 50%, shrinking the harvest by three fourths. Mongolia is three times the size of France with a population of only 2.6 million, yet it is now forced to import close to 60 percent of its wheat.[75]

Geology Professor at Oxford University Andrew Goudie reports that once rare Saharan dust storms, are now commonplace. He estimates that during the last half century they have increased 10-fold. The most affected countries in the region are northern Nigeria, Niger, Chad, Mauritania, and Burkina Faso. In Mauritania, in Africa's far west, the dust storm frequency has increased from 2 a year in the early 1960s to 80 a year today.[76]

Amazingly, the Bodele Depression in Chad is a source of an estimated 1.3 billion tons of wind-borne soil a year, up 10-times since measurements began in 1947. Africa is constantly being drained of its fertility and biological productivity as 2-3 billion tons of fine soil particles leave the continent in dust storms each year. These dust storms leaving Africa travel westward across the Atlantic, depositing so much dust in the Caribbean that they cloud the water and damage the coral reefs.[77]

Satellite images now record these dust storms emanating from the new dust bowls. On January 9, 2005, the National Aeronautics and Space Administration (NASA), released images of a vast dust storm moving westward out of central Africa. This immense cloud of tan-colored dust stretched over some 5,300 kilometers (roughly 3,300 miles). The storm would cover the whole of the United States and extend into the oceans on both sides if it were relocated over this country.[78]

Rivers are silting and getting muddier in some places due to water erosion. In Pakistan, the Indus River water is stored in two large reservoirs called, Mangla and Tarbela for its vast irrigation network. But they are losing 1 percent of their storage capacity annually as they fill with silt from deforested watersheds.[79]

Ethiopia is a mountainous country with highly erodible soils on steeply sloping land. It is losing close to 2 billion tons of top soil a year, being washed away by rain. This explains why Ethiopia is always on the verge of famine: perpetually unable to produce enough grains to feed its people.[80]

PLANT & ANIMAL SPECIES GOING EXTINCT

Humans have been the most harmful species—to both animals and to the planet's ecosystem. During its long geological lifetime, the Earth has experienced five great extinctions. The last being the mass extinction of the dinosaurs—perhaps caused by a meteorite that struck Yucatan Peninsula of Mexico some 65 million years ago. All these five extinctions were as a result of natural phenomena. But now, we are on the verge of sixth extinction; one caused by humans.

Habitat destruction, pollution, and constant human encroachment on their habitat, are threatening the very survival of countless other species around the planet. Rising temperatures, chemical pollution, and the introduction of foreign species are decimating both plant and animal species. While we humans are breeding exponentially, other species are shrinking in numbers and varieties. It should be understood that we humans depend on other species with which we share the planet, for our own survival. If other life forms go extinct, we will most certainly follow in their path. Today, some 39 percent of fish, 20 percent of world's 5,416 mammals, and 12 percent of the world's nearly 10,000 birds species are now vulnerable or on the verge of extinction.[81] We humans are one of the 25 million other species in the world. Unfortunately, we force 200 other species into extinction every day.[82]

Merciless human expansion is putting stresses on forests, animal species, fisheries and rangelands to the extent that they can no longer compete with us. We are destroying a wide range of plant and animal species with which we share this planet. Worldwide, species are now disappearing at 1,000 times the rate at which new species evolve. As Lester Brown of Earth Policy Institute says, "we have put the extinction clock on fast-forward."[83]

The 2007 IPCC report has noted that a rise in temperature of one degree Celsius will put up to 30 percent of all species at risk of extinction. As various species disappear, the services provided by them—nutrient recycling, insect and other species control, seed dispersal and pollination—diminishes. This mounting loss of various forms of life—which are vital for survival and proper functioning of the Earth's ecosystems—is weakening the fabric of life, leading to irreversible ecological changes, a dangerous development.

Roughly, 70 percent of 9,817 known bird species are declining in number. Out of them, some 1,217 species are in imminent danger of going extinct. Loss of habitat and deforestation affect 91 percent of all threatened bird species. In Pakistan, the great bustard, once widespread, is being hunted to extinction. Due to global warming, ten of the world's 17 species of Penguins are threatened or endangered. In Singapore, 61 bird species have become locally extinct due to extensive loss of lowland rainforest.[84]

Some 296 known species of primates are most at risk. According to The World Conservation Union-IUCN, 114 of these species are threatened with extinction. Ninety five of the world's primate species live in Brazil, where habitat destruction poses a particular threat. In West and Central Africa, hunting also threatens their existence where deteriorating food situation and new logging roads have combined to create a dangerous market for "bush-meat."[85]

The great apes called bonobos of West Africa are genetically and in social behavior close to us humans. But this close relation does not help them from the bush-meat trade or the destruction of their habitat by loggers. Inhabiting the forests of The Democratic Republic of Cong, a collapsing state with a prolonged civil conflict, they have declined from an estimated 100,000 in 1980 to as few as 10,000 today. About 90 percent of bonobos have disappeared in one human generation.[86]

Meanwhile, a strange and dangerous phenomenon is taking place in the United States since 2006. It is that of the disappearance of the honeybee. It is the main pollinator of U.S. fruit and vegetable crops. According to the survey of U.S. beekeepers, conducted from September 2006 to March 2007 by Apiary Inspectors of America, the bees in nearly one fourth of U.S. bee colonies had simply disappeared as a result of what experts are calling "Colony Collapse Disorder." Similar disappearance of large numbers of colonies has taken place in Brazil, Guatemala, and Europe.[87]

The scientists are puzzled by this whole phenomenon. The French call this "Mad Bee Disease". Bees seem to leave their hives on pollination forays, apparently become disoriented and never return. It is suspected that the Israeli acute paralysis virus that originated in Australia is the prime suspect. If the scientists cannot diagnose the culprit soon and find the remedy, the world could face unprecedented catastrophe due to depletion of fruit and vegetable production.[88]

The world's fish face the greatest threat. The main causes are pollution, overfishing, and excessive extraction of water from rivers and other fresh water ecosystems. In North America alone, an estimated 65 percent of the fish species evaluated by IUCN that once inhabited the streams and lakes are either extinct or are in danger of vanishing. In Europe, 109 species of fresh water fish out of 265 that were evaluated are threatened, or endangered. Even one third of the species in South Africa are in danger of extinction.[89]

According to the documentary, 'The End of Line', around 75% of the world's fish stocks are severely depleted. It further warns that world's fish will be extinct by the middle of this century if we continue to plunder the oceans. It blames increasing demand from consumers, supermarkets and restaurants, fishermen breaking their quotas and politicians ignoring the problem. Every year around 7 million tones of unwanted fish—bycatch—is thrown back into the sea. For example, in UK waters, stocks of some fish, like cod, have been reduced to less than 10% of what they were 100 years ago.[90]

As mentioned earlier, one of the biggest and fastest growing threats to the flora and fauna today is extraordinary agricultural expansion under way in Brazil as vast tracts of forestland is cleared to plant soybean, graze cattle, and produce sugarcane and corn for ethanol production. Ranchers and farmers there are clearing vast areas in the Amazon basin and in the *cerrado*, a savanna-like region the size of western Europe, in the south of the Amazon basin. The government is not able to enforce the laws which require the landowners not to clear more than one fifth of their land.[91] The *cerrado* is very rich in animal species. It is home to a variety of large mammals, including giant armadillos, giant anteaters, deer, maned wolves, and several large cats such as jaguars, puma, jaguarondi and ocelot. 607 species of birds live in the *cerrado*, including the rhea, the cousin of the ostrich that grows up to five feet tall, indeed a beautiful creature. 1000 species of butterflies have also been identified. There could be more. According to Conservation International, the *cerrado* also contains some 10,000 plant species. At least, 4,400 of them are endemic, not found anywhere else.[92]

Costa Rica, home to thousands of leatherback turtles, has seen their numbers decline dramatically from 115,000 in 1982 to 34,500 in 1996. The number of nesting females at its Playa Grande and Playa Langosta nesting ground has dropped significantly too. If these turtles are to be saved, their fishing mortality has to be minimized and the hatchling production has to be increased.[93]

Global warming is causing the ice to melt in the Polar Regions at an alarming rate and that in turn is threatening the very existence of polar bear, walrus, narwhal and ringed seal populations. Polar bears probably existed across the arctic for several hundred thousand years, researchers say. These are resilient animals, eating walrus, grasses and even snow goose eggs when they cannot hunt their preferred prey, bearded and ringed seals. The bears were greatly depleted across much of the arctic due to unregulated hunting until the Soviet Union clamped down in 1956, followed by other countries resulting in a 1973 treaty. At present, the polar bear population is estimated at 22,000 to 25,000.

Five countries that signed this treaty in 1973, the United States, Canada, Russia, Norway, and Denmark met recently in March 2009 at Tromso, Norway for three-days to protect polar bears through limited hunting. They concluded that worldwide cooperation is needed to address the looming risk to the species: the prospect that global warming from emissions of greenhouse gases would continue to erode the sheath of Arctic sea ice that half-ton bears roam in pursuit of seals.[94]

Thus everywhere we see, the plant and animal life is either being threatened or is going extinct. Every plant and living creature on this Earth has some important function to fulfill. They serve some useful purpose for the planet's ecosystems; some of which we don't even understand. Preserving and protecting them is vital for the very survival of humanity. Just creating parks and reserves, though essential, is not enough. Stabilizing the climate and controlling overpopulation of and encroachment by us humans is vital for the survival of all the species on the earth.

FAILING STATES

Lester Brown's stark warning in his amazing article in *Scientific American* should be read by the leadership in every government. The world grain production has fallen short of consumption in the six of the past nine years. This has forced steady drawdown in stocks. In the beginning of 2008, the world carryover stocks of grain (the amount in the bin when the new harvest begins) were 62 days of consumption, a near record low. As a result, there was a steep spike in the world grain prices in the spring and summer of 2008, climbing to the highest level ever.[95]

According to Brown, as food demand rises faster than the supplies are growing, the resulting food-price inflation exerts severe pressure on the governments of countries that are already teetering on the edge of chaos. Hungry people, with no money to buy expensive grains or land to grow it, take to the streets in large numbers. The number of failing states was already expanding before the steep price rise of 2008. Many of their problems emanate from their governments' failure to control their burgeoning populations while their food-growing land area remained the same or even shrank. As the food situation deteriorates, entire nations start breaking down at an ever increasing rate as we see in Darfur or what we saw in Rwanda in 1994. When national governments cannot protect their people either from food and water shortage, cannot provide basic social services such as education and healthcare, or protect their people from terrorism or civil wars, the entire nation becomes a failed state. We see them in increasing numbers around the world, on the verge of collapse or likely to collapse as in Congo, Somalia, Nigeria, Sudan, Zimbabwe, Ivory coast, Central African Republic, Guinea, Haiti, Burma, North Korea, Iraq, Afghanistan, and Pakistan.

In the 20th century, the main threat to the international security stemmed from superpower conflict. Today, in the 21st century, it emanates from failing states. At the root of the conflicts—wars and disputes around the world—are resources such as water, food, land, minerals and oil.

The question is, could water and food shortages we see now in several regions of the world, engulf the whole planet and bring down our industrial civilization?

CHAPTER 7
EMERGING WATER SCARCITIES & OTHER SYMPTOMS

Humankind has not woven the web of life. We are but one thread within it. Whatever we do to the web, we do to ourselves. All things are bound together. All things connect.
—Chief Seattle, 1855

AUSTRALIA, A CONTINENT IN TROUBLE

The world's most arid inhabited continent is perilously low on water. Australia, which once served as a food bowl to the world, is in search of a future. The world's 15th largest economy is learning hard lessons about the limits of natural resources in an era of climate change. The national production of rice has dropped from a million tons a year to just 21,000 tons, contributing to the food shortage across the globe. No industrialized country or a continent is facing water scarcity as does Australia today. The country is in deep trouble for the first time in its history. From outside, it may not look like that, as its ex-president, John Howard unwisely joined George Bush in its foolish and immoral war against Iraq from the beginning in 2002. But since 2002, Australia's troubles are mounting. Not in Iraq as much as at home. The country is dry and thirsty as for seven years, the rains have failed. The drought is seven years old now and there are no signs of rains. The current seven year drought is the most devastating in this country's 117 years of history. The erratic precipitation patterns bear the ominous imprint of a human induced climate shift. It is widely accepted there that global warming has increased the frequency and severity of natural disasters like this drought. According to Australian environmental scientist Tim Kelly, a three-quarter degree (Celsius) increase in temperature over the last 15 years in Australia has driven lot more evaporation of their water.

Flooded by Hume Dam in the 1920s, Murray's riverbanks were once thick with red gum trees that captured moisture and helped continue the cycles of rainfall. But due to the dam, the trees were submerged and destroyed, disturbing the rain-cycle. Some of Australia's lakes such as Lake Boga or Lake Alexandrina are almost dry or only partially full.

"The Europeans," writes Robert Draper, "who descended on the slopes of Murray-Darlin Basin—a vast semiarid plain about the size of Spain and France combined—were lulled by a string of mid-19th century wet years into thinking they had discovered a latter-day Garden of Eden. Following the habits of their homelands, the settlers felled some 15 billion trees. Unaware of what it would mean to disrupt an established water cycle by uprooting vegetation well adapted to arid conditions, the new Australians introduced sheep, cattle, and water-hungry crops altogether foreign to a desert ecosystem. The endless plowing to encourage Australia's new bounty further degraded its soil." [1] The Aboriginal people who lived in the basin of the Murray River for 30,000 years never disturbed its ecosystem; they lived by the nature, always respecting it and worshiping it like the Native Americans in the Americas until the Europeans arrived.

The new arrivals felled billions of trees, and destroyed its ecosystem. Does this remind us of the Easter Islanders who came to the Easter Island and destroyed its ecosystem several hundred years earlier?

Thousands of farmers in the Murray-Darlin Basin are in distress today because, due to highly reduced water levels in the Murray River, their water allocations have been drastically cut, forcing them to sell their animals, auction their farms, and go out of business. Towns are becoming ghost towns. Whole crops have been wiped out because of heat stress and low moisture. Entire growing sectors such as citrus, cotton, and rice face collapse. The government has made such drastic cuts in water allocation to these farmers in the once fertile Murray-Darlin Basin that there is 98 percent drop in rice production from 2006 to 2008.[2]

Similarly, for the first time public fountains in Barcelona, Spain, are dry. The city is so parched, there's $13,000 fine if you're caught watering your flowers. Recently, a tanker ship was docked there in the summer months carrying 5 million gallons of precious fresh water—and officials were scrambling to line up more such shipments to slake public thirst.

Barcelona's thirst predicament is not solitary. Greece will have to ferry water to Cyprus this summer. Australian cities are now buying water from that country's farmers and building desalination plants. Thirsty China is now planning to divert Himalayan water; and 18 million southern Californians will have to brace for their first water-rationing in years.

Water, Dow Chemical Chairman Andrew Liveris warned the World Economic Forum in February, 2008, "is the oil of this century." So far, developed nations have taken cheap, abundant fresh water for granted. But now, an ever increasing population, pollution and climate change have forced a change in shaping a new view of water around the world as "blue gold." [3]

Some see a tragic scenario of "peak water" displace "peak oil" as the central resource question. "What is different now is that it's increasingly obvious that we are running up against limits to new (fresh water) supplies," says Peter Gleick, a water expert and president of the Pacific Institute for Studies in Development, Environment, and Security, a nonpartisan think tank in Oakland, Calif. "It's no longer cheap and easy to drill another well or dam another river. The idea of 'peak water' obviously is an imperfect analogy," he says. Water, unlike oil, is not used up. It simply changes forms. The world still possesses the same 326 quintillion gallons, NASA estimates. But at least 97 percent of it is salty. The remaining accessible fresh water supplies of the planet are divided among agriculture (70 percent), industry (20 percent), and domestic use (10percent), according to the United Nations.

In the meantime, fresh water consumption worldwide has more than doubled since World War II to about 4000 cubic kilometers annually and is likely to increase by 25 percent by 2030, says a 2007 report by a Zurich-based Sustainable Asset Management (SAM) group investment firm.[4]

There should be plenty, as up to triple that amount is available for human consumption, the report says. But climate change, waste and pollution have left clean water supplies running short.

Population increase along with economic growth across Asia and the rest of the developing world is a major reason driving fresh-water scarcity. The human population of the Earth is likely to rise from 6.7 billion to 9 billion by 2050, as per U.N. report. Feeding those means more irrigation water for crops.

Unfortunately today, private companies are taking over water resources around the globe. In the U.S. today, 33.5 million Americans get their drinking water from privately owned utilities that make up some 16 percent of the nation's community water systems, according to the National Association of Water Companies, a trade association.[5]

But often, these private companies charge lot more than if these waters were in the public hands. For example, Bolivia kicked out the giant engineering firm Bechtel in 2000 when after taking over water systems of the city of Cochabamba, they spiked the cost of water beyond the means of average Bolivian's ability to pay.

Few people realize that the connection between water and food is strong. Each of us drinks 4 liters of water daily on average, in one form or another. But it takes 2,000 liters—500 times more—to produce our daily food. So it is obvious that 70 percent of all water use goes to irrigation while 20 percent is utilized by the industry. The remaining 10 percent is used for residential purposes. But as demand is increasing in all these three categories, the competition for water is intensifying and agriculture is losing this battle. Few people realize that water shortages means food scarcity.[6] "Can we run out of fresh water? Yes…" warns Maude Barlowe, head of the Council of Canadians and founder of Blue Water Project, "It is still here somewhere. But we humans have depleted, polluted, and diverted it to such an extent that we can now actually say the planet is running out of accessible, clean water, fast. The fresh water crisis is easily as great a threat to the Earth and humans as climate change (to which it is deeply linked) but has had very little attention paid to it in comparison."[7]

According to her, the world is running out of available, clean water at an exponentially dangerous rate just as population of the world is set to increase again. She advises the current political leaders to set aside their ethnic and religious differences, come together to find a solution to this dangerous common threat lurking in the horizon against humanity as a whole. Indeed the water situation is dire. Unfortunately, the average person in the industrialized world does not know this. Only the hundreds of millions who don't have access or have limited access to clean water in the developing world know the problem well as they experience it every day of their lives.

Not long ago, the former Australian Prime Minister John Howard hosted a high-level summit in Sydney to deal with what one scientist called "the worst drought in Australia in 1,000 years. His answer? Allow the farmers to "trade" country water to the city, thus draining already thirsty rivers of yet more water; drain the wetlands to supply the cities and ship in tankers full of water from Tasmania; and look into technology such as desalination plants. All of them are unsustainable. The government said not a single word, according to Barlowe, about conservation, protecting the watersheds, replenishing water systems, cleaning up toxic dumps or stopping the massive export of Australia's water stock-in-trade with China.[8]

Even Canada, one of the world's most water abundant countries is feeling the effects of water pollution and over-extraction of its water systems according to a 2005 report from Environment Canada. Huge amounts of water are being wasted in Canada's Alberta Tar Sands where water is pumped underground to mine the heavy oil from the ground.[9]

In contrast, Europe has taken some steps to manage its water better. In 2000, the European Commission launched the Water Framework Initiative, a European Union-wide plan for water conservation, clean up, and joint management of river basins. According to their plan, all European waters must achieve "Good Status" by 2015. It seems the European Union acts more responsibly in all aspects combating climate change, water management, and other issues affecting the planet than the rest of the world.

Currently, ninety percent of the raw sewage in both poor and not so poor countries is still discharged untreated. Massive amounts of water are being lost from leaky infrastructure in most of the megacities of the Third World. More than 50 percent of municipal water is lost because of faulty systems in the global south at present.

Today, industrial agriculture which is prevalent in most major countries is exacerbating the water crisis. Large factory farms create a staggering amount of manure and use extensively antibiotics, pesticides, and nitrogen fertilizers. All these toxic chemicals end up in the water supply. This has created "Dead Zones" in the oceans where millions of sea creatures have perished. Enormous amount of water is wasted in flood irrigation used by farmers in many parts of the world. The main form of irrigation in China is this type of irrigation. There, close to 80 percent of water used this way, is lost to evaporation. Flood irrigation over-tills the soil, and leads to desertification as the soil is then carried away by wind. Still, the World Bank and the World Trade Organization promote this model in the developing world while the wealthy countries are already wedded to unsustainable industrial agriculture.[10]

It is known that agriculture is the biggest user of water at present but that is changing now. Industries in the developed world now account for 59 percent of total water usage while, in developing countries, industry is gaining ground as a water gobbler. For example India, in the next decade, will triple its water use for industry. Water use and waste is growing exponentially as China, India, Brazil, Malaysia and a host of other countries undergo industrialization at an unprecedented rate. Yet, nobody, no political leader has the realization or the courage to question this model anywhere. The biz word is 'industrialize', and grow at any cost, damn the consequences. The world faces major water scarcity and inequity. We have the knowledge to fix this. But political leaders lack the foresight and the courage to act. The future of the world's depleting water supply is progressively disappearing into the hands of multinational corporations who see this as a great opportunity to make money. [11]

FALLING WATER TABLES

Across the world, water tables are falling. In their struggle to satisfy their increasing water needs, scores of countries are over pumping aquifers. Many aquifers are replenished, but not all. When India's and North China's aquifers are depleted, the maximum rate of pumping will automatically go down to the rate of recharge. But fossil aquifers are not replenishable. For example, for the vast Ogallala aquifer in the U.S., the North China Plain's deep aquifer, and the Saudi aquifer, depletion brings pumping to an end. If rainfall is enough, the farmers in these areas can resort to lower-yield dry land farming. But in arid regions such as in the southwest United States and the Middle East, the loss of irrigation water means the end of agriculture.

Falling water tables are already affecting several countries' harvests, including that of China which rivals the United States as the world's largest grain producer. An August 2001, groundwater survey released in

Beijing reported that the water table under the North China Plain, an area that produces over half of the country's rice and wheat harvest and a third of its corn, is falling rapidly. The shallow aquifer is now depleted due to over pumping, forcing the farmers to turn to the region's deep aquifer, which is not replenishable.[12]

The survey reported that in the heart of the North China Plain, the Hubei Province, the average level of deep water aquifer was dropping close to 3 meters (10 feet) every year. In some cities in the province, it was dropping at double this rate. Head of the ground water monitoring team, He Qingcheng warns that as the deep water aquifer is depleted, the region is losing its only water reserve.[13]

The World Bank Report mirrored the same concern: "Anecdotal evidence suggests that deep wells (drilled) around Beijing now have to reach 1000 meters (more than half a mile) to tap fresh water, adding dramatically to the cost of supply." In unusually strong language for a bank report, it foresees "catastrophic consequences for future generations" unless water use and supply can be brought back under control. [14]

China's grain harvest is shrinking due to falling water tables and the conversion of cropland to non-farm uses, resulting in the loss of farm labor in provinces that are rapidly industrializing. Particularly vulnerable to water shortages is the wheat crop, grown mainly in semiarid northern China. It has dropped to 105 million tons in 2007 after peaking to 123 million tons in 1997, a decline of 15%.[15]

As per The World Bank Report, China is mining underground water in three nearby river basins in the north—those of Hai, which flows through Beijing and Tianjin; the Yellow; and the Huai, the other river south of the Yellow. As it requires 1,000 tons of water to produce one ton of grain, the shortfall in Hai basin of 40 billion tons of water per year means that when the aquifer is depleted, there will be drop in the grain harvest by 40 million tons—sufficient to feed 120 million Chinese.[16]

While China's water situation is in dire conditions, India's groundwater woes are, in places, at crisis levels. Water shortages in India—where the margin between the food availability and survival is so precarious—are even worse than that in China. As of now, India's 100 million farmers have drilled 21 million wells with the investment of around $12 billion in wells and pumps. Fred Pearce in a survey of India's water situation reported in the *New Scientist* that half of India's traditional hand dug wells and millions of shallower tube wells have already dried up, resulting in a spate of suicides among farmers who depend on them. Electricity blackouts have reached epidemic proportions in states where about half of electricity is used to pump water from a depth of up to a kilometer. [17]

In the southern state of Tamil Nadu where some 62 million Indians live, water wells are drying up everywhere. According to Kuppannan Palaniswami of Tamil Nadu Agricultural University, the irrigated areas in the state have been reduced by 50 percent as falling water tables have dried up 95 percent of the wells owned by small farmers. Hence, many farmers have resorted to dryland farming. [18]

Well-drillers are forced to go as deep as 1000 meters as water tables fall. In many communities, all agriculture is rain-dependent as underground water sources have dried up; drinking water is trucked in. In the Saurashtra region of Gujarat, where I come from, the water shortage is severe to extreme. The head of Water Management Institute's groundwater station in Gujarat warns, "When the balloon bursts, untold anarchy will be the lot of rural India." [19]

Since 2000, India's grain harvest, squeezed both by water shortage and the loss of cropland to non-farm uses, has plateaued. That is the reason India reemerged as a leading importer of grain in 2006 after a long time. According to a study by The World Bank, 15 percent of India's food supply is produced by mining groundwater. That means, some 175 million Indians feed with grain produced with water from irrigation wells that will soon go dry. [20]

Hence, in countries such as India and China, as water tables fall, more and more electricity is used to pump water from deeper and deeper wells. This rising electricity demand is being met by increased electricity production by building coal-fired power plants, a high emitter of greenhouse gases and pollution.

Here in the United States, as reported by USDA, parts of Oklahoma, Texas and Kansas—the three leading grain producers—the underground water tables have dropped by more than 30 meters (100 feet). Wells have gone dry on thousands of farms in southern Great Plains. This has forced farmers to resort to lower-yielding dryland farming. This mining of underground water is affecting adversely the U.S. grain production, but irrigated land accounts for only one fifth (20 percent) of U.S. grain harvest. Compare this with close to three fifths (60 percent) of the harvest in India and four fifths (80 percent) in China.[21]

The seven U.S. states—California, Colorado, Nevada, New Mexico, Arizona, Utah, and Wyoming—draw on Colorado River water. But the river is drying up more every year and is losing its water capacity year by year. Irrigation areas in these states have declined over the years according to the USDA survey.

In Pakistan, a country of 164 million people and growing by 3 million a year, water tables are falling just like in India. Water shortage there is acute. Richard Garstang, a water expert with the World Wild Life Fund and a participant in a study of Pakistan's water situation, said in 2001 that "within 15 years Quetta will run out of water if the current consumption rate continues." Well, if at all, the consumption rate is likely to increase.[22] The same can be seen in the Baluchistan Province of Afghanistan, where water tables are falling dangerously low.

Saudi Arabia, a country of 25 million people, though super-rich with oil, is terribly poor in water resources. It has developed an extensive irrigated agriculture based largely on its deep fossil aquifer. Its wheat harvest has declined from a high of 4.1 million tons in 1992 to 2.7 million tons in 2007, a drop of 34 percent. Some Saudi farmers are now forced to pump wells that are 4,000 feet deep, nearly 1.2 kilometers or four fifths of a mile. A 1984 national survey reported its fossil water reserves at 462 billion tons. According to Craig Smith, in his *The New York Times* article, half of that has most likely disappeared by now. This means irrigated agriculture could last for another decade perhaps and then will altogether vanish.[23]

As Lester Brown rightly warns in his praiseworthy book, Plan B 3, Water tables are dropping everywhere. From the United States to India, from China to Mexico, Pakistan, Afghanistan, Yemen, Israel and a host of other countries, the aquifers are running dry as water tables are falling. [24] What implications does this entail? This means food supply of the planet is threatened. Our world could face dangerous food shortage in coming years. Millions of poor people around the world could starve.

DRYING RIVERS

Falling water tables or drying underground aquifers are not visible to us, but the signs of drying rivers or their reduced flow around the planet can clearly be discerned. There are two river systems where this can be observed. They are the Yellow River, the largest river in northern China, and the Colorado River of southwest United States. Others that either run dry or come close to it during the dry season are the Ganges, in whose basin huge population of Indians live, the Indus, which supplies most of Pakistan's water and the Nile, Egypt's lifeline for thousands of years.

A huge population increase and growing industrialization has tripled the world demand for water in last half century; the demand for hydroelectric power has grown even faster resulting in the construction of dams and diversion of river waters draining many rivers dry. Springs that feed some of these rivers are going dry as water tables drop, reducing their flows. [25]

Astonishingly, since 1950, the number of large dams—over 15 meters high—has increased from 5,000 to 45,000. Each dam reduces its river flow. In arid and semiarid regions where evaporation rates are high, on average, 10 percent of reservoir water is lost due to evaporation.[26]

Today, the Colorado River rarely reaches the sea. The states of California, Colorado, Arizona, Utah, and Nevada are heavily dependent on its water, and there is little or no water left when Colorado River reaches the Gulf of California. Due to this heavy demand for its water, its ecosystem and its fisheries are being destroyed.[27] According to a study published in *Science* in 2007, the southwest region of the United States will enter permanent drought by 2050, and that is an optimistic view. The seven states dependent upon the Colorado River Basin—Arizona, California, Utah, Wyoming, Colorado, Nevada, and New Mexico—will most likely fight over what remains of its diminishing water resources. The thirsty population of these regions will be beset by rampant firestorms, as portions of snowpack that remains bypass the liquid stage and evaporate into thin air.[28]

China is the land of rivers and lakes. It boasts the world's fourth biggest water source. But over 70% of China's lakes and rivers are polluted according to government research. Thirty of its thirty-two largest cities suffer from water shortages.[29]

The mighty Yellow River of China, which flows some 4,000 kilometers through five provinces and then reaches the Yellow Sea, is under increasing pressure for many decades due to over use. In 1972, for the first time, it ran dry. Since 1985, it has failed to reach the sea. [30]

The Nile, in whose bosom grew one of the oldest civilizations, now hardly makes it to the sea. According to water analyst Sandra Postel, in *Pillars of Sand*, some 32 billion cubic meters of water flowed into the Mediterranean each year before the Aswan Dam was built. The dam construction, evaporation, increased irrigation and other demands, has reduced its discharge to less than 2 billion cubic meters.[31]

Pakistan's population is essentially river-based, heavily dependent on the Indus River. This river originates in the Himalayas and flows southwestward to the Indian Ocean. It provides surface water and fills the underground aquifers that irrigate the Pakistani countryside, feeding millions of people. Now, due to growing demand, it has started running dry in its lower reaches. Pakistan's population of 164 million is projected to grow to 292 million by 2050; even now Pakistan is one of the ten failed states. How will it feed its ever increasing millions with ever decreasing water flow of the Indus? A catastrophe awaits this nation.[32]

The Mekong River of Southeast Asia is facing reduced water flow because of China building dams on its upper reaches. The downstream countries of Cambodia, Laos, Thailand and Vietnam receive less and less water now. Their complaints to China have no effect on their giant neighbor.[33] The situation is similar with the Tigris and Euphrates Rivers which originate in Turkey and flow through Syria and Iraq on its way to the Persian Gulf. Mesopotamia, one of the oldest civilizations on the Earth, began here. Its water is overused. Due to dams constructed by Turkey and Iraq, the water flow to the once "fertile crescent," is reduced, destroying some 80% of the vast wetlands that formerly made the delta region so fertile. [34]

Thus, we can see how river systems around the planet are being depleted by dams and over usage, reducing their water flow significantly. Add to this problem the melting of the glaciers, and the world faces a major catastrophe in the near future.

DISAPPEARING LAKES

Some three hundred and four million lakes are estimated to exist across the globe, but researchers are noticing that many inland lakes are beginning to dry. Whether in North America, Central Asia, East Africa or Siberia, lakes unable, to compete with the man made alterations to the environment, are drying at an alarming rate. "These are not just small lakes," reports Abigail Brown, who manages water resources in

Washington State, "some of the lakes with dropping water levels are gigantic in size."

There are 122 large lakes on the planet, each over 1,000 square kilometers (386 square miles).

Lake Victoria, at 68,000 square kilometers (26,560 square miles), is the largest tropical lake in the world. Mounting water-level decline is slowly destroying the livelihood of farmers, local fishermen, ranchers, and industrial water users near this lake. Scarcities of decent drinkable water supplies are becoming more common in the region, according to Abigail Brown.[35]

Last year, the morning edition of NPR aired a segment on Lake Victoria by correspondent Jessica Partnow: "Battle for Resources Grows as Lake Victoria Shrinks." For the World Vision Report, she has also reported on dropping water levels in Lake Haramaya in Africa. It is normal sometimes to have fluctuations of water levels in some lakes. But the current rate at which many lakes are going dry all over the world is not normal.

Once, Africa's Lake Chad was a landmark for astronauts while circling the earth; now it is difficult to spot. The lake, surrounded by Chad, Nigeria, Niger and Cameroon—countries with fast growing populations—has already shrunk 96 percent in last 40 years. The rivers and streams that feed the lake are draining dry due to the region's soaring appetite for irrigation water coupled with declining rainfall. Consequently, Lake Chad may soon disappear entirely; future generations may find its whereabouts a mystery. [36]

Water levels in the lakes decline due to humans altering the natural environment nearby. We construct dams, over-use groundwater, over-pump rivers, build roads and parking lots in natural recharge areas, build industries in locations without adequate water, over irrigate our crops, and waste too much water in our homes; add to this the effect of climate change on water resources.

There are other lakes around the world with dropping water levels. Some of them are Great Lakes in the United States, the Lake Baikal of Russia, Aral Sea in Central Asia, Lake Chad in Egypt, the Sea of Galilee (also known as Lake Tiberius) and Lake Chapala of Mexico.

The Jordan River enters Israel from Syria. It is shrinking so much that it can be called a creek in many places according to Reuter's reporter Megan Goldin. It mainly supplies water to the Sea of Galilee, which it enters at the north end and exits in the south end. Then it continues southward about 105 kilometers when it empties into the Dead Sea.[37]

As the Jordan River's flow further reduces while it passes through Israel, the Dead Sea is shrinking even faster than the Sea of Galilee. Its water level has dropped by some 25 meters (about 80 feet) in the last 40 years. By 2050, it could entirely disappear.[38]

No water body exhibits the plight of shrinking lakes and inland seas as vividly as the Aral Sea. Once busy centers of commerce, its ports today are abandoned and resemble the ghost mining towns of American West. At one point the world's biggest freshwater body, the Aral Sea has lost four fifth of its volume since 1960. Ships, which once plied its routes, are now stranded in the sand of the old sea bed, with water nowhere in sight.[39]

In 1960, the Soviets planted the seeds for the Aral Sea's death. The central planners in Moscow decided to make the region of Syr Darya and Amu Darya basins, a vast cotton bowl to supply the country's textile industry.[40]

As cotton planting expanded, the water flow in these rivers constricted as water was diverted from the two rivers that fed the Aral Sea. As the sea shrank, the increased salt concentration killed all the fish. The thriving fisheries that once provided 50,000 tons of seafood annually disappeared along with the jobs on the fishing boats and in the fish processing plants.[41]

The water flow in the above rivers is now reduced from 65 billion cubic meters annually to 1.5 billion cubic meters. Now, vast areas of sea bed are exposed as the sea shoreline is now up to 250 kilometers (165 miles) from the original port cities. Every day, thousands of tons of salt and sand are lifted from the dry seabed and are spread as airborne particles on the surrounding grasslands and croplands, reducing their fertility. [42]

One can see most vividly the disappearance of lakes in China as well. Once there were 4,077 lakes in western China's Qinhai province through which the Yellow River's main stream flows. More than 2,000 have disappeared over last 20 years. In the Hebei province which surrounds Beijing, the situation is far worst. With reduced water tables all around Beijing, Hebei has lost 969 of its 1,052 lakes.[43]

Growing population is outpacing the water supply in Mexico. Lake Chapala, Mexico's largest lake is the primary supply of water to 4 million residents of Guadalajara. Due to increasing irrigation in the region, the volume of water in the lake has declined by 80 percent.[44]

Scientists have warned that Lake Van in the southeastern part of Turkey will disappear in the next 10-15 years if no radical measures are taken to save it. Lake Van is regarded as the fifth biggest lake in Europe. Thousands of Turks take their summer holidays on Lake Van's shores, although 40 percent of them are no longer fit for health or fishing purposes.[45]

Thus due to excessive water diversion from rivers and over pumping of underground aquifers; the lakes are disappearing from continent to continent with disastrous effect on human and animal species.

The Great Lakes—Lake Erie, Lake Ontario, Lake Huron, Lake Michigan, Lake St. Clair, and Lake Superior—are a vast inland sea representing over one-fifth of all fresh water on the planet. More than 40 million Americans and Canadians depend on these lakes for their drinking water which play a vital role in public health, environment, industry, commerce, and leisure. But now there are causes for alarm: declining water levels, uncertain quality of drinking water, invasive species and pressures to divert water from and into the Great Lakes-St. Lawrence basin.

As many as 182 invasive species including the Zebra Mussel, have entered the lake system, and have begun disrupting the food web on St. Clair in 1988 and has clogged many water intake pipes since, at an annual cost running in the billions of dollars.[46]

Zebra Mussels make the lake water look much cleaner but when the water is clearer, sunlight penetrates deeper, and organic material proliferates and absorbs much-needed oxygen in the water that is needed by fish and microorganisms. The result is "dead zones" for the fish and other water creatures.

Water levels in these lakes are falling. 'Healing Our Waters'—Great Lakes Coalition predicts that lake level could drop this century by a foot on Lake Superior, three feet on Lakes Michigan and Huron, 2.7 feet on Lake Erie, and 1.7 feet on Lake Ontario. Lower water levels prohibit larger ships from navigating in the lake.

Lake Superior's temperature is rising, mentions Jay Austin, an oceanographer at the Large Lakes Observatory of the University of Minnesota at Duluth. "Temperature is the most important environmental variable" in a lake, he says. It determines "the chemical reaction rates, the metabolism rates of fish, phytoplankton, and zooplankton, and the spawning rates of fish." He also warns that "the surface water of Lake Michigan and Lake Huron also seem to be experiencing the accelerated warming phenomenon, although not Lake

Erie." Warmer water temperature means less ice cover in winter, which means more evaporation. That in turn lowers water levels, stressing ecosystems. According to Austin, the warming of the Great Lakes is its latest challenge, perhaps its most serious one.[47]

FAILING CROPS-INCREASING FOOD INSECURITY

Ten to eleven thousand years of farming history has evolved our agriculture as it exists today while the climate has changed little. Varieties of crops were developed in this long period to maximize yields. But with the rise in temperatures, agriculture will be out of sync with its natural environment. The most egregious evidence of this is found in the relationship between crop yields and temperature. Even a minor increase of 1 to 2°C in temperature can adversely affect the grain harvest in major food-producing regions, such as the U.S. Corn Belt, the North China Plain, and the Gangetic Plain of India. Higher temperatures can reduce or even stop photosynthesis, prevent pollination, and lead to crop dehydration.[48]

Two Indian scientists, Jyoti Parikh and K.S. Kavi Kumar, observed the effect of higher temperatures on wheat and rice yields. They concluded, based on their model on data from 10 sites, that in north India, a one degree rise in mean temperature did not meaningfully reduce wheat yields, but a 2 degree rise lowered yields at almost all the sites. Observing temperature change alone, they found that a 2 degree rise led to a decline in irrigated wheat yields ranging from 37 percent to 58 percent. Combining the negative effects of higher temperature with positive effects of CO2 fertilization, the decline in yields among the various sites varied from 8 percent to 38 percent. For a nation likely to add 500 million more people by the mid-century, this is a troublesome prospect.[49]

MORE POWERFUL STORMS

Higher temperatures cause further problems. In tropical oceans, rising surface temperatures release more energy into the atmosphere, driving stronger and more destructive storm systems. Rising seas and more powerful and destructive storms generate higher surges which could be devastating—as evident when the August 2005 hurricane, Katrina, hit the Gulf Coast near New Orleans. Katrina's 28-foot-high surges, in some Gulf Coast towns, left no structures standing. Though, New Orleans initially survived the impact, the inland levees were soon breached and large parts of the city were submerged. Thousands of people were left stranded on rooftops. Katrina was one of the most devastating—and expensive—storms to ever hit the Gulf Coast of the United States; it was one of eight that struck the U.S. in 2004 and 2005.

Global warming will increase the frequency of wild-fires in the western United States, particularly in California. "Wildfires are just one of the disasters we can expect if we don't act now to curb global warming," the Sierra Club's spokesperson Kristina Johnson says. "There will also be widespread floods, famine, and disease." The nation will be dramatically reshaped—from the fallout from these natural catastrophes—in ways that are unimaginable and dystopian to the extreme. Natural Californian species such as coastal redwoods and fire poppy could retreat or die off entirely due to warm temperatures. Rising mercury has invited all manners of pestilence, including the bark beetle, whose decimation of plant life across California, New Mexico, Colorado, and elsewhere has left behind dead husks just begging to ignite from freak lightning storms, which have also increased in number.[50]

In the fall of 1998, hurricane Mitch, one of the most powerful storms to emerge out of Atlantic, battered the coast of Central America. Two meters of rain were dumped on parts of Nicaragua and Honduras. Thousands of homes, factories, and schools collapsed, leaving them in ruins. Roads and bridges were destroyed as well. Some seventy percent of the crops and much of the top soil in Honduras were washed away: top soil that had accumulated over long periods of geological time. Hundreds were buried due to huge landslides. About 11,000 people were confirmed dead. Many thousands more washed away into the sea; they were never found. President Flores of Honduras rightly commented: "Overall, what was destroyed over several days took us 50 years to build." The storm damage exceeded both countries' annual domestic product and set back their economic development by 20 years.[51]

Meanwhile in Asia, in 2004 Japan suffered from 10 typhoons which caused $10 billion worth of damage. In the same season, Florida was hit by 4 out of 10 most costly hurricanes in U.S. history. Insurance claims generated by these four hurricanes were worth $22 billion.[52]

China suffered terrible flooding in the Yangtze River basin in 1998 which cost an estimated $30 billion, a price equal to the value of its rice harvest. Greater industrial and urban development in the coastal areas and river floodplains are to blame, in addition to a greater frequency of more intense storms.

The regions most vulnerable to such storms are the Atlantic and Gulf Coasts of the United States and the Caribbean countries. In the east, China, Japan, East and Southeast Asia, Taiwan, the Philippines, and Vietnam are going to bear the brunt of these storms crossing the Pacific. The Bay of Bengal, especially Bangladesh and the east coast of India are also vulnerable.

Europe is not spared either. Western Europe has historically experienced a heavily damaging storm once in a century. But in 1987, it had its first winter storm with a total cost exceeding $1 billion, one that caused $3.7 billion in destruction. Since then, Western Europe has had nine major winter storms causing billions of dollars in damage.[53]

In the first week of October 2009, deadly floods triggered by heavy rains swamped the southern Indian states of Karnataka and Andhra Pradesh. More than 220 people were killed while 2.5 million were left homeless. "These are the worst floods in 100 years," said Andhra Pradesh's minister of revenue and relief.[54]

Patterns such as these paint an obvious picture that climate change will bring more extreme weather catastrophes around the planet. Will the world be able to cope with such expensive disasters in the future? Their frequency will steadily increase with warmer weather.

There is perhaps more in store for us than just storms. On September 16, 2009, at the first major three-day conference of scientists in London, researching the changing climate's effects on geological hazards, scientists said that quakes, volcanic eruptions, landslides and tsunamis may become more frequent as global warming changes Earth's crust. "When the ice is lost, the Earth's crust bounces back up again, and that triggers earthquakes, which trigger submarine landslides, which cause tsunamis," Bill McGuire, a professor of earth sciences at the University College London, told Reuters.[55]

SHRINKING CO2 SINKS

The escalating scale of human emissions could not have come at a worse time. Scientists have discovered that the Earth's forests and oceans could be losing their ability to soak up carbon pollution. Most climate projections assume that about half of all carbon emissions are reabsorbed in these natural sinks. Computer models predict that this effect will weaken as the world warms up and a series of recent studies suggest that this is already happening.

Since 1981, the southern ocean's ability to absorb carbon dioxide has weakened by about 15% a decade, while in the North Atlantic, scientists at the University of East Anglia have found a dramatic decline in the CO2 sink between the mid-1990s and mid-2000s.

Another separate study published in 2008 found that the ability of forests to soak up anthropogenic carbon dioxide was weakening, because the changing length of seasons alters the time when trees switch from being a sink of carbon to a source.

Even soils could be giving up their carbon stores: in 2005, evidence emerged that a vast expanse of western Siberia was undergoing an unprecedented thaw. Since its formation some 11,000 years ago, the region, the largest frozen peat bog in the world, has begun to melt for the first time. Scientists believe the bog could begin to release billions of tones of methane locked up in the soils, a greenhouse gas 20 times more potent than carbon dioxide. The World Meteorological Organization recently reported the biggest yearly rise of methane levels in the atmosphere for a decade.[56]

PEAKING OIL

Few people realize that Earth's resources are finite. With few exceptions, almost everything we consume today is limited. Whether it is fossil fuels such as oil or coal—or the vast number of items derived from it such as fertilizers, pesticides, plastics, chemicals, tars etc.—or metal, the Earth has only finite quantities of these items. All these resources will some day run out.

The greatest threat our modern industrialized world faces today is from the fact that our fossil fuel dependent world will have to face a day when these resources will run dry. Although coal deposits, being much larger, will last longer, oil on Earth will run out in the not too distant future. M. King Herbert, an oil industry geoscientist, came out with the 'Peak Oil Theory' by which he claimed that the depletion of oil in the Earth will follow a bell shaped curve. (See below).

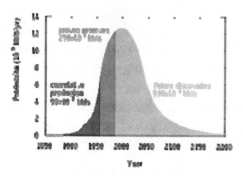

A bell-shaped production curve, as originally suggested by M. King Hubbert in 1956.[57]

Peak oil is the point in time when the maximum rate of global petroleum extraction is reached, after which the rate of production enters a terminal decline. The concept is based on the observed production rates of individual oil wells, and the combined production rate of a field of related oil wells. The aggregate production rate from an oil field over time usually grows exponentially until the rate peaks and then declines—sometimes rapidly—until the field is depleted. This concept is derived from the Hubbert curve, and has been shown to be applicable to the sum of a nation's domestic production rate, and is similarly applied to the global rate of petroleum production. Peak oil is often confused with oil depletion; peak oil is the point of maximum production while depletion refers to a period of falling reserves and supply.

Most energy experts now believe that we have consumed close to half of the planet's original petroleum reserves and are very close to a peak in production. No one knows for certain whether it will happen in 2015, 2020, 2030, or beyond, but we will soon find out. Additionally, most energy professionals now believe that global oil output will occur at much lower levels than only recently believed—a figure of 90-95 million barrels a day, not the 115-125 million barrels projected by the U.S. Department of energy previously.[58]

RISE IN ENVIRONMENTAL REFUGEES

With deserts and droughts spreading in many countries, millions of refugees are moving to neighboring countries. For example, in sub-Saharan Africa, mainly in Sahelian countries, expanding deserts are displacing millions of people, forcing them to migrate to North Africa or move southward. According to a 2006 U.N. conference on desertification in Tunisia, by 2020, up to 60 million refugees could migrate from sub-Saharan Africa to Europe or North Africa. For many years, this flow has continued.[59]

Thousands of people from south and central America (including Mexico itself) are trying to legally or illegally come to (Mexico and) the

United States because their countries have experienced terrible poverty caused by environmental damage, wars, and globalization.

Vast numbers of water refugees are likely to become commonplace when by 2050, yet another 3 billion people will be added to the world where underground water tables are already declining. Especially in arid and semi-arid regions, such refugees will be common where water supplies are shrinking but populations are growing. In northwestern India, villages are being abandoned due to depleted aquifers and people can no longer find water. In many parts of India, water is only available one hour a day or only by tanker truck. A dearth of water will force millions of villagers in northern and western China and in parts of Mexico to relocate elsewhere.[60]

Thousands of towns are also being abandoned in Iran because of spreading deserts. Near Damavand, a small town not too far from Tehran, 88 villages have been abandoned. Spreading desert is forcing farmers and herders in Nigeria to move into productive lands which are already shrinking.[61]

Yet another source of environmental refugees, perhaps the biggest one the world would ever see, would be from rising oceans. When the Greenland ice sheets and Polar Regions' ice sheets melt, the sea-level will rise several meters. This will create hundreds of millions of refugees who live in the coastal regions of the world. They will lose their homes and their livelihoods and will be forced to move upland and interior. Imagine the scenario that will unfold. These are indeed compelling reasons to drastically curb carbon emissions to stop global warming.

Millions of poverty refugees from Bangladesh have already illegally moved into India for a better life. Some reports put their number at 25 million. Already bent with the burden of millions of its own poor, India is forced to bear the burden of these additional people. It will be a catastrophe when some 62 million environmental refugees from Bangladesh will be forced to abandon their homes, losing their livelihoods when a quarter of their country is inundated and submerged in sea-water when sea-levels rise a few decades from now. Where will they go? India will have its own coastal refugees by then to support.

A report by the Charity said that Pacific Islanders were already feeling the effects of global warming, such as food shortages, rising incidence of malaria, and more frequent flooding and storms. The report warned that some had already been forced from their homes and the number of displaced people is climbing.

The report, "The Future is Here: Climate Change in the Pacific," predicted that many Pacific Islanders would not be able to relocate within their own countries and would become international refugees. Half the population of the Pacific lives less than 1.5 kilometers from the coast and are incredibly vulnerable to sea-level rises and extreme weather. It is estimated that some 75 million people in the Asia-Pacific region will be forced to relocate by 2050 if climate change continues unabated.[62]

CHAPTER 8
PERILOUS SIGNS OF DECAY

Our environmental problems originate in the hubris of imagining ourselves as the central nervous system of the brain of nature. We're not the brain; we are a cancer on nature.
—Dave Foreman, Harper's, April 1990

WASTEFUL AMERICAN ECONOMY & ITS INDULGENT WAYS

Mother Earth cannot bear the burden of the American way of life. Since the Roman Empire, no nation or empire has experienced such luxury and indulgence as we Americans enjoy today. But it has come at a horrible cost to the planet. America gobbles up 25% of world's oil and even higher percentages of world's other vital resources while it consists of just 5% of the world's population.[1] This is not just unfair to the billions of poor of the world who subsist on just a dollar or two a day. It is outright vulgar. We are the second greatest emitter of greenhouse gases in the world; China has just surpassed us in that distinction. It is rightly said that if the rest of the world lives like America, we need several Earths to sustain us.

Let's see how wasteful we are in America. In Las Vegas, Nevada, just one street, named Fremont Street, a six block long area uses 16 million light bulbs. New York's time Square uses 300MW (Mega Watts) of energy per year. That is enough energy to power 300,000 homes for a year.[2] Not just Las Vegas or New York, but every U.S. city you travel, you will see dazzling lights burning everywhere—everything is lighted: streets, public buildings, office buildings, public squares, bridges, ports—throughout the night, even on weekends and holidays. Why? Why should the lights be on for the entire night at all these places? Thousands of kilowatt hours of precious electricity are wasted this way. All this waste, yet in so rich a country there are still 88,000 to 90,000 homeless people in Los Angeles alone![3] What an inequality! What a waste of so much human resource in such a wealthy country.

The average food item in an America plate has traveled 1,500 miles. Can you imagine how many gallons of gasoline it has burned to reach our plates? Think about the hundreds of thousands of man-hours wasted hauling millions of tons of food on average 1,500 miles to land on our plate every day. Think about the gasoline consumed, and the wear and tear on the trucks.

Over the years, America has evolved into a wasteful throw-away economy with an indulgent life-style which is unsustainable on the long term. Every year we throw away old clothes and buy new ones. New fashions and modern styles encourage us to shed our older clothes, older cars, and other accessories for the new ones. Growing up in India, when we were kids, we learned that you don't throw away old things but have them repaired whether they are clothes, shoes, appliances, bicycles or cars. I remember we used to have a visit from the newspaper collector-buyer; we called him 'pasti-walla'. He used to come three to four times a year or more. He would buy the old newspapers and magazines that my mother would have collected in that time interval. He would weigh them and pay us accordingly. He would then take them, make paper bags from them and sell them to hawkers who sell their snacks in these paper bags. In these times in India, there were no plastic bags. All the newspapers were recycled. Same way, everything else—clothes, utensils, bicycles, old furniture, shoes, drink bottles – was repaired if necessary, or resold, recycled, and reused. Nothing was wasted. Nothing was ever thrown away. It is still the same way today—although that is changing.

Coming here in this country in the sixties, we realized (wrongfully) that there is no need to have anything repaired. Simply throw away the older things and buy new ones. That is the American way! Imagine how much material and man-hours we waste by such an attitude. In America, disposable paper towels have replaced cloth towels. Tissues have replaced handkerchiefs. Glass wares—dishes and cups—have been replaced with paper dishes and cups. Refillable beverage containers are replaced with throwaway aluminum or glass containers. Even the plastic shopping bags are used once and thrown away. The Earth simply cannot keep giving more and more metals, oil, plastics, paper or wood products (though wood and paper are regenerated) year after year, generation after generation. There is a limit. The Earth's resources are finite, not limitless. Our throwaway economy is surely on a collision course with the planets geological limits. According to a U.S. Geological Survey data on economically recoverable reserves, assuming a 2 percent annual growth of extraction, the world has 25 years of copper, 19 years of tin, 17 years of lead, 54 years of iron ore, and 68 years of bauxite reserve left.[4]

Browse through our newspapers and magazines. They are filled with advertisements all over to entice Americans to buy the products, more and more. We are told, the more we spend, the better the economy! Billions of dollars and millions of tons of paper are wasted thus, in selling to Americans a wide range of products, many of which they may not even need. In every one of our mail boxes, at home or at the office, we find a bunch of letters, advertisements, and useless (garbage) mails which we throw away every day. Imagine how many thousands of trees are cut every day to produce this huge quantity of paper that is totally wasted away! That is unsustainable capitalism.

Worldwide, the garbage generated by burgeoning cities is exceeding the landfills available. Cities are simply running out of available space as are their landfills. The costs of hauling garbage far to another state are rising as gas prices are going up. New York City was one of the first one to run out of landfill space, in March 2001. Hence it is forced to haul its garbage to New Jersey, Pennsylvania, and Virginia, some sites being as far away as 300 miles.[5]

Look at the quantity of garbage our cities generate. On average, New York City generates 12,000 tons of garbage every day. Assuming 20 tons of garbage for each tractor-trailer used for the long-distance hauling, as many as 600 rigs are needed to carry the garbage from New York City daily. These tractor-trailers form a nine mile long convoy creating traffic jams, polluting air, and increasing carbon emissions.[6]

New York City is not alone. Many other cities are in similar predicament. Toronto, Canada's largest city closed its last remaining landfill on 31st December, 2002. It now ships its garbage to Wayne County, Michigan. Athens, Greece also has its garbage problems, 6000 tons' worth daily. When local governments refused to accept this huge quantity of garbage from Athens, 6000 tons of garbage started piling up in the streets, creating a huge garbage crisis. During our trip to Athens in March 2008, we were witness to such a crisis when tons of garbage had accumulated all over the streets of Athens, this time it seems there was a strike by the garbage collectors of that city. Perhaps they were overworked.[7]

Nowhere is the garbage crisis more acute than in the fast growing Chinese economy. In its cities, the quantity of garbage is growing rapidly. The Chinese wire service, Xinhua, reports that there are 7,000 garbage dumps, each larger than 50 square meters in the suburbs of Beijing, Shanghai, Chongqing, and Tianjin. Though China recycles, burns or composts large share of its garbage, a larger share is still dumped in landfills wherever they are available or is simply piled up in unoccupied areas, many times in the outskirts of these cities.[8]

City governments around the globe must think about how to reduce generating the garbage in the first place and how to recycle as much as possible. Otherwise, the world will be flooded with garbage everywhere.

OCEAN GARBAGE FROM HAWAII TO JAPAN

A clear sign of our world being flooded with plastic dump is visible if you come across the "plastic soup" floating in the Pacific Ocean—that is growing at an alarming rate and now covers an area *twice the size of the continental United States* according to scientists. This vast expanse of debris—in reality the world's largest rubbish dump—is held in place by swirling underwater currents. This drifting "soup" stretches from about 500 nautical miles off the California coast, across the northern Pacific, past Hawaii and almost as far as Japan. An American oceanographer named Charles Moore who discovered the "Great Pacific Garbage Patch" or "trash vortex" believes that about 100 million tons of flotsam is circulating in the region. Marcus Eriksen, a research director of the US-based Algalita Marine Research Foundation, Long Beach, which Mr. Moore founded, has said: "The original idea that people had was that it was an island of plastic garbage that you could almost walk on. It is not quite like that. It is almost like a plastic soup. It is endless for an area that is maybe twice the size of continental United States." Dr. Eriksen and his group have been monitoring the monstrous garbage patch for last 10 years.

The "soup" consists of two linked areas, on either side of Hawaiian Islands, known as the western and eastern Pacific Garbage Patches. About 20 percent of the junk—consisting of everything from footballs and kayaks to Lego blocks and carrier bags—is discarded off the ships or oil platforms. The rest, the vast majority of the plastic garbage begins its journey as onshore trash.

On February 5, 2009, Mr. Moore warned that unless consumers cut back on their use of disposable plastics, the plastic stew would double in size over the next decade.[9]

Chris Parry, public education manager with the California Coastal Commission in San Francisco said that "ocean current patterns may keep the floatsam stashed in a part of the ocean few will ever see, but the majority of its content is generated on land." He opined further that "at present, cleaning it up isn't an option, it is going to get bigger as our reliance on plastics continues…the long-term solution is to stop producing as much plastic products and change our consumption habits." Further, Mr. Parry said that "using canvas bags to cart groceries instead of using plastic bags is a good first step; buying foods that aren't wrapped in plastics is another." [10]

It is nice to know that the San Francisco Board of Supervisors banned the use of plastics grocery bags earlier in 2007. A slew of state bills were written to limit bag production. But many of the bills failed after meeting strong opposition from the industry lobbyists, according to Christie, a legislative director with the California Coastal Commission.

Meanwhile, the stew in the ocean continues to grow. Millions of tons of plastic products are manufactured around the world in industrial nations. Modern plastics are so durable that objects half-a-century old have been found in the north Pacific dump. "Every little piece of plastic manufactured in the past 50 years that made it into the ocean is still out there somewhere," said Tony Andrady, a chemist with US-based Research Triangle Institute.

According to Warner Chabot, vice president of Ocean Conservancy, "The Great Pacific Garbage Patch is especially dangerous for the marine life…Sea turtles mistake clear plastic bags for jellyfish. Birds swallow indigestible shards of plastic. These animals die because plastic eventually fills their stomach. It doesn't pass, and they literally starve to death." He said further that cleaning it up will require a massive international effort. What must be done is to ban plastic fast food packaging, substitute it with biodegradable materials and improve enforcement laws. [11]

According to the UN Environment Programme, plastic debris causes the deaths of more than a million seabirds every year, as well as more than 100,000 marine mammals. Cigarette lighters, syringes, and toothbrushes have been found inside the stomachs of dead seabirds, which mistake them for food.

Ninety percent of the rubbish floating in the ocean is made up of plastics. In 2006, the UN Environment Programme estimated that every square mile of ocean contains 46,000 pieces of plastic. Dr. Eriksen said the slowly rotating mass of rubbish-laden water poses a risk to human health too. Hundreds of millions of tiny plastic pellets or nurdles—the raw materials for the plastic industry—are lost or spilled every year, working their way into the ocean. These pollutants act as chemical sponges, according to Dr. Eriksen, attracting man-made chemicals such as the pesticide DDT and hydrocarbons. Then, they enter the food chain. "What goes into the ocean goes into these animals and onto your dinner plate. It's that simple," warned Dr. Eriksen.[12]

DYING CORALS

The world's corals are dying at an alarming rate. In the Coral Triangle—surrounded by the Philippines, Singapore, Indonesia, and Papua New Guinea—by 2099, corals will be gone thanks to human induced global warming. Fish populations are dense in these coral regions. But as these corals diminish, some 100 million people depending on the fish will be on the hunt for food. Many communities will be destabilized as their economies will be ruined.[13]

Representatives of the Federation of Australian Scientific and Technological Societies told the Canberra parliament in November 2009 that the future of the Barrier Reef and a large chunk of Australia's tourist industry were under grave threat from rising sea temperatures. According to them, Australia's Great Barrier Reef will be severely bleached and eventually die unless carbon emissions are cut drastically. Just a small increase in average temperatures could cause massive coral-bleaching on the reef. Also, they said that a rise of more than 2 °C. would be 'catastrophic' for the reef and tourism in North Queensland.

The World Heritage-protected Great Barrier Reef sprawls for more than 133,000 sq. miles off Australia's coast and can be seen from space. It is the world's largest living organism. To give it a 50% chance of survival, global emissions must be cut by at least 25 percent by 2020. The UN's IPCC report has concluded that the Great Barrier Reef could be "functionally extinct" within decades, with deadly coral bleaching likely to be an annual occurrence by 2030.

Australia, one of the world's biggest carbon emitters per capita, has so far only pledged to cut its emissions by 5 percent from 2000 levels by 2020 but is ready to cut 25 percent if international climate agreement was reached at the Copenhagen Conference in December, 2009. [14] No agreement was reached.

Are these not clear symptoms of decay and the beginning of the self-destruction of current industrial civilization?

OUR OVERPOPULATED WORLD

In 42,000 B.C., the population of the world was estimated to be around 2 million people. By 1800 A.D., it was 1 billion. It swelled to 2 billion by 1930, 3 billion by 1960, 4 billion by 1974, 5 billion by 1987, and 6 billion by 1999.[15]

Let's face it. We humans are foolishly breeding ourselves to extinction. All the measures to thwart the destruction and degradation of the Earth's ecosystem will be futile if we fail to curb the burgeoning population growth. According to a recent U.N. report on population, today there are 6.7 billion people on the Earth. The world population on average grows by 1.18% annually today. That means, every year, the planet bears the burden of supporting and sustaining 80 million more humans. According to a recent U.N. forecast, if we continue to reproduce at the current rate, by 2050, between 8 billion to 10 billion people will inhabit the Earth. The increase of at least 2.5 billion—between now and 2050—was the population of the world just 50 years ago;[16] yet, the governments and politicians of India, Bangladesh, Pakistan, Indonesia, and Brazil, Congo or Egypt— and many more the world over—do not mention the word *overpopulation*.

The United Nations predicts that by 2025, 1.8 billion people will be inhabiting countries or regions with absolute water scarcity. Unsustainable farming practices cause the destruction and abandonment of almost 30 million acres of arable land each year.[17] So besides water, arable land is diminishing too.

All this is indeed sad and dangerous. Even if the world succeeds in drastically cutting down the use of fossil fuels, shutting down all the coal-fired power plants, and builds miles and miles of wind farms, solar farms, builsd solar electricity driven cars etc., the simple addition of billions more to the current population of the planet will certainly plunge us into an age of extinction and desolation not seen since the end of Mesozoic era, some 65 million years ago, when the dinosaurs went extinct.

Today, an accelerated obliteration of the planet's life forms is taking place. An estimated 8,760 species die off every year because, simply stated, there are too many of us humans. Most of these extinctions are direct result of human encroachment: the ever expanding need for energy, food, housing and other resources. As E. O. Wilson says, "Population growth is the monster on the land." Today, species are vanishing at a rate of a hundred to a thousand times faster than they did before the arrival of the humans. It is likely that if the current rate of extinction continues, Homo sapiens will be one of the few life-forms left on the planet, its members searching and scrambling violently among themselves for the last remaining water, food, and fossil fuels until they too vanish from the Earth. According to Wilson, humanity is leaving the Cenozoic, the age of the mammals, and entering the Eremozoic-the era of solitude. As long as the Earth is considered the personal property of the humans—a view held by nearly everyone, early on in Europe and on the North-American Continent, born-again Christians, Marxists, and free-market economists—we are destined to soon inhabit a biological wasteland.[18]

The European colonial powers stunted or blocked the natural agricultural and industrial revolution from taking place in their colonies, keeping them destitute and poor while their own countries passed through these revolutions to achieve higher standards of education and living. In due time, their population growths were under control as certain prosperity was achieved. But their colonies were left to fend for themselves, in a state of destitution and mass poverty. As a result, the population in these ex-colonies—India, China, Bangladesh, Indonesia, African nations, the Middle East, Latin America and other parts of Asia—have grown unabated. It is a proven fact that lack of education, especially amongst women, breeds poverty and population increase and that is exactly what has happened in these once colonized countries. That is the reason we always find that most of the time, the poor nations of the world with higher population rates are those which were once colonized. While these developing countries are struggling shake off poverty and the population explosion trap, the rich European nations and the United States have had their natural agricultural and industrial revolutions accompanied with an education of their populace. Their population rates as a result are highly controlled and maintained (with the exception of the U.S.). They maintain their life-style because they have the military and economic power to consume a disproportionate share of the world's resources. The developing countries are left with emergent population crises.

Countries like India, Bangladesh, Pakistan, South Africa, Indonesia, Egypt or China—whose one-child policy has prevented the birth of some 400 million people—have all tried and instituted birth control measures with varying degree of success. But they are not sufficient. On most of the planet, population is exploding. According to the United Nations, 200 million women have no access to contraception. The population of the

Gulf States, including the Israeli-occupied territories, will double in two decades, an increase that will ominously coincide with the peak oil.[19]

Take for example Egypt. It is a poster child for the imbalance between food production and population. It has experienced serious food riots. Its population, now 74 million and growing by 2.1 percent a year, will top 95 million by 2030. It is close to 98 percent desert and has only 6.6 million acres of cropland, a little more than half of that available to the state of Indiana. It is no wonder that Egypt is forced to import more than a third of its food today and the situation is worsening.[20]

The overpopulated countries of the world, in desperate bids to grow more food will ravage their own environments, cutting down forests and remaining wilderness areas, while depleting their water resources. This depletion of resources will eventually create scarcities that will be felt worldwide, creating overpopulation problems in industrialized countries as well. The resources that the developed or industrial nations consider their birth-right will be harder and more expensive to obtain. Millions displaced by rising water levels on the world's coastal regions will attempt to flee their own regions and legally or illegally enter other regions or countries where these resources are still available. Rising temperatures and more frequent droughts have already started destroying croplands in Australia, Africa, California and Texas. Countries like Bangladesh or Congo will first feel the effects of such devastation but it will soon spread to other countries. The developed or industrialized nations will not be immune to such food and water scarcity driven devastation. Ultimately it will consume them too. Overpopulation will become a serious threat to the viability of industrialized nations the moment cheap consumption of the world's resources can no longer be maintained. This moment may be much closer than we'd like to think.

A world where 8 to 10 billion people fiercely competing for diminishing resources will not be peaceful. Violent clashes or wars could ensue among and between regions and nations. The industrialized nations will use their militaries as they have done in Iraq recently, to ensure a steady supply of fossil fuels, minerals, and other non-renewable resources in vain efforts to sustain a life-style that, in the end is unsustainable. Industrial farming at present is made possible by massive overuse of fertilizers. Its sudden collapse will lead to mass starvation, famine and disease. Those who have little will certainly resort to violence, wars, and terrorism. Those who have the most to lose from such catastrophe will be the developed and industrialized nations. One just hopes that the leaders of these nations will pay equal attention to curbing the curse of population growth—and help other needy poor countries to do the same—as much as they should worry and take drastic measures to avoid global warming.

HUNDREDS OF THOUSANDS DYING

According to the first comprehensive study of the human impact of global warming, 300,000 people are already dying every year today due to global warming. The latest report comes from former UN Secretary General Kofi Annan's think-tank, "The Global Humanitarian Forum".

The report projects a bleak scenario of increasingly severe heat waves, floods, storms and forest fires that will be responsible for as many as 500,000 deaths a year by 2030, making it the greatest humanitarian challenge humanity faces.

Today, economic losses due to climate change amount to more than $125 billion a year which is more than all current world-aid. But the report says that the climate change could eventually cost $600 billion a year.

The report says further that civil unrest may also increase due to weather-related events. It warns, "Four billion people are vulnerable now and 500 million are now at extreme risk. Weather-related disasters…bring hunger, disease, poverty and lost livelihoods. They pose a threat to social and political stability."

If emissions are not brought under control within 25 years, the report makes clear, the following will occur:

- 310 million people will suffer adverse health consequences related to temperature increases.
- 20 million more people will fall into poverty.
- 75 million extra people will be displaced by climate change.

Water supplies will be most severely impacted by climate change, according to the same report. Shortages in the future are likely to threaten food production, reduce sanitation, hinder economic development, and damage ecosystems. It will cause more violent swings between floods and droughts. Hundreds of millions of people will become water stressed by climate change by the year 2030.

The study says it is impossible to be sure who will be displaced by 2030, but that tens of millions of people "will be driven from their homelands by weather disasters or gradual environmental degradations. The problem is most severe in Bangladesh, Egypt, Africa and coastal zones and forest areas."

It also states that the people most affected will be from poor and developing countries. Nearly 98% of the people seriously affected, 99% of all deaths from weather-related disasters and 90% of the total economic losses are now borne by developing countries. The populations most seriously at risk are sub-Saharan Africa, South Asia, the Middle East and the small island states of the Pacific. Ironically, the countries that have created global warming, the rich developed ones, at the moment bear few of its consequences.

The 12 countries that are least at risk are all industrially developed, save for one. They together have made close to $72 billion available to adapt themselves to climate change but have pledged only 400 million to help the poor countries. "This is less than one state in Germany that is spending on improving its flood defenses," says the report.

The study came as diplomats from 192 countries were preparing to meet for UN climate change talks aimed at reaching a global agreement to reduce greenhouse gas emissions in December, 2009 in Copenhagen. "The world is at crossroads. We can no longer afford to ignore the human impact of climate change. This is a call to the negotiators to come to the most ambitious agreement ever negotiated or to continue to accept mass starvation, mass sickness and mass migration on an ever growing scale," said Kofi Annan, who launched the report on May 29, 2009. Considering the conference's results, Kofi Annan must have been greatly disappointed.

Barbara Stocking, head of Oxfam said: "Adaptation efforts need to be scaled up dramatically. The world's poorest are the hardest hit, but they have done the least to cause it."

The data for the calculations for the report are based on data provided by the World Health Organization, The World Bank, the U.N., the Potsdam Institute for the Climate Impact Research, leading insurance companies, and Oxfam. Authors do agree that the estimates are uncertain and could be higher or lower. The paper was reviewed by 10 of the world's leading experts including Rajendra Pachauri, head of the UN's Intergovernmental Panel on Climate Change, Jeffrey Sachs, of Columbia University and Margareta Wahlstrom, assistant UN Secretary General for disaster risk reduction.

Nobel peace prize winner Wangari Maathai has said: "Climate change is life or death. It is the new global battlefield. It is being presented as if it is the problem of the developed world. But it is the developed world that has precipitated global warming."[21]

RISING HUNGER AND UNDERNOURISHMENT

According to U.N. Food and Agriculture Organization, there are 862 million people hungry and undernourished while a larger number, about 1.6 billion people are overweight and over nourished. Most of these people have excessive caloric intake, and suffer from exercise deprivation. The tragedy is close to 1 billion people worry about where their next meal would come from, while another 1.6 billion are concerned about eating too much.[22]

The majority of underfed and undernourished people are concentrated in the Indian subcontinent and sub-Saharan Africa, the regions where 1.4 billion and 800 million people live respectively. Twenty five years ago, China was also in similar situation but in the last quarter century, China has eliminated most of its hunger; India has made only limited progress. According to some reports, 40 % of India's children are undernourished. Though India produced much larger quantity of grains in that period, most of it was absorbed by the increase in its population while China's 'one child policy' helped overall in raising the consumption levels of its people.

Malnutrition takes a heavy toll on children under five during their rapid physical and mental development. In Bangladesh, almost half of all children under five are underweight and malnourished. In Nigeria, this number is 29%, while in Ethiopia, 47% of children are undernourished. These are Africa's most populous countries.[23]

Malnourishment and hunger are widespread in the poorest nation of the Western Hemisphere, Haiti. The entire country has been deforested. 3.3 million Haitians are food insecure and about 25% of the children are chronically malnourished like in sub-Saharan Africa. According to *World Focus*, the hunger is so widespread that significant section of the poor Haitians, especially the children are forced to eat cookies made from dirt.[24] In the aftermath of its catastrophic 2010 quake, the future of Haiti is uncertain.

Undernourishment begins at birth. Each year, according to a U.N. report, 20 million underweight infants are born to mothers who are also undernourished. The study shows that these children suffer from permanent damage resulting in "impaired immune systems, neurological damage, and stunted physical growth." As observed by David Barker of Britain's Southampton University, "60 percent of all new-borne in India would be in intensive care had they been born in California."[25]

Disease patterns reflect the widening gap between the rich and the poor. Infectious diseases such as Malaria, dysentery, respiratory infections, AIDS and measles are rampant among the poorest billion. Small and malnourished children are even more vulnerable to such infectious diseases. Millions of children die each year from water-borne diseases as clean drinking water is unavailable to a billion or more people.

In the developed countries of Europe and other regions such as Japan, populations are stable. In countries such as Russia, it is even declining. So development in any area of these countries benefits all the people. But in the poorer or developing countries, fast increasing populations absorb development, so the well-being of the people remains the same or even worsens as limited resources are now shared between more people. Literacy rates, education, healthcare, housing, clean water, and transportation: all these services are on the verge of breakdown in the certain developing countries. Food is already scarce. So imagine what will happen when to those who living in countries where population is projected to double by 2050 or earlier? The other billion people, who live in the countries where population is stable, are much better off, for the present.[26]

WATER AND AGRICULTURAL POLLUTION/DEAD ZONES

While millions are going hungry and malnourished around the globe, current industrial agriculture and factory farming is polluting the ground, river, and ocean water with high quantities of nitrogen, phosphorous, and other fertilizers.

The U.S. EPA estimated in 2007 that about 18% of the U.S. carbon footprint came from the agriculture—as it is practiced in the United States today—which is huge, as the U.S. is one of the largest polluters in the world. This doesn't even include the manufacture and use of pesticides and fertilizers, fuel and oil for tractors, equipment, trucking and shipping, electricity for lighting, heating and cooling, and huge emissions of carbon dioxide, methane, nitrous oxide and other green house gases. The EPA estimate additionally overlooks large portions of fuel, nitrous oxide (the synthetic nitrogen fertilizer, all of the CFCs and bromines, and most of the transport emissions involved in agriculture. When all of them are added up, U.S. agriculture's share of the carbon footprint will be at least 25% to 30%.[27]

High levels of nitrates and nitrites were found in 25 community wells that supplied drinking water to many Americans. More than 15 million people in 280 communities are drinking water contaminated with phosphorous or phosphates which stem mainly from industrial farming operations.

Huge quantities of nitrates and phosphorous fertilizer runoff flow into the rivers that ultimately end up in the ocean. When it reaches the ocean, river water rides up over the heavier salt water and algae blooms develop on the fertilizer rich water. When the algae die, the bacteria use up all of the oxygen in decomposing them. This creates an oxygen dead (hypoxic) zone. In 1995, scientists identified 60 such dead zones around the world.

Results published in 2008 identified 405 oceanic dead zones. The primary cause of dead zones is the extensively over-used highly soluble synthetic fertilizers to achieve maximum yields.[28] Dead zones mean all oceanic creatures, including fish, die off by millions due to lack of oxygen in these zones, some of which are gigantic. The Gulf of Mexico carries huge dead zones created by the flow of the Missouri, Mississippi, Rio Grande, Pearl, and a host of other rivers carrying with them enormous quantities of fertilizers, pesticides, and other chemicals used in farms all over their watersheds.

DISEASES AND EPIDEMICS

Numerous and rapidly evolving diseases and viruses are infecting increasing numbers of people around the world. West Nile, H1N1, Avian Flu, SARS, and HIV have emerged, threatening millions of people around the globe. Vast numbers of chemical pollutants present in the environment, food and water have made their way into humans. Cancer rates, heart diseases, asthma, bronchitis etc. are on the rise. For example, India has 2.5 million cancer patients. [29] Nowhere, are the damaging effects of air and water pollution more pronounced than in China. There, cancer deaths are alarmingly on the rise. Deaths from cancer now eclipse those from heart disease or cerebrovascular disease. Some 30 cities and 78 counties were surveyed there by the Ministry of Health. The survey released in 2007 found a rising cancer rate. Populations of some villages were decimated.[30]

Situated on the coast just north of Shanghai, Jiangsu Province is one of China's most prosperous provinces. It is also one of its most cancer-laden. It has only 5 % of country's population but has 12 % of country's cancer deaths. One river in that province was contaminated with 93 different carcinogens, most of them coming from untreated factory waste. Chinese people are paying a high price for progress. Each year China becomes richer, it also becomes sicker. [31]

The Environmental Working Group working with Commonweal, in July 2005, released an analysis of umbilical cord blood from 10 randomly selected newborns in U.S. hospitals. They found 287 chemicals in the blood. "Of the 287 chemicals we detected…we know that 180 cause cancers in humans or animals, 217 are toxic to the brain and nervous system, and 208 cause birth defects or abnormal development in animal tests." Infants are at a much higher risk.[32]

As reported by the WHO, an estimated 3 million people die worldwide annually from air pollution. In the United States, some 70,000 lives are lost to air pollution each year, compared with the country's 45,000 traffic fatalities.[33]

According to a U.K. research team, a surprising rise is observed in Alzheimer's and Parkinson's diseases as well as in motor neuron disease generally, in 10 industrial countries—6 in Europe plus Canada, the U.S., Japan, and Australia. England and Wales saw deaths from these brain diseases rise from 3,000 annually in the late 1970s to 10,000 annually in the late 1990s. Death rates from these diseases, mainly from Alzheimer's, more than tripled for men and doubled for women in 18 years' time. This increase in dementia is likely connected to a rise in the concentration of pesticides, car exhaust, polluted industrial effluents, and other pollutants in the environment. A Harvard School of Public Health study in 2006 found that long-term low-level exposure to pesticides raised the risk of developing Parkinson's disease by 70 percent.[34]

Scientists warn us about the danger of mercury, a potent neurotoxin that now permeates in the environment in practically all countries with coal-fired power plants and in many with gold mines. Gold mines release an estimated 290,000 pounds of mercury into the Amazon's ecosystem every year while coal-burning power plants emit nearly 100,000 pounds of mercury into the air in the United States alone. According to the U.S. EPA, "mercury from power plants settles over waterways, polluting rivers and lakes, and contaminating fish."[35] Malaria still claims more than a million lives annually, 89 percent of them in Africa. Millions more suffer from it most of their lives.[36]

Perhaps the greatest calamity to strike humanity since the smallpox decimation of Native Americans in the sixteenth century and the bubonic plague that decimated one fourth of the population of Europe during the fourteenth century is the scourge of AIDS and HIV today. Purportedly originating among monkeys in Africa and having been transmitted to the humans, this epidemic has claimed millions of lives so far in Africa, he Indian subcontinent, China, Europe, and the United States. Since it was identified in 1981, HIV has spread worldwide infecting some 86 million people by 2006. Of these, more than 40 million have perished so far. Sub-Saharan Africa has more than 25 million HIV-positive people, out of whom only 1 million receive anti-retroviral drugs. Africa has paid the highest price, with 25% of its people suffering from this disease today.[37]

The AIDS epidemic has created millions of orphans in its wake. It is estimated that Sub-Saharan Africa will have 18 million orphans—their parents succumbing to AIDS—by 2010. For some girls, the only option has been to resort to prostitution. With prostitution on the rise, the AIDS epidemic is also waxing. With HIV reaching epidemic proportion, Africa is losing millions of man-hours of useful work. Children are missing school. Africa's progress is being stunted. AIDS has threatened Africa's food security, its educational system, and its healthcare, drying up foreign investment. The epidemic is overwhelming African governments, creating failed states as we have seen in Sudan, Rwanda, or in the Democratic Republic of Congo.[38]

A former Special Envoy for HIV/AIDS in Africa, Stephen Lewis has opined that the infection trend can be reversed and it is possible to curb the epidemic, but it will take help from the international community. He said further that the failure to fully fund the Global Fund to fight AIDS, Tuberculosis, and Malaria, is "mass murder by complacency."[39]

According to the World Health Organization (WHO), approximately half of the world's population is at risk for malaria. Nearly, 250 million people are inflicted with malaria every year. The disease also takes heavy economic tolls in countries with high incidences of malaria, where as much as 1.3% of their growth rates are cut each year from their economies.[40]

RISING RESOURCE CONFLICTS

Rising population, declining land availability, and a shrinking water supply is leading to depletion of food supply. This is especially acute amongst the poor masses of the world. A combination of these scarcities is giving rise to resource conflicts worldwide.

The prime source of tension is decreasing access to land and other vital necessities of life stemming from the 70 million people added to world each year. This burgeoning world population has cut the grainland per person in half, from 0.23 hectares in 1950 to 0.10 hectares in 2007. These shrunken land holdings make it difficult for the world's farmers to feed themselves. It threatens their livelihoods, so their very survival. Hence tension within communities is mounting in these developing countries.[41]

One such area of spreading conflict is the Sahelian zone of Africa which has the fastest growing African population. In a long-standing conflict of more than 20 years between the Christian south and Muslim north, some 2 million people have died and over 4 million have been displaced in troubled Sudan. In the Darfur region of western Sudan, the recent conflict that began in 2003 illustrates the mounting tensions between two Muslim groups, the subsistence farmers and the camel herders. The government soldiers are backing Arab militias, who are committing a wholesale slaughter of black Sudanese in order to drive them off their land, forcing them out into refugee camps in neighboring Chad. By now, some 200,000 people have been killed in the conflict and an additional 250,000 have died of hunger and disease in the refugee camps.[42]

Nigeria is another case in point. There, 148 million people are crammed into an area not much larger than Texas. Overgrazing and overplowing are converting grassland and cropland into desert, forcing herders and farmers into a war for survival. As reported by Somini Sengupta in *The New York Times* in June 2004, "in recent years, as the desert has spread, trees have been felled and the populations of both herders and farmers have soared, the competition for land has only intensified." [43]

The great tragedy of modern times, the genocide in Rwanda in 1994 is a classic case of social tension and resource war emanating from mounting population pressure in a resource poor land. Rwanda's population was 2.4 million in 1950. It tripled to 7.5 million by 1993, making it the most densely populated country in Africa. With the growth in population, demand for firewood soared. By 1991, the demand was more than double the sustainable yield of local forests. Straw and other crop residues were used for cooking fuel as trees disappeared. The land fertility declined as organic matter supply to the soil decreased.[44] Rwanda's Minister of Agriculture and Environment (1990-92), James Gasana warned in 1990 that he did not see how Rwanda would reach 10 million inhabitants without social disorder "unless important progress in agriculture, as well as other sectors of the economy", were achieved. Gasana's warning turned out to be prophetic.[45]

With the loss of soil fertility, people's health too deteriorated. In the end, there wasn't enough food to go around. The population was half starved and desperate. It was now ready to explode into an inferno with a small spark. That spark came when on April 6, 1994, President Juvenal Habyarimana's plane approaching the capital Kigali was shot down. The president along with others was killed. The incident unleashed an organized attack by the Hutus leading to an estimated 800,000 deaths of Tutsis and moderate Hutus in just 100 days. In some villages, entire families were slaughtered so that no survivors were left to claim their land.[46]

Other countries are not immune from such tragedies. Social conflicts in India could dwarf Rwanda. The collision between ever rising human population and shrinking water supplies in India is inevitable with India's population projected to increase from1.2 billion in 2007 to 1.7 billion in 2050. Major social conflicts could erupt there if water scarcity and food insecurity drastically increases.[47]

The World Bank's 2008 report is most troubling. According to the survey, with zero economic growth in the developing world and rising food prices, as Michael Clare puts it, "you have a perfect recipe for unrelenting civil unrest and violence. The eruptions seen in 2008 and early 2009 will then be mere harbingers of a grim future in which, in a given week, any number of cities reel from riots and civil disturbances which could spread like multiple brushfires in a drought." [48]

Violent riots from rising unemployment, falling wages and rising prices have occurred in many countries. Longnan (China), Athens (Greece), Port-au-prince (Haiti), Santa Cruz (Bolivia), Riga (Latvia), Sofia (Bulgaria), Vilnius (Lithuania), and Vladivostok (Russia) have seen violent riots by the have-nots. Protests—though orderly due to heavy police presence—have been reported in Paris, Rome, Reykjavik, Zaragoza to Moscow, and Dublin over rising unemployment and falling wages.[49]

Food riots have now become a common occurrence around the world. In 2008, many regions of China witnessed economically-driven clashes. Such events are labeled "mass incidents" by Chinese authorities. They usually involve protests by workers over sudden plant closure, lost pay, or illegal land seizures. Many protests are against terrible air and water pollution as China is facing an immense pollution crisis.

International political conflicts and disagreements are on the rise among nations who share water from a common source, especially where populations are outgrowing the flow of rivers. Nowhere is this conflict more acute than between Egypt, Sudan, and Ethiopia in the Nile River valley. Agriculture in Egypt, where rains are scarce, is totally dependent on water from the Nile. It gets the lion's share of this water. But its population is projected to rise from the current 75 million to 121 million by 2050, thus requiring significantly more grain and water. Sudan too depends heavily on food produced with Nile River water. It is expected to grow from 39 million people at present to 73 million by 2050. Ethiopia controls 85 percent of the river's headwaters and is projected to expand from 83 million to 183 million. How would these countries cope with this problem? [50]

Syria, Turkey, and Iraq share the waters of the Tigris and Euphrates River system. Turkey controls the headwaters and is now building a massive project on Tigris River to increase the water used for irrigation and power. Syria and Iraq will need more water too as they are both projected to double their populations of 20 and 29 million respectively. They are greatly concerned about Turkey's forthcoming project.[51]

There is an uneasy arrangement among the five countries in the Aral Sea basin in Central Asia about sharing waters of the two rivers, Amu Darya and the Syr Darya, that drain into the sea. The demand in these countries—Kazakhstan, Tajikistan, Uzbekistan, Turkmenistan and Kyrgyzstan—already exceeds the current flow of the river by 25 percent. Turkmenistan which is located upstream on the Amu Darya is planning to develop another half-million hectares of irrigated agriculture. The region, racked by insurgencies, lacks the cooperation required to manage its scarce water resources. In addition, Afghanistan, controlling the headwaters of Amu Darya, plans to use some of the water for its development.[52]

A World Bank study has reported that Israel draws four times more water than the Palestinians from critical aquifers in the occupied West Bank. The Palestinians are allowed just one fifth of the water since the fifth consecutive drought.[53] The growing demand for water in water scarce Israel could be one of the veiled reasons behind the occupation of Palestine since the 1967 war.

Advancing deserts are displacing peoples and squeezing bigger populations into smaller geographic areas. The U.S. Dust Bowl displaced 3 million people; advancing deserts in China's dust bowl provinces could create millions of refugees.

Another potentially huge source of refugees would be the rising seas inundating vast coastal areas around the world. These numbers could eventually reach into hundreds of millions. At the Global Warming

Conference in Poznan, Poland, former U.S. vice-president Al Gore said that there will be 450 million climate refugees around the world.

Is the world witnessing just the beginning of the massive upheaval? Is human civilization on the brink? The recipe for the disaster is already in the making. These are just the early symptoms.

Reducing carbon emissions and stabilizing the climate is not optional; it is an urgent necessity, a life or death situation for hundreds of millions of people around the world, and for the survival of humanity itself.

CHAPTER 9
THE CURSE OF TECHNOLOGY & GLOBALIZATION

Modern technology owes ecology an apology
—Alan M. Eddison

AUTOMOBILES

The world round, every modern person aspires to own a car. In some developed countries and in suburb surrounded cities such as Los Angeles, owning a car has become a necessity. But in most developing countries including India, Brazil, Indonesia, Pakistan or even China, car ownership is a luxury and a symbol of status and wealth just like owning cows are an emblem of wealth and status in the Masai culture of Kenya and Tanzania,. So are we any different than these primitive tribes such as the Masai? They covet cows; we do cars! At least cows are a necessity: they form the lifeline of billions of people around the world as a source of milk, cooking-fuel, dung and hide, are beasts of burden plowing the farms of hundreds of millions of farmers around the world today and they don't pollute, when used sustainably. Meanwhile automobiles are the greatest polluting machines ever designed, in whose manufacture billions of tons of water, chemicals, paints, steel, plastics and rubber are guzzled and continue to gulp petroleum for the duration of their use. The ever increasing consumption of oil, and the resultant CO2 emissions from it, is a direct result of dramatic growth in oil-burning motor vehicles the world over.

Motor vehicles are fundamentally unchanged from a century ago. Surely, today's cars are vast improvements over the first Model T. But, the vast majority of them are still powered by an inherently inefficient technology. The four-stroke internal combustion engine was first developed by Nikolaus Otto in 1867 and was first incorporated into a car by Karl Benz in 1885. These ancient engines are still powered by petroleum, essentially the sole fuel for all worldwide mobility. Gasoline engines still waste more than two-thirds of the fuel they burn and directly emit 20 pounds of CO2 into the atmosphere for every gallon of fuel burned. Diesel engines perform a little better.[1]

America, several decades back, pioneered the motorization of human society and leads the world in auto ownership today, with more than one car per every licensed driver. Other nations are following its lead. Car ownership and use is on the rise everywhere. The desire for car is profound. An estimated 85% of the people of the world without cars revere and desire the same mobile lifestyle as the Americans. A poll conducted in 2004 by A. C. Nielsen found that more than 60 percent of residents in each of the seven fastest-growing nations, including India and China, aspire to own a car someday. Imagine, if each one of them owns a car, what will be the status of the air-quality and CO2 emissions in the world?

As global wealth grows, especially among the 2.4 billion people of China and India, so will auto ownership. Auto makers are focusing their marketing efforts in these emerging markets.[2] But before we look to the future, let us analyze some statistics regarding this human invention:

In 1900 only 4,192 passenger cars (and no trucks or buses) were built in the United States. At the start of the century, when America had only 8,000 cars and 144 miles of paved roads, an automobile break resembled that on a horse buggy: a padded stick pressed against a wheel. We all know that the world's human population is increasing dangerously. So is the world's car population. In 1970, there were 200 million cars in the world. As of 2001, about 450 million passenger cars traveled the streets and roads of the world. There were over 600 million motor vehicles in the world in 1997. With that trend continuing, the number of cars on Earth would double in the next 30 years.

> By September, 2003 the Bureau of Transportation Statistics reported there were 107 million US households, each with an average of 1.8 drivers and 1.9 cars, trucks, or sport utility vehicles. That corresponds to 204 million vehicles but only 191 million drivers.[3]

Marveling at these statistics, Marina Stasenko wrote in 2001:

> If an alien were to land on earth, the first thing he would notice about the "green planet" is the amount of cars there are on the streets. He would see that they come in all shapes and sizes, colors and are of many different brands. He would attempt to count the cars, but would get lost quickly because no brain can comprehend a number so large...
>
> It is estimated that there are approximately 600 million motor vehicles being driven on the streets of earth, the alien would be dumbfounded with this number. The biggest manufacturers are Japan, producing 8,056,000 cars in 1998, the US, with 5,554,000, and Germany with 5,348,000. With passing time, these numbers experience a rapid growth. For example, in 1960 Japan produced 185,000 cars, but by the end of the 1990s it was producing nearly 10 million a year. It is believed that at this growth rate, the number of cars on earth will double within the next 30 years. In this time scientists predict that traffic congestion will become 10 times worse than it is today. If in 2001 it is difficult to cross a major street without having to wait five minutes for the traffic to stop, how long will one have to wait in 2050?
>
> Today the alien will notice that with such a large number of cars and people on earth, there are approximately ten people

per car. But what will happen when he returns for a second trip in a hundred years? Will there be as many cars as people, or maybe by that time we'll have discovered a new method of transportation that is much more efficient and eco-friendly than the car? Only time can tell.

Richard Register points out following additional statistics in his 2006 book, *Ecocities*:

Today there are more than 600 million cars in the world and about sixty million new ones arriving from the assembly line each year.

Nearly half a million people worldwide and millions of mammals, amphibians, reptiles and a wide range of birds are killed every year by automobile accidents.

About a third of a million people die every year from air pollution, and cars are the single biggest source of this pollution worldwide.

When it rains or snows, water is polluted from oily, salty, and sooty runoff from roads. According to the EPA, this rivals sewage in damaging water resources.

The average American motorist uses about 600 gallons of gasoline a year for his car.

Owning a car is a costly affair. From its purchase, insurance, gasoline, repairs and maintenance, to registration, smog devices, accidents, and parking, cars are expensive. According to Runzheimer International, based on 2005 figures, in 2006, the total direct costs of operating a mid-sized average car in American cities was from $7,400 per car per year in Knoxville, Tennessee, to $11,844 in Detroit, with an average of about $9622. Multiplying that cost by the number of cars in the US (close to 160 million in 2006), the costs of operating cars climb to one trillion dollars, a staggering amount that could instead have gone into developing green energy, and ecocities for the people. Millions who were employed by the car industry could easily be employed by the green energy industries.

Imagine all the noise created by cars and trucks, especially people who unfortunately live near highways and roads.

The military-industrial complex builds its power partially on the manufacture and sale of cars, highways, and gasoline. Car manufacturers also make weapons: Chrysler makes tanks, GM makes military trucks, and oil companies make jet-fuel.

Cars are the weapons of choice in bombings in Iraq, Afghanistan, Beirut and Pakistan, killing many innocent victims.

One out of ten people on Earth owns a car; this is class-structure in society.

While 40 percent of the driving age adults in developed countries own cars, only one percent of those in developing countries do. North America, Europe, and Japan possess 16 percent of the world's population, but own 81 percent and manufacture 90 percent of the world's cars.

V. Shetty Pendakur of the University of British Columbia points out that around the developing world bicycles are the major or only vehicle for hundreds of millions of people. Countries such as India have a 7 to 1 ratio of bicycles to cars. He points out further that in India and other developing countries, the bicycle and its three-wheeled pedal-powered equivalent serve both as personal transportation and as a way of making a living. They are used to carry and transport people, carry loads, and make deliveries. In India, the average bicycle occupancy is 1.4 people per bike, which is higher than the car occupancy on many of America's highways and roads.[4]

Daniel Sperling and Deborah Gordon in their 2009 book, *Two Billion Cars*, project that the number of motorized vehicles around the globe—cars, trucks, buses, motorcycles, scooters, and electric bikes—will increase 3% annually. According to their projection, by 2020, a staggering two billion vehicles will populate the Earth, with at least half of them cars! Car growth will be slowest in the US with a less than 1% rise, Western Europe with a 1% to 2% rise, while China's and India's fleets are expected to grow by around 7% to 8% annually.[5] Growth in India will be rapid with Tata Motors' $2,500 cheap car 'Nano'—one wishes Tata Motors should rather mass produce affordable electric cars or at least hybrid cars—while growth in China is frantic and escalating with increasing affluence.

In an amazingly short period of time, China has skyrocketed to the number one world position in auto sales. It overtook the United States by selling 13.5 million vehicles in 2009 and became the world's largest market, according to *Xinhua News Agency*. The U.S. sold 10.4 million cars and light trucks in 2009. The Chinese tally includes 650,000 heavy trucks but without those sales, the Chinese figure is still higher. China's urban roadway network is expanding simultaneously at amazing speed to accommodate the burgeoning auto vehicle population. Between 1990 and 2003, it more than doubled in length from 60,000 to 130,000 miles. By 2004, more than 21,000 miles of high-speed motorways crisscrossed the country. By 2020, this network of high-speed roads is expected to double, achieving a length on par with the U.S. Interstate Highway System.

By 2020, China will likely have 150 million cars, trucks, and buses—an almost six fold increase over 2004. By 2030, China's vehicle population is projected to surpass that of the United States and will reach 500 to 600 million by 2050. This doesn't even include motorcycles and rural vehicles.[6]

Today, cars seem to have taken over industrial civilization just like corporations have. City after city around the globe, wherever one goes, cars, trucks, and their ensuing traffic jams abound. Hundreds of thousands of man-hours are wasted sitting in traffic which is an everyday occurrence. Many cities, especially in the United States, have been built around a car culture. They are structured for cars, not humans! Shopping centers in the US basically serve car-riders, not pedestrians or bicycle riders nor even bus or train mass transit commuters. If you don't own a car, it will be difficult for you to go to shopping malls. Cities like Los Angeles, Phoenix, or Houston developed with car-culture. There are masses of suburbs scattered with small commercial districts; they do not easily serve mass transit riders. I live in the suburb of Los Angeles and my movements would be quite restricted without a car.

Cars are already one of the largest sources of greenhouse gases today. Imagine when China surpasses the US in number of cars! Add India with its increasing number of auto vehicles and we should not forget the ambitions of the rest of the world's developing middle class population.

Within car and truck manufacturing, millions of tons of steel, plastics, rubber and paints, and billions of gallons of valuable water are consumed. Each vehicle will then consume additional gasoline. Even supposing the world succeeds in replacing gasoline with other renewable sources to power these vehicles such as electricity or hydrogen fuel-cells, manufacturing these autos themselves diminishes valuable non-renewable resources.

It is no question that cars provide with a useful and pleasurable service: luxurious car-rides have enabled us to enjoy beautiful scenery and given humans the freedom to travel fast and far. But the big question is, overall, have cars been beneficial to human civilization or have they done irreparable harm to us, to our environment, to other species, to mother Earth? Are we any happier today than say one and a quarter century ago when there were no cars, and we humans used to travel by horses, and later by trains?

If we really soul-search, the answer is obvious. The mass production of cars has not made us any happier. Setting aside selfish individual pleasures and luxury for the few, in fact cars have brought upon human civilization—90 percent of which do not even own cars—the destruction of a once beautiful environment, and the triggering of global warming that has brought this planet to the brink of a disaster the likes of which it has never faced before in its entire history.

Now that the Genie is out of the bottle, it will be impossible to stop the manufacture and ownership of cars. But at least we should totally replace gasoline cars with renewable energy powered vehicles. Our cities should be restructured to serve pedestrians, mass transit users, and bicycle riders rather than car owners. If the planet Earth is to survive and stay beautiful, shouldn't the number of cars in the world be minimized, and just like carbon emissions, each country be allocated a small fractional number of cars based on its population size?

Here, a big lesson should be learned by humans. Before creating a new gadget or technology, we should thoroughly examine its long-term impact on nature, on humans and on the environment. Some technologies are a curse rather than a blessing for humanity. Nuclear technology is yet another one that ranks high on this list.

NUCLEAR TECHNOLOGY

Besides the invention of cars, nuclear technology is yet another invention by humans in their quest for dominance over others, that has done irreparable harm to the environment and to all the living creatures on Earth.

Granted, nuclear energy has certain advantages. It is 'clean' energy as it emits no carbon dioxide. Once built and operational, it serves us for many years, some 30 to 40 years. But few people realize the fatal flaws inherent in nuclear power: cost, waste, safety, security, and proliferation.

Building new nuclear reactors whether in the US, India, or China is prohibitively expensive due to its high capital costs and long construction times—unless they are heavily subsidized by taxpayers. Around 2006, building a 1,500 megawatt nuclear power plant was estimated to cost in the US, $2-4 billion. As of late 2008, that figure had climbed past $7 billion.[7]

These costs will be less in countries like India or China. Yet, even reduced costs are still very high for these countries. Additionally, billions of dollars are required to maintain nuclear power plants and they require many years of construction before producing electricity. Instead of spending billions in building nuclear plants in any country, it is much better, cheaper, and faster to channel that capital to other alternative sources of energy such as wind or solar power.

Unlike popular belief, nuclear power is not a clean energy source. In fact, it produces both low and high-level radioactive waste that remains dangerous for several hundred thousand years. Generated throughout all phases of the fuel cycle, this waste poses a serious danger to human health.

To understand the futility of nuclear energy, we need not look beyond the United States. In the United States, at present over 2,000 metric tons of high-level radioactive waste and 12 million cubic feet of low level radioactive waste are produced annually by 103 operating reactors. To date, no country in the world has found a solution for this dangerous waste. Constructing new nuclear plants means more of this waste with nowhere for it to go. The waste will be too dangerous to keep lying around or near any place.[8]

Additionally, Uranium must be mined and enriched to serve as a fuel for nuclear plants. Both these procedures result in radioactive contamination of the environment and risks to public health. Most uranium mining in the US was done in Utah, New Mexico, Colorado, Arizona, and Wyoming—areas that are still suffering from its adverse effects. In uranium mining, uranium ore is physically removed or it is extracted in a newer process known as in situ leaching. Conventional mining has caused the workers to inhale dust and radon which has resulted in high rates of lung cancer and other respiratory diseases; both types of mining have contaminated groundwater.

Uranium metal, when conventionally mined must be separated from the rock in a process called milling, which forms large radon-contaminated piles of material known as tailings. Often, these tailings are abandoned aboveground. For instance, twelve million tons of tailings are piled along the Colorado River near Moab, Utah, threatening communities downstream. In the case of situ leaching, a solution is pumped into the ground to dissolve uranium. When the mixture is returned to the surface, the uranium is separated and the remaining waste water is evaporated in slurry pools. After this, the uranium is shipped to a facility for enrichment, a process that concentrates the amount of fissile uranium. The enrichment generates toxic hydrogen fluoride gas and large quantities of depleted uranium. The depleted uranium poses a threat to public health and must be disposed of in a geologic repository.

Over 54,000 metric tons of irradiated fuel has accumulated at the locations of commercial nuclear reactors in the United States. Though there are several proposals to dispose of this highly radioactive waste, at such locations as Yucca Mountain, none of them have been satisfactory.[9]

In their recent incisive analysis, "The Nuclear Illusion," Armory B. Lovins, Imran Sheikh, and Alex Markevich price the cost of electricity from nuclear power plant at 14 cents per kilowatt hour and that from a wind farm at 7 cents per kilowatt hour.[10] This includes the costs of fuel, capital, operations, maintenance, transmission, and distribution. Beyond this, there are other costs, such as disposing the waste, insuring plants against accidents, and decommissioning the plants when they wear out. So if all the costs of generating nuclear electricity are counted in the price to a country or to its consumers, nuclear power is dead in the water.

There are 439 operating nuclear reactors worldwide. Their average age generously could be counted as 40 years. After that, they have to be decommissioned at huge costs.

But first, let's look at the mounting costs of US nuclear waste problems. The United States leads the world with 101,000 megawatts of nuclear-generating capacity (compared to 63,000 megawatts in second-ranked France). The US government plans to store nuclear waste from its 104 nuclear power reactors in the Yucca Mountain nuclear waste repository, about 90 miles from Las Vegas, Nevada. The original estimate of the cost for this was $58 billion in 2001. Then it climbed to $96 billion by 2008. This comes to a staggering $923 million per reactor or almost a billion dollars each.[11]

In the United States, nuclear power plants currently operate at 64 sites in 31 states.[12] It should be a top priority of the US government to ensure the protection of these plants considering the devastation that would result from a terrorist attack. Unfortunately, Public Citizen reports that the US Nuclear Regulatory Commission (NRC) and nuclear industry are leaving plants vulnerable. India weathers multiple terrorist attacks per year, perhaps more than any other country except Iraq, Pakistan, and Afghanistan. With several more nuclear power plants scattered across India, the possibility of terrorist attacks poses much greater threat. The safety of nuclear power plants becomes a great concern for every country that follows this unadvisable route.

Another major risk of nuclear plants is a possibility of a catastrophe like Three-mile Island in the USA or, even worse, like the Chernobyl accident of 1987 in the Ukraine, then a part of the USSR.

There are fewer and fewer nuclear power plants being built worldwide. Smart leaders in various countries are realizing that nuclear energy, though appearing clean, comes with huge baggage, and is not worth the enormous expenditure and uncertain future for nuclear waste. No country, including France or the United States, has found a sensible way to dispose of the nuclear waste.

Thankfully, more and more wind or solar farms are being built worldwide. The reason for this gap is simple: wind or solar farms are much more attractive and beneficial. They yield more energy, more jobs, and more carbon reduction per dollar invested than nuclear plants; and, they are totally safe.

According to a new analysis by Public citizen based on the work of governments, universities, and other organizations in the United States, Europe, and Japan, it is indeed economically and technically feasible for a diverse mix of currently available renewable technologies to completely fulfill US energy requirements over the coming decades. Clean, safe renewable energy sources—solar, wind, advanced hydroelectric, some types of biomass, geothermal—can reliably generate as much energy as conventional fuels without significant carbon footprints, destructive mining, or the production of radioactive waste.[13]

With nuclear genie now out of the bottle, there is the huge problem of nuclear weapons and its proliferation. Now besides the United States, Russia, Britain, France, China, India, Pakistan, Israel, and North Korea too possess them.

COMPUTER TECHNOLOGY

The computer has opened up countless new frontiers for humanity and combined with the information technology of the internet, they are fantastic developments indeed. Though computers are highly useful items for the modern world, the fact remains that with technology comes colossal garbage problems of which we must take notice. We now have millions of computers around the world. But let's see what happens when our computers become electronic junk. For example, United States alone sends out 100 million junk computers to other countries as garbage per year, mostly to China. These computers contain hazardous materials such as mercury, cadmium, lead, and PVC plastics. Most of it goes to southern China where in one village, a huge computer and other electronic garbage dump is created. There, hundreds of poor Chinese look through this hazardous garbage trying to salvage copper and other materials for little pay. As a result, most of them suffer from dire health problems. There, 7 out of 10 kids have high lead contents in their bodies. This area has highest cancer rate in the world.[14] We must realize that technology doesn't come without a price. Technology and its exported waste is covered in more details in chapter-5.

THE GLOBALIZATION

Economic advance is not the same thing as human progress.
—John Clapham, A Concise Economic History of Britain, 1957

In July of 1944, the United Nation's Monetary and Financial Conference was held at Mt. Washington Hotel, Bretton Woods, New Hampshire. The world was in the throes of the Second World War, with Mussolini overthrown, and Hitler would last another ten months. Allies had landed at Normandy, the war also was to rage in the Far East, and Japan was not to surrender for another thirteen months. It would be another year before the UN Charter would be drafted. The economic leaders who gathered quietly here were looking beyond the end of this war hoping the world to be united in peace and prosperity. Their goal was to establish the institutions that would fulfill that vision.

The Bretton Woods Conference did give shape to institutions that molded the post-war global economic activity since that time, but experts believe that plans for these institutions go back still further, to the 1930s and to the U.S. Council on Foreign Relations. The council was the meeting ground for powerful members of the U.S. corporate and foreign policy establishment, and though it styled itself as a forum for expressing opposing views, a creator of ideas and leaders with this outlook unified in their vision of world-economy controlled, it was dominated by U.S. corporate interests.

Early on, members of this elite group figured that, at a minimum, the U.S. national interest necessitated free access to the raw materials and markets of the Western Hemisphere, the Far East, and the British Empire. On July 24, 1941, a council memorandum conceptualized the grand areas: the part of the world that the United States would need to dominate militarily and economically to ensure raw materials for its industries. The council also recommended the creation of global financial institutions for "stabilizing currencies and facilitating programs of capital investment for constructive undertakings in underdeveloped and backward countries."[15]

After three years, at the opening session at Bretton Woods, then U.S. Secretary of State and president of the council, Henry Morgenthau, read a welcoming message from President Roosevelt and gave his own opening speech, setting the tone and the spirit of the conference. He envisioned "the creation of a dynamic world economy in which the peoples of every nation will be able to realize their potentialities in peace and enjoy increasingly the fruits of material progress on an Earth infinitely blessed with natural riches." He called upon the participants to embrace the "elementary economic axiom...that there are no fixed limits to prosperity. It is not a finite substance to be diminished by division."

Thus, Morganthau set forth some of the assumptions of the economic paradigm that guided the work of the architects of the Bretton Woods system. Many of these assumptions were reasonably valid, as David Korten, a Harvard economist, points out. But two of the most important ones were deeply flawed. The first faulty assumption was that everyone would benefit from enhanced world trade and economic growth. The second one was there was no limit to economic growth, that we are not constrained by the planet.

At the end of this historic conference, The World Bank and International Monetary Fund (IMF) were created and the groundwork had been laid that finally culminated in GATT. Over the years, these institutions faithfully promoted their mandates of economic growth and globalization. The IMF and the World Bank, through its Structural Adjustment Programs (SAPs), have pressured country after country of the south to open their borders for Western goods and change their economies from self-sufficiency to export production.

When one looks back after some 55 years, the Bretton Woods institutions have fulfilled their mandate: there has been a fivefold expansion of global-economic growth, international trade has multiplied twelve times, and foreign direct investment has been increasing at two to three times the rate of trade expansion. Tragically, though these institutions have met their goals, they have failed in their purpose. There are more poor people around the world now than ever before. The gap between rich and poor countries has accelerated around the world, and the ecosystems of the planet are under extreme stress and deteriorating at an alarming speed. Well, globalization has served only one segment of the global society, the rich powerful companies and those who control them.

Today, there persists a huge misunderstanding regarding globalization. Political leaders, businessmen, academicians, economists, educated professionals, well-known journalists, and people belonging to upper economic stratum of societies around the world misguidedly believe that the globalization is beneficial for the world and is the "way of the future." It is unstoppable and the world is far better off with the globalized economy. Many are wrongly convinced that it gives employment to the world's poor; otherwise they would be starving.

Nothing could be farther from the truth. Part of this misconception is due to the colossal amount of propaganda perpetrated by the western powers, by the developed nations, and by their mass-medias all of whom have vested interests. In globalization, it is the developed nations who benefit the most. It is the rich nations and the rich, among both wealthy and poor nations, who mainly reap the fruits of a globalized economy.

For example, after NAFTA was passed, Mexico was forced to open its market to US goods. Soon, the United States dumped millions of tons of cheap, highly subsidized (below actual cost) corn—which is a staple food in Mexico—into Mexico. This forced millions of small Mexican corn farmers to go out of business. They lost their livelihoods and were forced to flock to already overcrowded cities to seek employment. This is but one of countless examples around the world of what globalized economy does to small farmers and others.

A few years ago, the city of Cochabamba, under globalization, allowed an American company, the Bechtel Corporation, to take over its water system. In a short time after this take over, Bechtel raised the price of water two to three fold. The poor people of Cochabamba could not afford to pay such a high price for the water which they always got cheaply. Thousands of them took to the streets. Violent clashes between the Western controlled government and the people took place. Finally, Bechtel Corp. was forced to quit and the water system was returned to the local authority, prices came down and people of Cochabamba won a hard fought victory.

In a globalized capitalist economy, the goal is growth, growth and more growth: growth of business and capital, growth of manufactured goods, and growth of raw material extraction. In the process, the ecosystems of many countries around the globe are trampled upon. But how long can our planet Earth, which is already saturated with destructive pollution, bear it? There is a limit to unbridled growth. The Earth has limited resources and its pollution absorbing capacity has already been reached. The signs are everywhere as we see more living species varieties going extinct every year.

In a sobering study published in the Proceedings of the (U.S.) National Academy of Science, a research team has tried to calculate the environmental costs of economic globalization since 1961 as expressed in terms of climate change, deforestation, ozone depletion, over-fishing, mangrove conversion, and agricultural expansion. After adjusting for relative cost burdens, they found that the richest countries, by their activities, had generated 42 percent of environmental degradation across the world, while shouldering only 3 percent of the resulting costs.[16]

Corporations seeking, through globalized trade, to profit by stimulating and feeding our insatiable appetite for consumer goods have trampled upon the livelihoods and ways of life of indigenous rainforest dwellers, Mexican farmers, Thai factory workers, and African miners— just to name a few.

Mahatma Gandhi had said: "There is a sufficiency in the world for man's need but not enough for man's greed". How visionary his words were! There isn't enough in this world for the greed of the multinationals.

Globalization continues as long as huge multinationals keep making profits and thus enriching the pockets of their CEOs, their stock-holders, and the coffers of their mother country, most likely a western developed nation. In the meantime, the poor working peoples of the third world who produce these goods with their sweat and blood stay poor and they don't even make a living wage. Is this a fair and justifiable system? Who needs such an unjust system? Pro-globalization 'experts' say it is an equal playing field for all countries of the world. But how can that be? How can tiny poor Honduras compete with the giant, wealthy United States or poor Kenya keep up with advanced Japan or powerful China? It is certainly not an equal playing field.

No wonder there were huge protests in Seattle, Washington in 1999, at the WTO Summit. Activists, NGOs, unions, and farmers from around the world descended there to express their disgust at such a system where the poor are exploited beyond limits. The world's average citizen and the poor had finally caught up with the globalizers and their nations. They said, "Enough is enough. We don't need this globalization"! Luckily, the developing nations of the world have realized. India, China, Brazil, and South Africa with others are fighting back, forcing changes in the WTO structure. The NGOs around the world are fighting back even harder. They want to do away with the WTO altogether as it is highly undemocratic in its structure. Fortunately for the world, they are succeeding. The WTO is in disarray, stopped in its tracks. Wherever they hold their meetings, mass protests are taking place. People have awaken it seems.

What are the implications of this arrangement of free trade? That communities and nations abandon self-reliance and embrace dependence. That all nations abandon their capacity to produce all items and concentrate only on a few. We export what we produce and import what we need. Kenya and Egypt for example were once fully self-sufficient for their food supply. Today, thanks to WTO mainly, they are highly dependent for a major percentage of their food on international import, a dangerous development for any country. Now there are many more in this category.

"Bigger is better". "Competition is superior to cooperation". "The world is interconnected". "Material self-interest drives humanity". "Dependence is better than independence". These are the pillars of a 'free trade' that is far from free! We give up sovereignty over our affairs in return for a promise of more jobs, more goods, and a better standard of living.

What we are witnessing in current globalization is Corporate Colonialism. In the old times, the European powers colonized other nations, exploited their resources and cheap labor by the power of their superior military and naval forces. They occupied other nations and ruled over them in order to exploit them. In today's Corporate Colonialism, they don't have to occupy other nations militarily. They now have a devised system called the WTO, which through globalization, through its institutions of the World Bank and International Monetary Fund, enable them to exploit other poor and developing countries' resources and cheap labor. Additionally, they have a huge market for their mass-produced goods in these poorer countries.

Once again, Mahatma Gandhi's quote as relevant then as it is today: "What we need is not mass-production but production by the masses." How right he was! Then everybody will be employed and self-sufficient. He had also promoted: "Local production for local consumption."

Under a globalized economy, goods produced in China, Japan, South Korea, and India are shipped over ocean to the United States or Europe, thousands of miles away. Imagine the amounts of oil burned, CO_2 emitted, and man-hour wasted amid this unnecessary intercontinental transportation where thousands of ships, planes, and trucks roam the world's oceans, roads, and skies ferrying goods which can (and should) be produced and consumed locally. In addition, local peoples should get the jobs they so rightly deserve. Today, if a corporation doesn't like manufacturing in one country for whatever reasons, they will just pack up and move to another country which gives them better terms. They could care less for those who lose their jobs in this transfer. Their loyalty is not to the employees but to their shareholders and profits.

Globalization needs to be brought under control quickly or needs to be dismantled totally if we don't want to see virtually all nations of the world end up subservient to corporate control, a new form of an ancient economic system known as feudalism.

Under the globalized world, with multinational corporations controlling our political, social, and everyday lives—especially in the developed countries of Europe, America, and Japan, and increasingly so in the developing countries like India and China—we humans have become like robots, or clones. 85 percent of us are working for somebody else. Day in, day out; Monday through Friday; 9 to 5, we are rushing to work and then back home to watch TV where corporations brainwash and condition our and our children's minds, molding our very opinions. We have no time to relax, to enjoy our kids growing up, to appreciate the beauty of nature, or to dwell on the real values of life. We are rushing, rushing, rushing...but for what.

To ensure the survival of humanity with humane values such as compassion, love, selflessness, and appreciation of nature's immense beauty, we must slow down, and synchronize with the more subtle rhythms of the natural world. In our cyber-cell-phone-iPod-fax-phone-TV-car-airplane and satellite world, we have virtually become slaves of this high-speed technical reality where the values and concerns of nature tend to become opaque to our consciousness; we have lost our humane values; we have lost sight, the purpose of life. Are we living to work or are we working to live? Is our work harming other humans, ecosystems, and nature, or does it sustain us, nurture the environment, and help the other inhabitants of our planet flourish? These are some fundamental questions we must ask about our work on this planet.

It is not technical progress that is important; it is our inner happiness, the advancement in human values such as care for other humans, animal and plant species—nature as a whole—the preservation of the environment, and the maintenance of peace and tranquility around the planet that is of prime significance. Technological progress is not going to bring happiness to us humans; rather, it is our values as decent human beings respecting our fellow man and the nature around us that will someday make this wonderful planet that we inhabit a heaven on earth. We are at a crossroads; by our actions, we are either going to destroy this planet with its beautiful forests and living things, along with ourselves, or by our wise and timely actions, we will create an Earth where all living creatures and nature are respected, protected, and allowed to flourish. The choice is ours.

SECTION IV
THE SUSTAINABLE WAYS

CHAPTER 10
WHAT WE THE PEOPLE CAN DO

Waste not the smallest thing created, for grains of sand make mountains, and atomies infinity.
—E. Knight

Nothing will benefit human health and increase the chances for survival of life on Earth as much as the evolution to a vegetarian diet.
—Albert Einstein

We must face the prospects of changing our basic ways of living. This change will either be made by our own initiative in a planned way, or forced upon us with chaos and suffering by the inexorable laws of nature.
—Jimmy Carter

Most of us are in the habit of wondering what difference my little steps will or could make to help the planet. This is misguided thinking. Every little step we take or don't take has a definite impact on the environment. When these little steps are multiplied by millions, the effect is a million fold. So how can we ever underestimate the power of an individual act?

There is much we can do to help our mother Earth:

We can own only one car per family, ride the bus, carpool, drive less but walk more, ride bicycles, shut lights, use fluorescent bulbs, have wind mills installed, have solar powered house, insulate our houses, lower our thermostats, avoid air-conditioners, be vegetarian or eat less meat, eat more natural rather than processed food, grow vegetables and fruits in our gardens, grow vegetables on terraces, use less water, don't run water while brushing or shaving, refuse to use plastic bags or bottled water, use less plastics, avoid fast foods, fly less, have no lawns and use no fertilizers nor pesticides or weed killers, avoid using insect killers, don't use paper dishes or plastic cups, have old items repaired rather than throwing them away and buying new, waste no paper, recycle, don't take long showers, advise others about green economy and being green, write to newspapers about being green, support and form other green groups, teach our children about being green, hold green seminars and teach-ins, support green candidates for political office, invest in green industries, and boycott non-green and enemies of green industries.

The following table gives us some idea of which of our activities contribute the maximum and which ones add the minimum of carbon dioxide emissions. Based on that, we can determine what actions each one of us can take.

The percentage of total U.S. individual/household energy consumed by end use, ranked in order of magnitude:

END USE PERCENT

Transportation

Private cars/vehicles	38.6
Air travel	3.4
Mass transportation & others	1.4

Subtotal	43.4
In-home uses	
Home heating*	18.8
Air conditioning	6.2
Total on heating/cooling	25.00
Water heating	6.5
Lighting	6.1
Refrigeration & freezing	4.3
Electric (heating elements, small appliances and Small motors)	3.9
Clothes washing/drying	2.5
Color TVs	2.5
Cooking	1.5
Computers	0.6
Propane and natural gas (Swimming pool heaters, grills, and lamps)	0.5
Dishwashers	0.2
Other	3.0

Subtotal   56.6

TOTAL   100.0

*Hot water for "Clothes washing" is included under "Water heating."
Source: Environment Magazine, September/October, 2008, p.16

SEVEN IMPORTANT STEPS WE CAN TAKE:

It is obvious from the above table that the best step each one of us can take to reduce carbon emissions is to get rid of our low-gas-mileage car or vehicle and start driving one with better fuel economy. There are plenty of choices: high-gas-mileage hybrids such as the Toyota-Prius, Honda-Insight, Nissan-Altima Hybrid, other non-hybrids with good fuel economy such as the Toyota-Corolla, Honda-Civic or similar cars, electric cars are also slowly emerging. Take public transportation as often as you can. Carpool whenever possible. Combine several trips for errands into one so. Keep tire pressure correctly inflated. Whenever possible, use a bicycle (it's also healthier).

The second most important action we can take is to reduce our home heating emissions by lowering our thermostat, especially at night and turning it off whenever possible. Have the attic of your house insulated along with your doors and windows. This will save a lot on your heating bill too.

The third most important step we can take is to reduce our water-heater temperature from 140 °F to 120 °F and shut it off when we are out of town. The best possible course would be to do away with the regular water heater altogether and have solar water heater installed. You will have free hot water for many years and will be proud of your contribution to save the planet.

The fourth most important step is to turn off air-conditioning whenever possible and raise the room temperature to 68-70 °F.

This step is about lighting in our home. Replace all the burnt-out regular incandescent light bulbs with energy saving compact fluorescent bulbs (CFL). The regular incandescent bulb gives off 90% heat and only 10% light from the electricity it uses. The CFL will give the same amount of light with only one a quarter the power used. In other words, replacing 100 watt regular light bulb with 25 watt CFL will give the same amount of light with only one quarter the amount of electricity used. That means only one fourth of the amount of CO_2 will be emitted from the coal-fired power plant. Jeffrey Langholz and Kelly Turner in their excellent book *You Can Prevent Global Warming*, point out that if every household in America replaced its next burnt-out light bulb with a CFL, more than 13 million pounds of CO_2 emissions could be avoided. This is equal to taking 1.2 million cars off the road for an entire year.[1]

The refrigerator is massive user of electricity in an average home. Raise the cooling temperature in the refrigerator enough to keep the food fresh yet use less energy. When it comes time to replace, always buy the highest energy saving model available in the market. In Europe, Greenfreeze has developed an environmentally friendly refrigerator that uses 38 percent less energy than a comparable one using Hydrochlorofluorocarbons (HCFCs). Check if they are available here in the U.S. or purchase the most energy efficient brand available.[2] The same applies to the washer and dryer. Always purchase the most energy efficient models available. Some highly motivated people altogether avoid using the dryer by drying their clothes in the backyard in the sun. That saves lot of energy. This is the way our clothes were dried when I was growing up in India. We had, at the time, no washers or dryers. This not only helps CO_2 emissions reduction, but also saves money.

Choose all your home appliances—refrigerators, water heaters, TVs, cooking ovens, toasters, lamps, computers, printers etc. for their energy efficiency.

Install a house meter in your home. This device enables you to see in a portable digital console how much energy you are using and its cost during the day, week or month. You can otherwise use plug-in meter that allows you to measure energy use by any appliance in your home.

There are other steps we all can take to reduce global warming and help the planet:

To produce one pound of meat, it takes 10 to 20 pounds of vegetables or grains. This is not for everyone. But those who are highly motivated to help the planet, become vegetarian. Avoid meat in your diet. As proven by medical science, the vegetarian diet is much healthier than non-vegetarian one. People who are vegetarian have better chances to be healthier and to live longer. Of course, everyone cannot become vegetarian. But those who can, this will be a terrific step to help reduce CO2 emissions. Or practice one meatless day per week by joining the "Meatless Monday Campaign." Watch Michael Pollan's documentary "Food Inc." It offers a stomach-turning look at factory farming and slaughterhouses in America. In the video, the scientists tell us that if all Americans switched from eating chickens and pigs to eating grains, beans, and vegetables just one day per week, that would curb global warming to the same extent as everyone in the U.S. shifting to Toyota Hybrids (a weekly equivalent of consuming 12 billion fewer gallons of gasoline). If all of us stopped eating animals completely and shifted to vegetarian diets, it would save 84 billion gallons of gas per week. Additionally, we will feel healthier and live longer.[3]

The average food item on our plate in America travels about 1200 to 1500 miles before it lands in our plate. Imagine how much energy is wasted in its packing, transportation, and refrigeration besides millions of man-hours lost in its transportation. As a result, the fruits and vegetables you buy are at least one week old. This is due to corporate control of our food. Whenever possible, buy your fruits and vegetables from local suppliers, farmers markets, or grow your own.

Buy organic produce. Enormous quantities of fertilizers, pesticides, and herbicides are poured into our soil on large farms, all of which are based on fossil fuels. They all add to climate change and create "dead zones" in the oceans where millions of fish and other sea creatures die due to a lack of oxygen. The best way to fight this is to buy organic from local farmers markets or from Community Supported Agriculture (CSA) Farms; there are several hundred in the United States; they use manure, and other organic fertilizers to grow food. Buy from them and buy local. By buying local, you are supporting the local economy, not some multinational company that buys from a foreign country or which may even be located in a foreign country. In addition, locally grown food and locally made items are fresh, travel less, and spend less CO_2 emitting energy. Large corporations leave bigger carbon footprints on the planet. By supporting smaller businesses, you are also reducing your own carbon footprint.

Avoid using bottled water. Bottled water is the biggest scam perpetrated by multinational corporations. According to reliable reports, bottled water is no safer than the tap water you get in the United States and most Western countries. Chemicals from the plastic of bottled water also leak into the water that you drink. In addition, the plastic bottles are made from petroleum, a major greenhouse gas emitter. Billions of these bottles are, once used, discarded and pollute our environment.

Whenever possible, avoid using plastic bags. They are big polluter of the environment and the ocean where they find their way. Countless sea creatures die from swallowing them.

There is a huge continental United States' size floating plastic garbage in the Pacific Ocean consisting of billions of plastic bags, plastic bottles, and a host of other plastic items. Use paper bags whenever you go to the grocery store or, even better, carry your own cloths bags and use them again and again.

Grow your own vegetables and fruits organically. This is not possible for everyone but those who can and are really motivated should try this. You will save money, will get delicious vegetables and will immensely benefit from the exercise and pleasure of gardening in your backyard. Many books are available that teach you about this.

Avoid eating fast food. Fast food is one of the most damaging phenomena that is so prevalent in America and now in other countries, unfortunately. It is highly damaging both to the world environment and to human health. It has drastically increased heart disease and obesity in America. The beef and chicken in billions of burgers and other items is factory-produced at enormous costs to the environment. Over-packaging in the form of both paper and plastic pollute the environment and accelerate deforestation. Also avoid canned foods.

Avoid using paper dishes, cups or plastic items. They are conveniences that we can live without. They pollute the environment and accelerate deforestation.

Avoid using packaged goods and disposable items as much as possible.

Avoid using any "weed killer" chemical. They are poisonous no matter what manufacturers tell you and are terrible soil polluters. Also avoid using insect, cockroach, rat or ant poison unless they are non-toxic and biodegradable.

Trees are big absorbers of carbon. Always plant trees wherever possible. Never cut any tree unless there is no choice.

Never dispose off used household paints or other chemicals in the garbage. They should be dropped off at the appropriate collection centers.

Do not buy new paper pads. Cut and make blank discarded papers into small size scratch-paper pads. This could be for your home as well as for your office.

Whenever possible, instead of paper towel, use cloth towel or napkin, wash it and use it again and again. Remember, paper of any kind adds to deforestation worldwide.

SOCIAL ACTIVISM:

Socially, we can be active and help other people realize the importance of saving our planet. Encourage your friends and neighbors to be environmentally aware and persuade them to take similar "Green Steps" and to live "Green".

Form your own local group, meeting once a month, discussing environmental issues, individual problems, experiences and achievements toward "Green Living."

Write to your local newspapers—letters and op-eds—regarding the environmental issues.

Get your children and your friends' and neighbors' children involved in the environmental movement explaining them the importance of "Green Living" and encouraging them to form their own "Green Youth Groups." Awareness at a young age is the best way to create a generation of environmentally aware, responsible citizens. Perhaps this is the most important step every parent can take. Our children and grand children are the future of this planet.

POLITICAL ACTIVISM:

It is said that "people get the government they deserve." This is very true. It is extremely important to get politically involved in the "Green Movement." No country moves in the right direction without political decisions, especially in a democracy like ours. Without peoples' support or opposition to the decisions by our ruling elite, the country can court disaster like we saw in our disastrous war in Vietnam in the 1960s or recently in Iraq or perhaps even in Afghanistan (though only time will tell about Afghanistan, to be fair). It was a student's movement that forced our political leaders to withdraw from Vietnam.

So get involved politically. Get involved in your local Democratic, Republican, or Green Party meetings. By the way, the Green Party has excellent ten point manifesto that every American should read. Write to your local Congressman or Senator and better yet, meet and discuss the necessity for alternate fuel economy in our country. They should know that you care very much about the "Green Economy" that United States must pursue and that they will only get your and other like minded people's votes if they actively support "Green Economy" initiatives. Remember, they are supposed to follow their constituent's opinions and wishes. In a true democracy, they are our servants, not masters. This applies to every democratic country on the planet. This is not for America alone and the "Green Movement" is not solely an American responsibility. It is everyone on this planet's business if this Earth of ours is to survive the human onslaught.

Join other major groups that are involved in environmental causes. The number of people in a group makes a lot of difference. Participate...participate...participate. Politicians have to listen to groups that consist of large numbers.

Write letters, and make phone calls to as many politicians locally as well as in Washington DC as possible. Even the president should be written to or called to express what issues concern you the most and what your opinion is.

Participate in every protest, rally or gathering of any legitimate group that espouses environmental causes or the green movement.

If you can, support those groups and individuals who are dedicated to the environment and other progressive green causes by generously donating money to and/or time volunteering for such groups.

INVESTING INTELLIGENTLY

As an investor, you can take several steps that will both help the environment and allow you to benefit financially. Here are some suggestions:

Invest in companies that are not harmful to the environment. Specifically invest in green companies such as solar power, wind energy, organic food producers, etc.

Avoid companies that do harm to the environment or to humans or other creatures. That means, do not invest in mining companies, oil corporations, defense industries, defense contractors, plastic bags, plastic toys, plastic cup and dish mfrs., tobacco companies, huge agricultural companies, chemical companies that are involved in genetically modified foods, seeds, pesticides mfrs, etc. the list is long and inexhaustible.

Avoid investing in countries that do not work hard to control their greenhouse gas emissions. Avoid countries that are occupying other people's lands, are often at wars or are suppressing other people. Do not invest in companies that do business with such countries.

Invest in mutual funds or companies that support environmental causes.

As a personal example, we sold our older 2002 ML-320 Mercedes, 18-20 mpg and replaced it with 2008 higher mileage, 32-33 mpg Altima Hybrid. Additionally, we just signed a contract to install a solar power system on the roof of our house. In 60 days or around mid-April, 2010, all our electricity will be free, derived from sun. In 8 to 9 years, with an almost 50% governmental rebate and tax write-off, the system will pay for itself. Our next car will certainly be an electric one. Additionally, we are buying two solar cookers. In a few weeks, we plan to cook our evening meals several times a week by solar energy from our back yard.

CHAPTER 11
RISING TO THE CHALLENGE

We shall require a substantially new manner of thinking if mankind is to survive.
—Albert Einstein

To live a pure unselfish life, one must count nothing as one's own in the midst of abundance.
—Buddha

Few people realize it but the current civilization of ours is on the brink. If humanity is to survive the biggest challenge it faces in thousands of years, it will have to take drastic steps to switch from a fossil fuel based economy and life style to a renewable energy based economy and a sustainable way of living. We have no choice. Not only must we make these sweeping changes in our lives but we must undertake them within a decade or so. We have little time. We are not far from a tipping point. If we fail to act before the tipping point, climate change will be irreversible. The time is running out. Act we must.

Our civilization will have to perform on several fronts at the same time. We must eradicate poverty, stabilize the population of the world, and stop the destruction of our planet while restoring it to its former vibrant state. That means we must restore forests by curbing deforestation and planting billions of trees worldwide, stop soil erosion by conserving and rebuilding the soil so as to grow an adequate food supply to feed the world.

Industrialized agriculture such as practiced in America, other western countries, and some developing countries too in last few decades is fossil fuel based agriculture, dependent on oil based fertilizers, pesticides, and herbicides. It is unsustainable as when the oil runs out, the supply of these materials will stop. The world has time still to convert to organic sustainable agriculture. All countries need to follow Cuba's wonderful example as to how they shifted from industrial fossil fuel based agriculture to totally organic agriculture, after the collapse of the Soviet Union.

Current civilization needs to switch to a renewable energy economy and to organic agriculture. It needs to achieve zero population growth, poverty elimination across the world, localized and not globalized economy, universal education, and reforestation not deforestation. The world needs to build ecocities, mass transportation systems, electric cars and buses, and localized agriculture.

The IPCC has reported that human activity globally emits 32 billion tons of CO_2 in the atmosphere each year, out of which 15 billion tons actually stays in the atmosphere and adds to climate change.[1] These carbon dioxide emissions will have to be reduced drastically to stop global warming. Coal-fired power plants must go as they are a huge source of carbon dioxide emissions along with poisonous mercury and sulfur dioxide pollution. Indeed, all carbon dioxide emitting industries will have to go, even at the expense of certain goods and comforts.

Globally, wind and solar farms will have to be spawning up, converting the inexhaustible supply of wind and solar energy into vitally needed electricity for our current unsustainable industrial civilization to continue functioning in a sustainable way. Other sources of energy such as hydrogen fuel, hydro-electric power, and geo-thermal energy will have to be harnessed for humanity to survive.

Look at the potential of solar energy. Every day, the sun bombards our planet with 9,000 times more power than we need to warm every home, power every electrical appliance, or to run every car on Earth. If we manage to capture just a slice of one percent of it, we can kick fossil fuels into the archives of ancient history. According to some experts, the technology is already here. Professor Anthony Patt has shown that all the energy that Europe needs could be supplied by lining 0.3 percent of the Sahara desert—an area the size of Belgium—with concentrating solar power technology. A consortium of Germany's leading corporations is raring to go. They just need the money; up front, $50 billion. But this is nothing compared to what we would spend sucking and chasing the last drops of oil from the planet's belly as the industrialized world goes into meltdown.

Other continents have similar options. Just by covering 200 square kilometers of its empty deserts with solar plants, the entire energy needs of the United States could be met: it would cost just 10 years' worth of oil purchases with none of the invasions and wars, tyrannies, or Islamic blowbacks. Both China and India have similar options in their deserts. It is achievable if there is a will and colossal effort.

On the other front, energy efficiency will have to be raised. New cars, trucks or buses will have to be designed to give very high mileage. Even better, cars and other vehicles will have to run on alternative sources of energy, not the usual gasoline. Electric cars, hydrogen fuel cars, buses, hybrid cars and trucks will have to be the future vehicles of transportation. Even the numbers of cars and trucks will have to be reduced. Billions of people will have to travel by trains, buses, or bicycles.

Cities must be redesigned to serve people, not cars as we see them today in the western world. Ecocities will be the future of urban human living. Businesses and other governmental buildings will have to be redesigned to be energy efficient.

It should be obvious that nuclear energy is not the answer to our energy problems. Also, biofuels such as ethanol are not the right choice.

Yes, it gives a country some independence from fossil fuel such as oil and natural gas or coal. But producing ethanol is highly energy intensive. Its production from sugar cane or corn leaves even bigger carbon footprints on the planet than extracting oil. According to the Agriculture Department, about 27% of the U.S. corn crop was to be used up in ethanol production in 2007. Thus it was the switching of some 25% to 30% of U.S. corn towards ethanol production during the Bush administration that triggered the worldwide hike in food prices. [2]

ALTERNATIVE ENERGY BY COUNTRY

Today, fortunately, country after country is on the move towards alternative energy sources: The United States, Denmark, the Netherlands, India, China, Brazil, Germany, Spain, Portugal, Peru, the Caribbean nations and others. All of them seem to have realized that fossil fuels are not the way to go, that they must shift to sustainable forms of energy supply and have started doing so. Clean, renewable sources of energy are growing at 27 percent worldwide. But despite such significant growth, wind energy is still considered a marginal source of energy as just one percent of global electricity consumption comes from wind today.

But some countries are more advanced in exploiting wind energy: 20 percent in Denmark, 13 percent in Spain, 11 percent in Portugal, and 9 percent in Italy.[3]

According to a recent (June, 2009) report by the UN Environment Programme (UNEP), "Global Trends in Sustainable Energy Investment 2009", the green energy sector saw fourfold growth in investment around the globe in 2008. Due to economic crisis, developed countries such as the US and those of Europe showed poor growth, but developing nations were the bright spots in clean energy investment.

"Investment in the US [in green energy] fell by two percent and in Europe growth was very much muted," said Achim Steiner, UN Under-Secretary General and UNEP Executive Director. "However, there were also some bright points in 2008 especially in developing economies. China became the world's second largest wind market in terms of new capacity and the world's biggest photovoltaic manufacturer, and rise in geothermal energy may be getting underway in countries like Australia, Japan, and Kenya," Steiner said.[4]

China led the financing of new renewable energy projects in Asia with an 18 percent increase over 2007 to $15.6 billion, mostly in new wind projects and biomass. China already is the world's biggest manufacturer of solar panels, a large percentage of it being exported.

India saw a 12 percent rise in investment in clean renewable energy like wind, solar, biomass and small-hydro projects with $4.1 billion being pumped into this sector in 2008, as per the UNEP report. The wind sector received the largest share of investment, growing at 17 percent from $2.2 billion to $2.6 billion. While investment in solar energy rose from $18 million in 2007 to $347 million in 2008, most of it was channelized to setting up module and cell manufacturing facilities. Investment in small-hydro projects grew about fourfold to $543 million in 2008, but growth in biofuels fell from $251 million in 2007 to $49 million in 2008.

Brazil accounted for almost all renewable energy investment in Latin America in 2008 with ethanol receiving $10.8 billion, up 76 percent from 2007.

UNEP estimates that between 2009 and 2011, 37% of current economic stimulus packages and 1 percent of global GDP is needed to finance a sustainable economic recovery by investing in the greening of five key sectors of the global economy: agriculture, energy, water, buildings, and transport.[5]

THE UNITED STATES

By far the biggest consumer of fossil fuels, the United States is increasingly on the way to alternative sources of energy. Just like during the years of World War II when the U.S. economy was quickly transformed into a war economy by major U.S. industries who instead of producing cars and trucks, rapidly switched to manufacturing tanks and fighter planes by the thousands, this country has an amazing capacity to change fast if need be. Well, that time has come again now and the new leadership headed by the Obama administration, unlike the Bush era, realizes the urgent need to transform its economic-base to alternative sources of energy.

Take Texas. For years a leading oil producing state, it is now also a leading generator of electricity from wind, having overtaken California some three years ago. Currently, Texas boasts close to 8,000 megawatts of wind-generating capacity online and has a huge 39,000 megawatts in the construction and planning stage. When completed, Texas will possess 50,000 megawatts of wind-generating capacity, equivalent to 50 coal-fired power plants. This not only fulfills the need of its 24 million inhabitants, but will export the electricity to nearby states such as Mississippi and Louisiana.

Besides Texas and California, the other leading states with commercial-scale wind farms are Minnesota, Iowa, Washington, and Colorado. Other states too are emerging as wind superpowers. In eastern South Dakota, BP and Clipper Wind power are joining forces to build a 5,050 megawatt Titan Wind Farm, the world's largest. Already under construction, Titan will generate five times as much electricity as the state's 780,000 residents currently consume. This huge project includes constructing a transmission line along an abandoned rail line across Iowa, supplying electricity to Illinois and the country's heartland.

The transition from fossil-fuels to sustainable energy sources is moving much faster than we realize. In the U.S., coal use has declined 11% over the last two years and an estimated 190 new wind farms with over 16,000 megawatts of generating capacity have become online.[6]

In the Tehachapi Mountains, northwest of Los Angeles, California is developing a 4,500 megawatt wind farm complex. In the east, in Maine—

a wind energy beginner—plans are underway to develop 3,000 megawatts of wind-energy capacity. That is far more than the state's 1.3 million residents need. While to the south, Delaware is planning an offshore wind farm of up to 600 megawatts that will fulfill 50% of the state's residential need. New York State has 700 megawatts of wind-generating capacity, and plans to add another 8,000 megawatts. There, most of the power will be generated by winds coming off Lake Erie and Lake Ontario. Soon, the wind-rich Columbia River Gorge will enable Oregon to nearly double its wind generating capacity with a 900 megawatt wind farm.

Philip Anschutz, a Colorado billionaire, is developing a 2,000-megawatt wind farm in south central Wyoming. Already, he has secured the rights to build a 900-mile high-voltage transmission line to California. This project, when ready, will open the doors to scores of big wind farms in Wyoming, a state rich in wind source and inhabited by few people. Under development is another transmission line, to run north-south that will link eastern Wyoming's wind resources with other growing Colorado cities of Denver, Fort Collins, and Colorado Springs. Similarly, wind-rich Oklahoma and Kansas are planning to build a transmission line to the U.S. southwest to sell their renewable wealth of cheap wind energy.[7]

Wisely, wind seems destined to take the center-stage of the new U.S. energy economy, ultimately providing several hundred thousand megawatts of electricity.

Solar power is another story. It is the largest available source of energy in America though it accounted for less than 0.1% of electricity generation in 2006.[8] Now, the solar power is expanding on a fast track. It is being harnessed by the use of solar thermal power plants and photovoltaic cells to convert sunlight into electricity. With its "Million Solar Roofs" plan, California is by far the leader in solar cell installation. New Jersey is on the move too, followed by Nevada.

Solar energy deployment grew at a record pace in the United States as well as throughout the world in 2008, according to new industry reports.

On March 19, the Solar Energy Industries Association (SEIA) released its "2008 U.S. Solar Industry Year in Review". It found that the U.S. solar energy capacity increased by 17% last year, reaching the total equivalent of 8,775 megawatts (MW). The SEIA report tallies all types of solar energy, and last year the United States installed 342 MW of solar photovoltaic (PV) electric power, 139 thermal megawatts (MWTh) of solar water heating, 762 MWTh of pool heating, and 21 MWTh of solar space heating and cooling.

The growth rate was highest for grid-connected PV electric systems. It increased by 58% to a total of 792 MW. Meanwhile, domestic PV manufacturing capacity increased by 65% and preliminary estimates peg the total U.S. PV manufacturing capacity at 685 MW annually at 2008-end.

It is reported that by 2025, solar power's contribution could grow to 10% of the nation's power needs. Prepared by the research and publishing firm Clean Edge and the nonprofit Co-op America, the report projects close to 2% of the nation's electricity coming from concentrating solar power systems, while solar photovoltaic systems will supply more than 8% of the nation's electricity. Those figures correlate to nearly 50,000 megawatts of solar photovoltaic systems and more than 6,600 megawatts of concentrating solar power.

As noted in the report, solar power has been growing rapidly in the past eight years, at an average pace of 40% per year. The cost per kilowatt-hour of solar photovoltaic systems has also been declining while electricity generated from fossil fuels is getting more expensive. As a result, the report projects that solar power will reach cost parity with conventional power sources in many U.S. markets by 2015. But to reach the 10% goal, solar photovoltaic companies will also need to streamline installations and make solar power a "plug-and-play" technology, that is, it must be simple and straightforward to buy the components of the system, connect them together, and connect the system to the power grid.[9]

As per the latest "Monthly Energy Review" issued by the U.S. Energy Information Administration on Sept. 24, renewable energy accounted for more than 10 percent of the domestically-produced energy used in the United States in the first half of 2008.

Through June 30, the United States consumed 50.673 quadrillion Btu (quads) of energy — of which 34.162 quads were from domestic sources and 16.511 quads were imported.

Domestically-produced renewable energy (biomass/biofuels, geo-thermal, hydropower, solar, wind) totaled 3.606 quads — equal to 10.56 percent of U.S. energy consumption that is domestically produced. This is only slightly less than the contribution from nuclear power (11.98 percent).

While consumption of nuclear power dropped by 1 percent during the first half of 2008, compared to the same period for 2007 (4.091 quads, down from 4.119 quads), renewable energy's share increased by 5 percent (3.606 quads, up from 3.439 quads).

Biomass and biofuels combined presently constitute the largest source of renewable energy in the United States (1.883 quads) followed by hydropower (1.387 quads).

Wind power experienced the greatest growth rate — increasing by almost 49 percent from the first half of 2007 compared to the first half of 2008 (0.244 quad, up from 0.164 quad).
Geothermal and solar contributions were at roughly equal levels in 2008 as they were in 2007. However, both are poised to significantly expand their market share in the near future.

"The significant contribution being made by renewable energy sources to the nation's energy supply documented by the U.S. Energy Information Administration (EIA) is much greater than most Americans realize," said Ken Bossong, executive director of the Sun Day Campaign, a non-profit research and educational organization founded in 1993 to promote sustainable energy technologies as cost-effective alternatives to nuclear power and fossil fuels. "Repeated statements by nuclear and fossil fuel interests that renewables contribute only a tiny fraction of the nation's energy supply are not only misleading but flatly wrong."[10]

The 14-megawatt solar cell installation at Nellis Air Force Base in Nevada is the biggest in the United States currently. At the commercial level, photovoltaic electricity is about to expand significantly. PG&E has gone into two solar cell power contracts with a combined capacity of 800 megawatts. These plants will cover 12 square miles of desert with solar cells and at its peak, will have an output equaling a large coal-fired power plant. In hot climates, solar power plants are especially useful as their peak outputs fulfill peak demands for air conditioning.

On August 20, 2009, in Rosemead, California, First Solar, Inc. and Southern California Edison (SCE) announced plans to build two large-scale solar power projects in riverside and San Bernardino counties in southern California. The projects will be some of the largest of their kind, with a generation capacity of 550 megawatts of photovoltaic solar electricity, enough to provide power to about 170,000 homes. The agreements are subject to approval by the California Utilities Commission. The projects consist of the 250 megawatt Desert Sunlight Project near Desert Center, California, and the 300 megawatt Stateline Project in northeastern San Bernardino County. The construction is scheduled to start in 2012 for Desert Sunlight and 2013 for Stateline. Both these projects are expected to be completed by 2015. Several hundred jobs will be created at each site. When operational, the solar plants will generate 1.2 billion kilowatt-hours of clean energy annually.

California at present has a goal of generating 20 percent of electricity from renewable sources by 2010 and has further established the goal to 33 percent by 2020. SCE is the nation's leading buyer of renewable energy and, in 2008, delivered 12.6 billion kilowatt-hours of electricity to its customers from renewable sources—about 16 percent of its total energy portfolio. First Solar, Inc. manufactures solar modules with an advanced semiconductor technology and provides comprehensive photovoltaic system solutions. By constantly decreasing costs, First Solar is creating an affordable and environmentally responsible alternative to fossil-fuel generation. The company is based in Tempe, Arizona and employs 4,000 employees around the world with manufacturing facilities in Ohio, Germany, and Malaysia.[11]

Solar thermal power plants use mirrors to concentrate sunlight on a container with a fluid heating it to 750 degrees Fahrenheit or more to generate steam that turns a turbine creating electricity. They have become quite attractive recently. Spain is big on this technology. The world's largest solar thermal complex completed in 1991 is in the United States with a capacity of producing 350 megawatts of electricity. In addition, as of September 2008, there were ten large solar thermal power plants under construction in the United States. They range in capacity from 180 to 550 megawatts. Eight of them will be in California, one each in Arizona and Florida. In the next 2 to 3 years, the US will have a capacity of from 420 megawatts of solar thermal generating capacity to close to 3,500 megawatts, an eightfold increase.[12]

Similar to wind and solar, geothermal energy is developing at an explosive rate. The United States has close to 3,000 megawatts of geothermal generating capacity. 2,500 of it are in California. The U.S. geothermal capacity will double as 96 geothermal power plants are now under construction. Thus massive future developments of geothermal energy are planned with California, Nevada, Oregon, Idaho, and Utah leading the way.[13]

Many interests are now supporting renewable energy in the United States though some still want to expand fossil fuel energy capacity for their own selfish interests. There is no question that the world, especially the developed nations must switch to renewable energy sources to reduce and eventually eliminate their dependence on fossil fuels as otherwise, global climate change could destroy or heavily damage industrial civilization as we know it.

To ensure that all these renewable energy sources are distributed nationwide properly, building a strong national grid is a must. America has a highly creditable capacity to rise to the challenge and change fast. It was obvious when President John Kennedy launched a program to go to the moon in the early sixties and the U.S. landed a man on the moon a few years later in 1969. But this challenge is far greater than any they or the world has ever faced before. Still, the United States could lead the world in this enormous task and succeed too.

Coal seams run out, oil wells go dry, but renewable energy is forever. If utilized to the fullest, it will be the salvation of humanity on the Earth.

GERMANY AND JAPAN

Perhaps no other countries have made greater strides than Germany and Japan in solar energy generation in the last few years. Motivated variously by concerns over security, health, climate change, and high energy prices, these nations are now home to robust and fast growing solar industries. Solar panels are found on hundreds of thousands of rooftops across these nations. Both nations followed different paths in the public policy they employed and that led to different results. While Germany's solar industry is still dependent on subsidized power production costs, Japan's investments to drive down the costs of solar energy have successfully created a domestic industry that has been independent of government subsidies since 2005.

The Germans were faced with soaring energy prices in the 1970s. The energy security concerns were heightened due to successive energy crises sending price shocks throughout Europe. The environment became a central concern for the German public in the next two decades due to increasing pollution and the Chernobyl nuclear disaster.

No wonder, in 1998, Germany's Green Party won enough votes to form a coalition with the Social Democratic Party and gained control of the parliament. Meantime, international cooperation was necessary due to the moral imperative caused by global warming. So, under the Kyoto protocol, Germany committed to a 21% reduction in emissions from 1990 levels by 2012.[14]

All these developments changed the dynamics, marking the beginning of a massive investment in renewable energy deployment, especially photovoltaic. Emissions reductions presented a myriad of challenges and to surmount them, the German government invested in a new industry that would establish Germany as a global leader in a clean energy technology.

With the passage of the "1000 Roofs Program" of 1991, the German solar photovoltaic (PV) industry was launched. In this program, the government gave subsidies to individuals to cover the cost of installing a PV rooftop system. The program aimed to gain experience with solar installations, constructing new houses compatible with renewable electricity generation requirements, and to stimulate solar power usage by German consumers. By the mid 1990s, some 2,000 grid-connected PV systems had been installed on German rooftops.

To accelerate further expansion of this new industry, this successful initiative was soon expanded into the 100,000 Roofs Program. Aiming to drive down the costs of solar PV system, the program invited private entities to participate. A loan of 6,230 Euros per kilowatt (peak) was given to each participant for PV systems with an output less than five megawatts and 3,115 Euros per kilowatt if the output was higher. By the end of the program in 2004, some 100,000 grid-connected rooftop solar systems were successfully installed. By its end, Germany's PV solar industry had expanded beyond the small-scale market to one capable of mass production.

To support the nascent solar industry and the solar rooftop program, the German government established a policy known as feed-in-tariff. The feed-in-tariff guarantees higher than market price for electricity generated by solar PV which is fixed for 20 years beyond the installation date, thus providing investment certainty both for individuals and businesses. The tariff, a component of Germany's renewable energy law, has been a part of Germany's energy policy since 1991, and still continues to this day.

With the demonstrated success of its 100,000 Roofs Program, in 2000, the new government increased the feed-in-tariff rates for solar PV. Part of the updated tariff however consisted of a 5% decrease each year in reimbursement for newly installed systems, thus giving a clear incentive for the solar industry to develop more cost effective panels.[15]

Within the last few years, the German solar technology turnover has risen from around 450 million Euros to more than 4.9 billion Euros annually in the construction, expansion, and modernization of their solar factories in order to increase their production capacities with solar modules, solar cells, and inverters. According to the German Federal Association of the Solar Industry (BSW), the number of people employed directly and indirectly in the solar industry had risen to around 50,000 in 2006. Despite Germany receiving only moderate levels of solar radiation due to its geographic location, it has become the largest solar thermal market in Europe. It takes second place only to Japan in the world in photovoltaic power generation.

According to BSW, there were 1,300,000 solar plants in Germany in 2006. 220,000 new plants were erected in 2006 alone.[16]

Thus, successive German governments have been very sagacious, foresighted, and pragmatic to steer their country so efficiently towards alternative energy sources, decreasing their dependence on fossil fuels.

In 1993, meanwhile, the Japanese Ministry of Economy, Trade, and Industry (METI) embarked on the New Sunshine Project in an effort to create a Japanese solar photovoltaic industry and a domestic market for solar power. Through several publicly funded and coordinated research, development, demonstration, and deployment ventures, Japan has made significant progress in manufacturing and driving down the costs of reliable solar power generation.

A combination of factors such as public concern for global warming and high prices of energy in Japan—the country imports 85% of its coal—have made a national priority for solar power. METI came out with various incentives, initiatives and projects focusing on growing Japan's solar industry and its capacity. This included the aforementioned New Sunshine Project, as well as the "5-Year Plan for Photovoltaic Power Generation Technology Research and Development," and the "Residential PV System Dissemination Program."

METI has been incredibly effective in its efforts to grow both consumer demand and industrial capacity installing rooftop PV systems on almost half a million homes, while driving down solar power costs. In 1994, the cost for installing a rooftop PV system on a residential home was $60,000 (in 2007 dollars). By 2005, the costs for installations had dropped to $20,000. This made solar photovoltaic competitive with domestic electricity rates in Japan. Soon after, Japan terminated federal subsidies for rooftop systems. Today, Japan is home to several of the world's top solar companies.

This success can be traced to Japan's embrace of coordinated public investment in each stage of the solar technology innovation pipeline, including not just funding for research and development, but also demonstration and early-stage deployment efforts. This support for the demonstration and early-stage deployment of solar photovoltaic ensured a market for the emerging technology; it is quite likely that without these policies, photovoltaics would have faltered before reaching cost-levels that were competitive with market electricity rates. Thus the Japanese government acted very keenly in the whole effort.

Germany's booming solar PV industry is the result of its strategic public investment since 1991 and beyond. Today, Germany is the leader in solar PV installation and manufacturing. German companies make up 46% of the global market today, generating over 10,000 jobs for the German workforce. The feed-in-tariff has been at the core of the industry's success and still continues to be the main driver of solar installations in Germany.

On the other hand, Japan has successfully implemented a series of policies that have made solar photovoltaics competitive with domestic electricity rates and has stopped subsidizing solar. While METI still continues to play a robust role in research and development of next generation photovoltaic technologies, the solar industry is growing in Japan and its government now seems to be on track reaching its goal of bringing solar power to 30% of Japan's rooftops without any further direct subsidies for the deployment.[17]

It is refreshing to see that these two countries have embarked on solar power programs since the 1990s and are enjoying a thriving success in harnessing solar energy for their people, offering them a clean environment and energy security. Total energy security is still a long way for these advanced nations but they have made a great start. The rest of the world can learn a great deal from these two pioneers of solar energy.

WorldFocus reported in September, 2009 that the new Prime minister of Japan promised that Japan will reduce its CO_2 emissions 25% by the year 2020.

CHINA

Superlatives such as biggest, largest, and tremendous usually apply to China whenever one describes it. Wind power is no exception and is a positive one at that.

China could be the world's largest producer of wind power by 2020 according to its statistics-crazed government. From the gusts along its enormous coastline and its vast desert plains, it could draw 150 million kilowatts (kw), generating 10 percent or more of its needs. As of early 2007, the country has been seventh in the world for wind power production, growing 30 percent on an annual average since 2000, from 350,000 kw to 1.26 million kw in 2005. In 2007, according to one analyst, its wind power capacity was set to rise by 65 percent. In all, according to a (GWEC) report, China boasts a total capacity of 3.2 billion kw, of which one billion can be developed. But realizing such a huge capacity and attracting crucial foreign investment will require reforms of the country's wind pricing mechanism.[18]

Today, China is working on seven wind farm mega-complexes with a total generating capacity of 110,000 megawatts. This is in addition to the many smaller wind farms already in operation and under construction. A recent report in *Science* concludes that the country can increase its current electricity generation sevenfold from wind alone.

A major impetus for developing wind and the country's innovative mag-lev turbine is the central government's 2005 mandate that all the major power firms must generate at least 5 percent of their electricity from renewable sources by 2010 and 10 percent by 2020; but standing in the way is cheap coal, so common in developing countries, that makes up 75 percent of China's energy-mix (and also an unhealthy and integral part of its air). According to government minister Pan Yue, the country's energy reduction goals set out by China's EPA in the beginning of 2006— cutting energy intensity by 4 percent and emissions of pollutants by 2 percent—"have absolutely not been achieved".[19]

Blocking wind's progress is the country's bid-based pricing system that the GWEC says is seriously hindering the market. Under the current regime, powerful state-owned power companies can bid well below realistic market prices, offsetting their losses with profits from coal-fired plants (a new one coming up each week). For a number of projects in recent years, according to *WorldWatch*, the winning bids ranged from 4.6 to 6.5 cents per kwh. According to one expert, the current average cost of wind power in China is between 6.3 and 8 cents per kwh; thus, a net loss was suffered by all the projects authorized.

According to the *Xinhua* news agency, during the 11th Five-Year Plan period between 2006 and 2010, China was scheduled to set up about 30 large wind power projects of 100 MW at regions with abundant wind power resources like in eastern coastal areas, the Hubei Province, and the Inner Mongolia Autonomous Region in north China. In terms of small wind power projects, China has already developed the biggest market in the world. By the end of 2005, China has installed 320,000 small wind turbine generators with a total capacity of 65,000 kw, thus supplying power to residents of remote areas.[20]

According to *Bloomberg News Reports* of June 4, 2009, China, the world's second-biggest energy consumer now, will invest about $14.6 billion to more than double its wind power capacity by 2010 from last year, rising from 12,000 megawatts to 30,000 mw.

In an article, Shi Lishan, deputy director of renewable energy at the National Energy Administration, said that wind power is "vital" because it is the cheapest form of renewable energy. Almost 80 percent of China's power comes from coal.

China Longyuan Electric Power Group, which accounts for about 25 percent of China's wind power, plans to further boost capacity to 6,000 megawatts by next year and to 20,000 megawatts by 2020. China Guodian Corp.'s renewable-energy unit was capable of generating 2,630 megawatts of electricity using wind turbines last year. China is also planning a stimulus plan to develop renewable energy.[21]

Already, China's small scale hydro and solar systems—their solar-water heaters make up 60 percent of the world's—makes it the world leader in renewable investment.

Besides a leader in manufacturing solar panels and wind turbines, China is also a leading solar water heater manufacturer. In the seaside city of Rizhao in Shandong province, population 2.8 million, 99% of households use solar water heaters. In the city of Dezhou, population 5.5 million and hometown of China's largest and most advanced solar water heater maker Himin Solar Energy Group, 90% of its households have solar water heaters and its streets are illuminated with solar lights.

Every roof-top of a house in Rizhao bears a solar water heater. Scenes like these of crowded roof-tops with solar water heaters are repeated all over China, though often in the shadows of carbon spewing smokestacks and noxious chemical plants. Rizhao is one of a small but growing number of cities requiring solar heaters to be installed or subsidized. They cost just $220, compared to larger and more elaborate solar water heaters in the US that costs $1500.

These heaters will be vital if China is to meet its goal of reducing its reliance on coal which supplies 80% of its energy needs today. The central government plans to fulfill 15% of its energy needs through renewable sources by 2020. In the last decade or more, competition among solar water heater makers has become fierce as there are now 5000 manufacturers of these heaters in China. The prices have and are coming down with better and better quality products.[22]

On September 8, 2009, First Solar, a solar cells manufacturing company that makes more solar cells than any other company in the world, said it had received initial approval from the Chinese government to build perhaps the largest solar field in the world.

First Solar said it struck a 10-year contract with the government to build in China's vast desert north of the Great Wall. Ultimately, the project will blanket 25 square miles of Inner Mongolia—slightly larger than the size of Manhattan—with a sea of black, light absorbing glass. This solar field will dwarf anything that exists today in America or Europe. At 2 gigawatts, or 2 billion watts, the solar plant will pump as much energy onto China's grid as two coal-fired plants, enough to light up to three million homes. But it would not produce electricity at night like most solar plants.

"The potential is enormous," for projects like this in China, First Solar CEO Mike Ahearn told the Associated Press before the announcement. "The Chinese government is further along in its thinking about solar than we've imagined."

As Keith Bradsher of *The New York Times* reported on January 30, 2010, China vaulted past competitors Denmark, Germany, Spain and the United States last year to become the world's largest maker of wind turbines this year. In addition, China also has leapfrogged the west in the last couple of years to emerge as the world's biggest manufacturer of solar panels. It is also pushing hard to build nuclear reactors and the most efficient types of coal power plants.

The September, 2009 issue of *Science* magazine reported that China is moving rapidly on carbon capture or sequestration technology front to offset its huge CO2 emissions from coal-fired power plants. China is planning to launch two big carbon capture facilities, making enormous investments. One will be in Inner Mongolia and the other will be in Tianjin. If successful, these projects could redefine how power is generated in China, and later in other parts of the world.

Vestas of Denmark has just erected the world's biggest wind turbine manufacturing complex in northeastern China, and transferred the technology to build the latest electronic controls and generators.

Speeding towards the future mass transit front, in December, 2009, China launched the fastest train on the planet, with speeds averaging 217 mph. It will link Wuhan in central China to Guangzhou in the south, covering a distance of 663 miles. It will travel through 20 cities reducing the travel time from 6 hours to 2 hours and 45 minutes.

Jobs are being added rapidly here in renewable energy, reaching 1.2 million in 2008 and climbing by 100,000 a year, according to the government-backed Chinese Renewable Energy Industries Association.[23]

Thus, there is no question that China is on the move on the renewable energy front.

INDIA

It is crucial that India, the world's largest democracy and its second most populous country also moves swiftly from a fossil-fuel based economy to a sustainable renewable energy-based economy. It seems the government of India is quite aware of this and is moving in that direction. What India and China, these two Asian giants will or won't do regarding renewable energy will have far reaching repercussions around the globe.

As those who have been to India know, there are frequent power cuts all over the country due to shortages of electricity. From New Delhi to Chennai, Mumbai to Calcutta, there are always inconvenient power cuts in factories and in households.

The writing is clear on the wall. The world's resources are simply not enough to fulfill the demands of rising populations everywhere and in India. The mad scramble for alternative sources of energy is attracting big money. It is estimated that about $20 trillion will be invested in the energy sector till 2030 and the major portion is likely to go to low carbon projects developing in India and China. Not surprisingly, companies big and small are scrambling to cash in on this opportunity.

Thus, there has been awakening within the Indian government and top Indian industrialists. Tata Group, one of the big Indian industrial conglomerates has been on the forefront on the green energy. It is looking at straddling different sectors of green energy. From generating solar power to manufacturing green batteries to planting jatropha trees in barren lands, Tata Group wants its presence in every sector of green economy. To its credit, much before green gained currency in India, Tata has been building its green businesses. Its solar venture has become a Rs. 1,100 crore ($220 million) company in 20 years. In 1989, Tata established a joint venture with BP Solar, one of the largest solar companies in the world. The company supplies simple solar lanterns as well as complex solar photovoltaic modules to industries. Tata BP Solar offers customized solar solutions for lighting homes, and streets, pumping water to fields and heating water for commercial and residential customers. It also provides cost-effective and reliable solar power to wide-ranging sectors from banking to education to healthcare and telecommunications. Tata AutoComp is manufacturing green batteries for the Indian and European markets. Another eco-friendly consumer product that is in the works by Tata Motors is Indica EV, an electric car that will run on polymer lithium batteries. Tata Motors plans to introduce the Indica EV in select European markets this year in 2010.

There are others too in the green energy. Mahendra & Mahendra, a heavy vehicle maker, has commercialized its foray into electric vehicle sector by launching its first electric three-wheeler called Bijlee, a first of its kind battery-operated vehicle. Others such as Infosys, Wipro, and HCL have gone into recycling water, building computers and laptops without carcinogenic materials, and lowering their per-capita power consumption to generating at least 30 percent of their energy requirements from green energy. This is of course the story of only a handful of companies. Others have a long way to go. Except the top 250 companies in India, others are not even concerned about their carbon footprints. [24]

Wind energy is not new to India. It has several wind farms in the country especially in the south. India ranks fifth in the world in the production of wind energy. The country gets moderate winds during the monsoon season between the months of April and October.

Remote, exposed hilly areas in south India and the central peninsula region have been identified as places good for wind farms. While at present, most of the wind farms are based in south India in the state of Tamilnadu, one of Asia's largest wind farms is located in the Satara region of western Maharashtra state. Mumbai is the capitol of this highly industrialized state.

Areas around Pune, a thriving city just three hours' drive from Mumbai, have been found suitable for wind farms. One of Asia's largest wind turbine manufacturers, Suzlon Energy, is based here. It was started in 1995 and since then, it has grown phenomenally due to the investor interest in and need for wind energy.

In the last few years, the industry has added about 6,000 megawatts of power supply and plans to add an additional 8,000 to 9,000 megawatts by 2012—this is enough to meet Mumbai's power needs for three days.[25]

Vivek Kher, a Suzlon spokesperson told the BBC in 2007 that wind energy was now the centre of attention because of rising fuel prices, geopolitical uncertainties surrounding oil producing countries, and a growing concern about global warming and climate change.

Realizing the urgent need for wind power, major power companies such as Reliance Energy, Tata Power, and the state-run Hindustan Petroleum have all entered into multi-million dollar deals with Suzlon to increase wind power capacity. Vivek Kher said that global concerns were forcing them to go green. He said, "Transmission and distribution companies have been mandated to source a minimum percentage of their power from renewable energy sources, and therefore a lot of fossil fuel companies are moving towards it as a matter of social responsibility, to diversify their energy portfolio." [26]

Suzlon has been doing business with the United States, India, China, Australia, Spain, Portugal, and Italy. Smaller firms and individuals have also invested in wind turbines. There are other players in Indian wind turbine market such as the Danish manufacturer Vestas Wind Systems A/S, the US company GE Energy, the German manufacturer Enercon GmbH and Spain's Gamesa SA.

Of India's total installed capacity of 147,000 megawatts, wind power accounts for only 8,696 mw, and most projects have a plant load factor, or efficiency of only 10-15%. The low efficiency is because companies are more interested in claiming depreciation benefits rather than generating more power.

India has the wind energy potential of 45,000 mw and the ministry of New and Renewable Energy hopes to increase wind power capacity to around 18,000 mw by the year 2012. [27]

The government of India is promoting wind energy by offering tax incentives to investors. Still, it constitutes only 1% of the energy units supplied to grids. With India's massive energy needs, wind power can barely make a dent there. At the current rate of growth, the maximum generating capacity will be met in another 20 years' time. Wind energy will only make a small difference in India's energy-mix, but in such a rapidly developing country, it will still be a significant achievement.[28]

On the solar front, India is home to one of the most abundant solar resources in the world, with 2.97 million square kilometers (more than 1 million square miles) of tropical and subtropical land and an average of 250-300 clear sunny days a year. Thus, solar power offers tremendous potential to meet a large portion of the country's energy requirements using both centralized and decentralized production.

If realized, such changes could dwarf current solar leaders (Germany, Spain, Japan, and the United States) in both domestic market size and export manufacturing. It would also create a huge job market in solar manufacturing and installation in India.

Solar power is making excellent progress in India as apparent by the fact that between 1999 and 2005, electricity generated from solar power increased 300 percent. In Africa, it jumped 2,500 percent, compared to just 11 percent in North America.[29]

A leaked early version of the Indian government's National Solar Energy Plan indicates that India may be thinking and planning more ambitiously about a "clean energy" roadmap than was previously believed.

First published in *The Hindu*, the draft strategy outlines plans for a national target of 200,000 megawatts of solar power generation capacity by 2050. This is easily 1.3 times India's current installed power generation capacity of 150,000 megawatts across all energy sectors.[30]

As per the leaked document, India's "solar mission" will constitute measures for rapidly expanding the use of small-scale photovoltaic panels, solar lighting systems, and commercial-scale solar plants, so as to drive down the costs and promote domestic solar manufacturing. The efforts would take place in both rural and urban regions and target commercial as well as residential users. The plan also proposes scaling-up centralized solar thermal power generation, with the aim of realizing the cost parity with conventional grid power by 2020 and the full necessary energy infrastructure by 2050.

Compared to India's current installed capacity at a mere 3 megawatts, this would constitute the most ambitious solar plan that any country has laid out so far. The scope of the initiative also matches and ultimately will far exceed India's nuclear power generation plans.

Greenpeace, and the TERI studies both operate on the premise that global carbon emissions must peak by no later than 2015 to avert dangerous emissions levels. They make the case that not only it is feasible for India technically and economically to make the shift to renewable energy sources (if this is combined with energy-efficiency measures), but it is prudent to begin this transition now.

Both the reports point out that the primary obstacles facing India's transition to renewable energy, are the upfront costs required and the need for a strong political will.

What is needed, according to TERI, is a shift to a 92% renewable share in India's energy supply. It would result in doubling of domestic emissions by 2031 (compared with a seven-time increase under the current trajectory) and would cost an estimated 457 trillion rupees (US $9.6 trillion). This is contrasted with a 75% renewable share, which would end up tripling of emissions by 2031 and would cost an estimated 260 trillion Rupees (US $5.4 trillion).

According to *Energy (R)evolution*, it is possible for 69% of India's electricity and 70% of its heating and cooling needs to come from renewable sources by 2050. But capturing this opportunity "would require an additional investment of $154 billion," Teri said. But the government's leaked national solar strategy proposes investments amounting to some 85,000-105,000 crore rupees ($18-22 billion) by 2031. This falls far short of funding needs for such a massive and rapid development of solar energy if compared with the above estimates. So both Teri and Greenpeace suggest the use of international financing mechanisms to bridge the cost gap, a proposal in line with Indian government's rhetoric in the ongoing international climate negotiations.[31]

In a June 6, 2009 report of *The New York Times* authored by James Carter, it is accounted that India is planning towards becoming a global leader and a hub of solar power, similar to the nations like Germany, Spain and the U.S.. India is working on a draft report called the National Solar Mission. According to the report, India plans to add 20,000 mw of solar power generation capacity by 2020. Additionally, the plan envisages 100,000 mw by 2030 and 200,000 mw by the middle of this century. In recognition of abnormally high costs of solar panels at present, the plan sets out to promote and accelerate indigenous production through various measures and hopes that with high demand in India and China, the industry will try to reduce the cost of production and solar power costs could decline to a widely affordable Rs 4 to Rs 5 per kwhr which is 7-8 cents, the average US power tariff.[32]

The government of India initiated Solar PV projects up to a maximum capacity of 50 mw to be supported by financial incentives of a maximum of Rs 12/kwh (28 US cents) for PV projects and Rs 10/kwh (24 US cents) for solar thermal power projects for a period of 10 years. As investors are rushing up to set up solar power projects and adding up to 2500 mw of capacity, the ministry has requested the Planning Commission and the Indian cabinet to expand the 11th Plan Solar Power Programme beyond 50 mw.

In March 2007, the government announced a semiconductor policy under its Special Incentive Package Scheme (SIPS) which will provide 20% of the capital expenditure during the first 10 years for semiconductor industries that included manufacturing activities related to solar PV technology located in Special Economic Zones (SEZ) and 25% for industries not located in SEZ.

India has the skills and capabilities to expand its solar power industries. Its current installed capacity for solar panel manufacture is 700 mw per year and has the skill and capacity to increase it to 20,000 mw per year.[33]

Recently, the solar energy industry in India has certainly gained momentum. It should be able to keep pace with the government's objective of achieving 10% of the country's total electricity needs by 2012. Fortunately, India already has a high-tech manufacturing base, skilled labor force, and a balanced eco-system for the PV industry which will be sufficient to make it a booming industry. Yearly PV production has reached over 300 mw, 85% of which is being exported.

Amazingly, India receives solar energy equivalent to over 5 trillion mwh a year, which is many times more than its total energy consumption, and should therefore benefit from economies of scale that are not available to smaller countries. However, long-term — 20 to 25 years— solar energy policy is necessary and the availability and management of strong infrastructure requirements should be addressed by the Indian government. India's Renewable Energy Ministry has declared a new program designed to expand solar power generating projects up to a capacity of 50 mw. The government, facing inadequate power generation and big transmission and distribution losses, wants to generate at least 10 percent of its electricity through solar power by 2012. With government support, a total of 33 solar photovoltaic power plants connected to the Indian power grid have already been built. The plants are expected to generate 25.5 lakh (2.55 million) units of electricity annually. There are currently 19 manufacturers of solar photovoltaic modules in India and several big investments are forthcoming.

Hence the initiatives in the proposed National Solar Mission are on sound basis and present a good opportunity to global banks, investors, manufacturers, and system integrators to focus their eyes towards this Asian giant. [34]

An April 29, 2007 report by Catherine Brahic in the *New Scientist*, points out that since the last four years (before 2007), a thriving market for household solar panels has sprung up in India with the help of a United Nations Environment Programme which assists local banks in offering cheaper loans for the panels.

As per this report, since 2003 the 1.5 Million Programme has helped 16,000 Indians living in the southern state of Karnataka buy solar power systems for their homes and small businesses. "In 2003, close to 70% of people in India did not have electricity," said Jyoti Painuly, senior energy planner for the UN Environment Programme (UNEP). "Even being connected to the national grid did not ensure reliable power because of frequent power cuts. There might be electricity when you don't need it and then the power is not there when you need it," she said further. Household solar systems work by storing up energy in a battery which is then connected, for example, to a few light bulbs, a small radio, or a small black-and-white TV. The system costs between $300 and $500, though, making them unaffordable for many of India's poor.

"The banks decided that we should subsidize lower interest loans to buy solar systems," said Painuly. Before, the banks were charging 12% interest for the loans to buy solar systems. But through the project, the two participating banks dropped that rate to 5% and UNEP paid the difference. UNEP also convinced the banks to extend the time period from three to five years and to accept lower down-payments.

The result was that buying solar systems became more affordable. And in next two years, other banks too started offering similar low interest rate loans due to higher demand.

Thus, the potential is enormous to accelerate the use of solar power by offering such innovative financing mechanisms to the masses in developing countries. Similar projects are now being initiated and offered by UNEP in China, Indonesia, Mexico, Egypt, Algeria, Tunisia, Ghana, and Morocco.

On February 5, 2010, at the 10th Delhi Sustainable Development Summit held in New Delhi, Prime Minister Manmohan Singh announced the launch of a Mission on Enhanced Energy Efficiency at cutting carbon emissions by 99 million tones. According to Dr. Singh, this will put in place an innovative policy and regulatory regime to unlock the market for energy efficiency, estimated at over $15 billion. Within the ambit of National Action Plan on Climate Change, India has already unveiled one of the world's most ambitious plans for promoting solar energy, targeting an installed capacity of 20,000 MW by the year 2022, reducing CO2 emissions by 99 million tones. Additionally, India is establishing its own National Institute of Himalayan Glaciology in Dehradun. [35]

BRAZIL

The energy minister of Brazil described the commitment signed by federal and state authorities on June 18, 2009 as an "historic step" towards promoting wind power. Wind energy at present accounts for less than one percent of the power generated in South America's giant. Hence this so called "wind charter" is aimed at developing public policies and setting targets for the production of wind energy.

According to experts, Brazil has the greatest wind power potential in Latin America and the Caribbean. Brazilian environment minister Carlos Minc announced on the same day that the left-wing administration of President Luiz Ignacio Lula da Silva planned to gradually eliminate all taxes on wind power-generating equipment. This is a good way to promote wind energy worth following by other nations if they already are not giving big tax-breaks for wind and solar energy buyers.

Minister Minc also lamented that it was "shameful" that a country like Brazil, which has the biggest wind energy potential in the region, produces a mere 200 megawatts, according to the latest wind atlas.[36]

The short-term outlook there is to increase the total wind power generation capacity to 30,000 or 40,000 megawatts though the potential is much higher than that: around 140,000 megawatts, according to the latest wind atlas. However, the Brazilian Wind Industry Association's estimate is at 300,000 megawatts. This, according to the association's president, Lauro Fiuza, represents three times the current capacity of all energy sources in Brazil.

Rio Grande do Norte on the Atlantic coast in the extreme northeast of Brazil is one of the states with the greatest potential for expanding wind energy because of its strong and constant winds.

According to the United Nations Environment Programme (UNEP), Brazil is the world's largest renewable energy market, with 46 percent of the country's energy coming from renewable sources. This represents 85 percent of its power generation capacity due to its vast hydropower sources and its decades-long ethanol industry.

Furthermore, as per UNEP reports, Brazil accounted for 90 percent of new investment in renewable energy in Latin America in 2008. Over 90 percent of new cars run on any ratio of gasoline and sugar cane ethanol, which produces fewer greenhouse gas emissions than fossil fuels.[37]

Lauro Fiuza Jr., president of Brazil's Wind Energy Association, ABEEolica says wind energy in Brazil could increase capacity by 1 gigawatt (gw) annually in the next ten years. He believes, for that to happen, the Brazilian government needs to come up with a long-term wind power program. ABEEolica believes a long-term policy would attract major companies to Brazil, increasing the sector's competitiveness. "Brazil has limited suppliers and it's crucial to increase the number of investors to boost the sector", he said at an energy conference in Rio. He pointed out further that, "Current installed capacity in wind power in Brazil is only 256 mw and the country has 143 gw of estimated potential, not including offshore." A major obstacle for the renewable source is the belief in Brazil that the wind energy is expensive. "Wind power is less expensive than imaginable because it costs less than a third of a fossil liquid fuel-fired thermo plant," he said.[38]

As per solar energy, turning sunshine into electricity is still too expensive to become widespread, but using it to heat water is a viable option that is spreading in many countries and it could make great strides in Brazil.

Two initiatives by environmentalists and interested companies are providing a boost to the solar water heating in Brazil.

Around 2006, a final decision by Mayor Jose Serra in Sao Paulo was required for the legislation to go into effect that would make installing solar water heaters obligatory in new buildings and those undergoing major reconstruction. Inspired by a similar measure in Barcelona, Spain in 2000, a draft law proposed some time back by Vitae Civilis, a non-governmental organization had already been approved by Sao Paolo municipal secretariat for the environment.

"A similar plan in Barcelona led to a ten-fold increase in the number of solar water heaters within three years. It had repercussions throughout Spain," said Delcio Rodrigues, an energy expert at Vitae Civilis.[39]

With results like that in Barcelona, it seems every country around the world should follow Spain's example.

Solar water heaters are particularly important in Brazil which adapted a means of heating water based on cheap hydroelectric energy generated by its numerous rivers. More than two-thirds of Brazilian homes use electric heaters for their hot water. According to Vitae Civilis' estimates, these, together with a lesser number of hot water tanks, account for 6 to 8 percent of total electricity consumption in the country. This consumption is high between the hours of 6:00 and 9:00 PM. At these peak hours, the share of total consumption is 18 percent. Because of this, even electrical distribution companies want to expand the use of solar water heaters. They lose out selling cheap energy this way but they save much more by reducing peak demand, which causes immense waste.

As a result, CEMIG has adapted a policy of solar water use, and is promoting their installation in 100 buildings in Belo Horizonte and also in a housing project in low-income families. So today, this city of 2.4 million people has become the capitol of thermosolar energy in Brazil, with 1,000 buildings using solar-heated water.[40]

Wisely, in the last 30 years, Brazil has developed its own water heater technology and industry. This has reduced the cost of equipment and it is exporting the heaters, according to Brazilian Association of Refrigeration, Air conditioning, Ventilation and Heating (ABRAVA). It has an entire department dedicated to solar water heaters (DASOL).

There are now 25 companies associated with DASOL, and all their products are certified by the state quality control board.

There is a potential to generate 15 billion megawatt-hours by solar radiation in Brazil. This is 50,000 times the country's total electricity consumption, according to Vitae Civilis. What is needed is a national program, directed by the government itself, to promote the advantages of the system and offer incentives, Placidelli told *Inter Press Service*.[41]

SPAIN

Spain is one of the most advanced countries in renewable energy. It has the target of generating 30% of its electricity needs from renewable energy sources by 2010, half of it coming from wind power. By 2006, some 20% of the total electricity demand was already generated from renewable energy sources. By January 2009, renewable energy sources generated some 34.8% of its electricity demand.[42]

Some autonomous regions of Spain lead Europe in the use of renewable energy technology, and plan to reach 100% renewable energy supply in a few years. Galicia, Castile, and Leon are especially near achieving this objective, generating 70% of their electricity demand in 2006 from renewable sources and the other five communities producing more than 50% from renewable sources.

If we take into account nuclear power, then two autonomous regions in Spain have already managed to produce 100% of their electricity demand in 2006, being free from CO2 emissions: Extramadura and Castile-La Mancha.[43] But many environmentalists do not consider nuclear energy as CO2 free. Extramadura is the biggest generator of renewable energy and would displace nuclear energy in the not too distant future. Castile-La Mancha too is one of the biggest producers of renewable energy in Spain and is increasing its share.

Spain has distinguished itself as one of the world's three biggest users of wind power with an installed capacity of 15,515 mw as of January 2008.[44] *In 2007, wind power accounted for close to 10% of the electricity generated in Spain.*[45]
It is interesting to note that on a particular windy day, wind power generation has surpassed all other electricity sources in Spain, including nuclear.[46]

Spain became the first country in the world in 2005 to require the installation of photovoltaic electricity generation in new buildings and second in the world (after Israel) to require the installation of solar hot water systems.[47] Spain is also the first country to ever have a solar energy power tower, situated near Seville.[48]

No wonder, during our trip of Spain in 2007, we were amazed that while traveling by a coach in the countryside, from Madrid to Seville and further south, house after house had solar hot water systems on their terraces. Spain's example is worth following by every nation in the world.

Twenty miles outside Seville, in the desert of southern Spain, more than 1,000 mirrors are carefully positioned. Each is about half the size of a tennis court. The mirrors are a part of the world's biggest solar power plant, a technology that reflects sunlight to superheat water stored at a central tower. The water is heated to 1000 degree C., producing steam that can turn an electricity generating turbine. This Concentrated Solar Power (CSP) technology is a cheaper, simpler, and more efficient way to harness sun's power than methods such as photovoltaic (PV) panels. This 68 million pound plant is designed to generate 20 mw of electricity, enough to power 11,000 Spanish homes.

Spanish firms are moving forward aggressively with CSP: More than 50 solar projects around Spain have been approved for construction by the government. By 2015, the country will generate more than 2 gw of power from CSP, easily exceeding current national targets.[49]

DENMARK

We were pleasantly surprised during our visit in the first week of August, 2009, to Scandinavia. In Copenhagen, Denmark, we saw wind mill after wind mill scattered across the city, especially off shore. In the ocean, they looked like white creatures popping up over the coast line. The city is full of bicycle riders riding their way to work or for other errands or going on picnics in the week-ends. More than 50% of the population in the city rides bikes on a regular basis here. Denmark is one of the most sustainable energy aware nations. It is the most advanced nation as per wind-mill generated power. In last 20 years, Denmark economy has grown 78% but its carbon emissions have been cut in half in the same period.[50]

While biking is a major locomotion power here, wind power here has supplied 19.7% of electricity generation amounting to 24.1% of capacity in Denmark in 2007, demonstrating its wind power generation the highest in proportion to any other country.[51] Denmark has been a pioneer in developing commercial wind power since the 1970s, and today almost half of the wind turbines produced in the world are from Danish manufacturers such as Vestas.[51]

Denmark has very large offshore wind resources, and large areas of sea territory where the water depth is shallow, 5-15 m, where sitting is most feasible. These sites offer good wind speeds, ranging from 8.5-9.0 m/s at a 50 m height.[52] Denmark is connected by transmission line to other

European countries and therefore it does not need to install additional peak-load plants to balance its wind power. It buys additional wind power from its neighbors when needed. Denmark plans to further wind's share of generating electricity by a strengthening of its grid.

In 2008, a deal had been announced between Project Better Place (Palo Alto, US) and the Danish utility Dong Energy that will lead to mass production of electric vehicles and implementation of an extensive recharging and battery swap infrastructure. This will act as a storage capacity for the nation's wind power generation capability. Two million cars in circulation will supply a standby capacity around 5 times the size of Denmark's needs. Smart charging systems will charge batteries when the power is plentiful and feed back the power into the grid when necessary.[53]

Though wind power accounts for almost 20% of the power generated in Denmark, it covers only 10-14% of the country's demand. Power in excess of immediate demand is exported to Norway, Sweden, and Germany. The first two have significant hydropower resources, which can quickly reduce their generation whenever wind farms are generating surplus power, saving water for later. This is a cheap way for northern Europe to store wind power until it is needed.

To encourage investment in wind power, Danish families were offered tax exemptions for generating their own electricity within their own or in an adjoining commune. This could involve buying of turbines outright, but more often families bought shares in wind turbine cooperatives which in turn invested in community wind turbines. By 1996, there were some 2,100 such cooperatives in the country.[54]

The wind turbine industry of Denmark is the biggest in the world, with around 90% of its output being exported. The Danish companies accounted for 38% of the world's turbine market. The industry employed around 20,000 workers and had a turnover of about 3 billion Euros.[55]

It is worth noting that the development of wind power in Denmark has been characterized by a close collaboration between publicly financed research and industry in key areas such as research and development, certification, testing, and the preparation of standards.

Denmark's example is worth emulating by many countries around the world.

SOUTH KOREA

South Korea is like mini-Japan, a highly industrialized, big polluter nation. But it has started making significant progress towards sustainable energy. At present, it is building a $350 million plant on its west coast to harvest the power of the ocean-waves. By installing turbines which can turn by ocean waves generating electricity constantly, the plant will generate 254 megawatts of power, about a quarter of the output of a nuclear power plant. It will supply electricity to half a million homes. This project will be the world's biggest of its kind.

Though South Korea has become one of the world's biggest CO_2 emitters, it is now rapidly moving towards green-energy, planning to spend some $87 billion on reducing its greenhouse gas emissions. This will be one of the most ambitious environmental planning projects anywhere in the world.[56]

ARGENTINA

The Spanish energy company Grupo Guascor announced recently that it will build a $2.4 billion wind power park in southern Argentina that will produce between 900 and 5600 megawatts, according to Barcelona Reporter. The Planning Ministry official cited in the article said the wind park should produce 300 megawatts by the end of 2010 and the rest will be operational by the end of 2011. According to the state news agency Telam, the plant will be the size of the largest plant operating in Europe.

As per estimates, Argentina has about 29 mw of wind power capacity, equivalent to about 1 percent of the grid.[57]

KENYA

It is interesting to realize that the poor, developing African country Kenya is a world leader in the number of solar power systems installed per capita (not the number of watts added). More than 30,000 solar panels, each generating 12 to 30 watts, are sold here annually. For a little investment of $100 for the panel and the wiring, the PV system can be used to charge a battery which then can supply power to run a fluorescent lamp or a small TV for a few hours a day. Rather than connecting to the national electric grid, more and more Kenyans have started using the solar power this way.[58]

PERU

The Peruvian alternative energy company Iberoperuana Inversiones SAC has begun construction on a 240 megawatt wind energy farm. It is this country's first major wind and renewable energy project. Iberoperuana Inversiones plans to invest $240 million in the farm, which is projected to supply clean electricity to an estimated 80,000 families in Peru's southern desert region of Paracas. The wind energy park will be located near the city of Ica which is near the Paracas National Park and the famous Nazca Lines.

The coastal country of Peru is ideal for development of alternative energy with its abundant desert wind and strong sunshine. It is creditable that climate change awareness has started penetrating the small developing countries of Latin America.[59]

THE CARIBBEAN NATIONS

The Dominican ministry of environment awarded licenses for the construction of three wind parks that could produce up to 190 mw of energy. The parks will be built in Bani, Oviedo and Montecristi according to Environmental Minister Omar Ramirez. The Dominican Republic, he mentioned, is the third country in the region and seventh in the world to take part in the Clean Development Mechanism Project. There are already several companies in Santo Domingo which have installed this system, based on the recently passed Renewable Energy Development Incentive Law. This will prompt many Dominicans to invest in order to produce this type of electricity, due to significantly lower costs.[60]

Record breaking fuel costs have forced the Caribbean Utilities Company (CUC) to consider the possibility of harvesting wind power in the Cayman Islands. CUC is seeking experienced and qualified wind-power companies worldwide to look at investing in windmill infrastructure capable of producing up to 10 megawatts or about 13 percent of Cayman's current generation capacity. Already a step ahead of Grand Cayman, Cayman Brac plans on installing as many as 10 windmills on The Bluff. The towers, 199 feet tall, will be capable of supplying 30% to 40% of the island's 3.3 megawatt power needs.

CUC is also encouraging homeowners and small businesses to embrace the use of solar power and even look at technology that uses the temperature of the ocean to generate electricity. Ocean Thermal Energy Conversion (OTEC) is a process that uses the difference between the temperature of shallow water and deep water to run a heat engine. Due to its proximity, Cayman Island could benefit from this process immensely but the technology at present is not economical.

Other Caribbean countries looking into wind power include Jamaica, Granada, the Bahamas, and Barbados, with Jamaica being the leader. Jamaica has one wind farm boasting 23 turbines capable of generating enough electricity to power more than 6,000 households at peak capacity. This sounds insignificant, but this is only the beginning for this tiny nation.[61]

EUROPE'S PROMISING NEW PROJECTS

As mentioned earlier, a concentrating solar power (CSP) plant in Spain uses panels to reflect sun-light on to a central tower to produce electricity. Similar plants are proposed for North Africa. Most recently, a consortium of European corporations and investment banks have announced a proposal to develop a massive amount of solar thermal generating capacity in North Africa. Much of it will be for export to Europe. It could easily exceed 300,000 megawatts, a power roughly three times the electrical generating capacity of France.

According to reports in the Guardian of UK, a tiny rectangle superimposed on the vast expanse of the Sahara captures the seductive appeal of the audacious plan to cut Europe's carbon emissions by harnessing the fierce power of the desert sun.

Dwarfed by any of the north African nations, it takes up an area slightly smaller than Wales but scientists claim it could one day generate enough solar energy to supply all of Europe with clean energy.

Arnulf Jaeger-Waldau of the European Commission's Institute for Energy, speaking at the Euroscience Open Forum in Barcelona, said it would require the capture of just 0.3% of the light falling on the Sahara and Middle East deserts to meet all Europe's energy needs. [62]

As part of a plan to share Europe's renewable energy resources across the continent, the scientists are calling for the creation of a series of huge solar farms—generating electricity either through photovoltaic cells, or by concentrating the sun's heat to boil water and drive turbines.

Countries such as the UK and Denmark ultimately could export wind energy at times of surplus supply through a new supergrid, transmitting electricity along high voltage direct current cables or they could import other green sources such as geothermal power from Iceland. Energy losses on DC lines are far higher than on the traditional AC ones, which makes transmission of energy over long distances uneconomic.

Political support for the grid proposal has come from both Nicholas Sarkozy and Gordon Brown. It answers the perennial criticism that renewable power could never be economic because of unpredictable weather. But its supporters argue that even if the wind is not blowing hard enough in the North Sea, it will be blowing somewhere else in Europe, or the sun will be shining on a solar farm somewhere.

Scientists opine that harnessing the Sahara would be particularly effective because the sunlight in that region is more intense: solar photovoltaic (PV) panels in northern Africa could generate up to three times the electricity compared with similar panels in northern Europe.

Much of the expense would come in developing the public grid networks of connecting countries in the southern Mediterranean, which do not have at present the spare capacity to carry the electricity that the North African solar farms could generate. According to Jaeger-Waldau, the infrastructure of the transfer countries such as Spain, Greece, Italy or Turkey also needs a major re-structuring.

Spain, Portugal, and other southern Mediterranean countries have already invested significantly in solar energy. Algeria has begun work on a vast combined solar and natural gas plant which will begin producing energy in 2010. Algeria plans to export 6,000 megawatts of solar-generated power to Europe by 2020.

Working on the project, the scientists do admit that it would require many years and huge investments to generate enough solar energy from North Africa to power Europe but envisage that it could produce 100 gw by 2050, more than the combined electricity output from all sources in the UK, with an investment of about 450 billion Euros.[62]

Wind currents create waves in the oceans and if that energy is captured to produce electricity, it will be another good source of renewable energy. That is precisely what Portugal is attempting to harness. The world's first commercial wave farm opened in 2008 at the Agucadoura Wave Park near Povoa de Varzim in Portugal. It utilizes three Pelamis P-750 machines with a total capacity of 2.25 megawatts, enough for the annual needs of about 1,500 family homes. A second phase of the project is being planned to increase the installed capacity to 21mw using 25 more Pelamis machines. That will save 60,000 tonnes of CO2 a year compared with a fossil fuel plant.

The Portuguese are also investing heavily in other renewable technologies. They are spending 250 million pounds on more than 2,500 solar photovoltaic panels to build the world's largest solar farm near the small town of Moura in eastern Portugal. It will supply 45 mw of electricity every year, enough to power 30,000 homes. In the past four years, Portugal has more than trebled its hydroelectric capacity and quadrupled its wind power sources—northern Portugal has the world's biggest wind farm, with more than 130 turbines and a factory that builds 40-meter-long blades. Portugal's minister of economy and innovation predicted that his country will generate 31% of all its primary energy from clean sources by 2020.[63] In the spring of 2009, there were reports that Portugal's ambitious Pelamis wave power project was facing some technical and financial difficulties.

Riversimple, a U.K. company founded by former race car driver Hugo Spowers and backed by Porsche scion Sebastian Piech, unveiled on June 15, 2009 the prototype for a two-seat, hydrogen-powered car that promised fuel consumption equivalent to 360 miles per gallon. This car can go 80 km/hr (50 mph) and will be able to travel 322 km (200 mi) per re-fueling, with an efficiency equivalent to 300 miles to the gallon. The cars will be leased with fuel and repair costs included, at an estimated 200 pounds ($315) per month. The company plans to have the cars in production by 2013. It is interesting how newer technologies keep coming up worldwide.[64]

In August 2008, Sweden unveiled plans for new high speed train that promises to slash energy use by 30 percent. The Grona Taget or Green Train, developed by engineering giant Bombardier, in trial boasts a record top speed of 295 km/h (about 183 mph). The project would cut energy consumption by 20 to 30 percent and would lower journey times and operational costs.[65] Sweden and other Scandinavian countries are on the forefronts of green energy revolution.

It is creditable that Europe is ahead of the rest of the world in switching to sustainable energy. From September 1, 2009, the European Union has banned the manufacture and import of 100-watt incandescent bulbs. In the entirety of the European Union, people will have to switch from energy-wasting incandescent bulbs to compact fluorescent lamps (CFLs), which last longer and are up to 75% more efficient. Ditching old-fashioned bulbs will save close to 40 billion kilowatt-hours a year by 2020, equivalent to the output of 10 power stations. Australia has already abandoned incandescent bulbs, and the United States is set to begin phasing them out within the next few years.[66] This is good news. But the world is waiting for the rest of the countries to do the same. Imagine when China, India, Japan, Brazil, Indonesia and others follow suit, how much energy the world will save!

CHAPTER 12
OTHER VITAL STEPS

Human destiny is bound to remain a gamble, because at some unpredictable time and in some unforeseeable manner nature will strike back.
—Rene Dubos, Mirage of Health, 1959

CURBING POPULATION: EDUCATION AND POVERTY

As mentioned in an earlier chapter, no amount of progress by any country or by the world as a whole will be sufficient if the world's population keeps increasing at a rate that is unsustainable. The root causes of overpopulation are poverty and illiteracy. Illiteracy causes poverty, poverty breeds higher populations, and higher populations keep the country poor. It is a vicious cycle. Every country which took control of population growth has made remarkable progress. Those whose population kept increasing, however, lagged behind, mired in poverty no matter how much they tried. All European nations, Japan, Scandinavian countries, Russia, the United States etc. have had zero or low population growth for a long time. Some, like Russia, experience negative population growth. Even China's population growth has slowed as a result of the one child per couple policy. These countries have made remarkable progress and many are rich. Meanwhile, countries such as India, Indonesia, Bangladesh, Pakistan, Nigeria, and Congo etc. have higher rates of population growth and have been struggling to come up for countless years. How can they break free from this vicious cycle of poverty and overpopulation?

Several world leaders spoke about overpopulation at the U.N. Summit in Rome on *"World Food Security: The Challenges of Climate Change and Bioenergy"*, held in June, 2008. To his credit, UN Secretary General Ban Ki-Moon, who has called for a 50 percent increase in global food production by 2030, warned that the world population would reach 7.2 billion by 2015 and inaction now would only make solutions harder. Another noteworthy exception to the general disregard for overpopulation at the conference was Japan's Prime Minister Yasuo Fukuda. He warned that resources are being exhausted, environmental ruin is spreading, and cultivable land is barely increasing anywhere while the world's population is continuing to grow.[1]

UN projections once showed the world population topping 10 billion by mid-century. The 2006 update now projects it at about 9.2 billion, while the U.S. Census Bureau projects it at 9.4 billion. But in the past decade and a half, significant declines in world fertility have been observed. The good news is that the annual increase in world population, now 75 million, is projected by the UN to dwindle to around 30 to 35 million by 2050 with fertility falling to the replacement level.[2]

India was one of the first countries to incorporate population control measures in the early 1950s. With these measures India has reduced its population growth rate considerably and yet its population passed one billion people in 1999 and currently it stands at around 1.1 billion. It is growing by 1.8% annually. The United Nation's "medium" projection has the country's population exceeding 1.5 billion by 2050 and reaching over 1.6 billion before it stabilizes.[3] The assumptions underlying these projections can be questioned, however, as fertility is certainly falling and the course of mortality may not be smooth. Still, substantial growth lies ahead and 1.5 billion people at some time in the century is plausible.

I go to India every other year. I see that even today, India's transportation system, healthcare, roads and bridges, railways, traffic, and other city services are at a breaking point. How would India support another half a billion people? And that with global warming induced food and water shortages, rising ocean levels and millions of envirogees all across the country, destitute, seeking food, shelter, and jobs?

India's population has grown by 650 million in the past 50 years. Many of India's problems are rooted in social and economic conditions and due to policy failure rather than to rises in population. Decreased population growth rate, more environmentally friendly food production, efficient use of water, and reduced pollution are desperately needed and, for the most part, are affordable. The fertility decline needs to be sped up by improving literacy and child survival and extending family planning services; there is no need for draconian China-style measures.

Considerable progress has in fact been made in the past five decades as per population growth in India. With its family planning program, India has avoided millions of births over the last five decades. Living standards and life expectancy have risen. Millions have breached the poverty line. The proportion of poor fell from over 50% to near 30% although the actual numbers have nearly doubled. Fertility has fallen from over 6 children per couple to about 3.2 today.[4]

The economy has grown and diversified. Food production has more than kept pace with population growth—in fact India moved from frequent food crisis and dependence on imports to self sufficiency; though soon India will once again have to import certain food grains. But in this period, India's environment greatly deteriorated. The environment may pose the greatest challenge for India's future. Food shortages will be another major problem. Can India feed another 15 to 20 million more mouths every year? Can it educate and shelter them adequately?

The greatest challenge India faces arising from population growth, is likely to be with water and food security. Today, water scarcity is acute.

What will happen with millions more in the future? Agriculture takes 80 percent or more of country's water. As water is largely low-priced or free, there is no incentive to conserve. Irrigation water is charged for, but such low rates do not pay for essential maintenance of major irrigation schemes. Hence, canal systems are leaky and water is wasted. As much as 30 percent of irrigation water is wasted. There is great need for improvement.[5]

Some positive signs regarding this massive global problem of overpopulation do exist. Some 43 countries around the globe now have populations that are either stable or declining slowly. In countries such as Japan, Germany, Russia and Italy, populations are likely to continue declining over the next half century. A bigger group of countries has reduced fertility to the replacement level or just below. They are headed towards population stability after large group of people move past their reproductive ages. China and the US belong to this group. China, via its one child per couple policy has succeeded in avoiding some 400 million births since this strategy was implemented in the late 1970s.

Iran, in just one decade, lowered its high population growth rate to one of the lowest in the developing world after its government carried out a successful campaign of family planning—though during Ayatollah Khomeini's rule, the growth rate had climbed to 4.2 percent in the early 1980s.

It was almost like a crusade—with religious leaders also being involved—for smaller families. Iran adopted panoply of contraceptive measures including male sterilization, contraceptive pills, and other forms of birth control. These were supplied free of charge. In fact, Iran became a pioneer, the only country to require couples to take a class on modern contraception before receiving a marriage license.

Additionally, a broad-based effort was launched to raise female literacy, raising it from 25 percent in 1970 to 90 percent in 2000. Women's school enrollment went up from 60 to 90 percent. Taking advantage of

TV sets in 70 percent of rural households, television was used to disseminate vital information on family planning throughout the country. All these measures bore fruits. Family size dropped from 7 children to fewer than 3. From 1987 to 1994, Iran cut its population growth rate by half. As of 2006, its population growth rate of 1.3 percent is only slightly higher than that in the United States.[6]

Mexico also applied this approach rather successfully. Its National Television Network Televisa ran a series of soap opera segments on illiteracy. One of these soap opera characters visited a literacy office wanting to learn how to read and write. The day after, a quarter million people showed up at these offices in Mexico City. Finally, 840,000 Mexicans enrolled in literacy courses after watching the series. Miguel Sabido, Vice-president of Televisa, the pioneer of this approach, dealt with contraception in another soap opera. Within a decade, this drama series helped reduce Mexico's birth rate by 34 percent!

Quickly, other groups adopted this approach of Mexico. The U.S. based Population Media Center has initiated projects in some 15 countries and is planning to start in many others. In Ethiopia, for example, their radio dramas addressed issues of family planning, gender equity, health, HIV/AIDS, and the education of girls. Two years after the broadcast began, a survey found that 63 percent of new clients seeking reproductive health care at Ethiopia's 48 service centers reported listening to one of the dramas. Contraceptive demands increased 157 percent.[7]

Perhaps a country like India, which has the biggest movie industry in the world and whose population is crazy for watching melodramatic Hindi movies, soap operas on TVs, and listening to radios-dramas, can benefit tremendously in creating awareness among its millions of people if it adopted this approach. Movie stars in India are like Gods and Goddesses to hundreds of millions of India's masses. They can render an invaluable service to India by educating its millions with the value of population control.

Compared with their benefits, the costs of providing family planning and health services are small. It would take additional funding of close to $17 billion from both industrial and developing countries.

As per UN estimates, meeting the needs of 201 million women who do not have access to effective contraception could prevent 52 million unwanted pregnancies, 22 million induced abortions, and 1.4 million infant deaths each year. In simple terms, costs to society in not filling the family planning gap may be much greater than humanity can afford.[8]

Japan cut its population growth in half between 1951 and 1958. It was one of the first countries to benefit from the demographic bonus. South Korea and Taiwan followed suit. In recent times, China, Vietnam and Thailand have benefited from sharp reductions in birth rates. Though this effect lasts only for a few decades, it is enough to launch a country into a modern era. No developing country has successfully modernized without slowing its population growth. No country has slowed population growth without alleviating poverty, and educating its people, especially women.

REFORESTATION AND FOREST CONSERVATION

Centuries ago, the world was blanketed with dense forests. Major parts of every country, except in the Middle East or other desert nations, were covered with forests. With the advent of industrial civilization and usage of fertilizers, food production increased. So did the world population, especially in the poor and developing countries.

As the encroachment of humans penetrated nearby forests, deforestation began. Humans needed the fuel wood for burning and cooking. People started expanding their croplands to plant more crops in place of forests. Industry replaced forests in many regions. Hence, as humanity increased in population, the forests of the world started declining. Nowhere is this deforestation more acute than in developing countries such as the Indian sub-continent, China, sub-Saharan Africa,

Brazil, Indonesia, Malaysia, the Koreas, and Latin America. Even Europe suffers from terrible deforestation.

The Earth's shrinking forests are a major source of CO2. We need to expand the Earth's forest cover, growing more and more trees to absorb this CO2.

An enormous international effort will be required to restore the Earth; an effort far bigger than the Marshal Plan that helped rebuild war-torn Europe and Japan. Unless such a gigantic effort is undertaken at wartime speeds, environmental degradation could translate into economic decline, massive food and water shortage, soil erosion and state failure that could push the world to the brink—just as it did to earlier civilizations who ignored nature's cries and devastated their forests at their own detriment.

To restore the Earth to her previous vibrant self, it is vital to protect the nearly 4 billion hectares of remaining forest and replant those already lost. Stopping deforestation; reductions in rainfall runoff, flooding, and soil erosion; and restoring aquifer recharge, all will result from worldwide reforestation. There is a vast potential in every country to reduce demands which are shrinking their forest cover. Industrial countries can reduce the quantity of wood used to make paper and the developing nations can reduce fuel wood usage by finding sustainable alternatives.

Paper recycling is one way to protect forests. Paper recycling ranges widely in the top 10 paper producing countries. China and Finland are on the low end, with 33 and 38 percent of the paper they use, with South Korea and Germany on the higher end, at 77 and 66 percent. The world's biggest consumer of paper, the United States lags far behind South Korea, but it has raised its share of recycled paper from 25 percent in 1980s to 50 percent in 2005. It is interesting to note that if every country recycled as much paper as South Korea, the quantity of wood pulp consumed to produce paper worldwide would shrink by one third.[9]

The greatest demand on trees can be attributed to use as fuel wood—accounting for over half the wood removed from forests. To their credit, some international aid agencies, including the U.S. Agency for International Development (AID), are sponsoring fuel wood efficiency projects. In one of its promising projects, 780,000 highly efficient wood cook-stoves, which use far less wood and pollute much less, were distributed in Kenya.

It is also in Kenya where Solar Cookers International is sponsoring the solar cooker project. These cookers are inexpensive, made from cardboard and aluminum foil, and cost $10 each. They cook slowly, retaining flavor much like a crock-pot. Requiring less than two hours of sunshine to cook a complete meal, they can effectively reduce firewood use at a minimal cost. They can also pasteurize water, thus saving lives.[10] Inexpensive government sponsored solar cookers are also used in rural India, with the government encouraging their usage.

Replacing firewood usage by solar cookers, solar powered electrical hot plates, and cooking stoves powered by methane gas generated from cow-dung are some of the ways firewood consumption can be reduced in developing countries.

Many nongovernmental organizations (NGOs) have worked for years to protect forests from clear cutting, but sustainable forestry is now seen as another way to protect forests. A forest and its products can be maintained in perpetuity if only mature trees are felled. The World Bank has recently begun to undertake sustainable forestry projects. In 1997, the World Bank joined forces with the World Wide Fund for Nature to form the Alliance for Forest Conservation and Sustainable Use; they helped designate 55 million hectares of new forest protected areas, and helped certify 22 million hectares of forest by 2005. In mid-2005, the Alliance declared its goal of reducing global net deforestation to zero by 2020.

Six countries account for 60 percent of world's tree plantations. China, which has little original forest left, is by far the biggest, with 54 million hectares of plantations. India and the United States are next, at 17 million hectares each. Canada, Russia and Sweden are close behind.[11]

In July, 2009, India incorporated a $130 million proposal during its 11th plan (2007-12) for protection of its forests. The money will be spent in conserving and restoring unique vegetation, controlling forest fires, and strengthening forestry infrastructure, among other goals. Besides, another proposal under 'capacity building in forestry sector' worth $80 million was established for the training of officials concerned with the protection of forests. India's Minister for Environment and Forest, Jairam Ramesh, said that India's forest cover, presently around 20% of country's land or about 65 million hectares would be extended by another six million hectares over the next six years.

South Korea offers an excellent example of a reforestation success story and model for the rest of the world. The mountainous country was left largely deforested when the Korean War ended half a century ago. Around 1960, under the leadership of President Park Chung Hee, the government launched a National Reforestation Project. Village cooperatives were formed where hundreds of thousands of villagers were mobilized to dig trenches and to create terraces for supporting trees on barren mountains. A researcher named Se-Kyung Chong at the Korea Forest Research Institute writes, "The result was a seemingly miraculous rebirth of forests from barren lands." Today, forest covers 65 percent of the country, an area of about 6 million hectares.[12]

In Turkey, a mountainous country deforested over millennia, a well-known environmental group called TEMA has made reforestation its principal activity. It is founded by two Turkish businessmen, Hayrettin Karuca and Nihat Gokyigit. In 1998, TEMA launched a 10 billion-acorn campaign to restore tree cover and reduce runoff and soil erosion. Since then, 850 million oak acorns have been planted. The program has raised national awareness about reforestation in Turkey.[13]

In Niger, farmers faced severe drought and desertification in the 1980s. They consequently began leaving some emerging acacia tree seedlings in their fields as they prepared their land for crops. When these trees grew, they slowed wind speeds, reducing soil erosion. The acacia which is a legume, fixes nitrogen, thus enriching the soil resulting in higher crop yields. During the dry season, its leaves and pods provide fodder for livestock. The trees also supply firewood.

This approach of leaving 20-150 seedlings per hectare to mature on about 3 million hectares has revitalized farmers in Niger. Assuming an average of 40 trees per hectare growing to maturity, that amounts to 120 million trees. This practice has enabled these farmers to reclaim 250,000 hectares of abandoned land. A major factor to this success story was that tree ownership was transferred from the state to farmers, making them responsible for protecting the trees.[14]

Fortunately, now in many countries, the realization has sunk in to preserve and expand forests. Some, however, are still being deforested. But in most major countries, reforestation is gaining pace.

CHINA

Throughout much of the last century, China was concerned little with the cutting down of its forests. With 1.3 billion mouths to feed and a burgeoning economy, it needed both the land and the lumber. Naturally, deforestation continued at a rapid rate. The damage is apparent in the numbers. Despite millions of trees planted since the 1980s in a small-scale effort, now only a few percent of the country's original forests still stand.

In the 1950s, to fuel steel furnaces and to clear farmland, hills were stripped of trees. This has left hillsides unable to trap rainfall, worsening summer floods that often drown hundreds of people along the Yangtze River in central China, and in the northeast.

In the '90s, efforts to increase grain outputs led to the clearing of more hillsides and farming in areas with fragile soil that soon gave out and turned into wastelands. This has led to deserts spreading in the north and sandstorms that scour Beijing and other major cities.

Devastating floods in 1998 along the Yangtze River finally led Chinese authorities to ban logging in large areas of the vast western province of Schuchuan. There the forests had been turned into fields of stumps. Experiments began that year in planting trees on farmland. By then, Chinese authorities realized that this massive deforestation and soil erosion had to be stopped.

In May, 2002, China embarked on a 20 billion Yuan (US $2.4 billion), 10-year program to plant 170,000 square miles or 440,000 square kilometers of trees—an area about the size of Sweden or California, as reported by China Daily. The replanted area will represent about five percent of the Chinese landmass. The forestry officials said it is the largest reforestation project ever, further warning that only an unprecedented effort can stop expanding deserts, chronic droughts, and deadly flooding that wholesale logging has created. Lei Jiafu, deputy administrator of the State Administration of Forestry, acknowledged that the smaller—but still substantial—tree-planting program under way since 1980s was not sufficient to end the deforestation of China's forests.

Announcing the above plans at a news conference, Lei said, "China has not fundamentally reversed the trend of a deteriorating ecosystem." "One problem facing the new, bigger effort will be finding the trees. China has a thriving tree-farming industry but whether it can produce all the seedlings required remains to be seen," Lei said.[15]

To shield Beijing and other cities from sandstorms, officials plan to create barriers by planting trees on 10,000 square miles of farmland, Lei said. By planting such barriers on a smaller scale, barriers are already created there cutting the size of gritty dust storms that smother the Chinese capitol each spring.

Lei mentioned further that to replace logging in forests, China plans to start commercial tree farms this year, financed by private investors. According to Lei, plans call for 82 million acres of tree plantations to be created over the next 10-15 years. He said officials also hope to decrease demand for timber by boosting efficiency in China's lumber and paper industries.[16]

Since the last 20 years or more, China's forest cover has grown from around 12 percent to more than 18 percent because of a concerted reforestation program and a ban on logging across vast areas of the country. Much of the program's recent success has come from the involvement of poor farmers across the countryside. Years of back-breaking work have turned many hillsides into chestnut and other fruit orchards and have created thousands of tree plantations across the country. This has been part of the country's ambitious plan to restore the nation's forest cover.

For example, in the Anhui Province, forest cover has returned to close to 25 percent. This success can be attributed largely to the involvement of local farmers but also to the adoption of new expertise and the introduction of new techniques.

About 1.5 billion top-grade seedlings were produced to meet the demand created by the Forestry Development in Poor Areas Project in 12 provinces.

Dramatic environmental and social changes were observed in a 2005 evaluation of this project. From 1998 to 2004—in just six years—the average yearly per capita income in project areas increased by 150 percent. Most of that increase (85 percent) materialized from the products of 'economic' trees like chestnut, ginkgo, and bamboo while the rest came from off-farm employment. In project counties, poverty declined from 40 percent in 1998 to 17.5 percent when the project closed in 2005.[17]

Across the participating provinces, forest coverage increased by 6.7 percent over 1997 levels, according to the evaluation, helping to decrease water loss and soil erosion significantly. More than 375,000 hectares of new timber plantations were established and nearly 290,000 hectares of bamboo and economic trees were planted.

"China is the only country in East Asia and Pacific Region that is actually increasing its forest cover," Says Liu Jin, the World Bank's forestry specialist based in Beijing.

Altogether, the World Bank has assisted China with $1.2 billion in financing for eight forestry projects covering 21 provinces since 1985. The long-term program has culminated in the establishment of over 3.8 million hectares of forest plantations—an area roughly the size of Switzerland and about 12 percent of the country's total plantations established over the same period. China plans to increase its forest cover to 23 percent by 2020.[18]

But surprisingly, according to reports as of June 23, 2009, food shortage fears have prompted the Chinese government to suspend the reforestation of marginal arable land, a senior government official said. Abandoning key environmental restoration projects for crop production highlights the growing problem of feeding world's biggest population as cities encroach into farmlands and urban population has started consuming more meat and vegetables.

Lu Xinshe, deputy head of the ministry of Land and Resources, warned that the country was struggling to hold the 120 million hectare "red line" considered the minimum land area required for food self-sufficiency.

With industrialization eating into the countryside, he said authorities would halt the plans to restore arable land to nature. "We will not plan any new large-scale projects to return farmland to its natural state, beyond those that have already been planned," he was quoted as saying by the Reuters news agency.[19]

Any fear of food shortage causes unease in a country where the elderly still remember the devastating famines of early the 1960s that killed between 15 million and 40 million people.

Between reforestation and food security, food security takes precedent. By last year's end, the amount of arable land in China had decreased to within 1% of the "red line."

Due to rising global food prices, Chinese companies have bought the rights to farm swaths of land in the Philippines, Russia, Laos, and Kazakhstan. Also, they have invested in biofuel crops in Congo and Zambia. According to one estimate, there are now one million Chinese farmers in Africa.[20]

INDIA

India is a large country with diverse forest ecosystems and is also a mega-biodiversity country. India's forest ecosystems are critical for biodiversity, watershed protection, and the livelihoods of indigenous and rural communities.

For the last century and half, a massive deforestation of India's forests has taken place. The main cause has been poverty and the people's need for cheap fuel wood and other wood forest products for cooking, hut building, and other necessities for their lives in rural India.

Fortunately, the National Communication of the Government of India has reported to the UNFCCC that the forest sector is a marginal source of CO2 emissions. India has formulated and implemented a number of policies and programs aimed at forest and biodiversity conservation, aforestation (planting new forests), and reforestation. Additionally, India has a goal to bring one-third of its geographic area under forest and tree cover by 2012.

According to the Forest Survey of India (FSI), all lands more than one hectare in area, with a tree canopy density of more than 10 percent are defined as forest. As per the State of Forest Report 2003, total forest cover in India is 67.83 mha. Combining very dense forests, the dense forests which are about half, and tree cover areas which are about 3.04%, the total area under forest cover is 23.68% of the geographic area. According to the UN Food and Agricultural Organization (FAO), the area under forests and other wooded land in India has increased from 63.93 mha in 1990 to 67.70 mha in 2005.[21]

Since 1980, India has been implementing an aggressive aforestation program. It initiated large-scale aforestation under the social forestry program starting in early 1980. In 1980, the Indian government came out with the Forest Conservation Act. This act was enacted to reduce indiscriminate diversion of forest land for non-forestry purposes, and to help regulate and control recorded forest land-use changes. This act has been one of the most effective legislations contributing to reduction in deforestation. Under this act, for any reason if the forest land is used for infrastructure projects, it is mandatory to raise compensatory plantation on an equal non-forested land or equal to double the area on degraded forestland.

Additionally, India has been implementing large-scale aforestation/ reforestation since 1980 under Social Forestry, Joint Forest Management, Sivi-Pasture, Farm Forestry, and Agro-Forestry programs, covering 30 mha. This may have reduced pressure on forests.

The Forest Policy 1988 set the stage for participatory forest management in India. The Joint Forest Management (JFM) program recognized the rights of protecting communities over forest lands. The Forest Department and local communities jointly plan and implement forest regeneration programs and the communities are rewarded for their efforts in the protection and management. This program has enabled the protection of existing forests, rejuvenation of degraded forests, and raising of forest plantations, potentially contributing to conservation of existing forests and carbon stocks.

The Prime Minister of India announced not long ago, a Green India campaign of afforesting six million hectares of degraded forests on an emergency basis, spending close to $1.2 billion initially. It would help reach the national target of having forest and tree cover over 33 percent of the country's land area, up from the current 23 percent.[22]

Thus, India is one of the few countries, particularly among the tropical countries, where carbon stock in forests has stabilized or is expected to increase. This decreases carbon emissions from the forest sector, thus contributing to a stabilization of CO2 concentration in the atmosphere.

According to the Global Forest Resources Assessment, countries such as India and China have experienced an increase in forest area since 1990. That is good news. However, the majority of tropical countries with large forest areas, such as Brazil and Indonesia, have been experiencing large-scale deforestation since before 1990. [23]

SEQUESTERING CARBON BY REFORESTATION

The most important aspect of tree planting or reforestation is that these trees sequester or absorb large quantities of CO2 during their life-span. Note the following interesting proposal.

As reported by Lester Brown of the Earth Policy Institute, a leading Swedish energy firm, Vattenfall has examined the great potential of carbon dioxide sequestration by reforesting the wasteland. According to them, there are 1.86 billion hectares of degraded land in the world— land that was once cropland, forestland, or grassland—and that about half of this, 930 million hectares, has a decent chance of being profitably reclaimed. Some 840 million hectares of this total are in tropical regions, where reclamation amounts to much greater rates of carbon sequestration (each newly planted tree seedling in the tropics absorbs on the average 50 kilograms of CO2 from the atmosphere each year during its growth period of 20-50 years, compared with 13 kilograms of CO2 per year for a tree in temperate regions).[24]

Vattenfall calculates that the maximum technical potential of these 930 million hectares is to absorb roughly 21.6 billion tons of CO2 per year. If, as a part of a global climate stabilization strategy, carbon sequestration were valued at $210 per ton of carbon, the company believes that 18 percent of this technical potential could be realized. This would mean planting 171 million hectares of land with trees. This area, which is larger than that planted with grain in India, would sequester 3.5 billion tons of CO2 per year, or over 950 million tons of carbon. Hence the total cost of sequestering carbon at $210 per ton would be $200 billion. Spread over a decade, this means investing $20 billion a year would give a decisive boost to climate stabilization. This is a fraction of what the United States spends on its military every year!

Since, industrialized and developed countries generated most of this carbon, would it not be fair that they fund this project? An independent body should be set up to fund, administer, and monitor the vast tree planting initiative.

As Lester Brown of The Earth Policy Institute estimates, the cost to the world would be as follows: of planting trees to reduce flooding and conserve soil ($6 billion), also to sequester carbon ($20 billion), protecting top soil on cropland ($24 billion), restoring rangelands ($9 billion), restoring fisheries ($13 billion), protecting biological diversity ($31 billion), and stabilizing water tables ($10 billion). When combined, the total cost will be $113 billion. Can the world afford it? The question is rather silly. With human survival at stake, can the world afford not to undertake these projects? [25]

CONSERVING AND REJUVENATING SOIL

If the food supply of humanity has to be protected, then conserving and rejuvenating soil is of vital importance. Expanding deserts, soil erosion, and land degradation are major problems around the world. Let's see what the leading countries are doing regarding this problem.

The 1930s Dust Bowl threatened to turn the U.S. Great Plains into a huge desert. This was a traumatic experience and it led to some extraordinary changes in American agricultural practices, including the planting of tree shelterbelts (rows of trees planted beside fields to slow wind, thus reducing erosion) and strip-cropping (the planting of wheat on alternate strips with fallowed land each year). Soil moisture gets accumulated on fallowed land as a result of strip-cropping while alternating planted strips reduce wind speed, hence reducing erosion on lands that are idled.[26]

The U.S. Congress in 1985, with full support from the environmental community, created the Conservation Reserve Program (CRP) to reduce soil erosion and control overproduction of commodities. Under this program, farmers were paid to plant fragile cropland with grass or trees. Some 14 million hectares were retired under this program along with the use of conservation practices on 37 percent of all cropland, thus reducing soil erosion from 3.1 billion tons to 1.9 billion tons during the 15 years between 1982 and 1997. The world could learn from this American approach.[27]

One interesting planting method being used widely in America and other countries is that of conservation tillage. This method, instead of plowing land, requires discing or harrowing it to prepare the seedbed, and then uses a mechanical cultivator to control weeds in row crops. The farmers simply drill seeds directly through crop residues into undisturbed soil, controlling weeds with herbicides (one hopes these herbicides are not the polluting variety). A narrow slit is created only at the soil surface, while the rest remains undisturbed. Seeds are inserted into the slits, and the rest of the undisturbed soil is covered with crop residues, keeping it resistant to both water and wind erosion. Besides reducing erosion, this method helps retain water, raises soil carbon contents, and reduces energy use.[28]

In the U.S., to qualify for commodity price supports, farmers were required to implement a soil conservation plan on erodible cropland during the 1990s. Hence, the no-till area expanded from 7 million hectares in 1990 to 25 million hectares in 2004. Now the no-till method is widely used in the production of corn and soybeans; it has spread rapidly in the western hemisphere, covering 25 million hectares in Brazil, 20 million hectares in Argentina, and some 13 million in Canada. Australia has 9 million hectares of no-till croplands.[29]

To stop its desert encroachment, Algeria announced it is concentrating its orchards and vineyards in the southern part of the country so that these perennial plantings will halt the desertification of its cropland. The Moroccan government, in response to severe drought, announced in 2005 that it was allocating $778 million to cancel farmers' debts and to convert cereal-planted areas into less vulnerable olive and fruit orchards.[30]

A similar situation is facing sub-Saharan Africa. The desert is moving southward all across Sahel, from Senegal on the west coast, to Djibouti on the east coast. Grasslands and croplands are turning into desert, causing great concerns for those people displaced. In response, the African union has launched the Green Wall Sahara Initiative. This plan consists of planting 300 million trees on 3 million hectares of land, stretching far across Africa. Senegal which is losing 50,000 hectares of land each year, will be the starting point on the western end.[31]

Likewise, China is planting a long line of trees to protect its land from an expanding Gobi desert. Similar to its stone counterpart, this Green Great Wall, will be 4480 kilometers (2,800 miles) long, stretching from outer Beijing through Inner Mongolia. In addition, China is paying its farmers to plant their cropland with trees in threatened provinces. The goal is to plant 10 million hectares of grainland with trees which easily equals ten percent of China's grainland area.[32] Desert shrubs are being planted in Inner Mongolia in an effort to halt the advancing desert and to reclaim land and stabilize sand dunes. 7000 hectares of land have already been stabilized and reclaimed in Helin County, south of the provincial capital of Hohhot, by planting the desert shrubs on abandoned cropland. The reclamation effort is now being expanded due to this success.[33]

POVERTY ALLEVIATION

Global poverty has declined over the last many decades. It has fallen from over 90 percent of the world's population in 1820 to 51.3 percent in 1992. During the same time period, the average life expectancy has more than doubled from 26 years in 1820 to 60 years by 2002.

Region	$1.25/day				$2.50/day			
	1981	1990	1999	2005	1981	1990	1999	2005
East Asia & Pacific	77.7	54.7	35.5	16.8	95.4	87.3	71.7	50.7
China	84.0	60.2	35.6	15.9	99.4	91.6	71.7	49.5
Eastern Europe & Central Asia	1.7	2.0	5.1	3.7	15.2	12.0	21.4	12.9
Latin America & Caribbean	11.5	9.8	10.8	8.4	29.2	26.0	28.0	22.1
Middle East & North Africa	7.9	4.3	4.2	3.6	39.0	31.2	30.8	28.4
South Asia	59.4	51.7	44.1	40.3	92.6	90.3	86.7	84.4
India	59.8	51.3	44.8	41.6	92.5	90.2	87.6	85.7
Sub-Saharan Africa	53.7	57.9	58.2	51.2	81.0	82.5	83.8	80.5
Total	51.8	41.6	33.7	25.2	74.6	70.4	65.9	56.6

Poverty, in contemporary studies is usually defined as the percentage of households living below a certain income; this is known as the poverty line. World poverty lines are usually measured at somewhere between $1.00 and $3.00 per person per day. To compare poverty rates across countries, household incomes are typically converted to a common currency using purchasing power parity (PPP) exchange rates. PPP is calculated by comparing the costs of equivalent "baskets" of goods such as food, clothing, and housing in various countries. For instance, in 2007 China's gross national income per capita in $US was estimated at $2,360, but its per capita PPP was $5,370.[34]

World Bank calculations show that using a poverty line of $US 1.25 per day, between 1981 and 2005 the percent of the world's population living in poverty decreased from 51.8 to 25.2. Using a poverty rate of $2.50 per day, the decrease was from 74.6 per cent of the world's population to 56.6 per cent. Nevertheless, even if one uses the most optimistic figures, 322 million people lived below the WB $1 per day poverty line in 2000; 600 million lived below $2 per day and 1.2 billion below $3 per day. Using $2.50 per day as a benchmark, the majority of the world's population, 56.6 per cent, was still poor in 2005.

East Asia witnessed the greatest reduction in poverty from 1981 to 2005 and so did the Pacific, including China. Poverty also declined in South Asia as a region, in India, and in the Latin American and Caribbean region. According to other reports, India saw the percentage of its population living on less than a dollar a day progressively decline from 42 percent in 1981 to 24 percent in 2005.[36] By contrast, the poverty rate in Eastern Europe and Central Asia rose in the 1990s but began to decline again in the 2000s. In Sub-Saharan Africa the poverty rate increased between 1981 and 1999, but began to drop in the 2000s.

In 2006, India established the largest employment program in history. It began a program called National Rural Employment Guarantee Act that promises a minimum 100 days of employment each year to the head of every rural household. Since then, more than 90 million Indians have been temporarily employed usually on government-funded road and well-construction projects, earning minimum wages of about $1.60 a day. The program isn't simply extraordinary due to its scale—though, incredibly, it could affect close to 70 percent of India's 1.1 billion citizens. What is exceptional about the program is its transparency. Regular public reviews of all documents—wage cards, bank records, engineers' reports and work completion papers—make sure that the laborers are being paid fairly. If shady practices occur, the villagers can air their grievances at village meetings. For many of India's poor, employment means life-changing development. The program's accountability means local politicians and businessmen who often collude for kickbacks, are made accountable.[37]

Besides such promising programs, India certainly has come out overwhelmingly in support of rural assistance programs for its poor in its 2009 budget.

DESIGNING ECOCITIES

Richard Register, the urban ecologist, and city designer from Oakland, California, writes in his engrossing 2006 book, *Ecocities: Rebuilding cities in Balance with Nature*:

Cities are by far the largest creations of humanity. Designing, building, and operating them have the greatest destructive impact on nature of any human activity. As we are constructing them today, cities also do little social justice, not to mention the grace and subtlety of human intercourse. Yet our built communities, from village and town to city and megapolis, also shelter and launch many of our most creative collaborations and cultural adventures, arts and artifacts. When we build the automobile/sprawl infrastructure, we create a radically different social and

ecological reality than if we build closely-knit communities for pedestrians. Contrast American sprawl with traditional European cities. We will go way beyond that comparison soon enough—far enough, in fact, to demonstrate that cities can actually build soils, cultivate biodiversity, restore lands and waters, and make a net gain for the ecological health of the earth. [He writes further]...Ecocities proposes a fundamentally new approach to building and living in cities, towns, and villages, an approach based on solid principles from deep history and an honest assessment of a troubled future...Cities need to be radically reshaped. Cities need to be rebuilt from their roots in the soil, from their concrete and steel foundations on up. They need to be reorganized and rebuilt upon ecological principles.[38]

Today, the vast majority of Americans live in cities and their suburbs, travelling 30, 40, or even 50 miles to and from their work. We see massive traffic jams all over the world in big cities whether you are in New York, Los Angeles, Bangkok, New Delhi, London, Paris, Shanghai, or Mexico City. Cities are designed for cars, not humans. Large parking lots, parking buildings, underground parking, highways, bridges, mega roads—all dot cityscapes across the United States. Concrete jungle is everywhere; it has replaced our natural habitat. Trees are few and far between. One sees cars everywhere. Pedestrian or bicycle lanes are few and sporadic. If you are a pedestrian or bicyclist in a typical city in the U.S., you will fast be lost or tired because these cities are not designed for you. The buildings are separate, using vast amount of cooling or heating energy. Many buildings have no windows.

Ecocities will be people-pedestrian friendly. Pedestrians, bicyclists, and bus riders should be able to go traverse cities with ease and pleasure. The cities should be compact, as Register advocates. Access by proximity and diversity will be crucial. Cities should consist of walkable centers, transit villages, discontinuous boulevards and agricultural areas close to the center. Cities' food (a large proportion of it) should come from these surrounding agricultural farms. The metropolis must become smaller pedestrian cities, towns, and villages of varying size and character, linked by transit systems taking people longer distances. Cars, of course, should be banned from these ecocities. Only transit system buses or trains will ferry people to the centers of these cities. The sidewalks will have lots of trees and plants with building roof-tops bearing gardens of various sizes and varieties. Water streams, ponds, and lakes will be many within the city, along with green parks for people to stroll. The large buildings of the cities should be interconnected to conserve energy. These buildings should have lot of windows for cool breeze, reducing the need for air-conditioners.

Luckily, there are some cities existing today which can be called ecocities. Curitiba in Brazil, Waitakere in New Zealand, Vancouver in British Columbia, and Portland in Oregon, USA, are some of them. These cities are making good ecological progress and the international ecovillage movement is steadily growing.

CURITIBA

It is interesting to know some details about Curitiba, Brazil. Over the last 38 years, its visionary city planners' strategy was to accelerate transition to sustainable communities and societies. In other words, they strive to guarantee a good quality of life for its residents over the long term, and ensure social inclusion, accessibility, public amenities, urban transparency and environmental sustainability for the city and metropolitan area.

Curitiba, is the best planned city in Brazil and an international model for sustainable development, as a result of strategic, and integrated urban planning. Its strategy was to simply put people first: to improve the environment, cut pollution, waste, and make the quality of life in the city better. Its strategic vision was articulated by its famous and most visionary former mayor, Jaime Lerner, who led the transformation. He said, "There is no endeavor nobler than the attempt to achieve a collective dream. When a city accepts as its mandate its quality of life; when it respects the people who live in it; when it respects the environment; when it prepares for future generations, the people share responsibility for that mandate, and this stared cause is the only way to achieve that collective dream."[39]

Curitiba's most unique strategy is it maximizes the efficiency and productivity of transportation, land-use planning, and housing development by integrating them so they support one another to improve the quality of life for its residents.

The city pioneered the idea of an all-bus transit network with bus-only avenues created along well-defined structural axes that were also used to channel the city's growth. The transit system is rapid and cheap, and is currently being integrated with the metropolitan region. Its efficiency encourages people to leave their cars at home. Curitiba boasts the highest public ridership of any Brazilian city (about 2.14 million passengers a day), and it registers the country's lowest rates of ambient pollution and per capita gas consumption. The bus-fare is cheap, so it helps the poorer residents living in the periphery. A standard fare is charged for all trips, meaning shorter rides subsidize longer ones. One fare can take you 70 kilometers.

Though there are more car owners in this city than anywhere in Brazil, auto traffic has declined by 30% and atmospheric pollution is the lowest in Brazil.

Curitiba has a network of 28 parks (nearly one-fifth of the city) and wooded areas. In 1970, there was less than 1 sq. km. of green space per person; today, there are 52 sq. km. per individual. Its residents planted 1.5 million trees along its streets. The builders get tax breaks if their projects include green space. Flood waters diverted into new lakes in parks solved the problem of dangerous flooding, while protecting valley floors and riverbanks, acting as a barrier to illegal occupation, and providing aesthetic and recreational value to the thousands of people who use city parks. The city has 200 kilometers of bike paths.[40]

The city also has a "green exchange' employment program that focuses on social inclusion, benefiting both those in need and the environment. Low-income families living in shantytowns unreachable by truck bring their trash bags to neighborhood centers where they exchange them for bus tickets and food. This means less city litter, fewer diseases, less garbage dumped in sensitive areas such as rivers and a better life for the undernourished poor. The city also has a program for children where they can exchange recyclable garbage for school supplies, toys, chocolates, and tickets for shows.

Under the "garbage that's not garbage" program, 70% of the city's trash is recycled by its residents. Once every week, a truck collects metal, paper, cardboard, plastic, and glass that have been sorted in the city's homes. The city's paper recycling alone saves the equivalent of 1,200 trees a day. Besides environmental benefits, money raised from selling materials goes into social programs, and the city employs the homeless and recovering alcoholics in its garbage separation plant.

Downtown areas are transformed into pedestrian streets, including a 24-hour mall with shops, restaurants and cafes, and a street of flowers with gardens cared for by street kids.

Most of the downtown is a vibrant pedestrian zone. No wonder, tourism generated $280 million in 1994, 4% of the city's net income. Per capita income is 66% higher than the national average. The city's 30-year economic growth rate is 7.1%, much higher than the national average of 4.2%.[41]

This is the wonder that is Curitiba! If humanity is to survive the oncoming catastrophe of global warming, for sustainable living, all the cities of the world would be wise to emulate Curitiba's wonderful example.

CO2 EMISSIONS

Before the industrial revolution, before humans started burning oil, coal, and natural gas, the atmosphere contained about 280 parts of CO_2 per million. Since then, the world has been adding the CO_2 constantly because of the fossil-fuel based world economy. Today, that figure stands at 387-390 ppm. The warmer air holds more water vapor than the colder atmosphere of the old Earth; that means more water evaporates from the ocean, generating more clouds, more rain, and more storms. This is all part of global warming.[42]

There is a conflict between a powerful drive to use fossil fuel and the real threat of CO2 emissions that go with it. As author Wallace Broeker and Robert Kunzig have suggested in their book, *Fixing Climate*, one way to get an idea of both the scale of the problem and an equitable solution might look like, is to imagine a "carbon pie." The pie represents the total amount of CO2 we can still emit into the atmosphere without its disastrous impact. We don't know at what level the CO2 concentration will become truly dangerous—at what level the climate might shift so that the melting of ice sheets becomes unavoidable or say the intensity of drought in the American West which threatens the civilization we have built here. According to James Hansen, director of NASA Goddard Institute for Space Studies in New York, that threshold is at 450 parts per million. The Goddard climate model forecasts a one-degree Celsius warming from that concentration and Hansen thinks one degree warmer average temperature than today is enough to threaten the melting of the ice sheets.

Hansen's words have great credibility in this field. He was the first one to warn while testifying to the Congress in 1988 that global warming was already happening, and he was right. He may be right again that 450 ppm is the limit of safety for atmospheric CO2. The problem is, that goal of CO2 at this level is not attainable. At present, every 4 gigatons of CO2 we emit in the atmosphere adds about 1 ppm to the CO2 concentration. The size of the pie that takes us to 450 ppm—only 70 ppm away from the current level—is thus only 280 gigatons. At global emissions from fossil-fuel burning currently at close to 8 gigatons annually, we will reach the 450 ppm limit in 30 years even if we don't accelerate emissions—and at present we are accelerating.[43]

According to Broecker and Kunzig, a more realistic goal would be 560 ppm—a doubling of preindustrial CO2—for which the middle-of-the-range climate-model forecast is warming of 3 °C. Then our carbon pie would be 720 gigatons. But how should the pie be cut? A fair and equitable solution would be each nation getting a pie proportional to its population. As a group, industrialized countries would get 20% of the pie, or 144 gigatons. Currently, they are emitting about 5 gigatons annually; at that rate, they would gobble up their pie in less than 30 years. That means, three decades for them to reduce their emissions to zero. This gives us some idea of the challenge these countries are up against, if they want to take full responsibility for the consequences of their prosperity and do as much as possible to protect the planet from dangerous global warming.

It is clear; industrialized nations are not and cannot reduce their emissions to zero in thirty years. Most of them are not going to meet their much less challenging obligations under the Kyoto Protocol—which calls on them to reduce their emissions by 2012 to below the 1990 levels—on average 5 percent below. The U.S. which signed but never ratified the 1997 protocol has not even tried to reduce its CO2 emissions, though they declined somewhat due to a mild winter. One of the biggest short comings of the Kyoto Protocol is that it placed no obligations on developing countries, and that is becoming obvious now.[44]

The idea of a carbon pie offers us a conceptual way out of this dilemma. It impresses upon the developed nations that any way out of this requires a deal between the developed and the developing world. To avoid the choice between protecting the climate and torpedoing their economies, the former will have to buy extra pieces of pie from the later. In return, the developing nations will get technical and economic help with developing their economies while at the same time reducing their own CO2 emissions. The bigger slices of pie that an equitable division will allot them would enable them to use fossil fuels for a longer time, thus allowing them to develop.

The carbon pie simplifies the reality. To stabilize atmospheric CO2 at 560 ppm, the world may not reduce its emissions all the way to zero, the above authors contend, because oceans will continue to absorb CO2, but at a reduced rate for a couple of centuries. However, by the second half of this century, the world would need to emit much less CO2 than now— while energy demand would have doubled or tripled. In other words, humans will have to find a way to produce energy at two to three times the current demand while simultaneously reducing CO2 emissions below current levels—and finally to zero.[45]

* * *

It is noteworthy to look at per capita individual CO2 emissions for each country:

Each Country's Share of CO2 Emissions

The world's countries contribute different amounts of heat-trapping gases to the atmosphere. The table below shows data compiled by the Energy Information Agency (Department of Energy), which estimates carbon dioxide emissions from all sources of fossil fuel burning and consumption. Here is the list of 20 countries with the highest carbon dioxide emissions (data are for 2006).

As the data illustrates, China is the biggest emitter of CO2 while the United States is next, followed by Russia, India, Japan and Germany. However, when you look at per capita emissions, a different story emerges. By far the biggest per capita emitter is Australia with 20.58 tonnes per person, with United States second, with 19.78 tonnes, followed by Canada with 18.81 tonnes of CO2 per person. The Chinese citizen is way behind with only 4.6 tonnes, while an Indian clocks in at a mere 1.2 tonnes. African countries such as Kenya at 0.3 tonnes are some of the lowest.

The fairest way to judge a country's responsibility for restricting their CO2 emissions is to look at their per capita CO2 emissions. The above data suggests the majority of the responsibility belongs to the rich and developed countries as they are the biggest per capita polluters.

Fair and equitable distributions of per capita CO2 emissions rights should have been the core topic of negotiations at Copenhagen Conference. That means the rich and developed nations should reduce

	Country	Total Emissions (Million metric tons of CO2)	Per Capita Emissions (Tons/capita)
1.	China	6017.69	4.58
2.	United States	5902.75	19.78
3.	Russia	1704.36	12.00
4.	India	1293.17	1.16
5.	Japan	1246.76	9.78
6.	Germany	857.60	10.40
7.	Canada	614.33	18.81
8.	United Kingdom	585.71	9.66
9.	South Korea	514.53	10.53
10.	Iran	471.48	7.25
11.	Italy	468.19	8.05
12.	South Africa	443.58	10.04
13.	Mexico	435.60	4.05
14.	Saudi Arabia	424.08	15.70
15.	France	417.75	6.60
16.	Australia	417.06	20.58
17.	Brazil	377.24	2.01
18.	Spain	372.61	9.22
19.	Ukraine	328.72	7.05
20.	Poland	303.42	7.87

Top 20 Countries
2006 CO2 Emissions

their emissions drastically while allowing the poorer developing nations to increase theirs, slowly and sensibly to certain levels. Unfortunately, it was not.

From the above data, it is apparent that the poor nations of the world and the developing countries will need much capital investment. As we all know, it is the developed world, that is mainly responsible for the current dilemma that we are in: global warming and climate change. They are the ones who since the industrial revolution have emitted huge amounts of CO2 and other greenhouse gases that have pushed the world to the current crisis. It is only fair that now, they should help other developing and poor nations switch to renewable energy economy, mass education, and eradication of poverty. They need help: the financial and technological assistance to build the infrastructure to move towards sustainable development while developing their own economies. If the G-8 nations (industrialized democracies) fail to help the developing nations in this endeavor, then the developing nations might fail to switch to sustainable economy and lifestyle even if they try hard. They simply may not have enough wherewithal or technology. Not only are the developed nations obligated to lend this aid, as a matter of fact, it is in their interest to do so.

The picture that emerges from these figures is one where—in general—developed countries and major emerging economy nations lead in total carbon dioxide emissions. Developed nations typically have high carbon dioxide emissions per capita, while some developing countries lead in the growth rate of carbon dioxide emissions. Obviously, these uneven contributions to the climate problem are at the core of the challenges the world community faces in finding effective and equitable solutions

CHAPTER 13
SUSTAINABLE SOCIETIES &
FREEDOMOCRACY

Only to the white man was nature a "wilderness".
—Luther Standing Bear

We do not inherit the earth from our ancestors; we borrow it from our children.
—Native American Proverb

There are a few societies on Earth who have grasped the secrets to sustainable living and are doing just that. Here are some of them:

CUBA: A MIRACLE

Cuba's story is nothing short of amazing. The world can learn from this island nation how to convert from fossil-fuel based to totally organic agriculture.

Prior to the Cuban revolution when Fidel Castro overthrew Fulgencio Batista in 1959, Cuba was a highly unequal society with very rich people and extremely poor workers. Only 8% of the rich farmers controlled 70% of the land. The Cuban economy was under the control of U.S.

Corporations, including banking, communications, mining, oil refineries, sugar production, and most large plantations.[1]

The majority of rural workers consisted of landless seasonal laborers with no schooling, no healthcare, no electricity, and no running water. They worked only three months a year, at planting season and at harvest.

When the revolution came, most wealthy landowners fled to the United States. Their former holdings were expropriated and given over to the laborers or former sharecroppers. They formed cooperatives and the government provided them with technical training, supplies, guaranteed markets, and crop insurance.

The Cuban revolution has been succeeded by three periods of agrarian reforms: the first in 1959, second in 1963, and finally the current land reforms of 1990s. The first reform put a limit of 1000 acres on private land ownership. The number of small farmers tripled followed by the establishment of state farms replacing large plantations. The second land reform reduced the ownership limit to 165 acres per person. The land reform of 1990s can be more appropriately called a controlled privatization.[2]

By 1965, state farms controlled 63% of the arable land, and more than 160,000 small farmers owned and tilled an additional 20% of the arable land. The small farmers joined farmer associations, Credit and Service Cooperatives (CCSs), and Agricultural Production Cooperatives (CPAs), which together controlled some 22% of the arable land. The CCSs and CPAs are in turn, confederated in the National Association of Small Producers (ANAP), which provides training and a number of other services to its members. It also negotiates with the government on prices and credit.[3]

With this set up, by the 1980s, Cuba had surpassed most other Latin American countries in nutrition, life expectancy, education, and per capita GNP. The literacy rate had increased to astonishing 96%, and 95% of the population had access to clean water. But Cubans had achieved a large degree of industrialization and equity through a trade regime that was unfortunately highly dependent on imports.

From the beginning of the revolution till the 1980s, Cuban agriculture had become highly mechanized compared to any other Latin American country. Though it manufactured everything from computers to pharmaceuticals, their main export was sugar. State-owned sugar plantations covered more land than food crops by the 1980s. Some 75% of its export consisted of sugar and its derivatives, sold exclusively to the Soviet Union, Eastern and Central Europe, and China.[4]

As Cuban agriculture was overwhelmingly invested in sugar, tobacco, and citrus fruits, it had to import 60% of its food, mainly from Soviet bloc countries. Cuba also imported 48% of its fertilizers, 82% of its pesticides, 36% of its animal feed for livestock, and most of its oil and fuel used to produce sugar.[5]

But due to its heavy dependence on vital imports on Soviet Union and Eastern bloc countries, the country would be left highly vulnerable if anything happened to its trading partners. The day of reckoning came in 1989 when the Soviet Union started collapsing. The first few years after the collapse had a severe impact on Cuba. Additionally, the crisis was compounded as the United States tightened its economic blockade, thus increasing the suffering of the Cuban people. Cuba suffered some 7,500 excess deaths per year during this critical period that can be attributed to these brutal economic sanctions. Unfortunately, the economic blockade of Cuba, imposed in early 1960s, is still in effect.

Upon the collapse of the Soviet Union, almost overnight, Cuba lost 85% of its trade. Imports of fertilizers, pesticides, and animal feed were reduced by 80%. The petroleum supplies for agriculture were halved.[6]

Food imports which accounted for 60% of the food consumed in Cuba were halved. By 1994, agricultural production dropped to 55% of the 1990 level. Per capita protein, caloric, and dietary fat intakes dropped by huge margins. The average Cuban is reported to have lost some 20 pounds by 1994. Undernourishment jumped from 5% to over 20%.[7]

But two government policies are credited with preventing the crisis from reaching emergency levels: food programs targeting the most vulnerable populations (the elderly, the children, and pregnant and lactating women), and food distribution ration cards that guaranteed a minimum food provision for every citizen. This government enforced safety net kept the crisis from reaching the proportions comparable to those of North Korea, where millions starved. In the meantime, the government got the breathing space to redesign its agricultural sector to meet the new challenge.

Cuba, all by itself, emerged from a crisis that could have made another country destitute. It destroyed the myth that organic agriculture cannot support a modern nation. Today, the Cuban GNP has grown every year since 1995. Solid gains in employment, productivity, and exports have been reported. Fruit production has returned to its 1989 level and surpassed it in the case of plantains. Prodigious increases in vegetables and tubers production have been achieved. The caloric intake of the average Cuban has seen an increase of 33% from the 1994 level.[8] Around the world Cuba has been recognized as a success, without the help from the World Bank or the IMF, in total contrast to their usual structural reform policies.

Cuban scientists had been aware for decades of the negative effects of industrialized agriculture. Cuba had seen big problems with soil erosion and mineral depletion. Smartly, these scientists had already developed organic and ecological methods of farming before the 1990s' crisis came. Following the crisis, Cuba was ready. The Castro government embraced these new methods and promoted them with new agrarian policies.

The task before them was clear: to transform the nation's agriculture from high input, fossil-fuel dependent farming to low input, self-reliant organic farming. Farmers did this first by remembering the techniques their ancestors had used before the arrival of industrial agriculture—techniques such as intercropping and manuring. Secondly, they incorporated new technologies made available to them by the government as a result of scientific research—technologies such as biopesticides and biofertilizers. Biopesticides developed the use of microbes and natural enemies to fight pests, along with resistant plant varieties, crop rotation, and cover cropping to suppress weeds. With these techniques, biofertilizers were developed using earthworms, compost, natural rock phosphate, animal manure and green manure, and the integration of grazing animals. With no oil available, tractors were replaced with animals to plough the land.

Huge state farms were not compatible with this new program. Agroecological farming simply does not work on a large farm. In agroecological farming, the farmer must have intimate knowledge of every patch of his farm. The farmer must know where to add the fertilizer, how much, and where the pests are harboring or entering the field. Smaller farms are easier to manage, and are more suitable for sustainable agriculture.

In September, 1993, the big farms were broken up. The government instituted a new program to restructure state farms as private cooperatives owned and managed by the workers. These cooperatives were called Basic Units of Cooperative Production (UBPCs). The new program transferred 41.2% of the arable land—most of the state farms of the country—into 2,700 new cooperatives with a membership totaling 122,000 farmers. Thousands of families moved to rural areas where their land rights were guaranteed by the government.[9] Linking the farmer to the land, the cooperative owned the production and a member's earnings were dependent on his or her share of the cooperative's income. Members were compensated based on their productivity, not their timesheet. This provided a greater incentive within the cooperative, yet allowed for larger economies of scale, mechanization, and the communal spirit which the cooperatives offered.

Another unique feature of the reforms was urban agriculture. It actually started as a spontaneous development that was later backed by the government official policy. Today, half of the produce consumed in Havana is cultivated in urban gardens. Amazingly, urban gardens produce 60% of the vegetables consumed in all of Cuba. These gardens provide 215 grams of vegetables per person per day for the entire population.[10]

Today, neighborhood gardens and community horticultural groups not only produce food for their members, but they also donate to schools, clinics and senior centers, and still have enough excess produce to sell in the neighborhood. Neighborhood markets sell produce at well below the cost of the larger community markets, providing vegetables to those who cannot afford the higher prices. In early 2000, there were hundreds of vegetable stands operating, with prices one third to half of the prices at farmers' markets.

The government, recognizing the potential of urban agriculture, in 1994, created an urban department in the ministry of Agriculture. The Urban Agriculture department formalized growers' claims upon vacant lots and legalized the rights of growers to sell their produce. The department simply promotes urban agriculture without imposing its authority upon the movement. Laws require urban agriculture to be completely organic, and the raising of livestock in urban areas is banned. By law, all residents are given up to one-third of an acre of vacant land on the edge of the major cities. By the beginning of 2000, more than 190,000 people had applied for and received these personal lots. In addition, the government has opened a number of neighborhood agricultural stores to supply organic inputs and extension services.[11]

Though caloric intake has not reached the 1980s levels, it is beyond doubt that domestic food production in Cuba has made a remarkable recovery, and that too by organic agricultural methods. During the 1996-1997 growing season, Cuba attained its highest ever production level for ten of the thirteen items in the Cuban diets. Potato, cereal, vegetables, tubers, beans, and citrus production have increased substantially since

1994. Animal protein production still remains depressed partially because the market reforms do not apply to meat, eggs, and milk which are not easily sold in farmers' markets. Also, the agroecological model does not apply easily to animal production. But the biggest factor keeping animal protein production down is due to the fact that the transition from industrial animal breeding to sustainable, ecologically feasible animal breeding is a slow process.[12]

The World Bank has reported that Cuba is leading nearly every other developing nation in human development performance. Amazingly, the biggest Cuban export today is that of ideas. Today, Cuba hosts a number of visiting farmers and agricultural technicians from throughout the Latin Americas and elsewhere. Cuba has close to a 98% literacy rate. It has one of the highest per capita numbers of doctors. Cuban agriculture experts are currently teaching agroecological farming techniques to Haitian farmers and others. Cuba has proven that biodiversity is not just a conservation strategy but a production strategy.

Today, 80% of Cuba's food production is organic. It has developed and is now an exporter of biofertilizers and biopesticides. In 1980, Cuba used 21,000 tons of pesticides. Today, it barely uses 1,000 tons. Realizing the scarcity of oil, Cuba started breeding thousands of oxen. Today, it uses these farm animals for its agriculture, not oil consuming tractors. Cuba consists of 2% of Latin America's population but it has 11% of its scientists.[13]

Agriculture is not the only field where Cuba has made wonderful progress. It has also made great strides in sustainable development. Solar power is promoted everywhere. Solar power is used in many schools and universities. Recently, more than 2,000 schools were supplied with solar panels. In many rural areas, solar panels power schools, clinics, community centers and peoples' homes. All over Cuba, water is pre-heated using the strong tropical sun. Sugar-mills are turned into power plants as sugar fibers and other crop wastes are burned, producing heat that generates electricity.

Due to the oil crisis after the Soviet Union's collapse, Cuba had to develop its mass transit system almost overnight. Old trucks were converted to buses. Car pooling and hitchhiking are common. Government cars and vehicles are required to give rides to any who need it. Bicycles are encouraged and have become common. Car travel has been drastically reduced.

Cement production has been reduced. Houses are small. Rural houses, though, have more space and gardens to grow food. Schools are within walking distance in Havana and people usually live not far from their work places. Healthcare is free all over Cuba. Today, Cuba has 57 doctors per thousand people while the United States has 28. Surprisingly, for a poor country, the life expectancy and infant mortality rate are comparable to those of the United States.

Students in Cuba are now participating and learning how to grow food. They visit rural villages; working in fields is part of their community service.

At the time of Columbus, Cuba was covered with 90% forest. But by 1959, it had declined to 14%. Forests were recklessly cut for plantation purposes. Today, Cuba has active reforestation programs, and at present, forests cover some 27% of its land. Millions of trees are planted all over Cuba.[14]

As fossil-fuels run out, which they surely will, there will be a major crisis gripping the world, especially in those countries which are so heavily dependent on fossil-fuel based industrial agriculture. As declining fossil fuel production adversely impacts current industrial civilization, Cuba may find itself in a position to help lead the world into sustainable agriculture and living. The world must learn from the Cuban example. It may ignore Cuba's miraculous transformation of its agriculture at its own peril.

KERALA, INDIA

Though India has long done rather poorly in the United Nation's Human Development Index, ranking 132-134th, one Indian state has done remarkably well: the state of Kerala. It means 'God's own country; and it is indeed. From its development indicators, Kerala looks like a different country. It boasts nearly universal literacy—91% as opposed to the Indian national average of 65%. It is also one of the fastest growing states in India, second only to Goa.

So what is so unique about Kerala that is so difficult for other Indian states, let alone for other countries in Asia, Africa, and Latin America to follow? While the world is looking for alternatives to the industrial and economic fundamentalism model of development, Kerala may hold a secret to sustainable growth and development.

In addition to its outstanding literacy rate, Kerala boasts one of the nation's best healthcare systems, even for those who cannot afford to pay user fees and so depend on government hospitals. While India's infant mortality rate is 32 per 1000 births, Kerala's is half, 16 per 1000. The IT, service, and tourism sectors in Kerala are doing exceptionally well (as well as in the rest of India). Agricultural production and small-scale manufacturing are also growing. Kerala offers a lush green countryside, its back-waters area—which are a pleasure for boat rides—and lots of other tourist attractions. Tourism is a big industry there. The air is pure, unpolluted, and clean as there are very few industries.

But, a few features stand out about Kerala's political and economic history. The state had a matrilineal and matriarchal society, with a line of forward-thinking queens that still ruled Kerala in the early days of British Empire. For example, the queen of Trivandrum issued a royal decree in 1817 declaring that "the state should defray the entire cost of the education of its people in order that there might be no backwardness in the spread of enlightenment." Not even Britain or the United States provided such services for their own people until the later part of the 19th century.[15]

Kerala has been ruled for last 50 years by a single party, the Communist Party of India (Marxist) or CPI (M). Three successful reforms were pushed through in the 1960s and 1970s by the CPI (M). The first and the most crucial one was the land reform. It was an attack on capitalism's founding principles—the right to property. For 10 years, the central government intervened and blocked its implementation. But planners and unions realized that building a more egalitarian and equitable economy and society required attacking the old feudal system at its roots, and small farmers weren't going to stand for anything less. Finally the law came into effect.

Secondly, the CPI (M) intentionally and methodically invested in education, setting goals so popular with the electorate that when the communists lost power, the new governments did not dare to change the education policies.

Lastly, Kerala invested heavily in healthcare financed by the government. The state now boasts 160 patient-beds per 100,000 people, the highest rate in the country.[16]

Because of universal education in Kerala, one of the greatest benefits accrued is the slow and controlled rate of its population growth. Women's education is the key to low population growth. Kerala thus has the lowest population growth rate in India and in the world; a major achievement.

Another unique characteristic of Kerala is its multi-religious population—approximately an equal percentage of Hindus, Muslims, and Christians—all living in peace with each other.

Thus Kerala offers an alternative; invest in people by providing free education, free health-care, and land reforms which ultimately lead to the development of a strong middle-class. Income distribution is more equal here, so there are fewer rich people than in other parts of India. But then there are fewer poor people as well. For ensuring basic human rights and human dignity for all, along with sustainable green-living, Kerala offers the world a unique model that is worth following by the rest of India and the world.

AMISH PEOPLE

One group of people in North America who are well-prepared to survive the crash of industrial civilization are the Amish people. Originating in Switzerland in the early sixteenth century as a division of Mennonites or Anabaptists, their name comes from a Swiss Anabaptist, Jacob Amman, who taught the ethic of simple, non-resistant (they don't serve in the military) life, living close to the soil, sharing material goods, and following the bible literally. They were terribly victimized in Europe and were saved from extinction by William Penn, who granted them a haven from religious persecution in Pennsylvania, the New World.

Since early colonial times, the Amish have preserved their distinctive culture, their language, their religion, their dress, and their way of life. Most of them live in Pennsylvania, Ohio, and Indiana but they are present in nineteen US states, Canada, and Central America as well.

One finds them driving horse buggies in rural gravel roads in these states with men wearing broad-brimmed hats and plain-cut trousers, the women and little girls wearing bonnets and ankle-length dresses. They usually shun cars, airplanes, telephones, electricity or other modern gadgets and live the life of rural folks who lived centuries ago. The most important factor that will enable them to survive the collapse is their total independence from fossil-fuel based fertilizers in their farming. They don't use any. They farm organically and achieve decent yields. Thus they are a peaceful people, don't need any fossil-fuel based energy, live by the soil, simply and peacefully.[17]

FREEDOMOCRACY RATHER THAN CASINO CAPITALISM

What are the main mantras of capitalism? Growth, growth and more growth...profit, profit and still more profit...Capitalism is based on a continuous growth of economy and more profit for corporations. But continuous growth is in obvious direct conflict with sustainability (or quite frankly) common sense. There is a limit to growth. The Earth's resources, on which modern industrial civilization is based, are limited. They are not infinite! The World's major industries today derive their raw materials from the earth whether it is oil, natural gas, coal, forest products such as wood and paper, mined metals, plastics and chemicals from fossil fuels...the list is long. While multinational corporations rob this Earth of its vital resources and amass fortune, the vast numbers of this planet's children are forced to live on less than a dollar a day. Is not human being born to this mother Earth an equal inheritor of her bounty?

The fossil fuel based capitalist economy strives to keep growing bigger and bigger, but how long can it last? How can the growth be limitless? Oil is peaking and is going to deplete in a few decades. Coal, natural gas, and even metals will meet the same fate. Our fresh water supply is diminishing by the day. It is obvious that the unbridled growth that this casino capitalism preaches and thrives to achieve as we see it in the United States is unsustainable. In the long run, growth will have to stop.

We are feeling the pinch of over population in many countries such as China, India, Bangladesh, and many others. Just as no one imagined in the 1960s that communism would collapse in a few decades, how are we so certain that capitalism will survive forever? Could this casino capitalism which is based on corporate greed and utter inequality between both citizens of a country, and fellow humans of this planet, survive for another century? It is doubtful.

An economic system like we have in America today—and like ones to a lesser degree which exist in Europe and Japan—where everyone is in it for themselves, a dog eat dog mentality, cutthroat competition, where a

CEO of a fortune 500 company makes $10,000 a minute while a poor Mexican farm worker makes less than that amount in a year, or where a CEO makes 400 to 500 times more money than an average worker in the same company in America today—how long can such an unfair system survive? Should it survive? Can't humanity do better than that? Can't all humans be fairer than that to each other? Aren't all men created equal as the great U.S. constitution asserts? Why are some more equal than others? Why does such disparity exist between fellow citizens and fellow humans? Every one born on this planet should be equal, is equal, and has an inalienable right to a decent life. Yet capitalism offers us such an uneven treatment of different human beings. It almost gives those who have power, knowledge, education, and connections the rights to rob those who are not so fortunate as to have been endowed with these facilities. Why should a civilized society allow such an unfair treatment of those less fortunate at the hands of those who are powerful?

Something is certainly wrong with the system. There is a limit to growth. Sooner or later, it will collapse; just like fiefdom did, like monarchy did, like many dictatorships did, or like Soviet communism did. Soviet Communism allowed the dictatorship of the communist party and a few of its leaders—no different from this capitalism which allows the rich and the powerful to exploit, dominate, and subdue those who are weak, uneducated, and not united. A good, fair, and just system is one which protects all, the strong and the weak; is one which has provisions to protect the weakest class of the society; is one which ensures adequate food, decent housing, good healthcare and well paying jobs for all its citizens. Instead of a system which allows a few individuals to amass vulgar fortunes, a reasonable system will see that there is fair distribution of resources for all.

I must say that the Scandinavian countries of Denmark, Norway, and Sweden are the exception. These countries have perhaps the best and most equitable form of democracies. In these countries, there are few people who are too rich and few who are too poor. Their democracy is highly transparent and devoid of major corruption. During our visit to

Scandinavia in the first weeks of August, 2009, we took a tour of the Swedish parliament. There we realized that there are no lobbyists in Sweden and the functioning of the parliament and the government is extremely transparent. No one can lobby to the members of parliament to vote in their favorite cause if that serves the interests of any industry or that of an individual. Also, in these Scandinavian countries, every citizen is covered for his or her health from cradle to grave. Education is utterly free, from kindergarten to college. As a matter of fact, the government gives you a scholarship to go to college. If a woman is pregnant, she gets 10 months of paid leave and gets paid by the government for every child born. Certainly, these countries have the most evolved form of democracies that the world should emulate.

Coming back to fairness and equality in our democracy in the United States, I am not recommending any kind of government coercion or decrease of freedoms. There is already much freedom here in the United States, which is very creditable. In an ideal system however, every citizen should not only enjoy all the benefits that society can offer, but they should enjoy freedom to the fullest sense of the word. Perhaps we could call such a super democracy, a "Freedomocracy" where, in addition to personal freedoms, exist freedom from hunger, illiteracy, unemployment, or exploitation. All the citizens of a Freedomocracy should enjoy genuinely equal rights, nutritious and adequate food, fair housing, free education, universal healthcare, well-paying jobs, and safe environment; politicians are elected at every level by the citizens and act as peoples' true servants and not their masters; elected officials are truly accountable to the electorate and citizens are consulted at every major decision the government plans to take. Of course such a system does not exist anywhere today. But someday, somewhere, it might arise.

When it does, there would be no more wars and occupations because such foolish endeavors commonly are manufactured by leaders to satisfy their own egos, their own or their country's selfish interests, or to keep their political careers going. Freedomocratic countries will naturally become more civilized: not only will the exploitation of their own citizens cease, but their exploitation of other countries as well.

In a Freedomocracy, the people will be free from exploitation, poverty, hunger, illiteracy, homelessness, or a lack of healthcare. They will be able to live peacefully in clean environments pursuing their interests, working to their ability; everyone will enjoy life, free from exploitation by anyone and with no government infringement on their privacy; they will enjoy full government protection. The Scandinavian countries are closest to the ideals of Freedomocracy today; Freedomocracy is indeed possible.

The time has come for humanity to devise a new system, a more humane system of governance. I am sure, if such a system of government is devised and adapted, perhaps humanity might survive—because the assault on nature will stop too. Then as long as such a system survives, it will be the closest thing to heaven on earth. Humanity will then thrive as the one family that it is, where every human being loves and respects each other, and the nature on this beautiful planet of ours.

When nations will live under Freedomocracies on this planet, our world will truly be 'God's own country.'

CHAPTER 14
IS COLLAPSE REALLY IMMINENT?

My father rode a camel. I drive a car. My son flies a jet airplane. His son will ride a camel.
—Saudi saying

We're finally going to get the bill for the Industrial Age. If the projections are right, it's going to be a big one: the ecological collapse of the planet.
—Jeremy Rifkin, World Press Review, 30 December, 1989

Mass Extinctions

There have been at least five mass extinctions in the history of life on Earth, and four in the last 3.5 billion years in which many species have disappeared in a relatively short period of geological time. The most recent of these, the Cretaceous-Tertiary extinction event 65 million years ago at the end of the Cretaceous period, is best known for having wiped out the non-avian dinosaurs, among many other species.

According to a 1998 survey of 400 biologists conducted by New York's American Museum of Natural History, close to 70 percent believed that we are currently in the early stages of an anthropogenic mass extinction, known as the Holocene event. The same proportion of respondents in that survey agreed with the prediction that up to 20 percent of all living populations could go extinct within the next 30 (by 2028) years. According to biologist E. O. Wilson's 2002 estimate, if the current rate of human destruction of the biosphere continues, one-half of all species of life on Earth will be extinct in 100 years.[1] Of greater significance is the fact that the rate of species extinction is currently estimated at 100 to 1000 times the average extinction rate in the evolutionary time scale of planet Earth.[2] No wonder modern industrial civilization has become a weapon of planetary mass destruction.

Since early eighteenth century, the industrial revolution that began in England gave us tremendous advancement in technology, medicine, healthcare, globalization, trade, construction, city infrastructure, roads, bridges, dams, electricity generation, cars, airplanes, ships, trains, electronics, communications, TVs, radios, telephones, and computers. Technology has enabled us to reach the moon and mars. We now have rockets, nuclear bombs, tanks, supersonic jet-fighters, and a vast array of weapons of war. In many parts of the world, wars are being waged even today, where these modern weapons are being tested and used against people.

But, this industrialized, fossil-fuel driven, over-consuming economy has also dealt us shrinking forests, expanding deserts, eroding soils, rising temperatures, collapsing fisheries, melting glaciers, rising sea levels, drying coral reefs, more destructive storms, falling water tables, and disappearing species. It seems to be in direct conflict with nature.

Still more than a billion people around the world live in dire poverty, earning less than a dollar or two a day. Millions are starving around the globe. More than a billion people don't have safe drinking water to drink. Hundreds of millions of children are malnourished. Millions are dying from treatable diseases such as malaria, dysentery, or typhoid. Countless millions don't even have shelter over their heads.

Industrial Civilization's less than two century old "March of Folly' has ravaged the Earth beyond belief. From the Ganges, Yamuna and the

Indus, to the Yellow River, the Yangtze, the Brahmaputra, and the Nile, the world's rivers are drying at an alarming rate. They could soon become just seasonal rivers. This could uproot or starve hundreds of millions of people in India, China, Pakistan, Bangladesh, Nepal, Egypt, and in surrounding countries. From the Himalayas, the Hindukush, the Tibetan Plateau, the Tien Shan, to the Pamir, Alborz, the Andes and the Kilimanjaro in Africa, glaciers are melting and retreating at an unprecedented rate. Even the Arctic and Antarctic ice sheets are steadily melting with large chunks of icebergs the size of Rhode Island breaking off and floating in the ocean.

Water scarcity already is chronic all over the world, especially in China, India, Pakistan, the Middle East, and in many parts of Africa. Food prices—due to failed monsoons, crop failures, soil erosion, corn being diverted to ethanol manufacture for cars, and a host of other reasons— have skyrocketed around the world.

The planet forests are decimated and still being destroyed in Brazil, Bolivia, Ecuador, Indonesia, Malaysia, Burma, and Canada. Ecosystems disappear forever due to this forest destruction and human encroachment. As mentioned in an earlier chapter, due to encroachment, overexploitation, and pollution, the world's fish could be gone in 50 years.

Capitalist Industrial Civilization's supreme mantra of constant growth and profit has polluted our planet's air, water, soil and oceans, affecting millions of innocent people around the planet, especially the poor masses who haven't yet reaped any benefit from this unbridled growth—many are losing their livelihood and homes.

The world is warming due to the fossil-fuel based economic machine that has been running this industrial revolution for more than a century and half. Today, we are emitting 90 million tons of CO2 into the atmosphere every 24 hours, and the amount is increasing day by day.[3] The atmosphere is heating, as are oceans. Average temperatures are on the rise everywhere. Ecosystems the world around are on the verge of breaking point. It should be obvious to all of us: We are living within an economic system that is unsustainable not only over the long haul but in the near term; unsustainable systems, obviously, cannot be sustained.

So, what good has this industrial revolution—touted for so long as the greatest thing that happened to mankind—done for humanity? In fact, I think man was happier before this industrial revolution. At least he was living with nature that was pure and unpolluted, expressing its beauty through vast forested areas, with clean waters in the rivers, lakes and oceans, beautiful animals, birds and fish living side by side in harmony with each other.

But today, we are at the brink of a disaster, a man-made one from which humanity may not be able to escape. Such is the 'gift' of the industrial revolution.

ANCIENT COLLAPSES

Scientists have linked climate variations to the collapse of societies around the globe. History warns us that when once powerful societies collapse, they do so unexpectedly and quickly. But that shouldn't be a surprise: peak power means peak populations, peak needs, and peak vulnerability. While some societies have suddenly collapsed, others have managed to survive for thousands of years like the ancient civilizations of India and China. So what can we learn from history to avoid the forthcoming catastrophe awaiting us? The answers are complex. All will depend on how wisely and quickly humanity manages to cooperate with each other and with Earth's ecosystems, shift to sustainable ways of living and moderate consumption, population control, and stay its insatiable demand on the Earth's resources.

In Mesopotamia, a canal-supported agricultural society collapsed about 3,400 years ago. The paleoclimatic record suggests that a severe 200-year drought may have brought about that collapse. With wetter conditions, civilizations thrived in the Mediterranean, Egypt, and west

Asia. But just ten years after their economic peak in 2,300 B.C., a catastrophic drought and cooling spoiled agricultural production, forcing regional abandonment and finally collapse.[4]

As Jared Diamond outlines, five groups of interacting factors have been especially important: environmental damage by people; climate change; enemies, changes in friendly partners; and societies' political, economic, and social responses to these shifts. Each society has succumbed to one or more of these factors, leading to its ultimate collapse.

The Polynesian society of Easter Island caused irreparable damage to its environment that ultimately led to its collapse only a few centuries ago. But the demise of the Norse colonies of Greenland was due to several factors: damaging the environment, climate change, enemies, and the end of trade.

The Mayas of the Yucatan Peninsula and adjacent parts of Central America developed the New World's most advanced civilization before Columbus. From local origins around 2,500 years ago, Maya societies rose especially after 250 A.D., reaching their peaks in population and sophistication in the late 8th century. But soon after, they underwent a steep political and cultural collapse. Kings were overthrown, large areas were abandoned, and at least 90 percent of the population disappeared. What happened and why? [5]

The major cause was environmental degradation by people: deforestation, soil erosion and water management problems resulted in less food. These problems were exacerbated by droughts caused partly by deforestation. Chronic warfare added to their decline as more and more fought over fewer and fewer resources. Why didn't the kings see these problems coming, their forests vanishing and their hills eroding? Because they were busy fighting each other, keeping up their images through ostentatious display of wealth, and by insulating themselves from the problems of the society. The elite merely bought themselves the privilege of being among the last to starve.

The inhabitants of the Pitcairn and Henderson islands heavily depended on imports from Mangareva Island. When Mangareva collapsed, imports essentially stopped and the people of Pitcairn and Henderson starved to death. The Mangarevans, just like the Mayas, succumbed to deforestation, erosion, and warfare.[6]

BLIND FAITH IN TECHNOLOGY

Many of us are in the habit of perceiving that technology will be our savior. Political leaders around the world naively believe that our complex problems can be cured by human innovation, ingenuity, and technological efficiency, along with a few smart changes in our choices of energy systems. Most of us who have grown up in the western developed world, have a lot of faith in technology, while in developing countries, the people have more faith in God. We, in the west, believe that technology will somehow save us from this catastrophe. We foolishly hope that some technological breakthrough somewhere will enable the world to find an unlimited sustainable source of energy on which the world's $50 trillion economy would keep running and growing. But this faith could be laughably naïve and dangerously misplaced. Technology didn't save the Indus Civilization, the Mesopotamians, the Mesa Verde, the Easter Islanders, or the Mayas. Their civilizations succumbed to the environmental damage, climate change events, drought, or other factors beyond their control. What guarantee do we have now that technology will save us this time?

Many also have blind faith in the wisdom of those in power. This is both foolish and risky. If those in power had sufficient wisdom, then we would not have had the first and second world wars, the nuclear arms race, thousands of nuclear weapons, wars and occupation of other countries, in this time and age. Humanity's faith in technology and in the wisdom of those in power is utterly misplaced. Can we really trust our leaders and the leaders around the world to act suddenly in a responsible manner? If we do, we will repent for the rest of our lives and our grand children will blame us for our folly. All of us around the world must unite, protest, and force our leaders to act now. Someone has fittingly said, "If people lead, the politicians will follow"!

OTHER HISTORIANS, ENVIRONMENTALISTS AND THINKERS

Well known experts have dwelled on the subject of collapse in the last few years. Among them, Joseph Tainter and Jared Diamond have written so insightfully on Eastern Island's and other ancient societies' collapses. However, Tainter and Diamond allude rather mildly to our current civilization's connection to the plight of ancient collapses. Lester Brown's Plan B-3 is a highly informative and excellent book; however, it is bit too optimistic about the actions being taken worldwide to combat global warming and the ultimate future of mankind.

In 1970, The Club of Rome sponsored Phase One of the "Project on the Predicament of Mankind." Dr. Dennis Meadows of MIT led a team of 17 scholars who worked for two years to complete it. The study examined five basic factors that determine and therefore, ultimately limit growth on this planet: population, agricultural production, natural resources, industrial production, and pollution.

Phase One of the study was published in Donella (Dana) and Dennis Meadows', and Jorgan Randers' 1972 book *Limits To Growth*, with the 1992 follow up book *Beyond The Limits,* and the last updated 2004 book, *Limits To Growth: The 30-year Update*. They had painted even in 1992 a realistic picture of a world that is soon approaching the problems we are already facing today. Among these authors, Dana was the unceasing optimist about the future of humanity. Jorgan (of Norway) was the cynic. He believed society would pursue the short term goals of over-consumption, financial security, and employment to its bitter end. Meanwhile, Dennis' position was in the middle.

The tone of *The Limits to Growth: the 30 Year Update* is cautiously optimistic. The authors maintain that there is still time for the world to achieve sustainability, but society must shift quickly to a new sustainable course. However, by 2022, it will be too late. The 20-year delay in moving towards sustainability will send the world "on a turbulent and ultimately unsuccessful path. The policies that were once adequate are no longer sufficient." Well, we are already past 2009, and the world leaders are still debating what to do—as the Copenhagen Conference recently proved.

According to some experts, the overshoot and collapse of industrial civilization was assured once humanity became dependent on the rapid exploitation of nonrenewable resources on a finite planet. Moreover, according to others, our insatiable appetite for electric power has accelerated the collapse and steepened the decline.[7]

Perhaps the best of the lot is Professor Richard Heinberg's 2003 book, *The Party is Over* and his subsequent 2004 book, *PowerDown*. There, Heinberg paints quite a realistic picture of the fate of industrial civilization. He advises our current industrial civilization to powerdown, deindustrialize, and consume less. According to him, if we don't act wisely, our civilization is in profound trouble. I find his approach to be the most realistic and appropriate.

OUT OF CONTROL CO2 EMISSIONS

At a high-level academic conference on global warming at Exeter University in the summer of 2008, climate scientist Kevin Anderson stood before his expert audience and contemplated a strange feeling. He wanted to be wrong. Many in his audience felt the same. His conclusions had already caused a stir in scientific and political circles.

Anderson, an expert at the Tyndall Centre for Climate Change Research at Manchester University, was about to send the gloomiest dispatch yet from the forefront of the war against climate change. He was about to warn that carbon emissions were soaring out of control—far above even the bleakest scenarios mentioned by the 2007 IPCC report and the Stern Review.

The cream of the UK scientific community sat in stunned silence as Anderson pointed out that carbon emissions since 2000 have risen much faster than anyone thought possible, driven mainly by the coal-fuelled economic boom in the developing countries. According to him, so much extra pollution is being pumped out that most of the climate targets debated by politicians and campaigners are fanciful at best, and "dangerously misguided" at worst. He warned that it was "improbable" that levels could now be restricted to 650 parts per million.

Currently, the CO2 level is around 390 ppm, up from 280 ppm at the time of the Industrial Revolution, and it increases by more than 2 ppm every year. The (UK) government's official position is that the world should aim to cap this rise at 450 ppm. Though the science is fuzzy, experts opine that it could offer an equal chance of limiting the ultimate temperature rise above pre-industrial times to 2 degrees Centigrade, which the EU characterizes as dangerous. We have had 0.7 °C of that already and an estimated extra 0.5°C is guaranteed because of emissions to date.

The graphs behind Anderson's visage on the big screen told a different story. Line after line, representing fumes from exhausts, chimneys, and jet engines were heading for the ceiling instead of curving downwards.

At 650 ppm, the science says the world would face a catastrophic 4 °C average rise. Even that bleak future could only be achieved if rich countries adopted "draconian emission reductions within a decade," says Anderson.[8]

Anderson is not the only scientist to voice grave concerns that current targets are hopelessly optimistic. Many experts, politicians, and campaigners privately admit that 2 °C is a lost cause. After a few drinks at a gathering, most would vote for the projections of 650 ppm than 450 ppm as the more realistic outcome.

Bob Watson, the chief scientist at the Environmental Department (UK) and a former head of IPCC, warned in 2008 that the world needed to be ready for a 4 °C rise. That kind of increase in global temperature will bring extreme food and water shortages in vulnerable countries, it will wipe out hundreds of species, and cause floods that would displace hundreds of millions of people. The warming would be much more severe at the poles, which could accelerate the melting of the Greenland and West Antarctic ice sheets.

Watson warned: "We must alert everybody that at the moment we're at the very top end of the worst case (emissions) scenario. I think we should be striving for 450 (ppm) but I think we should be prepared that 550 (ppm) is a more likely outcome." Meeting the 450 ppm target, he said, would be "unbelievably difficult".[9]

In the autumn of 2008 the Australian government suggested that the 450 ppm goal is so ambitious that it will foil attempts to agree to a new global deal on global warming at the Copenhagen Conference of December 2009. The report from economist Ross Garnaut which was dubbed the Australian Stern Review, says nations must accept that a greater degree of warming is inevitable, and to risk a failure to agree "would haunt humanity until the end of time".

It says developed nations including Australia, Britain, and the US would have to slash carbon dioxide emissions by 5% each year over the next decade to hit the 450 ppm target. Britain's Climate Change Act 2008, the most ambitious legislation of its kind in the world, calls for reductions of about 3% every year to 2050.

Earlier in 2008, Jim Hansen, senior climate scientist with NASA, published a paper that said climate targets of the world needed to be urgently revised because of the risk of feedbacks in the climate system. He used reconstructions of the Earth's past climate to show that a target of 350 ppm—significantly lower than where we stand today—is needed to "preserve a planet similar to that on which civilization developed and to which life on Earth is adapted".[10]

Ban Ki-moon, the UN secretary-general said on July 9, 2009 that the leaders at the G8 summit in Italy had not gone far enough in their pledges to limit rises in the world's temperature. The eight rich countries and the major economies' forum, a group of 17 other economies including China and India have now agreed that average global temperature should not be allowed to rise more than 2 °C. However, there were few firm plans about how to achieve that goal and the leaders remained divided even about what the baseline temperature for the 2 degree limit should be. All these countries agreed on was that the starting point for the limit should be "1990 or later."

The G8 talks were part of preparations for a 200-nation summit in Copenhagen in December, 2009. G8 leaders dropped a plan to call for developing nations to cut their emissions by 50 per cent by 2050, after opposition from China—the world's largest polluter—and by India. The G8 position on climate change was further undermined when Russia signaled that the 80 per cent carbon reduction for rich countries that it signed earlier was not in fact viable. A Russian spokesman said the 80 per cent goal by 2050 was not acceptable to them nor was it attainable.[11] As we can see, there are already major disagreements among leading nations.

On the eve of the G8 summit in L'Aquila, Indian Prime Minister Dr. Manmohan Singh said that the west must bear the "historical responsibility" for the climate change now affecting India and other developing countries, which had been caused by decadent lifestyles and centuries of industrialization. In a proposal that astonished western officials, India suggested that the price of co-operation would be for industrialized countries to pay at least 0.5 per cent of their GDP to help developing nations invest in cleaner renewable sources of energy and reduce their carbon emissions. This means the west should pay developing countries 120 billion pounds ($195.77 billion) a year in exchange for their help in reducing greenhouse gas emissions.

The Indian spokesman said India had 16 per cent of the world's population but contributed only 4.6 per cent to greenhouse gas emissions, while the United States accounts for 5 per cent of the world's population but contributes to 20 per cent of emissions.[12] China has hinted along the same lines. It said that it would agree to substantial restraint at Copenhagen if rich countries—responsible for 90 per cent of all the warming gases belched into the atmosphere so far—agree to offer one per cent of its GDP annually to poor countries to adjust to clean fuels; another fair proposal for simple justice. The poor countries have contributed very little to cause this crisis, but they will be the first to suffer its worst consequences. We can see from the Indian and Chinese proposal and its rejection by the western powers, that divisions between developed and developing nations are deep rooted. As expected, they were not resolved by December 2009 for the 200-nation Copenhagen summit; and if the world's leaders fail to agree to sizable cuts in greenhouse gas emissions, humanity's survival would be at stake. We will see later how they failed at the Copenhagen Conference.

We know that to stay on the right side of this climatic point of No Return, global emissions must start falling by 2015—just five years from now—and drop by 85 percent by 2050.[13] The scientific debate is over. We know what humanity has to do to survive. But do the politicians of leading nations have political will to act?

Joachim Schellnhuber, chair of an advisory council known by its acronym, WBGU, is a physicist whose specialty is chaos theory. Speaking at an invitation-only conference at New Mexico's Santa Fe Institute, he divulged the findings of a study which has just been published in October, 2009. If its conclusions are correct—and Schellnhuber ranks among the world's half a dozen most eminent climate scientists—it has monumental implications for the future Copenhagen-type conferences on climate change where world leaders will try again to agree on reversing global warming.

Schellnhuber and his colleagues go way beyond the findings of the Intergovernmental Panel on Climate Change. The IPCC says that the rich industrial countries must cut emissions 25 to 40 per cent by 2020 (from 1990 level) if the world is to have a fair chance of avoiding the catastrophic climate change. But by contrast, the WBGU study says the United States must cut emissions 100 per cent by 2020—i.e., quit carbon entirely within ten years. Germany, France, Britain and other industrial nations must do the same by 2025 to 2030. China only has until 2035, and the whole world must be carbon-free by 2050. The study warns that the big polluters can delay their day of reckoning by "buying" emissions rights from poor developing countries, which will only extend their deadlines by a decade or so.[14]

This time table is light-years more demanding than what the world's major governments were contemplating about in the run-up to Copenhagen. The European Union has pledged 20 percent reductions by 2020 which it will increase to 30 percent if others—like the United States—do the same. The British prime minister has promised 25 percent reductions if others do the same. President Obama has not mentioned a number, but the Waxman-Markey bill, which he supports, would deliver less than 5 percent reductions by 2020. China's Hu took the higher ground than the U.S. president, pledging to curb greenhouse gas emissions growth by a "notable margin" by 2020. Obama dropped a bombshell however, by urging that all G-20 governments phase out subsidies for fossil fuels. "The time we have to reverse this tide is running out," Obama declared. But the WBGU study suggests that our time is in fact all but gone.

The G-8 leaders agreed in July, 2009 to limit the global temperature rise to 2 ° C (3.6 degrees Fahrenheit) above the preindustrial level at which human civilization developed. Addressing the Santa Fe Conference, Schellnhuber joked that the G-8 leaders had agreed to the 2

°C limit "probably because they don't know what it means." But in fact, the "brutal" timeline of the WBGU study, Schellnhuber warned would not guarantee staying within the 2 °C. target. It would give humanity a two-out-of-three chance of doing so, "worse than Russian Roulette," he wryly noted. "But it is the best we can do." Countries would have to quit carbon even sooner to even have a three-out-of-four chance.

Underlying the WBGU study, there is a fundamental political assumption: that the right to emit greenhouse gases is shared equally by all the people on Earth. In diplomatic circles, it is known as "the per capita principle". This approach has long been insisted upon by China, India, and other developing nations and thus was seen as essential to an agreement in Copenhagen. Among G-8 leaders, only Germany's Merkel has endorsed it. Considering 7 billion people on the planet, the WBGU study arrives at an annual emissions quota of 2.7 tons of carbon dioxide per person. That is bad news for Americans who emit the highest number, 20 tons per person annually. That also explains why the U.S. deadline is most important. China won't welcome it either. Its combination of high emissions and huge population gives it a deadline only a few years later than Europe's and Japan's.[15] It is doubtful if the world will be able to abide by such drastic but necessary deadlines to stop CO2 emissions recommended by the WBGU study. The consequences are anybody's guess.

THE OLDUVAI THEORY

The Olduvai theory, first presented by Richard C. Duncan in 1989 is intriguing. It states that the life expectancy of industrial civilization is approximately 100 years: circa 1930-2030. It is defined by the ratio of world energy production and population (e). It has four postulates:

The exponential growth of world energy production ended in 1970.
Average e will show no growth from 1979 to circa 2008.
The rate of change of e will go steeply negative circa 2008.
World population will decline proximate with e.

Several historians and thinkers such as Henry Adams, Ernest Samuels, Frederick Lee Ackerman, and M. King Hubbert have contributed towards the Olduvai scenario.

Basically, the Olduvai theory, based on time-series data of world energy production and population, theorizes that: 1) electrical power is the crucial end-use energy for industrial civilization; 2) big blackouts are inevitable; 3) the proximate cause of the collapse of industrial civilization, if and when it occurs, will be that electric power grids will go down and never come back up. Thus, ultimately world energy production will go down, electricity generation will drastically decline culminating in massive blackouts across the world; and, accordingly, the world population will have to shrink.

World energy production data shows that unlike earlier years' exponential growth in world energy production, from 1979 to 2003 and later, world energy production has slowed down to linear growth of about 1.5%, proving the postulate no.1. Similarly, various data show that world total energy production per capita, e, grew exponentially at 3.9% yearly from 1700 to 1909. Thereafter, it grew at linear rates of 1.4% annually from 1909 to 1970; 1.7% per year from 1970 to 1979; and at 0.0% per year from 1979 to 2003. In other words, the average e did not grow at all from 1979 to 2003 and beyond. Postulate 2 is confirmed. We have seen sky-rocketing hikes in oil prices worldwide, confirming the postulate no. 3.

The Olduvai scenario for world population peaks at 6.9 billion circa 2015. Thereafter the population declines to 2.0 billion in 2050 (Postulate 4). According to Duncan, a growing number of independent studies concur.[16]

All industrialized nations are now—some growing rapidly—heavily dependent on resources that are located in poorer third world countries. What will happen when these resource-rich countries begin to foresee the day when their own demand will require these available supplies? Will the developed nations just idly stand by while supplies are available in other economically or militarily weaker countries? Will resource wars not follow? [17] How is our world going to prevent such conflicts as they arise? Will our world descend into chaos? These are scary scenarios that deserve some thoughts.

Professor Richard Heinberg's latest, September 2009 report, *Searching For a Miracle: "Net Energy" Limits & the Fate of Industrial Society* is more compelling. In it, Dr. Heinberg presents three scenarios:

Scenario 1 depicts the world at American standards. He says if the world's population were to stabilize at 9 billion by 2050—a distinct possibility as per many experts—bringing the entire world up to U.S. energy consumption (100 quadrillion BTU annually) would require 6000 quads per year. This means the world would require more than 12 times current total energy production. If we assume that the cost of solar panels can be brought down to 50 cents per watt installed (one tenth of current cost and less than the current cost of coal), a massive investment of $500 trillion would be required for the transition. This is not counting grid construction and other ancillary costs. This is almost an unimaginably huge sum. Therefore, this scenario is extremely unlikely to be realized.

Scenario 2 imagines the world at the European standards. It is obvious that the American standard of living is an unnecessarily high goal for the world as a whole, and Europeans already live quite well but consume only half as much energy. Suppose we aim for a world per-capita consumption rate 70 percent lower than that of the United States. Again assuming a population of 9 billion, achieving this standard would require total energy production of 1800 quads per year. This is still over three times the current level. To produce this much energy through cheap solar panels would cost $150 trillion, a number over twice the current yearly GDP. Though this scenario is conceivable, still it is highly unlikely.

Scenario 3 supposes that the current energy consumption is maintained on a per-capita basis. That means if people in less industrialized countries start consuming more, that must be compensated for by reduction in consumption in industrial nations, again with the world's population stabilizing at 9 billion. In this scenario, the world will consume 700 quads of energy per year. If this level of energy usage were to come from cheap solar panels, it would cost $60 trillion in investment—still an enormous sum, but one that is achievable over time.[18]

It is interesting to see the wide ranges in per capita energy consumption. The world average is 61 gigajoules per year. However, for Qatar, it is 899 GJ per year, for the U.S., it is 325 GJ, for Switzerland, it is 156 GJ, for China it is 56.2 GJ, for India it is 15.9 GJ, for Bangladesh it is 6.8 GJ, and for Chad it is 0.3 GJ. Hence, to come down to world average, the Americans would require to reduce their consumption to less than one-fifth of their current level, while Bangladesh citizens could increase their energy consumption level nine-fold to meet the world average.[19]

Finally, Dr. Heinberg points out that one can arrive at an inescapable conclusion from above scenarios: unless world energy prices decline in an unprecedented and unforeseeable manner, the world-economy is likely to be increasingly energy-constrained as fossil fuel deplete and are phased out for environmental reasons. It is quite unlikely that the world will ever reach the American level, or even the European level of energy consumption; even maintaining the current energy consumption levels will require massive investment.

What does all this mean? Well, it is obvious that our world is headed for a massive energy crisis once fossil fuels are phased out or depleted, unless energy consumption and the global population are controlled.

WORLD'S RESPONSE

To counter the impending catastrophe our world is facing today—as shown in chapters-6, 7, and 8—the world is responding. Country after country, from the European Union countries—who are on the forefront—Japan, the United States, China, India, and other Asian countries to even some African nations, every country is taking steps, however small, to steer their country away from a fossil-fuel-economy to a renewable resources-based one. The construction and use of solar power, solar thermal, wind power, geothermal power, and hydrological power are all on the rise worldwide. Even nuclear power is being touted as the solution to our energy problems.

Peoples' movements are propping up worldwide. Countless grassroots movements are organized worldwide. Highly dedicated individuals from Europe, America, and Canada to India, China, Thailand, and Brazil are actively organizing people to create awareness and to force their country's leaders to responsibly take concrete steps to stop runaway climate change.

Electric trains, high mileage hybrid, electric cars, LPG-powered or alcohol powered buses, and electric bicycles are being progressively built and used globally. Some countries, particularly those of Europe, are encouraging their citizens to use bicycles, smaller cars, buses, and trains. We must acknowledge that awareness amongst people and nations is on the rise especially in the last decade.

But will all these steps and awareness among a small percentage of people and their nations be enough to thwart the global calamity looming on the horizon? Will humanity, and the industrial civilization behemoth it has created, be able to change their ways, and quickly enough before it is too late? Will politicians and leaders of major nations have the foresight to forego their short-term political gains and undertake major steps to steer their countries on sustainable-economic paths?

We cannot presently know whether all these renewable energy projects around the planet truly herald a new dawn for humanity or the last sunset of all our hopes. Only time will tell.

THE GRIM SCENARIO

To those who understand the enormity of the ecological disaster we are facing, the scope and depth of the cascading crisis we face has become painfully clear of late. The grim scenario that we face is around the corner. Our current level of First World consumption is exhausting the ecological basis for life. The rapacious fossil-fuel-based economy of industrial civilization is bringing the world swiftly to the brink of chaos. If collapse comes, the picture will be ugly.

The cornucopian view of world forever awash in cheap and abundant oil still prevails in some quarters. But reality tells a different story...

Our world will be engulfed in utter chaos. The unsustainable economy to which we have been addicted for more than 150 years will be drastically curtailed or even worse, will come to a grinding halt. The unsightly face of globalization will be cut and irreparably bruised. The world as we know it would dramatically change.

As the rivers of the Himalayas, the Tibet-Qinghai Plateau, the Colorado, and countless others lose their water source due to melting of glaciers and ice sheets, they will become seasonal or even go dry, reducing their life sustaining waters to a trickle. Hundreds of millions of people who subsist in the Gangetic Plains, the fertile plains of Tibet-Qinghai Plateau, the basins of the Yangtze and the Yellow river, the banks of the Indus River, the plains of the Nile and many others will go thirsty (and hungry). Millions could die but those who survive will be forced to move where they could find water, food, and jobs to survive. Utter chaos and disruption would follow.

IPCC's report headed by Raj Pachauri had warned in 2007; "it is the poorest in the world, and this includes poor people even in prosperous societies, who are going to be the worst hit," said Rajendra Pachauri, chairman of the IPCC.

As per the report's findings, 75 to 250 million people across Africa could face water shortages by 2020. Crop yields could increase by 20% in East and Southeast Asia, but decrease by up to 30% in Central and South Asia. Agriculture fed by rainfall could drop by 50% in some African countries by 2020. 20 to 30% of all plant and animal species are at increased risk of extinction if temperatures rise between 1.5 and 2.5 °C. The scientific work reviewed by the IPCC scientists included more than 29,000 pieces of data on observed changes in physical and biological aspects of the natural world.[20]

As the temperature of the planet rises, west Arctic and Greenland ice sheets are melting at an alarming rate. If the Greenland ice sheet and the Antarctic ice sheets were to melt completely—and they will at current rate—trillions of gallons of water will be dumped in the ocean. This will raise ocean levels by 23 feet or more, which would spell immense catastrophe for the world. Thousands of miles of coastal areas will be submerged under ocean waters inundating islands after islands. One quarter of Bangladesh will be under ocean water. A World Bank map of Bangladesh shows that even a 3 feet rise in sea level would inundate half of the rice-land of this country of 160 million during this century alone. It will also inundate one third or more of the Mekong Delta, which produces half of the rice in Vietnam, the world's number two rice exporter. In addition, it would submerge parts of the 20 or so other rice-growing deltas of Asia.[21]

Many coastal areas of India, China, the United States, and large coastal regions of Europe will be overrun by sea-water. This will create some 400 millions of envirogees (it may be beneficial to get accustomed to this term for environmental refugees) most of whom will be poor. They will lose their homes, all their belongings, and their livelihoods. They will be forced to move upland transgressing other peoples' lands or their countries, further disrupting millions of lives.

The World Glacier Monitoring Service in Switzerland has recently reported the eighteenth consecutive year of shrinking mountain glaciers.

Glaciers are melting in the Andes, the Alps, the Rocky Mountains, and throughout the mountain ranges of Asia.[22] Melting mountain glaciers in Asia now pose the greatest threat to the world's food security. Both China and India are the world's biggest producers of wheat and rice—the staples of humanity. China's wheat harvest is almost double that of the United States, which ranks third after India. These two countries are the biggest producers of rice, together accounting for over half of the world harvest.

According to the IPCC report, Himalayan glaciers are receding faster than previously thought. The giant Gangotri glacier supplies 70 percent of the Ganges flow and if it disappears, the Ganges could become a seasonal river flowing during the rainy season but not during the summer dry season when irrigation water is most needed.

A leading Chinese glaciologist, Yao Tandong, reports that the glaciers on the Tibet-Qinghai Plateau in western China are now melting at an accelerated rate. He believes that by 2060, two thirds of these glaciers will be gone. This will greatly reduce the dry season flow of the Yellow and the Yangtze rivers. The Yellow River that flows through the arid northern part of China could become seasonal. If this glacier melting continues, Yao says, "(it) will eventually lead to an ecological catastrophe."[23]
Over pumping is depleting underground water resources in both these irrigation dependent countries. Water tables are falling everywhere under the north China Plain, the country's main grain producing region. In India, water tables are falling and wells are going dry in most states.

Water from the Ganges is the largest source of surface irrigation in India, and is the leading source of water for the 407 million people who live in the Gangetic Basin. In China, the Yangtze and the Yellow rivers flow in the dry season because of ice melt in the Tibet-Qinghai Plateau glaciers. Because of the low rainfall in the Yellow River Basin, the fate of 147 million who live there is closely tied to the river. The Yangtze River is China's leading source of irrigation water, helping to produce more than half of China's 130 million ton rice harvest. It also fulfills many of the water needs of the watershed's 368 million Chinese.

The populations of people inhabiting these river-basins in both India and China are larger than any country other than India and China. The ongoing water shrinkage in underground water aquifers and the prospective shrinkage in these river water flows are occurring against a startling demographic backdrop: India is projected to add 490 million people by 2050 and China 80 million. In India, more than 40 percent of children under five years are underweight and undernourished. With these dire prospects, hunger there will intensify and the child mortality rate will climb. Water shrinkage alone will create massive hunger in both these Asian giants where the situation could fast escape control when millions go hungry.[24]

Scientists have confirmed the fact that for each 1 °C rise in temperature above the norm during the growing season, a 10 percent decline in wheat and rice yields will occur. Already, agricultural production is no longer keeping pace with population increases. In a world with limited grain stocks—a world that is only one poor harvest away from turmoil in grain markets—a crop-shrinking heat wave in a major grain-producing region, could cause politically destabilizing food shortages around the world.

As Lester Brown reports, for much of the 20th century, the number of hungry in the world was declining. But it bottomed out in the late 1990s at 825 million. Then it moved upward, approaching 870 million in 2005 and passed one billion in 2009. The combination of melting glaciers, rising oceans, and crop-withering heat waves could push these numbers up even faster, forcing millions or more families to starve or barely survive on a single meal a day.[25]

Add to the above the other global warming induced catastrophes. The world will face massive storms—hurricanes, cyclones, floods, typhoons, and heavy rains in some areas and deadly droughts in other regions—with more frequency. We are already experiencing the early signs of these storms.

With likely epicenters of drought and desertification like Mexico, Ethiopia, Maghreb and Pakistan, millions of hungry refugees will try to cross the borders of their neighboring
countries creating utter chaos. Those who have contributed the least towards global warming, the poor and underprivileged of the world, will suffer the most from the oncoming catastrophe.

The top global food policy think tank, International Food Policy Research Institute (IFPRI) predicts that global warming will be responsible for a 16% decline in agricultural gross domestic product globally by 2020. The Center for Global Development argues that developing countries, in particular, will be hit hard by climate change: According to their report, by 2080, India will see a staggering 30-40% drop in agricultural production and Senegal will plummet 50%.

Even in the most optimistic scenario, climate change will reduce the farm outputs of many poor countries. Farm outputs of Pakistan will be reduced by 20 percent, Northeastern India's by 30 percent along with those of much of Southern Africa, the Maghreb, the Sahel belt, the Middle East, the Caribbean, and Mexico. Some twenty-nine developing countries will lose 20 percent or more of their current outputs to global warming while the rich north are likely to receive on average, an 8 percent boost.[26]

With human-induced destruction of the Earth's natural habitat, animal and plant species are going extinct day by day, year after year. The way deforestation is spreading in Africa and other parts of the world, it is quite likely that by the middle of this century, there won't be any lions, elephants, leopards, rhinos, and cheetahs left in Africa; there won't be any lions, rhinos and tigers left in India; and there won't be any orangutans left in Borneo, koalas left in Australia, and any pandas remaining in China.

Our grand children might see them in zoos alone or in movies, museums, and pictures.

WHAT IS THE WAY OUT?

All wealth comes from mother Earth. It is the common heritage of all living beings, humans as well as other living species including animals, birds, fish, plants, and trees. No group of people or countries, however strong, smart, or rich, has the right to monopolize the natural wealth of the Earth for their own exclusive selfish use. Mother Earth's wealth is for all her children and living species; everyone has equal rights to it. Just as in a human family—all is shared or should be shared equally by all children, regardless of their individual strength or weaknesses—planet Earth's wealth should be equally distributed among all her living species. It is called 'the commons'. If this is understood and followed through by leaders and the people of the so called developed nations, the mother Earth and all her living species will flourish. But it is yet to be seen if these political leaders will abandon their own or their country's myopic short-term selfish interests and will work for the common good of humanity. For humanity to survive this man-made catastrophe, the following steps are absolutely essential:

Switch to Sustainable Energy Sources: Before the fossil fuels—especially the oil and gas—run out, every nation must embark on a massive program to switch their economy and life-style to sustainable energy sources. Peak oil is only 15 to 30 years away. Some believe it has already peaked.

Within this paradigm shift, rich developed nations who are responsible for 90% of greenhouse gases that have brought this catastrophe to our doorstep, must donate 1% of their GDP to developing nations to help them switch to sustainable energy sources. In addition, they must help them with the technology to reach that goal.

Reduce Consumption: It is obvious that over-consumption, especially in developed nations, has squandered the Earth's resources, polluted this planet, and devastated planetary ecosystems. Hence, every developed rich nation must voluntarily reduce its consumption level. The world cannot afford its current consumption level or the life-style of the Americans or even Europeans. Imagine, 1.3 billion Chinese are desperately striving to attain the American consumption level. Add to that number hundreds of millions of Indian middle-class who are also aspiring to achieve an American-style consumption level. Then we will need several planets. One Earth alone cannot sustain even the current level of consumption. But, the consumption levels of poor countries need to go up so that there is an equitable distribution of Earth's resources; the rest must reduce. For a sustainable world, the world will be better off living with the slogan, "Simple Living, High Thinking."

Control and Reduce Population: Today, the world's population stands at 6.7 billion. Each year, humanity adds 78 million people to this already overpopulated world. India will grow from 1.2 billion in 2007 to 1.7 billion people (an increase of half a billion) by 2050, while China will add another 80 million in the same period. Sudan's population climbed from 9 million in 1950 to 39 million in 2007, and is heading for 73 million by 2050. Nigeria, a highly overpopulated country no larger than Texas has 148 million today and is still growing rapidly. Egypt's population of 75 million today is expected to expand to 121 million by 2050. Tanzania will grow from 40 million in 2007 to 85 million by 2050. The population will triple in Congo from 63 million today to 187 million by 2050. The world will have astounding 9 to 10 billion people by the middle of this century. Similarly, enormous expansions in cattle population are taking place in Africa. How can the planet sustain such burgeoning population growth?
27

Though the overall rate of world population growth is slowing, no amount of grain harvest and ecosystem of the planet can support such massive exponential population growth. No amount of grassland can support such an expansion in cattle population. While the population is expanding dangerously, the world grain harvest is perilously falling. How can the planet cope with such dire situation?

Not only does every nation need to control its population growth, but some need to reduce their population. This sounds odd but it is true. It can be done with highly reduced or even negative—like Russia, Italy, or Germany have—population growth lasting several decades or a century. U.N. data suggests that meeting unmet needs for family planning would reduce unintended births by 72 percent, reducing the projected world population by half a billion by 2050 to 8.64 billion.[28] Thus, much can be done by rich countries by helping poor countries overcome their population control problems.

According to experts, the planet Earth can sustain well about 2 billion people, not 9 or 10 billion, not even the 6.7 billion as of today. Humanity needs to work towards this goal if it is to survive and prosper and provide descent life for all its children. Of course, this goal will be too difficult to achieve.

Equal Distribution of Wealth: One of the root causes of poverty around the world is unequal distribution of wealth with a nation and in-between nations. Poor people in poor or even rich countries increase their population for several reasons: as a security to their threatened life and old age, lack of education, especially among women, poor or non-existent healthcare, high mortality rates among children, and unavailability of family planning advice or contraception.

Today, the social fabric of civilization is unraveling as a consequence of extreme and growing inequality between nations. As David Korten warns, a world divided between the profligate and the desperate cannot long endure. He says it intensifies competition for Earth's resources and drives an unraveling of the social fabric of mutual trust and caring essential to healthy social function. Every year, Forbes Magazine proudly lists the richest people in the world. Each year, more and more are added to this unique list. In reality, there is nothing to be proud of about this list.

For every billionaire, there are millions who are poor. Shouldn't the world rather have very few rich and even fewer the poor? It is a shame to humanity that while more than a billion people don't have enough to eat, billionaires after billionaires are being added to this 'prestigious' list.

According to the U.N. study, the richest 1% of the world's people now own 51% of all the world's assets; while the poorest 50% own only 1% assets. Obviously, when the rich own everything, there is nothing left for the poor to own![29]

Unless rich nations and the rich within nations realize that equal distribution of wealth is vitally important for the sustainability of the planet, this planet is doomed. In an unsustainable planet where ecosystems are being destroyed, forests are decimated, and resources are rapidly depleted while the planet is heating up, simply being rich will not guarantee safety.

Millions of destitute and desperate peoples could flee their homes or their borders in the form of human tsunamis which then will be unstoppable. Obviously, poverty alleviation and more equal wealth distribution is the responsibility of every rich person and every wealthy nation. It is in their self-interest. In a desperate world, no one will be safe.

Cut CO2 Emissions: As mentioned above, every nation must cut its CO2 emission levels, especially those who have contributed to global warming the most. If the world is to avoid above civilization-threatening scenarios, then carbon emissions will have to be cut by 80 percent, not by 2050, but by 2020! Otherwise, it will be too late and we would likely have crossed the tipping point from which there is no return.[30]

According to James Hansen, the famous NASA scientist, we have only 10 years (from March, 2006) to reverse global warming before it will be too late. Unless current Industrial Civilization drastically decreases CO2 emissions, we will pass this brink by the next decade.[31]

Shift to Organic Farming: If the world is to survive the oncoming catastrophe, it will have to shift to organic farming. Large fossil-fuel based farms have never been sustainable. They use enormous quantities of fossil-fuel based fertilizers, pesticides, herbicides, and petroleum. The world needs organically grown food supply. As Vandana Shiva so eloquently articulates, biodiverse, organic farms, and localized food systems offer us more security in times of global warming while producing more and better food, and offering more livelihoods. The industrialized global food system is based on oil while biodiverse, organic, and local food systems are based on living soil. The industrialized system generates enormous waste and pollution while a living agriculture generates no waste. In fact it utilizes animal waste as manure and fertilizer. The industrialized agriculture is based on monocultures while sustainable systems are based on diversity.

Carbon is moved from the soil to the atmosphere in fossil fuel-based industrial agriculture. Ecological agriculture, however, takes carbon from the atmosphere and puts it back in the soil. If we were to convert 10,000 medium-sized US farms to organic farming, the reductions in emissions would be equivalent to removing over 1 million cars from the road. If we were to convert all US cropland to organic, it would increase soil-carbon storage by 367 million tons and would cut nitrogen oxide emissions dramatically. Organic agriculture reduces CO_2 emissions directly and indirectly, so it mitigates the negative impact of climate change in addition to restoring soil fertility. Besides, biodiverse organic farms produce more nutritious food and generate more employment worldwide.[32]

The world will not only have to eliminate coal-fired power plants and stop building any new nuclear power plants: it will have to deindustrialize. The fewer industries, the better off our world will be. Car use worldwide will have to be substantially reduced and replaced with mass transit systems. We will have to make do with the simple things of life, with less so called 'comforts' and with lower levels of facilities.

To reduce energy consumption, pollution, deforestation, and unemployment, globalization will have to go, be drastically reduced, or restructured to benefit local production. Local production for local consumption should be the mantra of the world, as it was just a century ago.

Developed nations who are mainly responsible for creating this climate crisis must pledge about 1 % of their GDP annually to developing nations to mitigate and adapt to the adverse impact of the climate change. It is fair to say that India's and China's position is reasonable. That means the developed countries must commit $400-$500 billion annually towards green technology transfer and initiatives for various mitigation strategies to be adapted by the developing nations. Sadly, the developed nations are averse to agreeing with even ½ % of their GDP annually going to help poor nations weather the climate crisis.[33]

Even more unfortunate, the Copenhagen Conference of 193 nations in December, 2009, was a failure. Thanks to the United States and a few other developed nations, the conference fell short of the already low expectations set for it. The agreement appeared to leave everyone unhappy. President Obama disappointed all of us by not committing to any kind of concrete emissions-cut. Nick Berning of Friends of the Earth-International wrote, "Copenhagen has been an abject failure. Justice has not been done. By delaying action, rich countries have condemned millions of the world's poorest people to hunger, suffering and loss of life as climate change accelerates. The blame for this disastrous outcome is squarely on the developed nations."[34] The well-known environmentalist Bill McKibben wrote, "He (Obama) formed a league of super-polluters, and would be polluters...it is a coalition of foxes who will together govern the henhouse."[35]

Britain's leading climate writer, George Monbiot wrote in the Guardian/UK, "this is a scramble for the atmosphere comparable in style and intent to the scramble for Africa...in this case, most rich and rapidly developing states have sought through these talks to seize as great a chunk of the atmosphere for themselves as they can, to grab bigger rights to pollute than their competitors…in all cases immediate self-interest has trumped the long-term welfare of humankind. Corporate profits and political expediency have proved more urgent considerations than either the natural world or human civilization…goodbye Africa, goodbye south Asia; goodbye glaciers and sea ice, coral reefs and rainforest.[36]

Joss Garman of Independent-UK lamented, "This 'deal' is beyond bad. It contains no legally binding targets and no indication of when or how they will come about. There is not even a declaration that the world will aim to keep global temperature rises below 1°C…Copenhagen was a historic failure that will live in infamy."[37]

Archbishop Desmond Tutu put the stakes this way: "We are facing impending disaster on a monstrous scale…A global goal of about 2 °C is to condemn Africa to incineration and no modern development."[38]

As shown by the failure of the Copenhagen Conference, selfish, prejudiced interests are likely to guide the major powers in future negotiations. Now perhaps, the people of the world rightly see them as enemies of the Earth.

We have already lost 17 precious years. All polluting nations on this Earth will have to reduce their emissions by 50% by 2050 and will need to be carbon-neutral by 2080—though some experts even advise an 80% cut by 2020. Yet if business continues as usual, as it did in Copenhagen, if such self-serving and short-sighted stances by major polluting nations persist into the future, resulting in failures to negotiate fairly for concrete emissions cuts, our civilization may as well already be over the brink. If just compromise and prompt action must wait until the symptoms of collapse are so overwhelming, that they will have come too late because by then we might have crossed the irreversible tipping point.

Notes

Chapter-1
The Anasazi, Mesa Verde, Mimbres, Hohokam and Norse

1- Robert Lister and Florence Lister, *Chaco Canyon* (Albuquerque: University of New Mexico Press, 1981)

2- Timothy Kohler and Meredith Mathews, "Long-term Anasazi land use and forest production: a case study of southwest Colorado" (American antiquity 51:370-375 (1986)

3- Eric Force, R. Gwinn Vivian, Thomas Windes and Jeffrey Dean looked into the arroyo channels that lowered Chaco canyon's water table in their reassessment "Relation of Bonito Paleo-channel and base-level Variations to Anasazi Occupation, Chaco Canyon, New Mexico (Tucson: Arizona State Museum, University of Arizona, 2002)

4- Michael Samuels and Julio Betancourt, "Modeling the long-term effects of fuel wood harvests on Pinyon-juniper woodlands" (Environmental Management 6:505-515 (1982); Also see Julio Betancourt, Jefrey Dean, and Herbert Hull, "Prehistoric long-distance transport of construction beams, Chaco Canyon, New Mexico" (American Antiquity 51:370-375 (1986)

5- Jared Diamond, *Collapse,* p.153

6- Christy Turner II and Jacqueline turner, *Man Corn: Cannibalism and Violence in the Prehistoric American Southwest* (Salt Lake City: University of Utah Press, 1999); Jonathan Haas and Winfred Creamer, *Stress and Warfare Among the Kayenta Anasazi of the thirteenth Century A.D.* (Chicago: Field Museum of Natural History, 1993); Steven LeBlanc, *Prehistoric Warfare in the American Southwest* (Salt Lake city: University of Utah Press, (1999).

7- Jared Diamond, *Collapse,* p.154

8- John Stephens, *Incidents of Travel in Central America, Chiapas and Yucatan* (New York: Harper, 1841)

9- Jared Diamond, *Collapse*, pp. 159, 166-67. Also see, Michael Coe, *The Maya*, 6th ed. (New York: Thames and Hudson, 1999)

10- David Webster, *The Fall of the Ancient Maya*. (New York: Thames and Hudson, 2002).

11- David Webster, Ann Corinne Freter and Nancy Gonlin, *Copan: The Rise and Fall of an Ancient Maya Kingdom*, (Fort Worth: Harcourt Brace, 2000)

12- David Hodell et al., "Solar Forcing of drought frequency in the Maya lowlands" (Science 292:1367-1370 (2001); Jason Curtise et al., "Climate variability of the Yucatan Peninsula (Mexico) during the past 3500 years, and implications for Maya cultural evolution (Quarternary Research 46:37-47 (1996) Richardson Gill, *The Great Maya Droughts*, (Albuquerque: University of New Mexico Press, 2000). Also see, David Hodell et al., "Possible role of climate in the collapse of Classic Maya civilization" (Nature 375:391-394 (1995).

13- Two articles by scientists, Michael Rosenmeier, "A 4,000 year lacustrine record of environmental change in the southern Maya lowlands, Petén, Guatemala" (Quarternary Research 57:183-190 (2002); and Jason Curtis et al., "A multi-proxy study of Holocene environmental change in the Maya lowlands of Petén, Guatemala" (Journal of Paleolimnology 19:139-159 (1998). Also see, Gerald Haug et. Al., "Climate and the Collapse of Maya Civilization" (Science 299:1731-1735 (2003).

14- Jette Arneborg and Hans Christian Gullov, *Man, Culture and Environment in Ancient Greenland*, (Copenhagen: Danish Polar Center, 1998).

15- See papers by Robert McGhee, "Contact between Native North Americans and the Medieval Norse; a review of the evidence" (American Antiquity 49:4-26, 1984; Also see, Joel Berglund, "The decline of the Norse settlements in Greenland" (Arctic Anthropology 23:91-107, 1986. Jette Arneborg, *"Contact between Eskimos and Norsemen in Greenland: a review of the evidence,"* pp. 23-35 in Tvaerfaglige Viking symposium (Aarhus, Denmark: Aarhus University, 1993.

16- Bent Fredskild, "Erosion and vegetational changes in the South Greenland caused by agriculture", (Geografisk Tidsskrift 92:14-21, 1992). Also see, Bjarne Jacobsen "Soil resources and soil erosion in the Norse Settlement area of Osterbygden in southern Greenland", (Acta Borealia 1:56-68, 1991.

17- Tom Amorosi et al., "They did not live by grass alone: the politics and paleoecology of animal fodder in the North Atlantic region" (Environmental Archaeology 1:41-54, 1998.

Chapter-2
The Easter Islanders

1- Diamond Jared, Collapse: *How Societies Choose to Fall or Succeed,* pp. 80, 81

2- Discover Magazine, Diamond Jared, "Easter Island's End", August 1995

3- Sharp Andrew, ed., *the Journal of Jacob Roggeveen,* Oxford University Press, London, pp. 89-106

4- Discover Magazine, Diamond Jared, Easter Island's End, August, 1995

5- Jared Diamond, "Collapse," p.87

6- Ibid, p.89

7- Ibid, p.90

8- Ibid, pp. 95-96

9- Ibid, p.98

10- Tilberg Jo Anne Van and Ralston Ted, "Megaliths and mariners: experimental archaeology on Easter Island (Rapa Nui)", and Johnson K.L., ed., Onward and Upward! Papers in Honor of Clement W. Meighan (University Press of America).

11- Journal of Archaeological Science 16:177-205 (1989), Steadman David's reports on identification of bird bones and other remains excavated at Anakena Beach, "Extinctions of birds in eastern Polynesia: a review of the record, and comparisons with other Pacific Island groups". Also see Science 267:1123 (1995), "Prehistoric extinction of Pacific Island birds: biodiversity meets zoo archaeology".

12- Journal de la Societe des Oceanistes 80:103-124 (1985), Ayres William, "Easter Island Subsistence. This provides further archaeological evidence of food consumed.

13- Diamond Jared, "Collapse", pp. 104-115

14- Ibid

15- Ibid

16- Ibid, pp.120-135

Chapter-3
America & its Earthly Footprints

1- Philip Wenz, "Go Green: Our Earth's Future Depends on It", San Francisco Chronicle, January 17, 2009.

2- Andy Rooney, *60 Minutes,* April 6, 2008

3- David Sandalow, Freedom from Oil, pp. 14-19

4- U.S. Environmental Protection Agency, "Draft Programmatic Environmental Impact Statement," 2003 and "Final Programmatic Environmental Impact Statement," October 2005.

5 - U.S. EPA, "Mid-Atlantic Integrated Assessment: Acid Mine Drainage," updated March 3, 2006. In addition, coal mining causes air pollution, including dust and particle pollution which results in respiratory problems such as black lung disease in coal miners. Coal mining also adds to global warming as it releases heat-trapping methane found in coal seams.

6- Pat LaMarche, "Deadly Sins Taking Toll On Earth," The Bangor Daily News, Maine, April 22, 2009.

7- "Modern Marvels," History Channel, May 4, 2009.

8- U.S. Environmental Protection Agency, "Inventory of U.S. Greenhouse Gas Emissions and Sinks: 1990-2005," April 2007

9- U.S. Department of Energy and U.S. Environmental Protection Agency, "Carbon Dioxide Emissions from the Generation of Electric Power in the United States," July 2000.

10-National Research Council, "Managing Coal Combustion in Mines," 2006.

11 - Ibid

12- Press Release by Reuters, "Tests Show Pollution near Ash Spill", January 3, 2009.

13-See an article by Joshua Frank, "The Pentagon is America's Biggest Polluter", posted on *Alternet.org* May 12, 2008, pp.1-2

14- Ibid, p.2

15- Ibid, p.2-3.

16- Anne Platt McGinn, "POPs Culture", *World Watch*, March-April 2000, 32.

17- Joshua Zaffos's article, 'Low Sperm Counts and Deformed Penises: The Chemical Industry has a Hold on your Reproductive Future' in *Colorado Springs Independent*, June 26, 2008.

18- Judith Cook and Chris Kaufman, Portrait of a poison: The 2,4,5-T Story, Pluto Press, London, 1982, 1.

19- Michelle Allsopp, Pat Costner, and Paul Johnston, "Body of Evidence: the Effects of Chlorine on Human Health", *Greenpeace International*, London, 1995.

20- Kristine Schaefer, "Nowhere to Hide: Persistent Toxic Chemicals in U.S. Food Supply", Press Release, *Pesticide Action Network of North America*, San Francisco, California, November 2000.

21-Michelle Allsopp, Ben Erry, Ruth Stringer, Paul Johnston and David Santillo, "Recipe for Disaster: A Review of Persistent Pollutants in Food." Greenpeace Research Laboratory and University of Exeter Department of Biology, Exeter, U.K., March 2000.

22-Thomas Streissguth, ed., Nuclear and Toxic Waste, p. 7

23- Bill Moyers, "Trade Secrets: A Moyers Report. Program Transcript, Public Broadcasting Service, March 26, 2001.

24- Robert Napier, "Hot Air on the Environment" *Guardian (London)*, August 16, 2001.

25- Thomas Streissguth Ed., Nuclear and Toxic Waste, p.6

26- Harry Hanbury, Video, "Rocket Fuels, Pesticides and Pharmaceuticals Swirl in America's Troubled Waters", *American News Project*, May 26, 2008.

27-World Wildlife fund 2000.

28- Anita Gordon, " New Report Concludes Nation is Awash in Chemicals that can Affect Child Development and Learning", press release, *Physicians for Social Responsibility*, Washington D.C., September 7, 2000.

29- Thomas Streissguth, Nuclear and Toxic Waste, p.5

30- Ibid, p.16

31 - Bruce E. Johansen, The Dirty Dozens, pp.34-5. Also, Amy Goodman, *Democracy Now*, May 18, 2009.

32- Will Allen, Agriculture *Is One of the Most Polluting and Dangerous Industries*, Chelsea Green Publishing, posted on Alternet.org, May 11, 2009. p.2.

33- Ibid, p.3.

34- Johansen, The Dirty Dozens, p.1.

35- Elizabeth Grossman, High Tech Trash, pp.5-6. About computer and cell-phone garbage, *60 Minutes TV Program*, August 30, 2009.

36- Ibid, p.7

37- Ivan Eland, "We Can No Longer Afford the Empire", CommonDreams.org, January 13, 2009

38- *Financial Times*, FT.com February 10, 2010.

39- See Phyllis Bennis article, "As its Economic Power Wanes, Does the U.S. Lean Harder on the Military?" Foreign Policy in Focus, October 15, 2008. Also see, Frida Berrigan, "No Recession for Arms Sales", Foreign Policy in Focus, September 19, 2008.

40- Travis Sharp article, "Goodbye to Defense's Gilded Age?" Foreign Policy in Focus, October 15, 2008.

Chapter-4
China and the Planet Earth

1-Elizabeth Economy in "The Great Leap Backwards", Foreign Affairs Magazine, September/October, 2007, pp.1. 2 - Ibid, p.1-2

2-Ibid, p.1-2

3-Jared Diamond, "Collapse: How Societies Choose to Fall or Succeed", pp.360-62

4 -Elizabeth Economy in Nation Magazine, "China vs. Earth: How China is Threatening the World's Environment", May 7, 2007.

5 -Elizabeth Economy, "The Great Leap Backward", Foreign Affairs, September/October, 2007.

6 -Jared Diamond, "Collapse", p.365-66.

7 -Elizabeth Economy, "China vs. Earth", The Nation, May 7, 2007

8 - Peter Navarro, "China's Pollution Olympics", Asia Times, July 15, 2008.

9 -Jared Diamond, "Collapse", p.368.

10 -Elizabeth Economy, "The Great Leap Backward", pp.2-3

11 - Jared Diamond, "Collapse", pp.363-4.

12 -Elizabeth Economy, "The Great Leap Backward", pp.3-4

13 - Ibid. Also see, Jared Diamond, "Collapse", pp.371-72

14 -Christina Larson, "China's Environmental Problem is a Political One", Washington Monthly, January 22, 2008. Also see, Elizabeth Economy, "China vs. Earth, The Nation, May 7, 2007 and also see, E. Economy, "The Great Leap Backwards?, September/October, 2007.

Chapter-5
The Other Nations

1 - Isa Karlsson, "Unchecked Arms Trade Fuelling Conflict, Poverty", p. 1, Inter Press Service, October 10, 2008.

2 - Ibid.

3 - Ibid.

4 - Reported by Allan Woods, "Tar Sands Smog Seen Worsening", *The Toronto Star*, January 21, 2009. Also see, Broecker and Kunzig, *Fixing Climate*, pp.186-87

5 - Richard Heinberg, "Power Down: Options and Actions for a Post-Carbon World", pp. 119-121. Also see, Lester Brown, Plan B-3: Mobilizing to save Civilization, p.33.

6 - Pat Costner, "The Burning Question—Chlorine and Dioxin. Taking Back Our Stolen Future: Hormone Disruption and PVC Plastic." *Greenpeace USA*. April 1997.

7 -Johansen, The Dirty Dozen, pp.31-2.

8 - *Population Reference Bureau*, 2001.

9 - Daniel Pepper, Chocking on Pollution in India," Spiegel online, 2007. htpp://www.spiegel.de/international/world.

10 - Ibid. "Solar Dimming" was reported by Catherine Brahic, ABC News, November 14, 2007.

11 - *Population Reference Bureau, 2001.*

12 - Country Profile: India, Library of Congress Country Studies. December 2004. Accessed: December 21, 2008. http://lcweb2.loc.gov/frd/cs/profiles/India.pdf.

13 - Russell Hopfenberg and David Pimentel, " Human Population Numbers as a Function of Food Supply," www.oilcrash.com Retrieved on- February 2008 Also, *National Geographic Society.* 1995. Water: A Story of Hope. Washington (DC).

14 -Hernandez V. and N. Jayaraman, 1998, *Greenpeace Report,* titled, "Toxic Legacies, Poisoned Futures: Persistent Organic Pollutants in Asia. Washington D.C.

15 - A Greenpeace report, "Persistent Organic Pollutants in Asia: an Ongoing Disaster.", November 10, 1998.

16 - "Indian Enviros Urge Ban on Pesticide Endosulfan", *Environmental News Service,* July 3, 2002. India is too vast a country with its teeming millions and problems like these are common until discovered.

17 - *Greenpeace,* Bhopal Disaster, July 8, 2008

18 - *Greenpeace News Release,* "No More Ships For Scrap to India or Bangladesh", July 11, 2005.

19 - *Greenpeace News Release,* "Bahut Ho Gaya!" March 22, 2005.

20 - *Greenpeace News Release,* "Fuel efficiency law need of the hour, says Greenpeace". July 8, 2008.

21 - "Indonesian NGO Backs Villagers in Fight against Palm Oil", *Agence France Presse,* January 29, 2009.

22 -Mel White, "Borneo's Moment of Truth", *National Geographic,* November, 2008, pp.46-56.

23 - Charles Rusnell, "U.S. Military Wastes Entering Canada: Ottawa Concerned with Political Fallout, Document Shows." *Edmonton Journal,* March 31, 2000.

24 - Ann M. Simmons, "Tanzania Begins to Deal with Toxic Wastelands…" Los Angeles Times, March 30, 2000.

25 - U.N. Food and Agriculture Organization Press Release, "U.N. Agency Calls for Faster Disposal of Toxic Pesticide Waste Stocks", May 9, 2001.

26 - Greenpeace article, "Persistent Organic Pollutants in Asia: an ongoing Disaster." 1998.

27 - Greenpeace news release, "Poisoning the Poor-Electronic Waste in Ghana", August 6, 2008.

28 - Jared Diamond, "Collapse", p. 370.

29 - "Geographical location and extent of radioactive contamination", Swiss Agency for Development and Cooperation, Minsk, 2001, pp.5-6.

30 -http:/www.nea.fr/html/rp/Chernobyl/c04.html, Nuclear Energy Agency, 2002.

31 - Mycio Mary (2005). Wormwood Forest: A Natural History of Chernobyl., Joseph Henry Press. Washington D.C., p.259.

32 - *Wall Street Journal*, 27, April, 2006. Also see, "20 years after Chernobyl-the ongoing health effects", IPPNW. April, 2006

33 - http//www.wreckedexotics.com/articles/011.shtml?%3F.

34 -Zhores A. Medvedev, Nuclear Disaster in the Urals, pp. 4-21, 164-68

35 -"Oil Companies Are Harmful Polluters", Essential Action and Global Exchange, Pollution, James Haley, Ed. Current Controversies Series. Greenhaven Press, 2003. See "Oil for Nothing: Multinational Corporations, Environmental Destruction, Death and Impunity in the Niger Delta", by Essential Action and Global Exchange. WWW.essentialaction.org, January 25, 2000.

36 - Maurice Carney, Executive Director of Friends of Congo, Washington DC, said on *Democracy Now*, January 23, 2008.

Chapter-6
Current Civilization in Trouble

1 - U.N. Environment Programme (UNEP), *Global Outlook for Ice and Snow* (Nairobi: 2007)

2 - Ibid.

3 - Lester Brown, Plan B-3, pp.48-9.

4 - Ibid, p.50.

5 - Intergovernmental Panel on Climate Change (IPCC), *Summery for Policymakers, in Climate Change 2007: The Physical Science Basis. Contribution of working Group I to the Fourth Assessment Report of the Intergovernmental Panel on Climate Change* (Cambridge and New York: Cambridge University Press, 2007), p. 13; IPCC, "Intergovernmental Panel on Climate Change and its Assessment Reports," fact sheet, at www.ipcc.ch/press.

6 - IPCC, *Summery for Policymakers,* above , p. 15.

7 - U.N. Environmental Programme (UNEP), *Global Outlook for Ice and Snow (Nairobi: 2007).*

8 - Emily Wax, "A Sacred River Endangered by Global Warming," *Washington Post,* June 17, 2007; also see UNEP, above .

9 - Christian Larson, "Shrinking Glaciers Have Put Tibetans in the Path of Climate Chaos," *Christian Science Monitor,* January 22, 2009.

10 - Ibid.

11 - Clifford Coonan, "China's Water Supply could be Cut Off as Tibet's Glaciers Melt," *The Independent* (London), May 31, 2007; also see UNEP, as cited above.

12 - Jonathan Watts, "Highest Ice fields Will Not Last 100 Years, Study Finds: China's Glacier Research Warns of Deserts and Floods Due to Warming," *Guardian* (London), September 24, 2004; "Glacier Study Reveals Chilling Prediction," *China Daily*, September 23, 2004.

13 - See above, UNEP.

14 - Sara Miller Llana, "Diminishing Latin American Glaciers Threaten Water Supply," *Christian Science Monitor,* April 10, 2008.

15 - Eric Hansen, "Hot Peaks," *OnEarth,* fall, 2002, p.8.

16 - Leslie Josephus, "Global Warming Threatens Double-Trouble for Peru: Shrinking Glaciers and a Water Shortage," *Associated Press,* February 12, 2007; *Citation World Atlas* (Union, N.J.: Hammond World Atlas Corporation, 2004).

17 - Ibid.; also see cited before, U.N. Population Division.

18 - James Painter, "Peru's alarming Water Truth," BBC News, March 12, 2007; U.N. Population Division, Urban Agglomerations 2005 Wall Chart, at www.un.org/esa/population.

19 - reported by *World Focus,* World Bank Report, February 18, 2009.

20 - Lonnie G. Thompson, "Disappearing Glaciers Evidence of a Rapidly Changing Earth," American Association for the Advancement of Science annual meeting, San Francisco, February 2001;"The Peak of Mt. Kilimanjaro as It Has Not Been Seen for 11,000 Years," *Guardian* (London), March 14, 2005; Bancy Wangui, "Crisis Looms as Rivers around Mt. Kenya Dry Up," *East Africa Standard,* July 1, 2007.

21 - Michael Kiparsky and Peter Gleick, *Climate change and California Water Resources: a Survey and Summery of the Literature* (Oakland, CA: *Pacific Institute*, 2003); Timothy Cavagnaro et al., *Climate Change: Challenges and Solutions for California Agricultural Landscapes* (Sacramento, CA: *California Climate Change Center*, 2006).

22 - John Krist, "Water Issues Will Dominate California's Agenda This Year," *Environmental News Network,* February 21, 2003.

23 - Michael J. Scott et al., "Climate Change and Adaptation in Irrigated Agriculture—A Case Study of the Yakima River," in UCOWR/NIWR Conference, Water Allocation: Economics and the Environment (Carbondale, IL: Universities Council on Water Resources, 2004); Pacific Northwest National Laboratory, "Global Warming to Squeeze Western Mountains Dry by 2050," Press Release (Richland, WA: February 16, 2004).

24 - Giles Tremlett, "Climate change lays waste to Spain's glaciers," *Guardian.co.uk*, 23 February, 2009.

25 - Ibid., p.2.

26 - Ibid., p.2-3. 27 - Ibid., p. 3.

27- Glaciers melt 'at fastest rate in past 5000 years', Mail & Guardian Online, March 16, 2008, www.mg.co.za/article/2008-03-16

28 - UNEP, Mehrdad Khalili, "The Climate of Iran: North, South, Kavir (Desert), Mountains," San'ate Hamlo Naql, March 1997, pp. 48-53.

29 - Kilimanjaro ice cap melting, reported by Amy Goodman, *Democracy Now,* November 3, 2009. For rising ocean levels, see report by Jane Kay, "Ocean Expected to Rise 5 Feet along Coastlines", the *San Francisco Chronicle*, March 12, 2009.

30 - UNEP, op. cit. p.103; IPCC, *Summery for Policymakers,* p.13, Paul Brown, "Melting Ice Cap Triggering Earthquakes," Guardian (London), 8 September, 2007.

31 - Arctic Climate Impact Assessment (ACIA), Impacts of a Warming Arctic (Cambridge, U.K.: Cambridge University Press); ACIA website, www.acia.uaf.edu; "Rapid Arctic Warming Brings Sea Level Rise, Extinctions," *Environment News Service*, November 8, 2004; UNEP, p.103.

32 - Julienne Stroeve et al., "Arctic Sea Ice Decline: Faster than Forecast," *Geographical Research Letters*, vol. 34 (May 2007); National Snow and Ice Data Center (NSIDC), "Arctic Sea Ice Shatters all Previous Record Lows," press release (Boulder, CO: October 1, 2007); Stroeve quoted in "Arctic Ice Retreating 30 Years Ahead of Projections," *Environment News Service*, April 30, 2007.

33 - Mark Kaufman, "Decline in Winter Arctic Ice Linked to Greenhouse Gases," *Washington Post*, September 14, 2006; Josefino C. Comiso, "Abrupt Decline in the Arctic Sea Ice Cover," *Geophysical Research Letters*, vol. 33, September 30, 2006.

34 - David Adam, "Meltdown Fear as Arctic Ice Cover Falls to Record Winter Low," *Guardian* (London), May 15, 2006.

35 - David Ljunggren, "Arctic Summer Ice Could Vanish by 2013," *Reuters*, March 6, 2009.

36 - Ibid.

37 - NSIDC, "Processes: Thermodynamics: Albedo," at nsidc.org/seaice/processes/albedo.html.

38 - UNET, op. cit. 1.

39 - H. Jay Zwally et al., "Surface Melt-Induced Acceleration of Greenland Ice-sheet Flow," Science, vol. 297 (July 12, 2002), pp. 218-22.

40 - U.S. Department of Energy, Information Administration, "Antarctica: Fact Sheet," at www.eia.doe.gov.

41 - Gordon McGranahan et al., "The rising Tide: Assessing the Risks of Climate Change and Human Settlements in Low Elevation Coastal Zones," *Environmental and Urbanization*, vol. 18, no. 1 (April 2007).

42 - Ibid.

43 - Robin McKie, "Scientists to Issue Stark Warning Over Dramatic New Sea Level Figures", *The Guardian/UK*, March 8, 2009.

44- Ibid, p.2.

45 - Ibid.

46 - U.N. Population Division, *World Population Prospects: The 2006 Revision Population Database, at esa.un.org/unpp,* updated 2007.

47 - International Institute for Environment and Development, "Climate Change: Study Maps those at Greatest Risk from Cyclones and Rising Seas," press release (London: 28 March, 2007); Catherine Brahic, "Coastal Living-A Growing Global Threat," *New Scientist.com,* March 28, 2007; UNEP, Global Outlook for Ice and Snow (Nairobi:

48 - Anna Mitchell, Oxfam International Media Officer, "Sea Level Rise Spells Increased Likelihood of Disaster for the World's Poorest People", *Oxfam International,* March 10, 2009. 2007).

49 - World forested area from FAO, *Global Forest Resources Assessment 2005* (Rome: 2006), p. 16.

50 - Ibid. pp. xii-xvi.

51 - FAO, ProdSTAT, electronic database, at faostat.fao.org, updated December 22, 2006.

52 - Alain Marcoux, "Population and Deforestation," in *Population and the Environment* (Rome: FAO, 2000); March Turnbull, "Life in the Extreme," *Africa Geographic Online*, April 4, 2005.

53 - as cited by Lester Brown, Plan B 3, p. 88, Nigel Sizer and Dominiek Plouvier, *Increased Investment and Trade by Transnational Logging Companies in Africa, the Caribbean, and the Pacific* (Belgium: World Wide Fund for Nature (WWF) and WRI Forest Frontiers initiative, 2000), pp. 21-35; Lester R. Brown, "Nature's Limits," in Lester R. Brown et al., *State of the World 1995* (New York: W. W. Norton & Company, 1995), p. 9.

54 - Peter Goodman and Peter Finn, "Corruption Stains Timber Trade," *Washington Post,* April 1, 2007; Evan Osnos, "China Feeds U.S. Demand for Wood as Forests Suffer," *Chicago Tribune*, December 18, 2006.

55 - Ibid.

56 - Andy White et al., China and the Market for Forest Products (Washington, DC: *Forest Trends*, 2006).

57 - Mario Rautner, Martin Hardiono, and Raymond J. Alfred, (Frankfurt: WWF Germany, June, 2005), p. 7. About the rain forest in Sarawak, *WorldFocus*, September 3, 2009.

58 - Lewis Smith, "85 Per Cent of Amazonian Rainforest at Risk of Destruction, Researchers Warn," *The Times Online (UK)*, March 11, 2009.

59 - Ibid.

60 - Thomas L. Friedman, When Mother Nature and the Market Both Said: "No More", *The New York Times*, March 10, 2009.

61 - Lester R. Brown, Plan B 3, p. 88-89.

62 - Greenpeace Report-Summary, "Slaughtering the Amazon", p.3-7, June 2009. Also see www.fao.org (2009).

63 - Ibid.

64 - Ibid, p.4, 9.

65 - Ibid, p.8-9

66 - Kelly Hearn, "Exclusive: Selling the Amazon for a Handful of Beads," AlterNet, January 17, 2006.

67 - U. N. Population Division, World Population Prospects: The 2006 revision Population Database, at www.esa.un.org/unpp, updated 2007, FAO, as sited earlier, p. 193.

68 - *World in Focus*, February 18, 2009.

69 - Ibid; also see "Madagascar's Rainforest Faces Destruction," Guardian (London), June 29, 2003.

70 - U. N. Population Division, as cited earlier; also, Malawi Ministry of Mines, Natural Resources and the Environment, State of the Environment Report of Malawi 2002 (Lilongwe, Malawi: 2004); FAO as cited earlier, p. 196.

71 - Lester R. Brown, Plan B 3, p. 91.

72 - Yang Youlin, Victor Squires, and Lu Qi eds., *Global Alarm: Dust and Sandstorms from the World's Drylands* (Bangkok: Secretariat of the U.N. Convention to Combat Desertification, 2002), pp. 15-28.

73 - FAO, *The State of Food and Agriculture 1995* (Rome: 1995), p.175 as cited by Lester R. Brown, *Plan B 3*.

74 - Ibid,; USDA, *Production, Supply, and Distribution*, Electronic database, aw www.fas.usda.gov/psdonline, updated July 12, 2007; yield from FAO, ProdSTAT, electronic database, at faostat.fao.org, updated June 30, 2007.

75 - U.N. Environment Programme (UNEP), Mongolia: State of the Environment 2002 (Pathumthani, Thailand: Regional Resource Center

for Asia and the Pacific, 2001), pp. 3-7; USDA, as cited before; U.N. Population Division, cited earlier.

76 - Paul Brown, "4x4s Replace the Desert Camel and Whip up a Worldwide Dust Storm," *Guardian* (London), August 20, 2004.

77 - Ibid.

78 - National Aeronautics and Space Administration (NASA) Earth Observatory, "Dust Storm off Western Sahara Coast," at earthobservatory.nasa.gov. as cited by Lester R. Brown, Plan B 3, p. 92.

79 - Asif Farukh, *Pakistan Grain and Feed Annual Report 2002* (Islamabad, Pakistan: USDA Foreign Agricultural Service, 2003).

80 - UNEP, Africa Environment Outlook: Past Present, and Future Perspectives (Nairobi: 2002), at www.unep.org/dewa/Africa.

81 - Species Survival Commission, 2007 IUCN Red List of Threatened Species, at www.iucnredlist.org, updated September 12, 2007.

82 - Jim Merkel says in his book, Radically Simple, November 1, 2007.

83 - Species Survival Commission, *2000 IUCN Red List of Threatened Species* (Gland, Switzerland, and Cambridge, U.K.: World Conservation Union-IUCN, 2000), p.1.

84 - Species Survival Commission, cited above. Also, see "Great Indian Bustard Facing Extinction," *India Abroad Weekly*, February 12, 2001.

85 - Ibid.; TRAFFIC, Food for Thought: The Utilization of Wild Meat in Eastern and Southern Africa (Cambridge, U.K.: 2000).

86 - Danna Harman, "Bonobos' Threat: Hungry Humans," *Christian Science Monitor*, June 7, 2001; "Video: New Bonobo Ape Population Discovered," *National Geographic News*, March 7, 2007.

87 - Dennis Van Angelsdorp et al., "An Estimate of Managed Colony Losses in the Winter of 2006-2007: A Report Commissioned by the Apiary Inspectors of America," *American Bee Journal* (July 2007), pp. 599-603; Alexie Barrionuevo, "Bees Vanish, and Scientists Race for Reasons," *New York Times*, April 24, 2007.

88 - Joel Garreau, "Honey, I'm Gone," *Washington Post*, June 1, 2007; Erik Stockstad, "Puzzling Decline of U.S. Bees Linked to Virus from Australia," *Science*, vol. 317, issue 5843 (September 7, 2007), pp. 1304-05.

89 - Special Survival Commission, 2004 IUCN Red List of Threatened Species (Gland, Switzerland, and Cambridge, U.K.: IUCN, 2004), p. 89; Species Survival Commission, cited before.

90 - Catherine Jacob, "The World's Fish Will Die Out within 50 Years," *Skye News*, June 6, 2009.

91 - David Kaimowitz et al., *Hamburger Connection Fuels Amazon Destruction* (Jakarta, Indonesia: Center for International Forestry Research, 2004).

92 - Conservation International, "The Brazilian *cerrado*," at www.biodivercityhotspot.org. Center for Applied Biodivercity Science, "Hotspots Revisited: *Cerrado*," at www.biodivercityscience.org/publications/hotspots/Cerrado.html. Butterfly diversity from Helena c. Morais et al., "Caterpillar Seasonality in Central Brazilian Cerrado," Revista de Biologia Tropical, vol. 47, no. 4, pp. 1025-33 as cited by Lester Brown, Plan B 3.0

93 - James R. Spotila et al., "Pacific Turtles Face Extinction," *Nature*, vol. 405 (June 1, 2000), pp. 529-30; "Leatherback Turtles Threatened," *Washington Post*, June 5, 2000.

94 - Andrew C. Revkin, "Nations Near Arctic Declare Polar Bears Threatened by Climate Change,"*The New York Times*, March 20, 2009.

95 - Lester Brown, "Could Food Shortages Bring Down Civilization?"- Scientific American, April 22, 2009.

Chapter-7
Emerging Water Scarcities

1 - Robert Draper, "Australia's Dry Run," *National Geographic*, April 2009, p. 35-57.

2 - Ibid.

3 - Mark Clayton, "How the World is Realizing that Water is "Blue Gold", *Christian Science Monitor*, May 29, 2008.

4 - Ibid.

5 - Ibid, p.3

6 - Jacob W. Kijne, *Unlocking the Water Potential of Agriculture* (Rome: U.N. Food and Agriculture Organization (FAO), 2003), p.26; also see, water use from I.A.Shiklomanov, "Assessment of Water Resources and Water Availability in the World," *Report for the Comprehensive Assessment of the Freshwater Resources of the World* (St. Petersburg, Russia: State Hydrological Institute, 1998).

7 - Maude Barlowe, "Our Political Leaders are to Blame in World Water Crisis." *The New Press,* April 24, 2008. p. 1.

8 - Ibid. p.1.

9- Ibid. p.2.

10- Ibid. p.3.

11- Ibid. p.3.

12 - Michael Ma, "Northern Cities Sinking as Water Table Falls," *South China Morning Post,* August 11, 2001; share of China's grain harvest from the North China Plain based on Hong Yang and Alexander Zehnder, "China's Regional Water Scarcity and Implications for Grain Supply and Trade," *Environment and Planning* A, vol. 33 (2001) and also, USDA, www..fas.usda.gov/psd/psdonline, updated June 11, 2007.

13 - Ibid

14 - World Bank, China: *Agenda for Water Sector Strategy for North China* (Washington, DC: April 2001) pp. vii, xi. Also see, John Wade, Adam Branson, and Xiang Qing, China Grain and Feed Annual Report 2002 (Beijing: USDA, February 21, 2002).

15 - see USDA data, as d above.

16 - see above , World Bank, p. viii; calculations of 1000 tons of water to produce 1 ton of grain are derived from FAO, *Yield Response to Water* (Rome:1979).

17 - Peter H. Gleick et al., *The World's Water 2006-2007* (Washington, DC: Island Press, 2006), p. 148; also see, Fred Pearce, "Asian Farmers Sucking the Continent Dry," *New Scientist.com,* August 28, 2004.

18 - Pearce, op. cit. Tamil Nadu population from 2001 census, "Tamil Nadu at a Glance: Area and Population," at www.tn.gov.in.

19 - Pearce, see above .

20 - Grain production and imports from USDA, op. cit. earlier above. See John Briscoe, *India's Water Economy: Bracing for a Turbulent Future* (New

Delhi: World Bank, 2005); population data from U.N. Population Division, see earlier .

21 - USDA, *Agricultural Resources and Environmental Indicators 2000* (Washington, DC: February 2000), Chapter 2.1, p. 6; irrigated share data from FAO, resource STAT, electronic database, at faostat.fao.org/site/405/default.aspx, updated June 30, 2007; harvest from USDA, op. cit. earlier ; Sandra Postel, *Pillar of Sand* (New York: W.W. Norton & Company, 1999), p. 77.

22 - U.N. Population Division, World Population Prospects: The 2006 Revision Population Database, at esa.un.org/unpp, updated 2007. Fall in water table from "Pakistan: Focus on Water Crisis," *U.N. Integrated Regional Information Networks News,* May 17, 2002. Also see, Garstang quoted in "Water Crisis Threatens Pakistan" *Agence France-Presse,* January 26, 2001.

23 - U.N. Population Division, as d before. Craig S. Smith, "Saudis Worry as They Waste Their Scarce Water," New York Times, January 26, 2003; grain production data from USDA, cited before.

24 - Lester Brown, Plan B 3, Earth Policy Institute, W. W. Norton & Company, New York, 2008. pp. 69-74.

25 - Colorado, Indus, Ganges and Nile rivers Postel, see earlier cited Sandra Postel, Pillars of Sand, pp.59,71-73, 94, 261-62; Also see, Lester R. Brown and Brian Halweil, "China's Water Shortages Could Shake World Food Security," World Watch, July/August 1998, p.11. Water use tripling from I.A. Shiklomanov, "Assessment of Water Resources and Water Availability of Freshwater Resources of the World," *Report for the Comprehensive Assessment of the Freshwater Resources of the World* (St. Petersburg, Russia: State Hydrological Institute, 1998), p. 52.

26 - As cited by Lester Brown, Plan B 3, p.75. Sandra Postel, *Last Oasis* (New York: W. W. Norton & Company, 1997), pp. 38-39; World Commission on Dams, *Dams and Development: A New Framework for Decision-Making* (London: Island Press, 2000), p.8.

27 - as cited by Lester Brown, Plan B 3, p. 75. Postel, earlier , pp.261-62; Jim Carrier, "The Colorado: A River Drained Dry," National Geographic, June 1991, pp.4-32.

28 - Scott Thill, "Lightning Strikes: Get Used to Catastrophic Wildfires and Worse," AlterNet, September 15, 2008.

29 - Amy Reeves, "Chinese Demand Drives Growth for Water Equipment Makers," *Investor's Business Daily*, November 6, 2009, p.A7.

30 - Brown and Halweil as cited earlier.

31 - Postel, as cited earlier, pp. 71,146.

32 - Postel, pp. 71, 147; also see, U.N. Population Division, cited earlier.

33 - Marcus Moench, "Groundwater: Potential and Constraints," in Ruth S. Meinzen-Dick and Mark W. Rosegrant, eds., *Overcoming Water Scarcity and Quality Constraints* (Washington, DC: International Food Policy Research Institute, October 2001).

34 - as cited by Lester Brown, Plan B 3, Curtis J. Richardson et al., "The Restoration Potential of the Mesopotamian Marshes of Iraq," *Science*, vol. 307 (February 25, 2005), pp. 1307-10

35 - Abigail Brown, "Water for The Ages", www.alternet.org, posted on June 17, 2008.

36 - U.N. Environmental Programme (UNEP), Africa's Lakes: Atlas of Our Changing Environment (Nairobi: 2006); M. T. Coe and J.A. Foley, "Human and Natural Impacts on the Water Resources of the Lake Chad Basin," Journal of Geophysical Research (Atmosphere), vol. 106, no, D4 (2001), pp.3349-56; population information from U.N. Population Division, World Population Prospects: The 2006 Revision Population Database, at esa.un.org/unpp, updated 2008.

37 - Megan Goldin, "Israel's Shrinking Sea of Galilee Needs a miracle," *Reuters*, August 14, 2001; Jordan River diminishing from Annette Young, "Middle East Conflict Killing the Holy Water," *The Scotsman*, September 12, 2004.

38 - Caroline Hawley, "Dead Sea to Disappear by 2050," BBC, August 3, 2001; Gidon Bromberg, "Water and Peace," *World Watch*, July/August 2004, pp.24-30.

39 - Quirin Schiermeir, "Ecologists Plot to Turn the Tide for Shrinking Lake," Nature, vol. 412, (August 23, 2001), p. 756.

40 - "Sea to Disappear within 15 Years," *News 24*, July 22, 2003; Caroline Williams, "Long Time No Sea," *New Scientist*, January 4, 2003,

pp. 34-37.

41 -Fred Pearce, "Poisoned Waters," *New Scientist*, October 21, 1995, pp. 29-33; Williams, as cited above.

42 - Janet Larson, "Disappearing Lakes, Shrinking Seas," Eco-Economy Update (Washington, DC: Earth Policy Institute, April 7, 2005). Also see, L. Brown, Plan B 3, pp.77-8.

43 - Li Heng, "20 Natural Lakes Disappear Each Year in China," *People's Daily*, October 21, 2002; "Glaciers Receding, Wetlands Shrinking in River Fountainhead Area," *China Daily*, January 7, 2004.

44 - Jim Carlton, "Shrinking Lake in Mexico Threatens Future of Region," *Wall Street Journal*, September 3, 2003; U. N. Population Division, *World Urbanization Prospects: 2005 Revision*, electronic database, www.esa.un.org/unup, updated October 2006.

45 - "Lake Van in Turkey May Disappear in Decade," *Huliq News*, May 15th, 2008.

46 - George Tombs, "Great Lakes in Peril: Why 40 Million People's Drinking Water Is Threatened," *Christian Science Monitor*, January 19, 2009.

47 - Ibid, p. 2-4.

48 - Lester Brown, Plan B-3, pp.51-2.

49 - K.S. Kavi Kumar and Jyoti Parikh, *"Socio-Economic Impacts of Climate Change on Indian Agriculture,"* International Review for Environmental Strategies, Vol. 2, (2001), pp.277-93; U.N. Population Division, *World Population Prospects: The 2006 Revision Population Database*, at esa.un.org/unpp, updated 2007.

50 - Scott Thill, "Lightning Strikes: Get Used to Catastrophic Wildfires and Worse," AlterNet, September 15, 2008.

51 - Storm death toll from the National Climatic Data Center, National Oceanic & Atmospheric Administration, "Mitch: The Deadliest Atlantic Hurricane Since 1780," at www.ncdc.noaa.gov, updated 1 July, 2004; Flores quoted in Arturo Chavez et al., "After the Hurricane: Forest Sector Reconstruction in Honduras," *Forest Products Journal*, November/December 2001, pp. 18-24; gross domestic product from International Monetary Fund (IMF), *World Economic Outlook Database*, at www.imf.org, updated April 2003.

52 - Michael Smith, "Bad Weather, Climate Change Cost World Record $90 Billion," *Bloomberg,* December 15, 2004; Insurers See Hurricane Costs as High as $23 Billion," *Reuters,* October 4, 2004.

53 - Munich Re, "Natural Disasters," Also see, "Significant Natural Catastrophes in 2005 and 2006."

54 - *World News, South and Central Asia, MSNBC News Service,* October 5, 2009. Similarly, worst floods were reported in Philippines around this time.

55 - *Los Angeles Times,* September 19, 2009, p. A29

56 - David Adam, "Too Late? Why Scientists Say We Should Expect the Worst," *The Independent/UK,* December 9, 2008.

57 - Hubbert, Marion King (June 1956). "Nuclear Energy and the Fossil Fuels 'Drilling and Production Practice'" (PDF). *Spring Meeting of the Southern District. Division of Production. American Petroleum Institute.* San Antonio, Texas: Shell Development Company. pp. 22-27. http://www.hubbertpeak.com/hubbert/1956/1956.pdf. Retrieved 2008-04-18.

58- Michael Klare, "The Energy Challenge of Our Lifetime," *Tomdispatch.com,* November 10, 2008.

59-"Scientists meeting in Tunis Called for Priority Activities to Curb Desertification," *UN News Service,* June 21, 2006.

60 - Tushaar Shah et al., about abandoned villages in India, *The Global Groundwater Situation: Overview of Opportunities and Challenges* (Colombo, Sri Lanka: International Water Management Institute, 2000); U.N. Population Division, World Population Prospects: The 2006 Revision Population Database, electronic database, at esa.un.org/unpp.

61 - Iranian News Agency, "Official Warns of Impending Desertification Catastrophe in Southeast Iran," *BBC International Reports,* September 29, 2002; Government of Nigeria, *Combating Desertification and mitigating the Effects of Drought in Nigeria,* National Report on the implementation of the United Nations Convention to Combat Desertification (Nigeria: November 1999).

62 - Bonnie Malkin, Sydney, "Climate change to force 75 million Pacific Islanders from their homes," *Telegraph.co.uk,* July 27, 2009

Chapter- 8
Perilous Signs of Decay

1 - see Chapter-3, p.33

2 - Modern Marvels, *History Channel,* November 17, 2008.

3 - *ABC News,* March 25, 2006.

4 - Determined from U.S. Geological Survey, *Mineral Commodity Summaries 2007* (Washington, DC: U.S. Government Printing Office, 2007).

5 - Eric Lipton, "The Long and Winding Road Now followed by New York City's Trash," *New York Times,* March 24, 2001.

6 - Lester R. Brown, "New York: Garbage Capitol of the World," Eco-Economy update (Washington, DC: Earth Policy Institute, April, 2002). Other data are cited by Lester R. Brown, Plan B 3.0, p. 115.

7 - Niki Kitsantonis, "Athens Is in the Grip of a Garbage Crisis," *International Herald Tribune,* January 28, 2007.

8 - "Fast Urbanization Dumps Garbage in Chinese Cities," *Xinhua News Agency,* August 18, 2006.

9 - Kathy Marks and Daniel Howden, "The world's Dump: Ocean Garbage from Hawaii to Japan," *The Independent UK,* February 6, 2009.

10 - Justin Berton, Chronicle Staff Writer, "Continent-size toxic stew of plastic trash fouling our ocean," San Francisco Chronicle, October 19, 2007.

11 - Ibid.

12 - Kathy Marks and Daniel Howden, as cited earlier above.

13 - *BBC News,* May 13, 2009.

14 - Bonnie Malkin in Sydney, "Great Barier Reef 'Will Die' Unless Carbon Emissions Slashed," The Telegraph/UK, November 17, 2009.

15 - Crude Impact Documentary.

16 - U.N. Report, BBC News, July 11, 2008.

17 - Deborah Rich & Jason Mark, "Hold Steady: Population Growth on a Shrinking Planet," *Earth Island journal,* June 9, 2009.

18 - Chris Hedges, "We Are Breeding Ourselves to Extinction," *TruthDig.com,* March 9, 2009.

19 - Ibid.

20 - David SEMCO, NPG Senior Advisor, "Population: An Unacknowledged Presence at World Food Crisis Talks," June 2008-UN-Food and Agricultural Organization (FAO) Summit in Rome.

21 - John Vidal, "Global Warming Causes 300,000 Deaths a Year, Says Kofi Annan think-tank," *The Guardian of UK*, May 29, 2009.

22 - U.N. Food and Agriculture Organization (FAO), *Number of Undernourished Persons*, www.fao.org/faostat/foodsecurity. Also, WHO, "*Obesity and Overweight*," fact sheet (Geneva: September 2006).

23 - FAO, *The State of Food Security in the World 2006* (Rome: 2006), pp.8, 32, 33; FAO, the State of Food Security in the World 2000 (Rome: 2002); U.N. Population Division, *World Population Prospects*: The 2002 Revision—Volume III. Analytical Report (New York: 2004), pp.136-58, 169. Also see, FAO, *The State of Food Insecurity in the World 2005* (Rome: 2005), p. 33.

24 - Reported by *World Focus*, May 27, 2009.

25 - Gary Gardner and Brian Hawley, "*Nourishing the Underfed and Overfed*," in Lester Brown et al., *State of the World 2000* (New York: W. W. Norton & Company, 2000), pp. 70-73.

26 - Stable populations cited from Population Reference Bureau, at www.prb.org/DataFind/datafinder7.htm; projections about doubling, see U.N. Population Division, as cited before.

27 - Will Allen, *Agriculture is One of the Most Polluting and Dangerous Industries*, Chelsea Green Publishing, posted on Alternet.org, May 11, 2009.

28 - Ibid, p.2.

29 - PTI, India Journal, April 17, 2009, p. A26.

30 - Jonathan Watts, "Beijing Blames Pollutants for Rise in Killer Cancers," *Guardian* (London), May 22, 2007.

31 - Ibid.

32 - Jane Houlihan et al., *Body Burden: The Pollutants in Newborns* (Washington, DC: Environmental Working Group, 2005).

33 - Lester Brown, *Plan B 3*, p. 113.

34 - Ibid. pp.113-14.

35 - Global Environment Facility, U.N. Development Programme (UNDP), and United Nations Industrial Development Organization,

"Removal of Barriers to the Introduction of Cleaner Artisanal Gold Mining and Extraction Technologies," *UNDP Global Mercury Project Inception Document GLO/01/G34* (Washington, DC: April 2002), p.8; Ilan Levin and Eric Schaeffer, *Dirty Kilowatts: America's Most Polluting Power Plants* (Washington, DC: Environmental Integrity Project, July 2007), p.2; EPA, "EPA Decides Mercury Emissions from Power Plants Must Be Reduced," press release (Washington, DC: December 15, 2000).

36 - U.N. Population Division, *World Population Prospects: The 2004 Revision* (New York: 2005).

37 - Total deaths and historical estimates from UNAIDS statistics in Worldwatch Institute, Signposts 2004, CD-Rom (Washington, DC: 2004) and in UNAIDS Epidemic Update (Geneva: various years); sub-Saharan Africa from UNAIDS, 2006 AIDS Epidemic Update (Geneva: December 2006).

38 - UNAIDS, UNICEF, and U.S. Agency for International Development, *Children on the Brink 2004: A Joint Report on New Orphan Estimates and a Framework for Action* (Washington, DC: 2004), p. 29.

39 - Stephen Lewis, press briefing, New York, January 8, 2003; Edith M. Lederer, "Lack of funding for HIV/AIDS is Mass Murder by Complacency, says U.N. Envoy, " *Associated Press,* January 9, 2003.

40 - World Health Organization (WHO), reported by *World in Focus*, April 24, 2009.

41 - U.S. Department of Agriculture (USDA), *Production, Supply, and Distribution Country Reports* (Washington, DC: October 1990); 2007 grainland area from USDA, *Production, Supply and Distribution*, Electronic database, at www.fas.usda.gov/psdonline, updated August 15, 2007; U.N. Population Division as cited earlier.

42 - "Time for action on Sudan" (editorial), *New York Times,* June 18, 2004; "A First Step to Save Darfur" (editorial), *New York Times,* August 3, 2007; Coalition for International Justice, "Estimates from Retrospective Mortality Surveys in Darfur and Chad Displacement Camps, Circa February 2003-April 2005," at www.cij.org, April 2005; "Sudan," in U.S. Central Intelligence Agency, *The World Fact Book*, at www.cia.gov/library/publications, updated September 10, 2007.

43 - Somini Sengupta, "Where the Land is a Tinderbox, the killing is a Frenzy," *New York Times*, June 16, 2004; U.N. Population Division, cited earlier. Government of Nigeria, *Combating Desertification and Mitigating the Effects of Drought in Nigeria*, National Report on the Implementation of the United Nations Convention to Combat Desertification (Nigeria: November 1999).

44 - U.S. Census Bureau, Population Division, International Programs Center, *International Database*, at www. census.gov/ipc/www/idbacc.html.

45 - James Gasana, "Remember Rwanda?" *World Watch*, September/October 2002, pp.24-32.

46 - Emily Wax, "At the Heart of Rwanda's Horror: General's History Offers Clues to the Roots of Genocide," *Washington Post*, September 21, 2002.

47 - U.N. Population Division, as cited earlier.

48 - Michael T. Clare, "Economic Brushfires for a Planet at the Brink," *TomDispatch.com*, February 25, 2009.

49 - Ibid.

50 - U.N. Population Division, as cited earlier; Also, Sandra Postel, Pillars of Sand (New York: W.W. Norton & Company, 1999), pp.141-49.

51 - Ibid.

52 - Michael Wines, "Grand Soviet Scheme for Sharing Water in Central Asia is Floundering," *New York Times*, December 9, 2002.

53 - World Bank Report, as reported by Amy Goodman, *Democracy Now*, May 28, 2009.

Chapter- 9
The Curse of Technology & Globalization

1 - Daniel Sperling and Deborah Gordon, *Two Billion Cars: Driving Toward sustainability*, Oxford University Press, Oxford, 2009, pp.3, 13.

2 - Ibid, p.4.

3-http://www.hypertextbook.com/facts/2001/MarinaStasenko.shtml

4 - All of the above statistics are from Richard Register's book, Ecocities, 2006, pp. 141-64.

5 - Sperling and Gordon, *Two Billion Cars*, p. 4.

6 - Ibid, pp. 209-11. For Chinese car sales, "China moves beyond U.S. to become top car market," The Global Edition of The New York Times, January 10, 2010, p.9

7 - Lester R. Brown, "The Flawed Economics of Nuclear Power," *Earth Policy Institute*, October 28, 2008.

8 - "Nuclear's Fatal Flaws: Summery," *Public Citizen*, updated April, 2006.

9 - Ibid.

10 - "Forget Nuclear," Amory B. Lovins, Imran Sheikh, and Alex Markevich, *Rocky Mountain Institute*, April 28, 2008.

11 - Lester R. Brown, "The Flawed Economics of Nuclear Power."

12 - Ibid.

13 - "Nulcear's Fatal Flaws: Summery," *Public Citizen*, April, 2006.

14 - *60 Minutes- CBS Program*, November 9, 2008.

15-Editors Jerry Mander and Edward Goldsmith, *The Case Against The Global Economy*, David C. Korten, "The Failures of Bretton Woods," 1996, pp. 20-21 President Franklin Roosevelt was duly informed of the council's views.

16- Mike Davis, "The Era of Catastrophe? Geologists Name New Era after Human Influence on the Planet, *Tomdispatch*, August 11, 2008

Chapter- 10
What We the People Can Do

1 - Robert K. Musil, Hope for a Heated Planet: How Americans Are Fighting Global Warming and Building a Better Future, p.185. Also see, Jeffrey Landholz and Kelly Turner, *You Can Prevent Global Warming (and Save Money): 51 Easy Ways* (Andrews McMeel, 2003, Kansas City, MO), p. 3-7.

2 - Ibid, p.186.

3 - Kathy Freston, "Meatless Mondays: Do Something Good for the Earth and Your Health," AlterNet, July 6, 2009

Chapter- 11
Rising to the Challenge

1 - See article, "One-fifth of fossil-fuel emissions absorbed by threatened forests," ScienceBlog.com, June 24, 2009.

2 - Tom Doggett, "Ethanol to take 30 pct of U.S. corn crop in 2012: GAO, *Reuters,* June 11, 2007

3 - Fabiana Frayssinet, Brazil: Historic National Commitment to Wind Energy, *Inter Press News Agency,* June 18, 2009. P.1-2

4 - PTI reports, *India Journal,* p. B2, June 19, 2009

5 - Ibid.

6 - Lester R. Brown, "New Energy Economy Emerging in the United States," *Earth Policy Institute,* October 15, 2008. Also see his article, "Stabilizing Climate: Beyond International Agreements, December 21, 2009.

7 - Ibid.

8 - See, http://apps1.eere.energy.gov/news/news_detail.cfm/news_id=12475.

9 - News Release, "Wind Energy Grows by Record 8,300 MW in 2008, *American Wind Energy Association* (AWEA) report, January 27, 2009

10 - "Renewable Energy Tops 10 Percent of U.S. Production," *Southwest Farm Press,* October 16, 2008.

11 - *India Journal,* August 28, 2009. p. A39. Also, *CBS Evening News,* October 18, 2009

12 - Ibid, pp.1-2.

13 - see www.earthpolicy.org/updates/2008/update77_data.htm.

14 - Posted by Jesse Jenkins, "Soaking Up the Sun: Solar Power in Germany and Japan," *Breakthrough.org,* April 7, 2009.

15 - Ibid, pp.1-2.

16 - www.german-renewable-energy.com, "Solar Power".

17 - Posted by Jesse Jenkins, "Soaking Up the Sun: Solar Power in Germany and Japan," *Breakthrough.org,* April 7, 2009. Pp.2-3; also see, "Solar Panels to go in 30% of Houses by 2030", *Japan Times,* January 1, 2008.

18 - Alex Pasternak, "China Could Be World's Biggest Wind Power By 2020," *Treehugger.com/ science+technology*, New York, NY January 26, 2007.

19 - Ibid. Also Lester Brown, "Stabilizing Climate: Beyond International Agreements," December 21, 2009.

20 - Ibid.

21 - *The Bloomberg Report*, "China, Argentina Turn to Wind Power," New York, N.Y., June 4, 2009.

22 - David Pierson and Nicole Liu, "China, green? In the case of water heaters, yes," *Los Angeles Times*, Beijing Bureau, September 6, 2009.

23 - "First Solar, China Near Deal To Build Huge Solar Field," *Associated Press*, September 8, 2009. For fast train, Bridgette Meinhold, "China unveils the World's Fastest high speed Trains, *Inhabitat*, *inhabitat.com*, 12/28/09.

24 - Malini Bhupta, "Plug and Profit," *India Today*, pp.34-38. For Tata Motors' electric car, Reeba Zachariah, Tata Group plans to go green, Times of India, Times Business section, January 4, 2010, p.17, Bangalore, India.

25 - Monica Chadha, "India taps into wind power," *BBC News*, Mumbai, 2007/05/02.

26 - Ibid, p.2

27 - *Wind Energy News*, "India Wind Energy Slowdown," pp.1-2. March 23, 2009.

28 - Ibid.

29 - "Grand Theft Solar," *Foreign Policy*, January/February, 2009, p. 29.

30 - Anna Da Costa, "Solar Plan Could Revolutionize India's Energy Sector," Worldwatch Institute, May 29, 2009, Worldwatch.org

31 - Ibid, p.2.

32 - Analysis by Himadri Banerji, "India Mulls Ultramega Plans for Solar Power," www.glgroup.com, analysis of James Carter article, "Could India Become a Solar Leader?" *greeninc.blogs, New York Times,* June 8, 2009.

33 - Ibid.

34 - Ibid, p.1-2.

35 - Catherine Brahic, "Affordable Solar Power Brings Light to India," *New Scientist*, April 29, 2007, pp.1-2. For Delhi Summit announcement, see *India Journal*, February 12, 2010, p. A22.

36 - Fabiana Frayssinet, Brazil: Historic National Commitment to Wind Energy, *Inter Press News Agency,* June 18, 2009. P.1

37 - Ibid, p.2

38 - *Wind Energy News,* Brazilian Wind Power Potential, October 9, 2008.

39 - Mario Osava, Energy-Brazil- Hot Water from Sunshine, *Inter Press Service News Agency,* 2006.

40 - Ibid.

41 - Ibid, p.2, February 1, 2006.

42 - Las renovables ahorraron en enero 90 millones de euros en importaciones de gas, Energías-Renovables.com, (Spanish)

43 - Red Eléctrica de España Annual Report 2006.

44 - *"España instala en 2007 más megavatios eólicos que nunca* ", http://www.energias-renovables.com/paginas/Contenidosecciones.asp?ID=14&Cod=12262&Tipo=&Nombre=Noticias.

45 - Asociación Empresarial Eólica - Spanish Wind Energy Association

46 - Récord de energía eólica por el vendaval

47 - Renewables, Global Status Report, 2006 Update, http://www.ren21.net/globalstatusreport/download/RE_GSR_2006_Update.pdf

48 - First Ever Solar Energy Power Tower in Spain - 4/03/07 http://www.beyondfossilfuel.com/solar/tower_0403.html

49 - Alok Jha, "Power in the Desert: Solar Towers Will Harness Sunshine of Southern Spain," *The Guardian/UK,* November 24, 2008.

50 - *WorldFocus,* November 5, 2009.

51 -

Danish Annual Energy Statistics 2007" (PDF). Danish Energy Authority. October 2008. http://www.ens.dk/graphics/UK_Facts_Figures/Statistics/yearly_statistics/2007/energy%20statistics%202007%20uk.pdf.

51 - The world's leader in Wind Power, *Scandinavica.com,* published 2004, accessed 2007-06-22.

52 -Case Study: Wind energy in Denmark, www.manageenergy.net

53 - Lettice, *John (2008-04-27). "*

Denmark signs up for wind powered electric car switch".

The Register
. http://www.theregister.co.uk/2008/03/27/denmark_agassi_ev/.
Retrieved on 2008-11-24.

54 - *Paul Gipe (1996).* "
Community-Owned Wind Development in Germany, Denmark, and the Netherlands". Wind Works
. http://www.wind-works.org/articles/Euro96TripReport.html. Retrieved on 2007-06-21.

55 - The world's leader in Wind Power, *Scandinavica.com*, published 2004, accessed 2007-06-22.

56 - *Worldfocus*, October 7, 2009.

57 - *The Bloomberg Report*, "China, Argentina Turn to Wind Power," New York, N.Y., June 4, 2009.

58 - "The Rise of Renewable Energy," (http://rael.berkeley.edu/files/2006/Kammen-SciAm-Renewables-9.06.pdf)

59 - "Peru's First Wind Project," *Wind Energy News*, September 2, 2008.

60 - "Dominican Republic Bets on Wind Energy," *Wind Energy News.com*, March 31, 2008.

61 - "Caymans Invites Wind Power Proposals," *Wind Energy News.com*, July 31, 2008.

62 - Lester Brown, "Stabilizing Climate: Beyond International Agreements, December 21, 2009. Also see, "Solar Power from Saharan Sun could Provide Europe's Electricity, says EU," *The Guardian, UK,* July 23, 2008.

62 - Ibid

63 - Alok Jha, The Guardian/UK, September 25, 2008.

64 - Jason Palmer, "Hydrogen car to be 'open source', science and technology reporter, BBC News, June 16, 2009.

65 - By *BusinessGreen Staff,* "Sweden Rolls Out New high-Speed Green Train on Old Tracks," http://www.greenbiz.com August 10, 2008.

66 - Henry Chu, "He's light-years away from EU's bright idea," *Los Angeles Times*, October 18, 2009, pp.A1, A21.

Chapter-12
Other Vital Steps

1 - See Ban Ki-Moon's and Fukuda's statements at www.fao.org/foodclimate/conference/statements

2 - David Simcox, NPG Senior Advisor "Population: An Unacknowledged Presence at World Food Crisis Talks". Also see htpp://esa.un.org.unpp

3 - Govt. of India. *1991 Census: general tables.* New Delhi: Office of the Registrar General; 1991. Also, Dept. of Economic and Social affairs. *World Population Prospects: the 1998 revision.* New York: United Nations; 1998.

4 - Central Statistical Office. *National Sample Survey*, 55th round. New Delhi: CSO; 1996; also, Govt. of India. *Vital rates of India*, 1971 to 1996. New Delhi: Office of the Registrar General; 1998.

5 - Robert Cassen and Pravin Visaria, "India: looking ahead to one and a half billion people," p. 3-4, *British Medical Journal*, October 9, 1999.

6 - Lester R. Brown, Plan B 3.0, pp. 136-138, *Earth Policy Institute*, January 21, 2008.

7 - Ibid, pp.138-139.

8 - Ibid.

9 - Lester R. Brown, Plan B 3.0, p. 153.

10 - Ibid, pp. 153-54.

11 - Ibid, pp. 154-55.

12 - The Financial Express, "Developed nations must spend 1% of GDP for clean tech: India," August 1, 2009. Also Se-Kyung Chong, "Anmyeon-do Recreation Forest: A Millennium of Management," in Patrick B. Durst et al., In search of Excellence: Exemplary Forest Management in Asia and the Pacific, Asia-Pacific forestry Commission (Bangkok: FAO Regional Office for Asia and the Pacific, (2005), pp. 251-59.

13 - Turkish Foundation for Combating Soil Erosion (TEMA) at english.tema.org.tr

14 - Lester R. Brown, Plan B 3.0, pp.157-58.

15 - "China Begins Huge Reforestation Effort," *Xinhuanet*, May 15, 2002. htpp://news.xinhuanet.com/english/2002-05-15

16 - Ibid.

17 - "A Poverty Project that is Restoring China's Forests," *The World Bank*- News Release, December 6, 2007. htpp://web.worldbank.org

18 - Ibid.

19 - Jonathan Watts, Beijing, "China suspends reforestation project over food shortage fears," *Guardian.co.uk*, June 23, 2009

20 - Ibid.

21 - N.H.Ravindranath, Rajiv Kumar Chaturvedi and Indu K. Murthy, "Forest conservation, afforestation and reforestation in India: Implications for forest carbon stocks," *Current Science*, July 25, 2008.

22 - "Global Warming," *India Today*, July 14, 2008, p.32

23- Ibid.

24 - Lester R. Brown, Plan B 3.0, p.167.

25 - Ibid.

26 - Secretariat of the U.N. Convention to Combat Desertification, "The Great North American Dust Bowl: A Cautionary Tale," Global Alarm Dust and Sandstorms from the World's Drylands (Bangkok: 2002), pp. 77-121.

27 - Jeffrey Zinn, Conservation Reserve Program: Status and Current Issues (Washington, DC: Congressional Research Service, 8 May 2001)

28 - Lester R. Brown, Plan B 3.0, p. 159.

29 - Ibid, pp. 159-60.

30 - "Algeria to Convert Large Cereal Land to Tree-Planting," Reuters, December 8, 2000; "Drought-hit north Africa Seen Hunting for Grains," Reuters, July 15, 2005.

31 - Lester R. Brown, Plan B 3.0, p. 160.

32 - Evan Ratliff, "the Green Wall of China," Wired, April 2003; Wang Yan, "China's Forest Shelter Project Dubbed 'green Great Wall'," Xinhua News Agency, July 9, 2006; Sun Xiufang and Ralph Bean, China Solid Wood Products annual Report 2002 (Beijing: USDA, 2002).

33 - Lester R. Brown, Plan B 3.0, p.161.

34 - Rhoda E. Howard-Hassmann, "Globalization, Poverty Reduction, and Economic Rights, Canada Research Chair in

international human Rights; *Wilfrid Laurier University*, Canada, posted March 9, 2009.

35 - Shaohua Chen and Martin Ravallion, "The Developing World is Poorer than We Thought, But No Less Successful in the Fight Against Poverty," Washington, D.C.: World Bank, 2008. Table 7, pp. 33-34.

36 - Kishore Mahbubani, "Power and Impending Glory," *India Today*, August 24, 2009, p.24.

37 -"India's New Deal," *Foreign Policy*, January/February, 2009, p.28.

38 - Richard Register, *Ecocities: Rebuilding Cities in Balance with Nature*, New Society Publishers, Gabriola Island, BC, Canada, 2006, p.1-5.

39 - Orienting Urban Planning to Sustainability in Curitiba, Brazil. ICLEI website, http://www.3.iclei.org/localstrategies/summary/curitiba2.html, visited October 3, 2009.

40 - Ibid.

41 - Ibid.

42 - Bill McKibben, "Earth2," *The Atlantic Monthly*, May, 1998. Also see, www.350.org for latest CO2 emissions figures.

43 - Wallace S. Broecker and Robert Kunzig, *Fixing Climate: What past Climate Changes reveal about the Current Threat—and How to Counter it*, pp. 190-91.

44 - Ibid, pp.191-92.

45 - Ibid

Chapter-13
Sustainable Societies & Freedomocracy

1 - Cuba, Going against the Grain: Agricultural Crisis and Transformation; Chapter 2, Cuba's Distinction: Land Reform and a Modernized Peasantry, Sinclair M, and Thompson M. *Oxfam America Report*, June 2001. http://www.oxfamamerica.org/pdfs/cuba/distinction.pdf

2 - Household incomes in Cuban Agriculture: A Comparison of the State, Co-operative and Peasant Sectors, Deer, C. D., et al. In Development and Change, Vol. 26, Blackwell Publishers, 1995.

3 - Ibid.

4 - World Resources 2000-2001—People and Ecosystems: The Fraying Web of Life. Prepared by The United Nations Development Programme (UNDP), The United Nations Environment Programme (UNEP), The World Bank, and The World Resources Institute. UNDP, September 2000.

5 - Ibid.

6 - Dale Allen Pfeiffer, "Cuba- A Hope," *The Wilderness Publications*, www.fromthewilderness.com, p.4.

7 - Ibid

8 - See cited earlier: Cuba Going against the Grain

9 - Ibid

10 - See earlier, Cuba Going against the Grain.

11 - Ibid.

12 - Ibid.

13 - Documentary, "Surviving Peak Oil: How Cuba survived peak oil."

14 - Ibid.

15 - Shirin Shirin, "Economic Woes? Look to Kerala," *Foreign Policy in Focus*, December 11, 2008.

16 - Ibid.

17 - Richard Heinberg, "PowerDown: Options and Actions for a Post-Carbon World," pp. 151-52

Chapter-14
Is Collapse Really Imminent?

1 - Wilson, E.O., *The Future of Life* (2002) (ISBN 0-679-76811-4); also see Ulansey, David, "The current mass extinction" repeats this statement with links to dozens of news reports on the phenomenon. URL accessed January 26, 2007.

2 - J.H.Lawton and R.M.May, *Extinction rates*, Oxford University Press, Oxford, UK

3 - "Oil Sands Threaten Our Survival, Al Gore Warns," *The Toronto Star*, November 24, 2009.

4 - Jen Mapes, "Climate Change Linked to Civilization Collapse," *National Geographic News*, February 27, 2001.

5 - Please see Chapter-2

6 - Jared Diamond, "The Ends of the World as we Know them," *The New York Times*, January 1, 2005. Could this happen to current industrial civilization?

7 - Richard C. Duncan, "The Olduvai Theory: Energy, Population, and Industrial Civilization," winter, 2005-2006.

8 - David Adam, "Too Late? Why Scientists Say We should Expect the Worst," *The Guardian/UK*, December 9, 2008.

9 - Ibid.

10 - Ibid.

11 - James Kirkup in L'Aquila, G8 Summit, *Telegraph.co.uk*, July 9, 2009.

12 - Dean Nelson, South Asia Editor, *Telegraph.co.uk*, July 7 and 22, 2009.

13 - Johan Hari, "Collapse or Survive: The Stark Choice Facing Our Species," The *Independent/UK*, September 23, 2009.

14 - Mark Hertsgaard, "Climate Roulette", *The Nation*, October 13, 2009.

15 - Ibid.

16 - Richard C. Duncan, "The Olduvai Theory: Energy, Population, and Industrial Civilization," winter 2005-2006

17 - Forrester, J. W., World Dynamics, second ed., Pegasus Communications, Waltham MA. 1971-3, p.70.

18 - Richard Heinberg, "Searching for a Miracle: 'Net Energy' Limits & the Fate of Industrial Society," A joint project of the International Forum on Globalization and the Post Carbon Institute, (False Solution Series), September, 2009. pp. 61-62.

19 - Ibid.

20 - "Billions face climate change risk," *BBC News*, April 6, 2007.

21 - Lester R. Brown, "The Copenhagen Conference on food Security," *Earth Policy Institute*, November 10, 2009.

22 - Ibid.

23 - Lester R. Brown, "Melting Mountain Glaciers Will Shrink Grain Harvests in China and India,"

Earth Policy Institute, March 20, 2008.

24 - Ibid.

25 - Lester R. Brown, "The Copenhagen Conference on Food Security," *Earth Policy Institute,* November 10, 2009.

26 - Mike Davis, "The Era of Catastrophe? Geologists Name New Era After Human Influence On the Planet," *Tomdispatch,* August 11, 2008. Also see, John Feffer, "Mother Earth's Triple Whammy," TomDispatch.com, Foreign Policy in Focus, June 18, 2008

27 - Lester R. Brown, "When Population Growth and Resource Availability Collide," *Earth Policy Institute,* February 12, 2008.

28 - Tara Lohan, "Can Condoms Save Us From Climate Change?" *AlterNet,* September 19, 2009.

29 - David Korten, "How Do We Go from Empire to Earth Community?" *Yes! Magazine,* June 16, 2008.

30 - Lester R. Brown, "Melting Mountain Glaciers Will Shrink Grain Harvests in China and India," *Earth Policy Institute,* March 20, 2008.

31 - *60- Minutes, CBS News,* March 20, 2006.

32 - Vandana Shiva, "Soil Not Oil: Why We Need to Kick Petroleum Out of Our Farms," *South End Press,* December 3, 2008.

33 News Release, *The Financial Express,* "Developed Nations must spend 1% of GDP for clean tech: India, August 1, 2009

34-Nick Berning, "Copenhagen: A Disaster for World's Poorest," Friends of the Earth-International, December 18, 2009. The well-known environmentalist Bill McKibben wrote, "He (Obama) formed a league of super-polluters, and would be polluters...it is a coalition of foxes who will together govern the henhouse."

35-"Copenhagen Talks End with Agreement, But No Binding Deal: So How Screwed Are We? *AlterNet,* December 19, 2009.

36-George Monbiot, "Copenhagen Negotiators Bicker and Filibuster While the Biosphere Burns," *The Guardian/UK,* December 18, 2009. Joss Garman called it "a historic failure that will live in infamy".

37- Joss Garman, "Copenhagen: Historic Failure That Will live in Infamy," *Independent, UK,* December 21, 2009.

38- Naomi Klein, "Copenhagen: The Courage to Say No," *The Nation*, December 18, 2009.

LaVergne, TN USA
26 January 2011
214093LV00005B/109/P